Standard Handbook of Salt-Water Fishing

Cape Hatteras, North Carolina

STANDARD HANDBOOK OF

Salt-Water Fishing

ROBERT SCHARFF

Revised and Updated

THOMAS Y. CROWELL COMPANY, NEW YORK

ESTABLISHED 1834

L.C. Card 66-25435

Manufactured in the United States of America

ISBN 0-690-76926-1
    5 6 7 8 9 10

Acknowledgments

I wish to thank the following people and manufacturers for their help in making this book possible: James C. Miller of the Horrocks-Ibbotson Company; Frank Fitzpatrick of the James Heddon's Company; Harry D. Heinzerling of the Creek Chub Bait Company; S. R. Harper of the True Temper Corporation; Thomas B. Lipton of the Penn Fishing Tackle Manufacturing Company; Pete Zackek of the South Bend Tackle Company, R. M. McMillen of the Enterprise Manufacturing Company; Edward B. Maguire of the American Tackle & Equipment Company; B. A. Coleman of the B. F. Gladding & Company; Charles G. Hays of the West Palm Beach Chamber of Commerce; Edward H. Comstock of the U. S. Line Company; Albert H. Neff of the Ashway Line & Twine Manufacturing Company; C. C. Hamill of *Down South* magazine; Dick Wolfe of the Garcia Corporation; the Neptuna Tackle Company; Lawrence Vorhaus Advertising; Gudebrod Brothers Silk Company, Inc.; Shakespeare Company; and the authors and state departments mentioned in Chapters 13 to 15. I also wish to thank Julian M. Romeskie for the art drawings, Arline Martin and Edith Robbins for typing the manuscript, and George Heinold, salt-water fishing editor for *Outdoor Life,* for his helpful comments on the revision of this book. My grateful acknowledgment to all of them for help in making this book complete and up to date.

ROBERT SCHARFF

Contents

CHAPTER 1

Introduction to

Salt-Water Fishing

Fringing the beaches, sheltered bays, and inlets of the ocean shore line, or milling about the surface and depths of the far offshore expanses, a great variety and abundance of food and game fish, large and small, search for their livelihood while en route to or from their spawning grounds. These hungry hordes offer smashing action on rods and reels adapted to their sizes and fighting habits, and in many cases rank high from the epicure's standpoint. Annually tens of thousands of people in North, Central, and South America get rousing thrills from matching strength and skill against the power and cunning of the sea's fin-guided population. Along the Atlantic, Pacific, and Gulf of Mexico coast lines you'll see boat- and land-based fishermen of every description plying baits and lures throughout the year.

Why do so many people fish our salty waters? Fishing is often the excuse, rather than the reason, for using a rod and reel and taking trips to new places. Perhaps it is an excuse for a man to become a boy again—to lean back in the boat with a blue sky overhead and watch the white clouds build into dream castles. Perhaps it is a way to shatter the bonds of civilization and renew our experience of God and nature. Maybe fishing is just an excuse to delay mowing the lawn or weeding the garden. The things associated with fishing are much more important than the fish, or the actual catching of them. The man who recognizes this, and uses fishing as an excuse rather than a reason, perhaps derives the most from the sport.

Life is too short not to find time for salt-water fishing. There is a mystery about the sea that forever lures the angler. And there is always the possibility of a sudden and exciting catch. Starting out to fish for snook, the angler may end up with a record tarpon; searching for mackerel, he may boat a broadbill swordfish, rarest of all the sea's great angling trophies. The big, swift, ocean-roving fish may be caught in sheltered inland waters where they occasionally congregate. The catch may be measured in pounds or hundreds of pounds, but the pleasure of the sport can never be measured in numbers—only in thrills.

The angler who seeks his sport on the ocean, or on the more placid waters of the bays and inlets of our coasts, has such an unlimited variety of fishing offered him that he always can fit his sport to his pocketbook, to his inclination, and to the time which he has at his disposal. He can spend many weeks and impressive amounts of money in pursuit of marlin, giant tuna, and other big game of the sea; at more moderate expense in money and time he can enjoy the high-powered thrills of sailfish or tarpon fishing; he can spend an off day and an odd dollar or two on fishing for weakfish or stripers. Or he can cast from a sandy beach out into the lashing surf. There is a kind of salt-water angling to suit every mood and pocketbook, and there is good sport in each.

To the average layman, fishing is a nonsensical pastime. His idea of the sport is an angler sitting on the stringpiece of a dock with hand lines attached to an array of dock bells, awaiting the first jingle to haul in what has been hooked. He has never seen the real thing, so naturally he does not give fishing much credit. However, the fact that more money is spent on fishing than on any of our other national pastimes—baseball, golf, etc.— has him all ears.

Salt-water fishing is becoming sophisticated today: unless you use officially recognized equipment you are just another angler, because awards are based on tackle specifications. "Sport fishing" they call it, and those of the realm like to keep it so.

Sport fishing of marine waters has developed over a long period of time. The old flagpole rod and wooden reel are gone. Sporty tackle has taken their place. Now the salt-water angler is devoted to fishing equipment that lends the greatest thrill. In so doing, salt-water angling has become a greater diversion. You can fish inshore bays, inlets, sounds and rivers; or throw a line into the surf or you can go after big creatures far out in the ocean. In other words there is a type of salt-water fishing for everyone. And there are plenty of fish in all locations to suit your favor.

Aside from the variety of fish to be caught, one of the outstanding reasons for the popularity of salt-water angling is that you are afforded the opportunity of seeking these intrepid fighters during the entire year— day or night. At many places along our rocky and sandy coastlines there are innumerable fish ready to seize your bait or lure regardless of season or tide.

As in any other endeavor, though, the returns you receive from salt-water angling are in direct proportion to the effort you invest. True, a certain amount of luck enters the fishing picture, as anyone who has suffered the chagrin of being "low hook" to a novice can tell you. But luck is not the secret of successful fishing, nor is there any hocus-pocus either. Sure, a veteran angler has his bag of tricks—but there is nothing magical about them. He has learned them all through experience, often the hard way. Every step in angling is based on logic. In the remaining chapters of this book, we will discuss the "logic" of all types of salt-water angling. The skill will come with practice, as you put this logic to use.

CONSERVATION

While marine biologists are pretty well agreed that no important salt-water food or game fishes are, at the present moment, in serious danger of total annihilation, past experience with many land creatures in all parts of the world seems to warrant a policy of caution and farsightedness. The history of conservation in this country has been largely the story of locking the barn after the horses are stolen. Recently, the enormous interest that has been taken in big-game fishing has helped mightily to turn the conservation spotlight upon many salt-water fish; the broadbill swordfish, marlin, sailfish, tarpon, and tuna. Already a serious decline has been noted among several of these—a classic example is the bluefin tuna of the Pacific coast. Two or three decades ago several hundred were caught each year by members of the Tuna Club at Catalina, California, but now only three or four are taken annually. As a result of attention focused on the big game of the sea, increasing interest is also being taken in conserving smaller species, such as bluefish, channel bass, sea bass, weakfish, yellowtails—and even flounders and porgies.

Since marine species recognize no state boundaries, most states bordering our coast line require no license for salt-water sport fishing nor have any close seasons for salt-water fish. Unlike the fresh-water species, only a few states place any size or quantity restrictions on the fishes taken from the sea. (See Part II for details on state salt-water fishing regulations.) Also, no federal or state agencies stock our oceans as they do fresh-water streams or lakes. Therefore, it is up to you, the angler, to practice salt-water conservation. Do not take more fish than you can use and do not take undersized ones. (The regulations of the State of Texas given on page 3 are good guides for size.) Also, many of the big game fish—tarpon, sailfish, and marlin—are poor eating, so it is only sporting to release these as soon as they are "officially" caught. It is childish to bring fish to the docks merely to be seen and photographed with them. Sportsmen find liberating these fish more satisfying than leaving them on docks to rot. At Ocean City, Maryland, last season, releases totaled over forty per cent of the fish caught.

TAGGING FISH

The tagging of fish is a means of marking them so that they may be recognized at some future time. Fisheries biologists, concerned with learning more about the ways of fish and improving fisheries management practices, have three main objectives in tagging and releasing fish: (1) learning where and how the fish travels; (2) obtaining information concerning the identity (the degree of separation and mixing) of fish populations; (3) obtaining information on population levels, rate of exploitation, survival, growth, and other statistical matters important to fisheries management.

The general way in which this information accumulates is as follows: A certain number of marked fish are released into the ocean; subsequent sampling (by anglers or ichthyologists) then yields marked and unmarked fish; the percentage of marked fish recovered gives a measure of the degree of utilization of exploitation by the fishery. Under favorable circumstances it may also be possible to estimate the size of the fish population by proportional computations.

It is evident that the success of tagging programs is usually contingent upon the cooperation of fishermen. Therefore, if you catch a tagged specimen, keep the fish itself, but be sure to send in the tag (or tag number) to the agency noted on it. (Cornell University researchers once released some fish with tags reading, "Send to Cornell University." A few loyal cooperators took the instructions literally and boxed up the fish with tag still attached. Needless to say these packages cleared through the University mail room in record time!)

Sometimes the return of tags takes devious courses. An account was recently published of two tag returns from sockeye salmon released in British Columbia. The salmon and tags turned up in England—in cans!

IGFA WORLD RECORDS

Contrary to what a lot of anglers believe, you don't have to be a millionaire to land a world record fish. You don't have to own a forty-foot power cruiser with a flying bridge. You don't even have to take two months off each year to travel half way around the world. We can cite a number of cases where "casual" anglers have taken world record fish almost in their own backyards without the slightest notion that their catches would rate official listing in the IGFA record book. And, conversely, many of the world's most expert anglers and ardent big game sportsmen have never managed to make any kind of entry on the world record roster.

Now, we will grant that according to the law of averages, the more you fish, the better your chances are of bringing in a world beater. Also, using the right tackle and being able to choose the right fishing spots isn't going to increase the odds against you. And of course it helps considerably to have enough "know how" to turn the reel handle in the right direction, especially if you are fishing in the heavyweight division. However, you can take our word for it that the biggest single factor in filling up the pages of the IGFA record book is just plain, ordinary, unvarnished luck. There are more than six hundred record classifications (see Appendix A for a partial list) to shoot at in salt-water fishing. Remember that these listings range from the 2664-pound All-Tackle mark for white shark all the way down to a 3 pound, 12 ounce listing for sea bass in the 8-pound Line Test Class, and you can see that your chances are as good as any one else's if your luck is running at the same time the fish are.

The recognized agency for certifying and posting all records for salt-water game fish is the International Game Fish Association (IGFA). Before the IGFA was founded, the American Museum of Natural History and *Field & Stream* magazine together kept records. Since the IGFA's organization, it has kept detailed salt-water angling records, while *Field & Stream* has taken over the fresh-water function on a less elaborate, but universally accepted, basis.

The IGFA was founded in 1939, largely through the efforts of well-known international sportsman Michael Lerner, with Dr. William R. Gregory as its first president. It is a privately endowed, nonprofit organization with no commercial connections and no dues or assessments. Its organizational roster includes more than three hundred member clubs and seventy international committee members in leading fishing countries throughout the world. It also has a close affiliation with fourteen scientific institutions. All officers and representatives serve without pay. There are no dues for member clubs and no charge for publications.

The IGFA record classifications are separated into two main divisions: one including over-all record catches by either men or women anglers, and another special division for women anglers exclusively. In both these divisions, records are kept for forty-nine common species of salt-water game fish (three more species may be added shortly) in seven different categories based on line sizes. These categories include the All-Tackle Class for the heaviest fish caught on any line; the 12-pound Line Class for lines testing up to and including 12 pounds; the 20-pound Line Test Class (12- to 20-pound test line); the 30-pound Line Test Class (20- to 30-pound test line); the 50-pound Line Test Class (30- to 50-pound test line); the 80-pound Line Test Class (50- to 80-pound test line); and the 130-pound Line Test Class (80- to 130-pound test line). Record catches in all these classifications are entered on the rolls as they are confirmed by the IGFA Board, and complete current listings are issued to interested parties by the IGFA.

Now, getting down to brass tacks, let's assume that off Duckwaddle

When photographing a fish in establishing a claim to
a record, show it—unless, like a marlin or a tuna, it
is too large—against a light background with measuring tape clearly evident. This oceanic bonito was laid
out on a concrete walk. A photograph of fish on the
scales is also helpful.

Point you've just come up with a whopping 8-pound summer flounder.
In accordance with IGFA regulations for all species, you were using a
lure with not more than two hooks on it, spaced at least a hook-length
apart, and you brought your catch to gaff without assistance. (Many
charter boat skippers, wanting large catch records, do the striking for
their clients. An angler taking a fish this way ought not credit himself

with a "catch," but with an "assist." Those wanting to be honest in hanging a prize fish mount on the wall should strike the fish and play it to the boat themselves, where someone else may gaff it, or land it by seizing the leader.) You also boated the fish intact and complied with all the other regulations shown on the reverse of the IGFA affidavit form. Because you were using a light line of only 8-pound test, you have a sneaking suspicion that you might just happen to be eligible for IGFA record recognition (and the fact of the matter is, you definitely would be).

So what do you do next? Well, first of all, you take your fish to the nearest recognized weighing station and see if it scales up to your expectations. The chances are that if you made your catch near an active fishing center, there will be an IGFA record chart around to check against. (Appendix A in this book gives the major records as of 1966.) If you actually do top the weight in any record class, your next step is to get hold of an IGFA affidavit form. These forms are usually available on the docks of most coastal fishing centers and at many tackle shops as well. They may also be secured by writing directly to the Recording Secretary, International Game Fish Association, Alfred I. du Pont Building, Miami 32, Florida.

Meanwhile, although it is not essential, it will strengthen your claim if you can contact an IGFA club officer or international committeeman to serve as one of your two required witnesses. While weight is the deciding factor in determining world record fish, you also need the dimensions of your catch to fill out your affidavit form. Girth should be measured at the thickest part of the body, and length, from the mouth to the tip of the tail or, in the case of a "billed" fish, from the point of the bill to the tip of the tail. As indicated on the form, it is also essential to put in complete data on the tackle used and other details of the catch. When completed and notarized, your affidavit form should be submitted to the Recording Secretary at the address previously given. It should be accompanied by a clear, full-length photograph of your fish and a 10-yard sample of the actual line used in making the catch.

Your record claim will be reviewed by at least two officers of the IGFA for formal confirmation. If it is approved, you will shortly afterward receive the IGFA's official world record certificate inscribed with your name and details of your catch. Although the IGFA has been in full scale operation for over twenty years and handles an unusually heavy volume of record claims, each year, surprisingly enough, a relatively large number of records in some of the line test divisions are still unclaimed. More than that, many of the record catches already listed in the small fish categories are still sufficiently modest in size to place them well within the reach of the "week-end angler."

CHAPTER 2

Salt-Water Reels,
Lines, and Rods

BASICALLY, any salt-water tackle outfit consists of a reel, a line, and a rod. The line is knotted to the reel, and the reel is clamped to the rod. But the proper choice of any of these pieces of fishing tackle is liable to prove difficult if you don't know what each type will do.

SALT-WATER REELS

By definition, a reel is a spool set in a frame, usually of metal, which is attached to the rod butt near the hand for the easy control of the line when angling. Most of us are familiar with the modern salt-water reel, but it took many years to develop. At the end of the last century, there were only a very few big-game anglers who had courage enough to fish for tarpon and small tuna because they encountered many skinned knuckles from the whirling reel handle every time they battled a fish. They covered their hands with very heavy gloves to protect themselves from these "knuckle-buster" reels. But as more and more fishermen took up the challenge of giant-size fish, reel manufacturers tried many methods to give some protection between human flesh and a rapidly turning spool of coarse line. But none were successful until in 1911 William C. Boschen developed the idea of the star or internal friction drag. Then, in 1913, Joseph Coxe and Julius vom Hofe made reels incorporating this outstanding feature. From then on the salt-water reel developed rapidly and marvelously, thanks to the work of our famous reel manufacturers—Pflueger, Meisselbach, vom Hofe, Catucci, Holzmann, Kovalovsky, Coxe, Shakespeare, and others. Today we have two fine types of salt-water reels: the conventional revolving-spool reel (described below) and the spinning reel (see page 19).

Revolving-Spool Reels

The modern conventional revolving-spool type of salt-water reel is a highly efficient mechanism. With one of the proper size and with the other tackle in balance, an angler can subdue a fish at least ten times his own weight. Of course such things as rods, lines, and hooks are indispensable— but it was the development of the modern reel that is largely responsible for the great present-day interest in marine fishing.

Most manufacturers use standard code numbers to designate reel sizes. Though some tackle companies no longer use the code, especially for the smaller size reels, your local sports equipment dealer can always give you the size you want if you know the proper code designation. Salt-water reels are available in sizes 1/0 to 6/0 inclusive; 9/0, 10/0, 12/0, 14/0, 15/0, and 16/0. However, a 6/0 reel of one brand may not hold exactly the same yardage as a 6/0 of another manufacturer. Yardage also varies according to kind of line used. A few years ago all capacities recommended by manufacturers were based upon linen line. Today, braided dacron, nylon, and monofilament (*mono* for short) are all used as a so-called *standard*. The following chart, which is a generalization of several manufacturers' specifications, gives the approximate line capacities of three types of lines for the various popular-size reels. (Manufacturers who do not use the standard code usually stamp the reel's capacity somewhere on it, generally on the seat. Reels made in Europe are usually designated 6-inch, 8-inch, etc., according to the diameter of the reel plates.)

APPROXIMATE CAPACITIES OF COMMON SALT-WATER REELS

Line Test in Pounds *	Reel Size										
	1/0	2/0	3/0	4/0	6/0	9/0	10/0	12/0	14/0	16/0
20 lb. Dacron	225									
30 lb. Dacron	200	275	350	450						
50 lb. Dacron			200	250	400					
80 lb. Dacron				150	250	400	650	800	1050	1250
130 lb. Dacron						300	450	550	850	1000
20 lb. Monofilament	350	425								
30 lb. Monofilament	200	275	375							
18 lb. Nylon	250									
27 lb. Nylon	225	300	275							
36 lb. Nylon				350	600					
45 lb. Nylon				275	500					
54 lb. Nylon				200	400					
72 lb. Nylon					350	500	850			
90 lb. Nylon					300	400	600	800	1100	1400
108 lb. Nylon						300	500	600	1000	1200

* See page 26. Dacron and nylon are of the braided type.

The original American salt-water reels were single action—that is, one revolution of the handle produced one revolution of the spool. This is the way a single-action fly reel works, and, incidentally, many British heavy-duty salt-water reels are still manufactured employing this principle. But most salt-water reels made in the United States use the multiplying principle and are called multiplying reels. The chief improvement in the adaption of this principle is the lowering of the gear ratio to anything

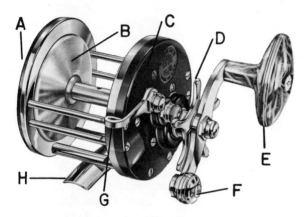

Parts of a conventional revolving-spool type of salt-water reel.
(*A*) Tail plate.
(*B*) Spool flange.
(*C*) Head plate.
(*D*) Star drag.
(*E*) Egg-shaped handle.
(*F*) Counterweight.
(*G*) Throw-off lever.
(*H*) Foot.

from 2-to-1 to about 5-to-1. (This means that the spool revolves two to five times for every turn of the handle.) While a reel with a lower gear ratio does not retrieve as much line per turn of the handle as one with a higher ratio, it makes cranking in the line easier. The leverage is also greater with a low ratio reel; thus less effort is necessary. Most big game and trolling reels have a 2-to-1 or 2½-to-1 ratio while those used for surf casting and jigging are 3-to-1 or 3½-to-1. Reels employed for bait casting usually have a 4-to-1 ratio; a few go as high as 5-to-1.

Drag Control

It is safe to say that no modern angler would willingly take on a large salt-water fish with one of the old-time reels. The handle of this kind of reel revolves backwards when the fish runs, and a speedy fish can convert the handle into a blur of motion about as dangerous as a circular power saw. Various efforts to provide a drag or brake have been made, but Boschen's star drag was the first practical one and it is still used by the majority of salt-water fishermen today.

A star drag takes its name from the star-shaped wheel located between the body of the reel and the crank-handle. The five points of the star wheel, with their rounded ends, are easily turned forward or backward by the angler's winding hand. The braking action is controlled by the star wheel which increases or decreases the pressure between the drag washers. By adjusting the star wheel, varying degrees of tension can be applied to the fisherman's line. Adjustment of the drag is controlled by turning the star wheel forward to tighten and backward to loosen. A little pressure between the drag washers results in light tension; a fish can pull the fisherman's line from the reel with little effort. Increasing the tension applies greater braking action on the spool and makes it increasingly difficult for a fish to run and take out line. Care should be exercised not to put more drag on the reel than the line can safely withstand. Actually, drag tension never should exceed the strain which will break the line. Drag tension should be set to tire out a fighting fish and slowly wear him down, rather than stop his run entirely. To check the amount of drag you have on your reel, put your reel in gear and pull on the line coming from your rod tip. The star drag should generally be set on light or medium, and when the fish strikes it may then be increased as needed. Since the drag on the line and the fish increases anyway, as the line lengthens the slight extra drag that may be momentarily desired will be automatically taken care of.

The star drag mechanism consists of a series of disks mounted on the gear sleeve. Some are anchored to the shaft rotating within, while others are keyed to the grooves inside the main gear. They will perform only if they are assembled in proper sequence, correctly alternating the various washers. Drag washers work best when dry, clean, and free from grease

The most commonly employed types of drag control: star (*top left*); starless (*top right*); friction drag (*bottom left*); leather thumbguard brake (*bottom right*).

or oil. For efficient operation, washers which are oil-soaked, charred, or glazed should be removed and replaced.

One of the long-standing criticisms of the star-wheel arrangement has been the lack of any kind of calibration. That is, the drag can't be decreased or increased with enough exactness when the reel is in use. You can preset the drag accurately with a spring scale, of course; but suppose you change it later, and then, during action, want to return to the preset mark. You have to be a pretty sensitive adjustor, and when drag pressures are critical you'd better be right. Furthermore, a star wheel isn't exactly the easiest thing in the world to adjust when a fish is being played, especially when beginners, who are inclined to fiddle with the mechanism, have changed the setting (and, nine times out of ten, set it up too tight). More than one fish has been lost that way. A new development by several manufacturers employs a friction drag.

This friction drag system possesses two new features. One is a knurled knob to preset or set the brake mechanism for a desired range of pressures. Another is a "fine-tuning" level which controls the drag through that predetermined range of settings, from free spool and strike through the running and fighting of a fish to a special "power shift" for extra drag in a battle's closing phase. Also part of the drag mechanism is an over-size brake disk which dissipates any heat generated when the drag is putting a strong arm on a fish. The braking unit functions in this manner: The drag is preset or set as desired by turning a smoothly operating knurled knob next to the crank. The scope of this knob is from free spool to maximum possible drag. Beyond the free-spool or "off" position, its setting at any point determines a specific range of drag pressures available by shifting the fine-tuning lever. In other words, once the coarse-adjustment knob has been set (it can be changed at will, of course) it determines a certain range of drag pressures which can be selected by the fine-adjustment lever. The lever operates through a quadrant of about 120 degrees, from free spool to power thrust.

Another drag arrangement, not as expensive as the friction preset just described, is called the "starless" drag. This system permits complete drag control, but it is also automatically adjusted by the pull of the fish and, when properly set, will not tighten beyond the line strength. When the line is spooled on the reel, the maximum drag is preset so the drag will not tighten beyond what the line will stand. (If the maximum drag is inadvertently set too low, or if the line must be broken, a special safety device may be thrown to release the maximum setting and permit the application of an increasing amount of drag.) The drag is lessened simply by backing off (reversing) the reel handle; thus the drag can be set at any given strength for a "strike," just as with the star. Then, as the fish is reeled in, the drag automatically tightens to compensate for the added pull exerted by the fish. But should the fish exert too much strain on the rod or reel, the drag can

Popular methods of antibacklash control:
simple friction device (*upper left*);
mechanical thumber control
(*upper right*); centrifugal brake control
(*lower left*); magnetic inductive type
control (*lower right*).

be instantly decreased simply by reversing the handle slightly. The starless
drag has proved especially useful for trolling. As the lure drops astern, the
reel handle can be backed off, decreasing the drag, rather than placing the
reel on free spool. Should a fish strike while the lure is drifting out, the
angler just starts winding in, and the drag automatically increases to compensate for the added pull.

All salt-water reels have some type of free-spool mechanism which
allows the spool to revolve freely without turning the gears. This device
is actuated by a lever or plunger; it is essential when casting baits out to
a far spot, when dropping baits back to tempt big-game fish into striking,
and for similar uses. Once the fish is hooked, the free spool is made inoperative. Most free spools work by means of a lever; you throw the lever
forward and the reel goes into free spool; you throw it back and the spool
goes into mesh with the gears. One leading manufacturer designs his reels
with a plunger to throw them into free spool. You merely turn the handle
forward to engage the gears.

Antibacklash Control

While most salt-water reels have no antibacklash control, a few do.
But, first, what is a backlash? What causes it? It is caused by the spool

moving faster than the line. At the start of the cast and with the reel in free-spooling the lure drags out line at a great rate of speed. Thus the reel spool is forced to turn at a high r.p.m. When the lure reaches its target and loses much of the initial speed, the spool, because of its friction-free construction, continues to revolve rapidly. Unless it is checked either by a sensitive thumb or a mechanical drag, the spool will continue to run after the line has stopped, thus making a tangled mess.

The simplest and perhaps the most widely used antibacklash is nothing more than an attachment which brings friction to the spool. This is controlled by a knob or lever located at the side of the reel. However, don't confuse this control with the "click" button. The click button, common on salt-water reels of all types, is nothing more than a noisemaker which merely gives you a warning as the line leaves the spool. In other words, it is on your reel simply to attract your attention when a fish picks up your bait and also to keep your spool from turning when you do not want it to. The click button should never be engaged while casting; but casting or antibacklash drag is designed for casting and should be so used. Most of these drags are adjustable for use with different weight lures. A good rule of thumb is to set the drag so that the weight of the lure will be just enough to drag line off the spool—*slowly*.

A variation of the friction attachment is the mechanical thumber which automatically thumbs the line just as your bait or lure reaches the end of its flight. This device operates only when the line is going out. An automatic clutch throws the mechanical thumber completely when the line is being reeled in. Another type of casting reel works on the centrifugal force principle and this simple device literally "thinks" for you, helping to prevent backlashes.

One of the finest types of spool control is the magnetic inductor control featured on some surf-casting reels. A row of magnets is mounted on a movable plate on the side of the reel. The spool of this type of reel has a special disk which is extremely sensitive to magnetic influence. The magnets set up a magnetic field which restricts the action of the spool. Since the magnets can be moved nearer to or farther from the sensitive spool, you can control the amount of drag to the minutest degree. When this contrivance is properly adjusted to the weight of the lure, the conditions of the wind, the peculiarities of the caster, etc., you can surf cast without thumbing the reel. Such an arrangement is ideal for night surf fishing, especially when the target cannot be seen.

Another kind of reel has air fins built onto the outside of the flange of the spool that operates opposite the tail plate. The fins pick up air as the spool revolves and increase the drag the faster it spins. Since high speed is what you want to control, this pneumatic principle works fairly well. The major difficulty here is that there is no way to adjust the drag for different conditions. It is exactly the same for the lightest lures as it is for

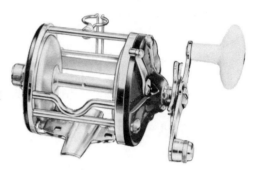

Popular types of level winders: simple double-threaded style (*left*), double-threaded level winder with line guide (*right bottom*), and brain wave line level winder device (*right top*).

the heaviest weights. Also, as your thumb becomes more proficient, you want to reduce the influence of the antibacklash. But an adjustment of the antibacklash is impossible because the vanes of the spool are fixed. One manufacturer makes available a second reel spool which has no antibacklash fins at all, so you can start with a finned spool and when you become used to it you can switch to the totally free spool.

There is another antibacklash attachment which should certainly be mentioned: the oil viscosity type. While the others are part of the reel itself, this is a separate unit which can be fitted to almost any reel. It looks like a large knob and is fitted to the reel axle at the left side of the reel. There are special models for all the different reels, so be sure you get the one designed for your own reel. This cup utilizes differing weights (viscosity) of oil to control the cast. The axle of the reel fits into the cup where it activates a mechanism bathed in oil. If you use a heavy oil, the reel spool will turn slowly. If a light oil is used, the spool revolves at a higher rate. But you cannot easily change the oil for different weather conditions, so the viscosity type is not as popular as the previously mentioned types. In the cool of morning, the oil is rather thick. As the day warms up, the oil thins out and is less effective. In cold winter weather some oils get like putty. Nevertheless, many anglers are still enthusiastic about the oil cup.

Because all of these antibacklash devices do limit the distance of casts, most expert surf casters prefer to use the thumb method of spool control described in detail in Chapter 6. But for the novice surf caster an antibacklash reel is probably desirable; most people do not wish to spend endless hours untangling snarled lines while they are learning to cast. With a good reel having antibacklash controls, the beginner can expect to cast a reasonably good distance the first day out. Even the expert will find reel spool control useful at times.

Level Winders

Few salt-water reels have level winders and none of the reels used for really big game fish have them. However, several manufacturers are equipping their surf reels with them. The typical level winder has a double-threaded shaft mounted parallel to the reel spool axle. Into the double thread is fitted a hardened steel pawl. As the crisscross shaft turns, it forces the pawl back and forth in the double thread. The line holder is part of the pawl. Thus the line is wound evenly throughout the width of the spool. A special side plate allows the removal of the level wind mechanism without the complete disassembling of the reel. This is very desirable since this part of the reel requires special care. A drop of oil and a good cleaning with a brush or pipe cleaner will make the level winder of a salt-water reel last for a long period of time.

The leveling attachment of another manufacturer—though it, too, is actuated by a double-threaded screw—is thrown out of gear when casting. In gear it moves all during the time you are reeling in the line, but when the reel is thrown into free spool, the holder is also free and does not move, so the spool becomes free of all drag. In order to reduce the friction as the line passes through the holder, the line guide has a special enlarged section. While it is being cast, the line does not come off the reel at the same angle as when you are reeling in. It has a tendency to fly up, away from the reel spool. The enlarged part of the line guide is lined up with the flying line and cuts down on the drag. There is some friction, naturally. Yet, this reel produces fairly good results.

Perhaps the most important development in the level wind department is the "brain wave" device found on some reels. This features a crossbar located so the line runs over it as it is wound in. Since the bar is slightly high on the reel, the line is forced up over the bar and down to the spool. Naturally any drag on the line as it is reeled in will cause the line to press against this crossbar. The bar, or "brain wave," as the manufacturer calls it, is made with a set of shallow grooves. The line, pressing on the grooves, is forced back and forth as the "brain wave" revolves. The makers tell me their biggest trouble is teaching the fishermen to relax, to let the reel do all the work and to keep their hands off the line. The spiral bar moves one full turn in eight revolutions of the handle. When the line reaches the end of its travel (at the edge of the spool), another groove picks it up for the return trip to the other side of the reel. Because of the position of the guide bar, it is desirable to have the first line guide on the rod approximately 30 inches from the reel position. This level wind mechanism is totally inoperative during the cast. As a matter of fact, the spool is entirely free when you throw out the free spool lever. Thus you have a level-wind reel which takes all the manual leveling out of your fishing yet produces the maximum efficiency of a reel with no auxiliary features.

Spools

Originally all salt-water reels had rather narrow, deep spools. Now, however, there is a considerable diversity of shapes; surf-casting and squidding reel spools, for example, are wide and shallow. When braided-nylon lines first became popular on the West Coast years ago, the reel manufacturers

Methods of supporting big-game reels: cradle suspension (*top*), clamp support (*lower left*).

were greatly disturbed at the number of broken reel spools caused by the elasticity of the nylon. In fact, the spools were breaking at such a rapid rate that one reel manufacturer wanted to discourage the use of nylon. However, reel manufacturers have overcome this difficulty by producing models of newer and stronger alloys with reinforced flanges on the spool.

The great popular use of monofilament lines has created another problem. These lines (see page 28) are decidedly springy in the sizes used on salt-water reels, and have the annoying tendency of working themselves back of a spool flange if there is any space between the flange and the body of the reel. Once the monofilament line gets into the works, the reel has to be taken apart to straighten things out. Many of the newer reels coming onto the market are either adapted to or especially made for monofilament lines—that is, they have spools that fit tightly into the bodies.

Some of the reels used for surf casting and to fish salt-water bays and tidal rips use wide, light metal or plastic spools that allow the line to exit freely with a minimum of backlashing. These special reels hold from 150 to 250 yards of line. Minimum for surf fishing should be 150 yards, and many times you may need more if the big fish are stubborn. The 150-yard size is for light fishing; the 200-yard size for all around surf fishing, and the 250-yard size for large fish and heavy duty.

For best casting performance, fill the spool of your reel to capacity with line, or with a backing arbor and line. By doing this you'll be able to cast farther and reduce wear and tear on your reel. Most reel manufacturers recommend the amount of line of the various pound tests that their reels will hold with an arbor and without one. Remember that as a rule an arbor is not practical when more than 100 yards of line are required.

The method by which the reel is fastened to the rod is a matter of some importance. Small salt-water reels usually have the same type of feet that fresh-water reels have. There is, however, a limit to the strength of the shoes and rings that hold such feet to rods, and for the bigger reels, an additional device is employed. This consists of clamps fastened by wing nuts. The clamps go around the rod. This system provides a much stronger and more secure fastening than the foot and ring system alone. The extra weight helps to steady the reel.

Because a very large reel mounted on the top of a rod is an unstable thing, efforts have been made to lower the center of gravity. One method is to construct a reel so that it can hang under the rod instead of being attached to the top of it in the usual way. Another method is to build the reel into the rod handle so that the axis of the reel spool is on the same plane as the rod. This cradle suspension is effective in producing balance, but has the disadvantage of preventing the free interchanging of the reel from rod to rod. These larger salt-water reels all have eyelets or lugs on top of their frames for attaching the snaps of the fighting harness (see page 177).

Some of the reel manufacturers have even taken into consideration the fact that there are many fishermen who operate from the port side of the plate. Reels for left-handed anglers are available in a variety of models, at a slight additional charge.

Reel designs and improvements are always being made. New ideas also are being marketed. For instance, there is a new electric reel on the market which has become very popular among those who fish deep for such game fish as amberjacks and the groupers. This is a boon to the aged and the handicapped, and takes a lot of the grunting and groaning out of bottom fishing.

A fishing reel does a lot of work and gives a great deal of service without demanding much attention. During casting, the spool makes about 5,000 revolutions per minute, so you can understand that its bearings need oil and a certain amount of other care. It is always wise to follow the reel manufacturer's instructions for both operation and care. For general reel care instruction see Chapter 11.

Spinning Reels

Since World War II, no method of casting has gained such momentum as that of spinning. The beginning angler will ask: What is spinning? Why did it increase so rapidly in popularity? Can large fish be caught with spinning tackle? As used in this book, the term *spinning,* except in salmon fishing, means casting with a stationary spool reel. Instead of being pulled from a revolving spool, the line spins over the rim of a fixed spool without restraint. Actually, the spool of a spinning reel moves only when a fish is taking line out. It rotates on a spindle at the resistance set by the drag control. Various technical advantages accrue to the fisherman as a result. First, since it is the revolution of the spool which causes backlash, the stationary spool eliminates one of the fisherman's most exasperating hazards. Also, the lack of restraint on the line makes possible a longer cast with a lighter lure for the average fisherman.

Many people attribute the popularity of spinning to its ease of casting, a marked advantage for beginners. However, spinning is more than a lazy man's answer to the casting problem. While it is true that the fundamentals of spinning are easily learned, the fine points of using spinning tackle will be mastered only with practice (see Chapter 9).

Spinning has opened many new avenues of fun for the salt-water angler. Truly amazing records are being established by spin-men these days. For

Comparison of the action of conventional revolving-spool reel (*left*) and spinning wheel (*right*).

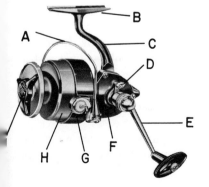

Parts of a salt-water spinning reel.
(*A*) Line pickup mechanism.
(*B*) Foot. (*C*) Leg.
(*D*) Antireverse control.
(*E*) Handle. (*F*) Gear housing.
(*G*) Spool cup. (*H*) Spool.
(*I*) Drag brake adjustment.

those who seek trophy fish in the light-tackle division, the field is wide open. A 150-pound marlin has been fought to a belly-up finish in running seas with an 8-pound test monofilament line. One angler, after a two-hour fight, landed a 261-pound mako shark on spinning gear with a 12-pound test monofilament line. With spinning tackle, whether you have hooked a big fish or a small one, every ounce of the fish's strength must be exhausted before it can be brought in for the net or gaff.

Spinning wasn't designed to replace conventional revolving-spool reel casting. Actually, spinning, as we know it, is simply a method of casting, not fishing. Although it is just another means of accomplishing the same thing as the conventional casting outfits, there is sufficient difference in the operation and action of the two to give them individual merit.

To sum up, the following are the major advantages of spinning tackle:

1. Casting is more easily learned.
2. Casts of greater distances are possible.
3. Light lures, including flies and live bait, are easier to cast.
4. Backlashing is eliminated; however, care must be taken to prevent tangles.
5. There is a more sensitive response to both small and large fish.

The major advantages of conventional revolving-spool-reel casting tackle are:

1. Big fish are handled more easily.
2. Greater accuracy in casting is possible.
3. Snag-infested waters do not give as much trouble.
4. Heavier lures are handled more easily.
5. Results are better when trolling.
6. Line is controlled more easily when playing a fish.

Line Pickup

As previously stated, spinning reels, unlike conventional reels with their revolving spools, have stationary spools from which the line peels or spills off the end when cast. There is no spool inertia to overcome, as with conventional reels. The weight of the cast lure is the only force that pulls the line off the spool of a spinning reel. As the line leaves the reel spool, it spins in a whirling motion, making about two turns, or whorls, for every foot cast. The line continues to peel off the reel spool only as long as the lure is moving forward. When the lure stops, the line stops unspooling. When the line is retrieved, the winding of the line is in an opposite direction to that of the whorls put in it during the forward cast, and the line, therefore, is respooled without twist.

In accepting the retrieved line, the spool of a spinning reel doesn't rotate like the spool of a conventional reel; it just moves in and out, or oscillates up and down, retrieving the line back on the spool evenly. A revolving cup turns around the spool to place the line back on it. Actually, a spinning reel's spool revolves only when the pull of a fighting fish exceeds the braking action of the drag, which is set just tight enough to let needed line peel from the reel spool.

There are three types of line pickup devices used on spinning reels. The line pickup device is that important part of the reel which catches the line and then winds it back on the reel spool after a cast. Each type has its advantages, and the choice is pretty much up to the angler. Two types—the full bail and the finger pickup—are automatic, while the third has a roller or manual pickup.

The full bail pickup is the most popular today. This type is characterized by a crescent of metal, wire-like in appearance. This half-circle of wire passes over the entire spool and is fastened on both sides of the cup or rotating head. In casting, the bail is pushed out of the way by passing it over the end of the spool. At the end of the cast, when the lure hits the water, or while it is still in the air, a turn of the handle flips the bail over the spool into the retrieving position. Expert anglers like this type of pickup because it is fast and is especially handy when fishing with lures, which must be reeled back the instant they strike the water. Beginners prefer the bail pickup because it is easy to use and requires little practice.

The finger pickup reel features an appendage similar in appearance to the human index finger. This piece of sharp, stiff metal wire is attached

This photo shows several major differences in the operation of a spinning reel as compared to a conventional reel. Note that the line is retrieved with the left hand and the spin reel hangs below the rod with the line guides also downward, while conventional reels are attached above the rod and the line is generally retrieved with the right hand.

to one side of the rotating head and is fastened in place by a hinge-like fixture. This finger swings into position as the lure strikes the water and catches the line for winding back on the spool. This is automatic and just requires the turning of the reel handle to pick up the line. The major difficulty of the finger pickup is that it often misses the line and sometimes the line tangles around the arm. The pickup arms are also often bent out of shape. For these reasons, plus the fact that it is easy to injure a finger on the sharp metal appendage, this type of spinning reel pickup isn't usually recommended for beginners.

The last method of line pickup, the roller, is manual. It consists of a hook or roller permanently attached to the side of the revolving cup. When casting, you lift the line from the pickup hook with your finger and make your cast. At the end of the cast or, to be more exact, while the line is still going out and the lure has almost hit the water, you extend the index finger of your casting hand and interrupt the flow of the line. As line strikes your finger, you catch it. By drawing it away from the spool toward the rod handle, you place it in position to be picked up by the hook. Then, as you turn the reel handle, the pickup hook comes around and catches the line. It requires some practice to achieve the proper finger technique, but many expert anglers like the manual method because line is more easily controlled. Also spin reels with manual pickups are a bit less expensive than reels with automatic pickups. Another big advantage of the reel with manual pickup is that it is sturdier, with fewer parts to break down.

The better spin reels have a roller over which the line runs when retrieved. This roller takes a lot of wear, especially when retrieving heavy lures or fighting big fish. These rollers turn freely and should, of course, be made of very hard metal, agate, or sapphire. Otherwise a groove will soon appear where the line rubs against them.

Drag Control

Since light lines are generally used in spinning, the drag is a very important part of any good spinning reel. When a fish desires to run, a good drag allows him to do so without placing too great a strain on the line. So a vital consideration when choosing a spinning reel is that the drag action must be smooth. And it must also keep the tension at which it has previously been set. There are still a few spinning reels available which do not meet these requirements. When angling with the heavier spinning lines and for fish which don't run or leap much, the drag is not too important. But for light spinning line and for the more active game fish, the drag should not jerk or bind. It should also have a gradual adjustment instead of a sudden one—when you increase the drag or decrease it you should be able to do it a little at a time. On a few reels a slight twist of the knob will increase the drag too greatly. During a fight with a fish you may break the line by applying the drag too quickly.

Drags for spinning reels vary somewhat in construction, but the majority make use of some type of slipping clutch which exerts pressure on the reel spool. These drags can be set so that the amount of pressure on the spool is regulated. On most reels this consists of a wing or knurled nut in front of the spool which can be tightened or loosened, as desired. But other reels have various attachments at different parts of the reel for controlling the drag. The amount of drag necessary for best results is a controversial subject among salt-water spin anglers. Some prefer to fish with a light drag; others like as much drag as the line will take. Regardless of the amount desired, the best method of adjusting the drag is to rig up your spin rod and reel as for actual fishing. Then get someone to run off approximately sixty feet of line. If you are alone you can tie the end of the line to a tree or similar solid support and then back up and let out that much line. Now tighten your drag slightly and back up. Keep backing up and tightening your drag until the rod takes its approximate maximum bend. When this occurs, try backing up a little farther. The line should still slip off the spool but not too easily. Now you have about the maximum fishing drag that this particular line and pole will safely stand. If you are fishing for small bottom species which don't run, you can leave that setting. However, if you are fishing for fish which run a long way, leap, or otherwise put up an active scrap you should make the drag somewhat looser.

Antireverse Lock; Choice of Spools; Left-Hand Winding

Another useful device found on most salt-water spinning reels is the antireverse lock. When this is at the "on" position it prevents the handle from turning backwards. Many anglers like it so much that they leave it at the "on" position all the time. But it was primarily designed for fighting a fish and should be put on as soon as a fish is hooked. This device is also helpful when you are fishing alone and want to land a fish. Then you can take your hand off the reel handle and use it for netting or gaffing a fish. The antireverse can also be used while you are still-fishing or trolling. In still-fishing or trolling you often put the rod down, and with the antireverse in the "on" position any strike is against the drag. Most spin reels with the antireverse "on" also have an audible click which warns of a bite or strike. When the fishing outfit isn't being used, it should also have the antireverse "on," or the handle will turn and the line will be taken off the reel if it gets caught on anything.

Salt-water spin reels come in various sizes and in weights from 10 to 20 ounces or more. The larger ones are used for offshore fishing and for surf fishing.

Spools and spool capacity are also important considerations in salt-water spin-fishing. The spools must be strong to take the strain of fighting a big fish. Synthetic lines, especially monofilament when packed tight on a reel spool during a fight with a fish, also exert terrific pressure and can easily break or damage a weak spool. The spool should also hold enough line for the type of fishing you plan to do. Most fishing done in salt water with a spin outfit employs the use of 10-, 12-, 15- and 20-pound test lines. In the heavier tests you cannot get much line on a small spool and you do not get much casting distance if your line unreels too close to the center of the spool. To make their reels more adaptable for different types of salt-water fishing and various sizes of lines, several manufacturers feature interchangeable spools. With such spools, you can have one for each type of line you will use. Unfortunately, spinning reel manufacturers have not set up a standard code of reel line capacities and thus you must check each individual reel as to the amount of line it will hold.

One of the biggest differences between spinning reels and most conventional reels, as far as the angler is concerned, is that the spin reel hangs below the rod, with the line guides also downward, while conventional reels are attached above the rod. And the spin reel usually comes with the crank handle on the left side, while most conventional revolving spool reels have right-hand cranks. Many persons who are novices in spinning but experienced in other methods of fishing object to the handle being on the left side, necessitating left-hand operation. But this inconvenience soon disappears, because left-hand winding is learned quickly and easily.

The major advantage of left-hand winding is that you can use a spin rod with your right hand, then immediately grasp the reel handle and wind in the line with your left hand. The rod doesn't change hands and you are ready for action at all times. When casting with the conventional reel, you cast with your right hand or on the right side, then transfer the rod and reel to your left hand or left side before you can turn the handle efficiently. While this is not a serious inconvenience if you make only a few casts, the extra motions become a burden on wrists, arms, and back if you are casting continuously. In addition, you must always support the conventional reel on top of the rod. A spin reel, on the other hand, enjoys a more balanced position under the rod. For left-handed anglers the handle should be on the right side, and some reels can be obtained with it there.

Closed-Face Spinning

In addition to the opened-face spinning reels just discussed, there is the closed-face type. While popular for years with the fresh-water angler, they are now being used by some of his salt-water brethren. As the name implies, the closed-face spinning reels have completely enclosed spools. The line, instead of running from the reel in large spirals, is conducted through a hole in the face of the cone. This hole reduces the spiraling of the line, thus making it more adaptable to night fishing and windy conditions. With a closed-face you have a little more control of the line than with the other type. Because of the cone, however, more care of the reel is required and the length of casts "seems" more restricted. Many experts claim that this isn't so, saying that casts are more accurate with closed-face reels.

The line pickup with a closed-face spinning reel is accomplished by a pin or lug which engages the line inside the housing. This type is more positive under all conditions than the opened-face reel, and accidental spilling of the line into uncontrolled loose spirals is impossible. There are few reels of this type that come with a "push-button" that allows thumb control of the line, too. There are also several types of drag arrangements, but the most popular seems to be the slip-clutch drag which takes the form of a micrometer-type arrangement in which the outer cone is adjustable. The micrometer ring is tightened for more drag, loosened for less. The antireverse lock feature and the line capacities are similar to those of the opened-faced reels.

SALT-WATER LINES

By definition, a line is that part of the fishing tackle which provides the link between the angler and the fish. Without question, the line plays the most important part in handling big fish. A poor line can be the weak link in the chain that connects the fish, thrashing around on one end, with the fisherman, thrashing around on the other. The improper line for a specific condition can even prevent the angler from hooking the fish in the first place.

Salt-water fishing lines take tremendous punishment. They chafe against the bottoms and sides of boats, against pilings and rocks; they are worn by the action of sun, salt water, and sand, rotted by slime, blood, oil, and acids, cut off by fish and propellers.

Fishing line is usually designated by its strength in pound test. In factories, the pound test of the common salt-water lines is established by a special traction machine. The sample of line to be tested is inserted in the machine, which pulls it until it breaks. At the point where the sample breaks, the machine registers the pressure. For example, if a line withstands pressure up to 36 pounds before it breaks, it is a 36-pound test line.

Only a few short years ago, the most popular and most widely used salt-water line was made from Irish and Belgian linen. This was an excellent type of line, despite many shortcomings, and is still used by a *very* few experienced anglers, especially when going after the big fellows. Linen lines came in two types, braided and twisted; the latter, known as "cuttyhunk," was the best and most widely used for salt-water fishing.

Linen lines were graded according to the number of threads in multiples of three, from 3-thread to 72-thread. The unit of strength of a thread was usually rated at three pounds, wet strength. A 3-thread line represented 9-pound test, a 54-thread line 162-pound test. The strength of the more common salt-water linen lines as based on the wet test (the standard most widely used in the fishing equipment industry) was:

No. of Threads	3	6	9	12	15	18	21
Wet Test	9 lb.	18 lb.	27 lb.	36 lb.	45 lb.	54 lb.	63 lb.
* IGFA Classification	12 lb.	20 lb.	30 lb.		50 lb.		

No. of Threads		24	27	30	36	39	54
Wet Test		72 lb.	81 lb.	90 lb.	108 lb.	117 lb.	162 lb.
* IGFA Classification		80 lb.				130 lb.	180 lb.

* See page 5.

Synthetic Braided Lines

Today, most of the lines used on conventional revolving-spool reels are of braided nylon or dacron. The spin-caster on the other hand usually prefers the use of a synthetic monofilament line.

Of the two braided types, dacron has become the most popular mainly because it has less elasticity than the nylon lines. Any degree of stretch in a line is undesirable because you don't receive instant strike response. That is, with dacron lines "action at the bait is 'telegraphed' immediately to the rod," not lost in the line as often happens with lines that stretch. Also, the hook sets faster because there is no stretch to overcome first. There is better lure control, too. Surface baits, bottom rigs, trolling lures, and live bait are worked more effectively. And again, there is better fish control, because you fight the fish, not the stretch.

The thin diameter of dacron puts more yards of line on any reel than lines of most other materials, except for the very *better* grades of nylon. In casting, the thin diameter helps improve accuracy and increase distance. "You hit the target area more often." Also, a thin line means less drag in the water, more positive lure and fish control, and faster retrieve because you're fishing with a tighter line. In addition, dacron retains maximum strength at the knot when "direct pull" knots are used. These knots are the most reliable since loops and folds do not cross each other, and thereby do not cut the dacron material.

As was stated in Chapter 1, world records are based on line test in seven classes—12, 20, 30, 50, 80, 130, and 180 pounds. To qualify for a record in any of these classes, the line used must not exceed the test allowed. For this reason, many manufacturers label their dacron lines according to "class," rather than "test," to make sure a fisherman knows he is using a line that qualifies for a particular IGFA class. A "class" line tests *up to, but not over* its class, while a "test" line does not test under its test. For example: a 30-pound class line tests *up to, but not over* 30 pounds. A 30-pound test line tests *not less than* 30 pounds. As a margin of safety, these "class" lines are made to test about 10 per cent below the class. A 30-pound class line tests about 27 pounds, a 50-pound class line tests about 45 pounds, and so forth. This assures a fisherman that the particular line he uses will qualify for a particular IGFA class. Dacron lines, of course, are also listed by test. The most popular test weights are 8, 12, 15, 18, 27, 36, and 45. Squidding or surf-casting lines are usually available in 18-, 27-, 36-, and 45-pound test weights.

The stretch disadvantage of nylon lines has been greatly reduced in the past few years. Also, the diameter of nylon line seems to be reduced each year while the test weight remains the same. Thus nylon lines are now on their way back, especially since they are less expensive than dacron lines. Some lines now available actually combine nylon and dacron.

Nylon lines are available in line pound test similar to the old linen types, but are not rated in accordance with the number of strands or threads.

Nylon Lines Commonly Available

*IGFA Classification	12 lb.	20 lb.	30 lb.	50 lb.		80 lb.		130 lb.
Pound Test	12 lb.	18 lb.	27 lb.	36 lb.	45 lb.	63 lb.	72 lb.	108 lb.

* See page 5.

Braided synthetic lines are usually available in spools of 50 or 100 yards and sold in boxes which contain two to six spools. (In larger test weights 500- and 1,200-yard spools are available in individually packed boxes.) Putting two to six connected spools of line on your reel is almost as easy as putting on a single spool, if you follow these simple directions. First, string all the spools (in the order in which they were spooled) on a pencil, a heavy wire, or anything that is long enough to hold all the spools and permit them to revolve freely together. Next, loosen the line on the end spool, either right or left, by using your fingernail, the small reel wrench that comes with your reel, or something else that does not have a sharp point or cutting edge. Now loosen the end of the line (usually it is tucked under itself about three times in tying-off at the factory) and tie it to the spool shaft of your reel or around the arbor. Start winding it on. All the spools will revolve. Then, as one spool is emptied, remove it, repeat the operation described above with the next spool, and so on until your reel is filled. As you loosen the line tie of the second and each succeeding spool it will be necessary to slip the entire reel through the "tie off" loops of the line. If you wish you can use cellophane tape to hold all the spools firmly together, but this is not necessary.

Synthetic lines are available in several colors—green, yellow, charcoal, tan, blue, black, various shades of gray, and even blended colors. Which color is best for salt-water fishing? Frankly, I doubt that it makes any great difference. Fish seem to take a lure that is tied to a black line about as readily as one tied to a tan one—or green, charcoal, or mottled gray. If a line always passed directly over the fish, so that the fish could see it against the silvery surface of the water, perhaps a light-colored line would be best; or if the line always passed under the fish, a color that matched the bottom —brown, charcoal, or black—would be the least conspicuous. Or, still again, if the line invariably passed to one side of the fish, perhaps it would be better if it matched the tone of the water—tan, gray, or perhaps even a somber tone of green. But since the line will be over, under, and at all sides of fish, it is difficult to see how one color can be preferred over another. But, don't tell that to a Southern angler because he'll debate that the dark green line is preferable to one of lighter color.

Monofilament Lines

Mono means one and monofilament simply means one filament. This is the name given to the hundreds of different kinds of lines made by the extrusion process and has nothing to do with any one brand. Monofilament, particularly the flat or oval type, is being widely used in salt-water spinning, but it is also used on conventional reels, and several manufacturers have produced reels specially designed for its use. The smooth transparent qualities of these lines are one of the reasons why they interest salt-water anglers. A smooth line means less water drag. The reduced drag allows the trolling fisherman to fish much deeper than he could with either of the two braided synthetics. For the bottom fisherman, it also means he can use much lighter sinkers and still hold bottom because water currents tend to lift a line with drag. Until the development of the ultra-soft and limp monofilament line, however, conventional reel casting was difficult.

Salt-water monofilament lines are most commonly available in 6- to 50-pound test. To install a mono line on your spinning reel's spool it is necessary first to determine the direction of the pickup. Most reels pick up and distribute the line clockwise; the pickup of right-side crank models (left-hand reels) revolves in a counterclockwise direction. To make the line installation task easy, some manufacturers are making their lines available in special containers or "spin-packs" rather than on regular spools. These spin-packs are factory-positioned to empty counterclockwise and to fill reels picking up clockwise. To reverse emptying of a pack, simply remove the lock pin, grasp both wheels together, and flop in place on the card. Replace the lock pin. Now the line will come off in a clockwise direction from the bottom of the pack wheel. To be sure that there is sufficient tension on the line, tighten the drag so there is no slippage, and with the spin-pack held by your foot, apply pressure with your finger on the cone hole so that the line spools on tightly.

To fill a reel from a regular spool, ask someone to hold the spool with his thumb beside the back spool lip. The spool should be positioned so that the line spirals off the facing of the spool edge as it's emptied.

The major reason why synthetic-fiber lines—both mono and braided— replaced linen was that they are extremely resistant to deterioration from salt water. While most lines require no *special* care (see Chapter 11), many anglers still wash them out in fresh water after use. I think this is a good idea, especially in the case of nylon lines—either braided or monofilament.

Wire Lines

Any angler who spends much time deep-water trolling invariably uses wire lines. Stainless steel, bronze, copper and other corrosive-proof metals have

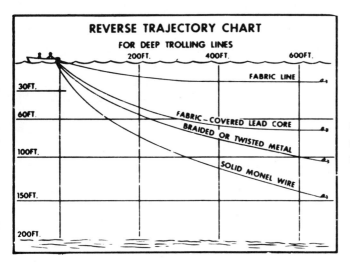

Comparison of deep trolling lines.

had their moments of popularity, but the present-day trend is toward Monel (a nickel alloy). Monel has a high tensile strength per diameter and a low surface resistance to water friction. Solid Monel wire, for instance, descends to greater depths than the other type lines under equal trolling speeds. It has a lower water drag and a greater density than the other types, so the sinking coefficient is greater. The solid wire is ideal for trolling below the 100-foot level because it does not require sinkers to get it down there.

There are four types of wire lines: solid, twisted, braided, and fabric-covered lead core. (The latter usually has a lead core inside a tightly braided nylon jacket.) While the twisted wire line will stand careless usage better than solid wire, it doesn't sink· so deeply or abruptly. The braided and lead-core lines do not sink so fast, nor so deep, as the solid or twisted line, but each has its purpose, depending on the type and depth of trolling you are doing (see Chapter 7). Wire lines range from 5- to 85-pound test, with the most popular sizes being 26- and 35-pound.

The one major disadvantage of all wire lines is that they are more difficult to control when playing a fish. Unless handled with the utmost care, wire can get into some terrible tangles. Letting it flow off the reel is the critical operation. If you let it overrun, you can get a mess that almost defies untangling. Also all wire lines kink readily, but the single-stranded (solid) line gets the most serious kinks, followed by the twisted line and the braided line. Most kinks are caused by letting the line spin out too fast behind a moving boat. If you get a loose kink, you can straighten it out with your fingers, but a tight one should always be cut out and spliced (see section on knot-tying in Chapter 3).

Resourceful bluefish and striped-bass anglers have worked out an excellent combination which nearly eliminates wire-line breakage due to kinks. The combination at Montauk, New York, for example, is this: 15 feet of 45-pound test monofilament leader, 200 feet of wire line backed by more monofilament line. The line is paid out astern until about a foot of the monofilament backing runs out of the tiptop guide. The monofilament acts as a shock absorber, preventing kinks and breakage due to kinks. It also makes the line more controllable. In other areas, the length of the wire line can be adjusted to the depth of the waters. It takes a little experimenting, but this combination is very popular from Cape Hatteras to Provincetown along the East Coast. Remember, when using wire lines, to be sure to use a reel specifically designed for wire.

Selecting Your Lines

In big-game fishing braided dacron and nylon are the most common; however, a few old-timers are still able to find enough linen line for this type of salt-water fishing. But since large amounts of line are required to fight big fish, be sure the reel you use is constructed to withstand the pressures that synthetic lines can create. Braided synthetics are preferred over monofilament lines by surf casters, too.

For bottom fishing and average offshore trolling, braided nylon or dacron is ideal. Nylon stretches a little, but that is not a great disadvantage. You must just be alert to set the hook quicker and harder in the fish's mouth. Use a sharp hook, too. These are the best all-around lines for the weekend fisherman.

Though braided nylon or dacron lines can be used for spin fishing, monofilament is best. Monofilament is very good for trolling with a 3/0 reel or smaller. Perhaps before long the very large reels will be made stronger and this line can then be used on these reels too. You can also use your monofilament line for bottom fishing.

The skill of the angler also determines what line strength to use. A beginner is better off with a slightly stronger line until he learns how to cast and play a fish. An expert with a light outfit and line can make "stunt" catches which a beginner should not even attempt. It takes quite a bit of experience before you can judge just how much strain your line will take before breaking. But even experts using the best tackle lose some prize fish because of broken lines—if you want the most sport and fun you have to accept that.

SALT-WATER RODS

By definition, a rod is a manufactured stick in one piece or in two or more sections joined together by ferrules or splices, which tapers progressively from butt to tip and is fitted with guides, hand grasp or grasps, and reel seat. There are stiff rods and limber rods; some are short, some long. Only by trial and error can you decide which is best for you. One decision that you don't have to make is that of material. Almost all rods manufactured today are made of tubular fiberglass (usually referred to as "glass" rods). A few bamboo, hickory, beryllium-copper, and tubular-steel rods still can be found in use, but no major companies are manufacturing them any more.

Salt-water rods can be divided roughly into five classes: surf-casting, trolling, still-fishing, bait-casting, and spinning rods. Generally it will be found that one rod is entirely suitable for use in several different classes.

Surf-casting Rods

The regulation surf rod is usually made in two pieces—the butt and the tip. (Rods with one-piece tips are very much stronger than those which are jointed in the middle. The two-piece jointed-tip rods are not designed for casting and will not give satisfactory service if so used.) A one-piece tip, 6, 6½, 7, 7½, 8, or 8½ feet long, its butt capped with a "male"-style metal ferrule, is fitted to a 20- or 30-inch club or spring butt, giving an over-all rod length of 8, 8½, 9, 9½, 10, 10½, or 11 feet depending on the length of the tip section. Rod length should be in proportion to the height and arm length of the fisherman. A good procedure to follow is to experiment first with a tip that measures six to fifteen inches longer than your own height and with a tip weight from six to fifteen ounces in proportion to the weight of the lure to be cast. Experienced surf casters generally agree that a surf rod should never feel too heavy at the tip and that, in casting, the angler should feel the pull of the lure being tossed beyond some distant breaker.

The length, weight, and action of the tip section is an important factor in casting. For squidding from a beach, under average conditions and with average lures, a medium-weight rod (9- to 12-ounce tip) of 6½ or 7 feet is very suitable. It should be fairly stiff in action since long casts are often desired. When fishing from piers, jetties, or rocky shore lines where the caster stands only a few feet above the water level and uses light lures, a shorter, lighter (6- to 9-ounce tip) rod with a softer action can be used. For bottom fishing or squidding from a beach where heavy lures, baits and sinkers are used, and long casts are needed, a long (7½ to 8½ feet), heavy (12- to 15-ounce tip), and somewhat stiffer rod is generally more satisfactory. See Chapter 6 for more details on the selection of rod for different types of surf casting.

The long rod butt of the surf rod gives the two-handed powerful leverage so essential in surf casting and is the necessary complement to the long, tapered tip section. The most common rod butt material is hickory, and you have a choice of two types of rod butts—the club pattern, which has the same diameter throughout, and the spring butt, which tapers to a smaller diameter in the middle. Of the two styles, the club pattern seems to be most popular with the average surf caster. But, regardless of the style, you should select the one that feels most natural when you grip it. Including the metal reel seat that accepts the tip ferrule as well as the reel, the rod butt lengths run from twenty to thirty inches, depending on the length and weight of the tip section. For bottom fishing with bait, the length of the butt is not of great importance because casts are few and far between, though the regulation 28- to 30-inch butt is most satisfactory for the average man with long arms. But in casting artificial lures, where casting must be done continuously, the butt must fit perfectly or else the casting task will become very awkward and tiring. Most light rods used for this purpose have a shorter butt than the heavier bait-casting rods. These butts usually run from twenty to twenty-six inches in length. A rubber butt cap is a useful addition, because of the confidence it seems to give the novice surf angler when grasping the rod butt securely for a cast.

Sizes of surf rod guides will be roughly ¾ inch for the light tip guide to ⅞ inch for the line guide nearest the reel, with those spaced between in proportion. But, in selecting the surf rod, the height, weight, arm length, and style of casting of the individual angler must all be taken into consideration.

Trolling Rods

Trolling rods for salt-water fishing are classified according to tip weight, the weight of the tip being indicative of the strength of the rod and, therefore, its suitability for a certain type of fishing. The general classifications are as follows:

4-ounce tip size. For ultralight tackle class. 5-foot tip, 17-inch butt. Reel seat diameter, ⅞ inch. An ideal rod for fish averaging from one to ten pounds.

6-ounce tip size. For the light tackle class. 5-foot tip, 14-inch butt. For weakfish, small striped bass, mackerel, bluefish and other fish averaging from five to fifteen pounds.

9-ounce tip size. Light-medium tackle class. 5-foot tip, 17-inch butt. Felt-covered foregrip. For albacore, small tarpon, salmon, striped bass, yellowtail, and other fish from fifteen to fifty pounds.

12-ounce tip size. Medium-weight tackle class. 5-foot tip, 17-inch butt.

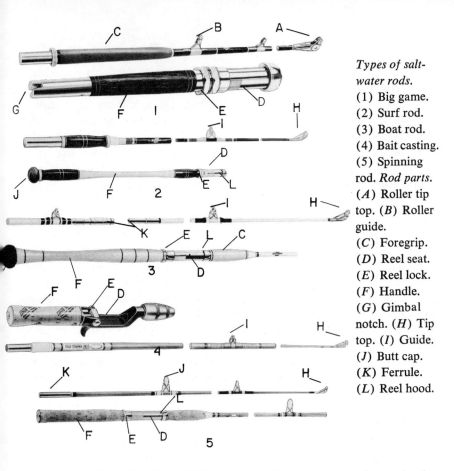

Types of salt-water rods.
(1) Big game.
(2) Surf rod.
(3) Boat rod.
(4) Bait casting.
(5) Spinning rod. *Rod parts.*
(*A*) Roller tip top. (*B*) Roller guide.
(*C*) Foregrip.
(*D*) Reel seat.
(*E*) Reel lock.
(*F*) Handle.
(*G*) Gimbal notch. (*H*) Tip top. (*I*) Guide.
(*J*) Butt cap.
(*K*) Ferrule.
(*L*) Reel hood.

Felt-covered foregrip. For sailfish, tarpon, school tuna, marlin, and other fish of fifty to one hundred pounds.

As a rule, a limber rod is an advantage over one that is too stiff, heavy, or large. It gives the victims a better fighting chance, and distributes the strain more equally over the length of the rod and onto the line. The line, of course, must be able to cushion the rod tip against the sudden shocks produced when the fisherman pumps and reels, and by the fish when he runs, lunges, or sounds. The problem, then, is to match the suppleness of the tip with the breaking strain of the line. The heavier the line, the stiffer the tip. In buying rods for general trolling, perhaps the best approach is to remember that the tip should not be less than five feet in length when measured from the shoulder of the ferrule.

For trolling with line of nine thread and heavier, a rod with a pulley tip is best. It is a great deal easier on your line, causing much less wear. If you can't get a pulley tip, be sure that you do not get an agate tip or agate guides. In surf casting they may help you attain a trifle more distance, but in boat fishing they are likely to get cracked or broken without the angler's noticing it. (Stainless steel guides and tips are the best for boat fishing.) Then, too, the boat fisherman usually has about twice as many guides on his rod as has the surf caster. Five guides is the correct number for offshore fishing. High guides, while not a necessity, are desirable because they help to take the strain off the rod and the line runs through them more easily.

On rods up to 12 ounces a cork grip is preferable. On the heavier sizes, a felt grip is best; it is more comfortable to the hand and it doesn't hold water. Be sure to get one that has not been dyed with some color that may run and get on your line. One good feature of the modern grip is the locking device which prevents the tip from turning in the butt.

The length of the butt for the trolling rod should be governed by two factors: the size of the angler and the manner in which he likes to fight a fish. First the butt must be suited as nearly as possible to the angler's reach so that the reel and forward grip will be in the least tiring position for pumping and winding. Next to be considered is whether the angler fishes entirely from a chair, using the chair's rod gimbals, or whether he plays the fish standing up, or sitting with the butt resting in a belt socket or pushed in against his waist. Do not hesitate to try the butt for size before taking it out of the tackle shop. A butt at all times should be substantial enough to carry a strong, solid reel seat. The seat should be heavy enough to hold a reel firmly against any side strain as well as the forward pull. (Specific recommendations for big-game fishing rods can be found in Chapter 8.)

Still-Fishing Rods

The most popular rod for bottom fish is the tubular fiberglass "boat rod" with one or two sections and from five to six feet in over-all length. Tips should be six to nine ounces and over-all characteristics of these sticks are the same as described for light or light-medium trolling rods. The butt should be twelve to eighteen inches long and should have a good screw-locking reel seat with grips above and below it. This shorter butt enables the angler in a sitting or standing position to place the butt firmly against the body for ease in reeling and in handling the fish. This rod can be used from piers, bridges, shore, and boats, and is best for the medium- and large-sized bottom fish and for fishing in deep water and in strong currents where heavy sinkers are required.

For bay fishing and other protected waters the smaller rods known as bay, weakfish or flounder rods are best. These run up to five or six feet in over-all length with a tip of two to four ounces. They should be as light as possible; they should have plenty of "give" because the fish caught in protected waters are not generally very heavy and you want to have as much sport with them as you can. A heavy, stiff rod takes most of the fun out of the fight. Furthermore, these fish bite rather delicately, and if you sit there with a rod built like a tent pole, you might not even feel the fish nibbling. You'll just spend the day putting bait on the hook for crabs, sea robins, blowfish, and other fish to steal.

Bait-Casting Rods

Many anglers use fresh-water bass rods for certain types of salt-water fishing (see Chapter 9 for details). These bait-casting rods should be 5 to 5½ feet in tip length and have medium or heavy action. Many heavy-action casting rods are designed with a rear cork grip two or three inches longer than the conventional cork grip, and this extra length is a decided advantage when playing a large fish, for it allows the butt to rest against the body and gives the angler more leverage. The reel seat should be of the screw-locking type that will hold the reel securely under all conditions. There is nothing more annoying than to have the reel come loose when you are playing a large fish. The guides and tip top should be of either carboloy or stainless steel with a chrome deposit.

The regular 100-yard size, quadruple-multiplying, level-wind casting reel is ideal. Some anglers prefer a 150-yard reel, and this is to be recommended when large fish are the principal ones encountered. However, it is more tiresome to cast than the 100-yard size, and does not lend itself to long casts as well.

Spinning Rods

It was not too long ago that the angler who wanted to try salt-water spinning had to use a fresh-water rod. What a difference today! Now we have salt-water rods to take care of almost every kind of spin fishing.

Salt-water spinning rods are of three kinds: light, medium, and heavy. The light salt-water spin rod, generally made of hollow glass, should be short enough and light enough to cast with one hand. This means the 6-, 6½- and 7-foot lengths are best for this work. Some of the rods in this class will handle lures up to 1½ ounces, but most of them work best with lures of one ounce or less. Such rods will also cast lures as light as ⅜ ounce a fair distance, using, of course, a light line. This makes the light salt-water spin rod a very versatile tool. The 8-pound test line is used with such a rod for most spinning, with the 10- and 12-pound tests occasionally needed. The light spin rod is ideal for boat fishing in rivers, bays, sounds, and other shallow waters. It can also be used from shore in quiet waters, and makes a good rod for wading and fishing in the Bahamas, Florida, the Gulf of Mexico, and other shallow flats and protected waters. For such fish as small striped bass, weakfish, channel bass, bluefish, snook, and small salmon, the light rod is sporty. Although used mainly for casting artificial lures, this rod can also be used for bottom fishing in shallow waters where currents are not very strong. Sinkers should not be much heavier than 2 ounces. The best reel for this rod is the smaller-sized salt-water model.

The medium rod is from about 7½ to 9 feet in over-all length. This rod has a butt of 14 to 24 inches and it is cast with two hands. The shorter, lighter rods in this class make good boat rods and also shore casting rods.

The longer ones can be used for light surf fishing. In this class you will find many of the salmon rods used in the Northwest for "mooching" for salmon. (See page 114.) The medium-weight rods can usually handle lures and sinkers weighing up to 2 ounces if flexible, and a bit heavier if stiff. Lines testing 12 to 15 pounds are suitable. This rod also makes a good pier, bridge, or jetty rod where long casts are not required and heavy lures are not used. It is also good for light trolling and for bottom fishing with bait. If a man had to choose one spinning rod for salt-water fishing, the medium rod is the most versatile. It is constructed of either solid or hollow glass.

The heavy rod measures from 8½ to 12 feet in over-all length, with most of these rods falling in the 9- to 10½-foot range. This is the most practical rod for most surf fishing along both the Pacific and Atlantic Coasts. Pacific Coast surf casters like the longer, more flexible rods, while Atlantic surf casters traditionally prefer their rods of shorter lengths, with a stiff action in the tip for casting heavy lures when needed. You can heave a lure or sinker weighing up to three ounces with some of these rods. The heavy rod also enables you to reach those distant holes, bars, and feeding fish. It will handle the largest fish found in the surf, with the exception of the bigger sharks and rays. Lines testing from fifteen to thirty pounds can be used on the larger reels with the heavy rods.

The construction of these heavy spinning rods varies widely according to the manufacturer. Some have heavy hardwood butts and hickory and heavy brass chrome-plated reel seats. Others have lighter hollow-glass butt sections with light aluminum reel seats and cork grips. This makes a somewhat lighter rod. For surf fishing, a one-piece tip section fitted into a separate butt section makes the strongest rod. The two-piece spin rods in which a ferrule is used at the middle are preferred for boat fishing. They are also easier to carry when you must transport them. These tips or sections may be of either solid or hollow glass.

Regardless of the class of spin rod, make sure that the reel you have fits the reel seat on the rod you are buying. There are so many spinning reels, both imported and domestic, that you will find they vary considerably in the size and thickness of the reel foot. If your reel does not fit, it can often be filed down to make it fit. For complete information on various rod, reel, and line combinations, see page 260.

Despite the wide variety of salt-water rods on the market, many anglers prefer to build their own boat rods and surf rods. Thus the angler can have the fun of experimenting with these adaptable materials and can build a rod to his own specifications. Or you can purchase a do-it-yourself rod kit and assemble it. The raw materials—glass blanks, cork grips, reel seat and guides—or a complete kit with full instructions can be purchased from any sporting goods dealer.

CHAPTER **3**

Terminal Tackle, Natural Baits,

and Artificial Lures

IN SALT-WATER FISHING, the term "terminal tackle" is applied to everything that is attached to the end of the actual fishing line—leader, swivel, sinker, hook, lure, bait, etc. In this chapter we shall discuss the individual components of the terminal tackle or rig. For specific terminal rigs in the different types of salt-water fishing—surf casting, inshore fishing, trolling, big-game fishing, etc.—see Chapters 5, 6, 7, 8, and 9.

LEADERS

The leader is a connecting length between the line and lure, or between the hook and the snap or swivel at the end of the line. It may be made of heavy synthetic or metal wire—either twisted, braided or single-strand. It usually has a snap at one end, a swivel at the other. The leader serves two main purposes: its relative invisibility deceives the fish by making the lure or bait appear to be unattached to a line, and it provides a cutproof and chafeproof link between the lure or bait and the more fragile line.

Most fishermen have at some time or other tried to fool noncooperative fish by throwing a handful of bait into the water, one piece of which was attached to a hook. Perhaps this seems like taking unfair advantage of the hungry fish. But usually the intended victim demonstrates its ability to take care of itself: it gulps every morsel of the bait except the one hiding the hook. This is not because of some supernatural prescience peculiar to fish. It is simply a matter of eyesight. A fish's usual dinner comes with no strings attached—especially, no long string that leads up to the surface of the water. For fishing results, the hook hidden in the bait or lure must, of course, in some way connect to the fisherman. But the trick is to let this connection show as little as possible and this means making the leader nearly invisible.

Most experts agree that, because invisibility is so important, the best leader you can use is the lightest one that will take the fish you are after. Some fish slash and cut at their food, others over-run the bait. The leader

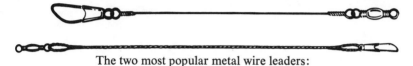

The two most popular metal wire leaders:
single-strand (*top*) and twisted (*bottom*).

used must be able to stand up to their sharp teeth. Others swallow their bait and will chafe through any but a sturdy leader. Some display fantastic strength for their size. Some, like the two-pound pirana of South American waters, have jaws that close with the bang of a steel trap and require heavy steel leaders and stout hooks. Others, like the mild-mannered and toothless pompano, allow even the most delicate leader to enjoy a long life.

Most successful fishermen are skilled in preparing their fresh bait so that it will troll, drift, or sink naturally in the water. Likewise, manufacturers of artificial lures do their best to produce lures with especially enticing action. But the action and appearance of a lure can be only as effective as the leader will let it be. Stiff leaders often partly or wholly upset the effect. Only with a good, flexible leader of low visibility is a lure really what it was intended to be.

In most salt-water fishing, it is necessary to have a metal or wire leader on your lures or hooks, because other types of leaders will be quickly cut by the sharp teeth of such fish as barracuda, bonito, and bluefish, and the gill and fin covers of many salt-water fish. These metal leaders will vary according to the type of fish you are seeking and the fishing you are doing.

Short wire leaders, 6 to 9 inches long, often have one end permanently attached to jigs, plugs, squids, and other lures. The other end has a small loop or eye to which the snap on the end of the standard line leader is attached. This makes for easy changing of lures.

For light spinning shorter leaders are best, but for surf fishing you may use somewhat longer ones running about 9 or 12 inches in length. In trolling for the larger gamefish you need still longer ones—up to 3 feet for albacore, bonito, school tuna, etc., and up to 15 feet for the billfish such as marlin, swordfish, sailfish, etc. (For specific species see Chapter 8.) Generally metal leaders are rated in pound tests or breaking strength in pounds in the same manner as line.

In general, three kinds of material are used for metal leaders: single strand, bare cable, and plastic-covered cable. Single strand, which is frequently used for the largest of fish, is usually of stainless steel or tinned piano wire. It is strong for its size and does not kink under tension, but it is frequently shiny, and these flashes of light from the leader can be a disadvantage. However, metal leaders of stainless steel or tinned wire are the most popular in salt-water angling today.

	BREAKING STRENGTH, POUNDS	
Leader Sizes	*Stainless Steel*	*Tinned Wire*
2	27	30
3	32	35
4	38	40
5	44	48
6	58	64
7	69	80
8	86	100
9	105	115
10	124	138
11	140	160
12	174	200
13	195	230
14	218	265

(There are still larger sizes for special purposes.)

Dark-colored cable, made of stainless steel, is exceptionally strong and will not throw off flashes of light. Its great disadvantage is that after being stretched it kinks badly. This type of leader is steadily increasing in popularity with big-game fishermen.

Plastic-coated wire cable is also available, but is generally fairly bright in color. This coated material is easier to handle than bare cable, being less likely to cut the hands, and it enjoys considerable popularity on this account. But the plastic coating seems to act as a magnifier to make the coated wire look larger than an equivalent size of uncoated leader. This makes the plastic-coated type unsuitable for leader-shy fish like sheepshead, mackerel, and corbina.

Because of their invisibility and flexibility, many salt-water anglers prefer to use synthetic leader materials for small-mouthed fish such as weakfish, flounder, fluke, etc. These species habitually mouth a bait for some time before swallowing it. As a rule, such fish will feel a rigid leader and spit out the bait before the hook can be set. Soft, flexible synthetic will be less often noticed, however, and the fisherman can delay setting the hook until the proper time. When you are angling for these fish but at the same time may get a strike from a fish that cuts or chafes the synthetic, use a short section of wire at the hook end of your leader. The length of this wire section can be a matter of only a few inches.

SYNTHETIC LEADER SIZES *

	Diameter	Pound Test
5X	.006″	1.25
4X	.007″	1.75
3X	.008″	2.25
2X	.009″	2.9
1X	.010″	3.5
0X	.011″	4.3
9/5	.012″	5.1
8/5	.013″	6.0
7/5	.014″	7.0
6/5	.015″	8.0
5/5	.016″	9.1
4/5	.017″	10.3
3/5	.018″	11.5
2/5	.019″	12.8
0/5	.021″	15.6
	.023″	20.0
*Nylon is the most used syn-	.028″	30.0
thetic leader material today and	.032″	40.0
thus its name has become synon-	.040″	50.0
ymous for all synthetic leaders.	.045″	60.0

Making Wire Leaders

Perhaps more large fish are lost because of improperly made wire leaders than for any other reason. Making up a leader is an art that you learn by patient practice, after becoming acquainted with the basic elements involved. While you can purchase wire leaders in standard sizes at your local tackle stores, many salt-water fishermen, in order to have the leader fit their exact specifications, do make their own. Metal wire leaders are usually purchased in coils of twenty-five feet, or in coils weighing one pound. It is well to practice with the thinner-gauged wires first, as these sizes are easier to work than the heavier-gauged sizes. A strong right thumb and index finger are needed for the job. This procedure should be followed:

1. Leader length should be from 4 to 15 feet. Push 3 to 4 inches of the working end of the wire through the eye of the hook, swivel, or whatever lure is to be tied. Hold the hook between the thumb and index finger of the left hand.

2. With the right thumb and index finger, sharply bend the wire across the hook eye, so that the wire end and the standing part of the wire (the long wire) point in opposite directions, and touch at the point of crossing.

3. With the wire thus crossed, the hook held in the left hand, with the right thumb and index finger firmly grip the wire at the point of juncture, and begin twisting the wire to the right, tightly, until ten to twelve hard,

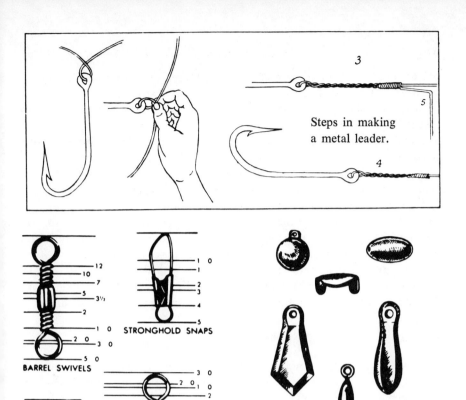

3

Steps in making
a metal leader.

5

4

BARREL SWIVELS

12
10
7
5
3½
2
1 0
2 0 — 3 0
5 0

STRONGHOLD SNAPS

1 0
1
2
3
4
5

3 WAY SWIVELS

3 0
2 0 — 1 0
2

SNAP SWIVELS

12
10
7
5
3½
1

Common sizes and types
of salt-water snaps and swivels.

Common types of sinkers
(*top, left to right*) round, pinch-on, and
egg-shaped; (*center*) diamond,
adjustable-ringed, and bank;
(*bottom*) pyramid and dipsy.

even twists have been turned into the wire. Both wires must be twisted
equally, and the twist must be short and hard in order to hold.

4. Make ten to twelve round turns with the short end of the wire around
the standing part, being careful tö lay each turn tightly against the preceding one.

5. Bend the remainder of the short end, in its middle, at an angle of 90
degrees, grip the bent end firmly with the right thumb, close to the 90-
degree bend. Lift the remainder of the short end of the wire in a 180-degree

arc toward the standing part of the wire, thereby breaking off the end of the wire close to the last round turn, leaving no sharp end.

When fishing for the big fellows, it is wise to use the double-wrap method. To do this, place the wire into the eyelet of the hook, lure, etc., and make a loose wrapping for about a dozen turns, tightly spaced. Then make a tight wrapping of a dozen turns and finish off as just described above. This double-wrap method will stand much strain because the two types of wrappings give a cushioning effect against any severe shocks.

In working with coated plastic wire, you should remove the coating so that the wire will go into the sleeves. If you want to, you can replace the coating after you have put the sleeve on; but doing this affects little the actual efficiency of the leader; it is purely a matter of appearance.

Most gut nylon leaders are purchased ready-made, but if you wish to tie your own, the material may be purchased from your local tackle shop. Methods of tying and knotting leaders are described later in this chapter.

SWIVELS

Swivels are always attached to the line end of the leader. They are essential with any revolving lure, to help prevent the line from becoming untwisted, or "unlaid," and growing weak. Most popular are the regulation barrel swivel and the three-way swivel. Both are generally constructed of brass or bronze and are joined together with a pin so that the links can revolve freely. The barrel swivel may be employed between the fishing line and the leader so that in the event a lure or bait spins unduly it won't kink or overlay or unstrand the fishing line. The three-way allows the line to be attached to one ring, the sinker to the second, the leader with the hook to the third. For surf casting, this type is usually essential. Both the barrel and the three-way are made in various numbered sizes as shown in the illustration. In most cases it is best to use the lightest and smallest size you can.

A snap is a convenient connecting link between the fishing line and the leader, lure, or sinker. It looks and works like a safety pin and is generally made of comparatively heavy stainless steel wire, such as No. 1/0 for game fishing and up to 20/0 for big-game fishing. The snap is tied to the end of the line or leader and appropriate other terminal tackle is snapped onto it. It enables you to speedily change hooks, lures, sinkers, leaders, etc.

It is possible to purchase a combination snap and barrel swivel. These swivels have a safety pin catch which can be quickly opened and closed for convenient changing of lures.

If light swivels are used, then do not tie on a heavy wire leader, or the swivels will be apt to stop functioning; and if you have heavy swivels on, then steer clear of using a light wire leader, or the wire may buckle or coil. Your whole outfit, you should remember, must balance to work efficiently.

SINKERS

Sinkers are weights of lead, molded in various shapes. The purpose of a sinker is threefold: to enable the lure or bait to be cast to a particular spot, to carry the lure or bait to the bottom, and to hold it on the bottom. To meet these three requirements both the weight and the design of the sinker vary for the type of fishing; for example, when fishing in still water only the lightest sinker is required to take the bait to the bottom, whereas fishing in deep water in swift currents makes necessary the use of sinkers up to two pounds in weight. Most salt-water sinkers are rated in ounces of weight.

The bank sinker is one of the most widely used sinkers, good for all-around fishing over rocky or sandy bottoms in moderate depths. The diamond sinker is another popular sinker for bottom fishing; it is widely used from party boats fishing in deep water. The square sinker also works well in deep water. These three sinkers have holes at one end to fasten the line.

The round sinker is best when fishing over rocky bottoms or where there is a chance that the lead may get stuck in rocks. Dipsey sinkers are also good here, but they come mostly in light weights and are good with the lighter spinning outfits.

The egg-shaped sinker which has a hole running through the middle is very popular for shy, wary fish which nibble at the bait. The line runs through this sinker and the angler can feel the lightest bite, but the fish cannot detect the sinker so readily. Another type of small sinker used in still-water fishing is the split shot. These range in size from about BB air-gun shot to ⅓ ounce, and barrel- or bean-shaped leads from ⅛ ounce upwards.

Pyramid sinkers are used mostly for bottom fishing in the surf. These are solid lead sinkers equipped with a ring on the top for fastening the line. For further information on this type of sinker, see page 125.

For certain types of trolling, special trolling leads add weight so that the lures travel down deep where the fish are. These are equipped with safety snap hooks on one end and swivels on the other. They are made of solid lead which is molded on a bronze center pin. Information on trolling keel sinkers may be found on page 141.

Every fishing catalog will list a dozen or more types of sinker, but the newcomer to the sport cannot go far wrong in his choice if he remembers the function of a sinker and how its shape affects its action. Different weights and types of sinkers should be carried at all times. If the water is shallow, the current is weak, and the tackle is light, the sinkers in lighter weights can be used. For deep water, strong currents, and heavy tackle, the heavier sinkers are needed. Many fish are lost because the sinker used by the angler is too heavy to feel a light strike at the instant it occurs. A fish finder (a line passing directly to the hook—see page 126) will eliminate this trouble. But a good rule is to use the lightest sinker with which a good cast can be made—you should always fish light. The most popular weights in sinkers for most salt-water fishing are 1, 4, 6, and 8 ounces.

HOOKS

No matter how good or how expensive the rest of your tackle, it is that little hook that holds and lands your fish. Or does not hook him because it is badly designed. Or breaks or bends because it is made of poor material. Wise salt-water anglers know this, and pay close attention to the selection of their hooks.

There are many types of hooks, each designed to do a particular job. No one hook will do every job. Many considerations enter into the proper choice of a hook. You should know something about the anatomy and habits of the particular species of fish (see Chapters 5 to 9) you are fishing for. In big-game fishing (Chapter 8), the mouths of sailfish, tarpon, marlin, and swordfish are bony and hard to penetrate, so sharp hooks made of especially heavy wire are required for their capture. On the other hand, the mouths of some bay species, like the kingfish and weakfish, are extremely tender, making light wire hooks essential. Other species, such as blackfish and porgies, have mouths strong enough to crush clams.

The habits of the fish also have a bearing upon the type of hook you should select. For instance, when you are trolling (Chapter 7) you must know whether the fish you are after will commonly hit the bait from the rear, from the side, or head on. Although various circumstances may cause a particular species to strike in an uncharacteristic fashion, this happens so seldom that striking habits remain important to know. The live bait fisherman knows that some species will nibble at a bait, others will swallow it, and still others will grab the bait and run some distance before swallowing. Likewise, fish vary in their fighting tactics. Some, such as the tuna, take off on long, powerful runs. Others, such as the sailfish, make shorter runs and do more leaping. Groupers and sheepshead run for nearby coral or rocks and have to be stopped. All of these things must be considered when selecting a hook.

It is very important to know the different parts of a hook as shown in the accompanying illustration: the point, barb, bend, shank, eye, gap, and bite. All of these have very important functions.

Types of Points

There are three types of commercial processes used today in fashioning hook points: grinding, forging, and upsetting. By any of these methods the common types of points suitable for salt-water fishing can be made and are shown in the accompanying illustration.

There are variations in the length of the point—that is, the distance from

Hook terminology.

Common hook points,
bends, eyes, and shanks.

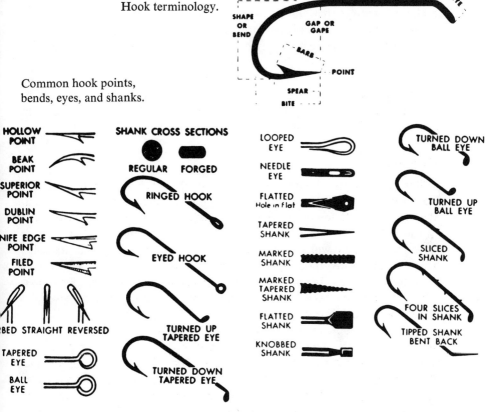

the tip of the point to the end of the barb. The long or standard point is best for all fish except those that have soft, thin-walled mouths. The long point provides better penetration, and it is more difficult for a fish to shake out. Moreover, it holds better in a torn mouth. The short-pointed hook, on the other hand, can be used efficiently on fish with thin, soft mouths. However, it's difficult to set because the angle between the point and end of barb is sharp, and will not penetrate with ease against resistance. In addition, it is an easier point for a fish to throw.

Types of Shanks

A hook penetrates into a fish by the leverage of the shank. At the moment the point penetrates, the hook shank exerts its leverage to bring the point of the hook forward to complete the bite. In general, hooks come with short, medium, and long shanks. For all-around fishing the medium or standard shank is best. The short shank is preferred in clear water, for wary fish, and for small baits. It can be buried inside the bait and a fish cannot see the hook. Usually, a short shank provides freer action, thus it is not as likely to hamper the action of the bait. It turns more easily in the fish's mouth and hooks deeper in the throat. Long shanks are used in fishing for species that are known to have sharp teeth which can cut a line or snell above the shank. They are also good for fish which swallow baits and when small baitfish are used. Being heavier, the longer shank will sink the bait faster in the fish's mouth.

Shanks are generally made straight, but some have bends or humps which are used in making artificial lures, such as certain surf-casting or trolling lures. Other shanks may have barbs or "slices" which help to hold baits, such as worms, more securely and naturally.

Hook Materials

Standard gauges of wire are generally used by fishhook manufacturers. However, there may be variations in the quality and temper of the metal. Steel is employed for most hooks, but special metal alloys are also used.

The smaller hooks and those made from light wire must have some "give" or else they will snap under a strain. Hooks for general fishing also bend a bit, but only under great tension. The larger hooks with heavy wire are rigid to prevent big-game fish from straightening them out. For most fishing, round wire hooks are satisfactory; but for extra strength, "forged" or flattened hooks are strongest.

The finish found on salt-water hooks is important since rust quickly weakens a hook. It may be blued, japanned, bronzed, tinned, or gold-, silver-, nickel-, or cadmium-plated. Blued and bronzed hooks rust quickly and should only be used once or twice. Silver- and nickel-plated hooks last somewhat longer. Tinned hooks also stand up pretty well and cadmium- or gold-plated hooks are better still. Hooks made of "Z" nickel are completely rust-free, but have a softer temper than steel hooks.

Dark and dull finishes are valuable for wary fish and clear water. The brighter finishes are used with artificial lures, such as metal squids, spinners, and spoons, where extra glitter and flash are desired.

Types of Bends

Hook designers have given a lot of thought to the hook shape in relation to the fish's physiology and habits. The bend of a hook can be round, oval, or with a sharp angle. Each shape meets a specific condition. For example, a hook with a round bend has a wide gap between the point and shank. It is good for large bait and sets best when the fish has a large mouth. With this type, however, a hooked fish applies less leverage against the shank than with other bends.

Sharp-angled hooks are used for small-mouth fish, such as flounders and eels. They are easily swallowed and the sharp angle sets the barb after the hook is taken.

For every hook the barb is located so it will be the first section of the hook to enter the part of the mouth into which the hook will set. There are three types of barb locations, or bends, used in relation to the point of the hook and the shank. They are (as shown in the illustration) reversed bend, kirbed bend, and straight bend.

For general salt-water fishing, the straight bend is the most widely used. The fish quite often feel an offset or kirbed hook more quickly and spit it out. Also, if a fish strikes a lure on the side from which the hook is bent away, it is almost impossible to hook him. Furthermore, when used in trolling and casting, such hooks often cause the lure to spin. The reversed or kirbed hooks are best for live baits.

Types of Eye Patterns

Salt-water hooks come with ball, tapered, looped, or needle eyes. The ball, or ringed, eyes are round and uniform in thickness and are strong. They are used for most salt-water fishing purposes.

A tapered eye is also round, but the wire is thinner to cut down weight. A little strength is sacrificed to make it useful for light artificial lures. The looped eye type is oval and, like the tapered eye, is thinned to reduce weight. Needle eyes, which resemble those found on sewing needles, are exceptionally strong and stand up under the great strains exerted by deep-sea giants. They are widely used for rigging whole baits for big-game fishing and trolling.

Hook Sizes

Hook sizes often confuse the novice angler. Though hooks are pretty well standardized in their actual dimensions, there is still a good deal of variance in actual size between different types (see illustration). Numbers start with 22, the smallest made—though 10 is about the smallest used for salt-water fishing—and increase in size as the number decreases. Combination numbers, such as 1/0, increase in size as the numbers increase; 20/0, the largest made, is used for giant fish such as sharks, swordfish, large tuna, and so forth. Hooks are measured from the bottom of the bend to the top of the shank (it doesn't include the eye).

SIZE (Number)	LENGTH (Inches)	DIAMETER (In 1/1000")
10	9/16	0.024
8	11/16	0.027
6	13/16	0.030
4	15/16	0.033
2	1⅛	0.037
1	1¼	0.039
0	1⅜	0.041
1/0	1½	0.043

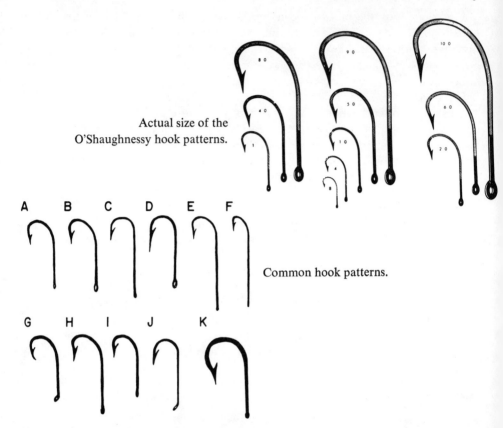

Actual size of the
O'Shaughnessy hook patterns.

Common hook patterns.

For 2/0 on up add ⅛ inch for each number. In general, odd-numbered
sizes (7, 9, etc.) are approximately midway between even-numbered sizes.
Deviations from regular sizes are indicated by x's and the word "Long"
or "Short." Thus, 1x Long (1xL) means that the shank is as long as the
standard length of the hook which is the next size larger counting the odd
as well as the even sizes. (For example, a size 2-1x Long is size 2 hook with
a length of 1¼ inches). Similarly 2x, 3x, 4x, etc., are all figured in the
same manner; that is, a 4x Long shank is identical to the length of the shank
on a hook four sizes larger than itself, and so on. Hooks are not regularly
made longer than 8xLong.

The same system is reversed in measuring the shortness of a hoop shank:
2x Short (2xs) means that the shank of the hook is the standard length of
the shank on a hook two sizes smaller, and so on. The most widely used
short-shanked hooks have shanks 5x Short and, in this respect, hooks are
not regularly made shorter than 5x Short. The box in which they are
packed is usually marked by the letters *xx* or ½ .

Hook diameters are also indicated by an *x* with the word "Fine" or
"Stout" next to it. Thus, a 2x Fine wire hook is made of the standard size

wire for the hook two sizes smaller. For example, size 4-2x Fine is size 4 on 0.030 diameter wire. Hooks are not regularly made finer than 2x Fine, or heavier than 4x Stout.

Hook Patterns

The following are the more popular salt-water hook patterns:

Sproat is a nearly round bend with a straight point. This pattern has a wider angle of penetration and is an old favorite for small and medium-sized fish such as weakfish, mackerel, kingfish, pollack, haddock, cod, small striped bass, etc.

Limerick is something like a half-round bend with a straight point, although the actual design varies slightly depending on the manufacturer. It requires considerably more effort to sink the barb of a Limerick than that of the Sproat, but it is still an old favorite of commercial fishermen for pollack, haddock, and cod. Sport fishermen use it for tying large wet, streamer, or bucktail flies for salt-water species.

Aberdeen is a fine, round bend hook with a wide gap and a sharp point. It is used with small baits for spot, herring, small croakers, and weakfish.

Siwash is also called a Salmon Hook. While it originated in the Pacific Northwest and takes its name from the Siwash (literally "fish-eating") Indians, this hook is now rapidly gaining favor with East Coast anglers for fish that leap, and put heavy strain on a hook, such as bonitos, albacores, blues, striped bass, etc. It's a round-bend style generally with an extra-long, sharp point made from very heavy wire. The point, which generally runs half the length of the shank, is its most unique feature. Long points have three functions: (1) to hold a large bait; (2) to give deeper penetration in cartilage and membrane; (3) to prevent a jumping fish from throwing the hook.

Carlisle is a round bend with a kirbed point, on an extra long shank. It is used for fish that swallow baits or which have sharp teeth capable of cutting a leader or snell. The Carlisle pattern is ideal in small sizes for flounders, small bluefish and eels, while the larger sizes are good for big blues, fluke, etc.

Chestertown is the flounder fisherman's favorite. Its long shank, light gauge wire, and narrow gap with sharp bend make this hook good for small baits and fish with small mouths that suck in baits.

Eagle Claw or Beak is most commonly used in fresh-water fishing but is rapidly gaining popularity with salt-water fishermen because of its "claw-like" turned-in point that penetrates easily and holds. This claw-shaped point comes close to the ideal practice of having the point of the hook in a direct line with the pull of the leader. The well-known gold-plated Eagle Claw is used for weakfish, striped bass, bluefish and bottom species.

O'Shaughnessy is very similar to the Sproat and the Limerick. The main difference is that the O'Shaughnessy has a point that bends inward. This hook is usually made from heavy wire to give it extra strength, and the wire is forged or flattened. Due to the turned-in point, this type of hook does penetrate very quickly; but for slow-biting fish the O'Shaughnessy is very popular. It may be used for bait-fishing and trolling rigs, and with feather lures, spoons, and metal squids.

Virginia is a heavy wire, short bite hook that is usually rigged with tarred line or heavy nylon leader for sheepshead, blackfish, and other fish that can bite through lines, lighter leaders, and bend hooks.

Kirby is a round shape similar to the Sproat, but with the point kirbed or bent to the side so that it is not in the same plane as the shank. This hook has been quite successful for certain kinds of fishing, being used chiefly for small sucking fishes, such as the flounder, ling, kingfish, and whitefish.

Big-game hooks are heavy forged wire with extreme round bends, slightly offset, for big fish with big mouths, such as sailfish, marlin, swordfish, tarpon, tuna, sharks, and other heavyweights that really strain a hook. One of the most popular hooks is the Sobey with its extreme round bend, in-point, heavy forged wire construction, and needle eye. It is used mostly for tuna, swordfish, tarpon, and marlin. Another good hook is the Martu which has a diamond outpoint insuring quick and deep penetration. It is used for marlin and tuna. Several other excellent hooks for big-game fishing are the Sea Master, Tarpon and Tuna, Sea Demon, and Giant Tuna styles.

Snelled hooks have a short piece of gut-nylon or wire fastened to their shanks. The snell may be from six inches to three feet in length, with a loop at the end opposite the hook for attaching the line or leader. Snelled hooks are very popular for bottom fishing in salt water because they eliminate the need of a leader. Most of the previously mentioned hook patterns, except for big-game types, are available with snells.

Double or treble hooks are used mostly for artificial lures such as plugs. For light fishing with light tackle, small lures, and small fish many treble hooks do the trick. But when you start fooling around with heavy tackle, big fish, and strong currents you need extraheavy trebles. Big fish like striped bass, hooked on plugs, can exert plenty of leverage and have straightened out many treble hook arrangements.

Finally, we have some of the largest hooks made—the shark hooks used with heavy lines. These come as long as 12 inches and may have a gap from the point to the shank of 4 to 5 inches. They are usually attached to chain leaders from 3 to 6 feet long.

Hooks are a small item in your angling budget—but they are all-important. The most expensive hook ever made is a real "buy" compared to your reel, line, rod, lure, bait, and other accessories. Saving a few pennies by purchasing a cheap hook, or by using one with a rusted barb, is very foolish. When it comes to hooks, study them, learn their uses—and then purchase the best. You will never regret it.

NATURAL BAITS

Purists may scoff at the bait fisherman, or "sinker-bouncer"; but there is no scoffing at success, and there are times when salt-water gamesters will respond only to natural bait. From giant tuna to tiny porgies most salt-water fish are a pushover for a properly presented natural bait. Actually all artificial lures are supposed to be imitations of some natural baits. The wise angler, then, is one who knows his natural baits, how they are caught or obtained, how they are hooked, and how they are presented to the fish.

The bait fisherman should also remember that for best results his bait should be as lively and fresh as possible. Luckily, most coastal tackle stores and boat liveries carry bait. The angler who gathers his own bait should check with his state and local laws since many states and areas have laws governing the taking of baits such as sea worms, clams, crabs, and bait fish.

The following baits are the most popular. If you make a study of how, when, and where these baits are used, you are certain to catch more fish. (More information on the use of natural baits can be found in Chapters 5 to 9).

Sea Worms

These marine worms are a favorite bait with salt-water anglers since so many fish take them and they are easily bought or obtained and are handy to carry and keep. The clamworms, also called "sandworms" along the Atlantic coast and "pileworms" or "musselworms" along the Pacific coast, are the most popular sea worms. This worm has a bluish or greenish iridescent back and pink or red undersides. They are found in mud flats and shelly sand, among barnacles and mussels on piles and under stones. At night they leave their hiding places or burrows and can be picked up on the tidal flats or scooped up in the shallow water. At other times they can be obtained by digging deep with a clam hoe or fork on the tidal flats at low tides. Most clamworms average from five to twelve inches in length.

Another popular sea worm or muckworm is the bloodworm. This worm is pink or flesh-colored and has a smooth body tapering on both sides. When touched or disturbed it shoots out a long proboscis which has four tiny, black jaws. It can be dug up with the same tools used for other sea worms, but usually lies deeper in the mud than the clamworms, near the low-water mark.

You can keep sea worms alive for several days by putting them into a well-ventilated box or can containing moistened seaweed, rock moss, or rockweed. Keep them in a cool or shaded spot and sprinkle them lightly with salt water occasionally. You must also separate them frequently, or

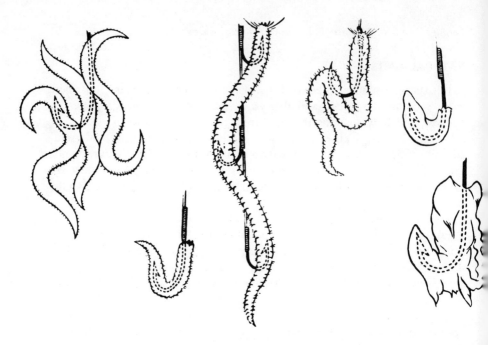

Common methods of attaching sea worms to the hooks.　　　Common shellfi

they may ball up under the vegetation and slit each other's throats with their sharp nippers. Never use dead sea worms as bait.

Sea worms will take flounders, croakers, weakfish, tautog, porgies, and striped bass in the Atlantic; and corbina, surf perches, spotfin, and yellow-fin croakers in the Pacific. For big fish one, two, or three worms on a hook are generally employed. For trolling, one or more are hooked behind the spinner leaving the ends trailing and fluttering attractively through the water. A gang or tandem-hook rig can be used to catch fish which strike short. With this rig, small or short-striking fish will be taken on the trailing hook, larger fish on the upper one. For small fish with tiny mouths, pieces of worm one or two inches long are good.

Sea worms are also excellent for bottom fishing; but since they are very soft, the beginner may find himself being "robbed" of his bait by trash fish (sea robins, blowfish, etc.) or crabs. For bottom fishing, use broken pieces of worms gobbed on a single hook, or use a worm gang.

Clams

There are many kinds of these bivalves which can be used for bait. The most important, especially on the Atlantic coast, is the surf clam, or sea clam, popularly called the "skimmer" clam. Another common and popular clam is the ordinary hardshell clam found in fish markets and often called the littleneck, the quahog, or the round clam. Still another is the soft-shell clam—also known as the long-necked clam, sand clam, and steamer clam —which is found along both coasts. Many other clams, such as the gaper clam, geoduck clam, pismo clam, and the jackknife, or razor, clam, can be used for bait when available. Most clams can be purchased from fish markets and bait dealers. Or you can obtain them along the beaches or in bays where they bury themselves in the mud and sand. You can wade in the shallow water and look for them or feel them with your bare feet and then dig them out. While on the exposed flats you can dig them out with a clam fork or hoe. Carry the clams to your fishing grounds in a small metal bucket.

Clams will stay alive for several days if kept on ice or in a cool location. For longer periods they can be submerged in salt water in a box. The clams, of course, must be removed or sucked from their hard shells. This can be accomplished correctly by inserting a long knife blade between the two shells and cutting the muscles which hold them together. To save time, however, many fishermen just hit the clams against some hard object such as a rock to crack the shells and remove the insides or meat.

The whole meat of one or more clams should be draped on the hook when it is used for striped bass in the surf or for haddock and cod off-shore. The neck, or siphon, of most clams also makes good bait if the dark skin is removed to show the light meat. For smaller fish, such as tautog, flounders, porgies, and sea bass, tiny pieces of clam are good. Use the tough, muscular foot and stringy mantles for the best results. Throw the empty shells into the water around the boat to serve as chum to attract fish. In some cases the clam shell is merely cracked and the whole thing put on the hook. Any strong-jawed toothed fish can cope with the situation.

Other Shellfish

Mussels, which are found in most salt waters, can be used for such fish as tautog, flounder, croaker, corbina, kelp bass, porgy, and surf perch. This bait can be picked up by the bushel at low tide from rocks, piles, or mussel beds, or may be purchased at bait shops. Since mussels are a soft bait and don't stay on the hook well, the "meat" should be wrapped around the hook with fine thread. Some fishermen boil, steam, or dry out the mussel meat a bit to toughen it. Mussels are also used as chum. They can be crushed and thrown overboard a little at a time or placed in a chum pot or basket and lowered into the water.

Other shellfish, such as scallops, oysters, sea snails, periwinkles, abalone, conchs, and whelks, can also be used for bait. In fact, almost any salt-water shellfish, if large enough to make a practical bait, can be used.

Squids

Although squids and octopuses are considered mollusks, like the clams, mussels, and oysters, their habits and uses as bait are radically different from the other shellfish. There are many species of squids found along both the Atlantic and Pacific coasts, from tiny one-inchers to giant 60-footers. But usually all of them can be used as bait for salt-water fishes.

Once in a while squids can be found stranded on shore or can be netted or snagged in shallow water. Most often they have to be purchased from fishmarkets, bait dealers or tackle stores. Since squids are difficult to keep alive, they are now generally packaged in frozen one-pound containers. If purchased fresh, they should immediately be put on ice or be frozen whole. Another method for keeping squids for long periods is to clean them, cut them up into good-sized strips and pickle them in heavy salt brine. If kept in a refrigerator in a jar, they will last a long time.

Whole squids are rigged for trolling offshore for marlin, tuna, and swordfish. Whole squids can also be hooked once or twice on 8/0 hooks and drifted or fished on the bottom for striped bass, channel bass, and other large fish. The head, tentacles, or body sections also make good bait for stripers and weakfish. Big strips are good for cod too. For smaller fish, such as bluefish, fluke, sea bass, winter flounders, or weakfish, cut the strips into triangles or rectangles of a size sufficient to cover the hook. A good idea is to combine squid strips with other baits, such as sea worms and clams. These softer, delicate baits are often stolen, but the tough squid remains. Thus the hook always has some kind of bait on it.

Crabs

These crustaceans are eaten by many salt-water fishes. They can be bought in fish markets and from bait dealers, or can be caught by hand, with long-handled nets, on lines baited with fish or meat, and in wire traps. Keep them in damp seaweed on ice for short periods of time or in cages submerged in the salt water for longer periods.

Crabs make good bait in all their various life stages. They shed their hard covering at intervals as they grow, and most fish prefer to eat them when they are in the helpless, soft stage. Just before they shed their hard covering they are known as peeler or shedder crabs. After they shed their shells, they are called soft-shell crabs and when their new shell is starting to harden, but still caves in when pressed, they are called leatherbacks or paperbacks. Finally the shell hardens completely and they are called hard-shell crabs again. Crabs are best as bait in the shedder or soft-shell state; therefore they are most expensive while in this state.

The most popular is the blue-claw or blue crab. In the hard condition, they can be hooked through the body, between the legs, or in the hole left when the large claws are removed. Whole large crabs can be used for

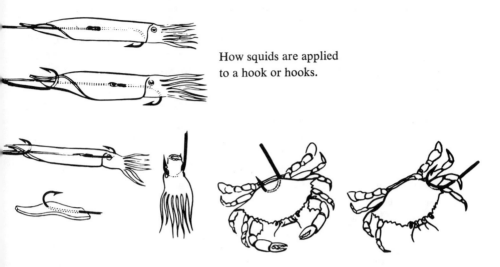

How squids are applied
to a hook or hooks.

Proper method of applying
hard-shell crabs to a hook.

big fish, while whole small crabs or sections of large crabs are fine for smaller fish. But the best baits are the soft-shell, or shedder, blue crabs. A whole shedder, tied to the hook with fine thread or rubber bands, is fine for big weakfish, channel bass, tarpon, bluefish, and striped bass. Small portions of a shedder are best for croakers, kingfish, porgies, and other small bottom feeders. Since soft-shell or shedder crabs are tender meat, the small parts must also be tied to the hook.

Another popular crab, especially for surf fishing, is the calico or lady crab. The larger ones should be soft-shells or shedders for best results. The smaller ones, about the size of a half dollar, can be used in the hard-shell stage. Calico crabs will take channel bass, cod, striped bass, weakfish, and other fish.

Fiddler crabs are a favorite with blackfishermen. There are two kinds; the dark marsh, or mud, fiddler and the lighter-colored sand, or chinaback, fiddler. The latter is generally preferred; it is sold by bait dealers in the fall of the year. Remove the big claw and run the hook through the hole which remains.

The green crab is also used for blackfish. It can be gathered at low tide along rocky shores and on jetties and breakwaters. Cut the large ones in half or quarters and use the small ones whole. Run the hook through the top shell from the underside. When using a hermit crab for bait, remove the shell and thread the body meat or insides on the hook so that the point and barb of the hook reaches the soft tail portion of the body.

Somewhat similar to crabs as a bait are lobsters, especially the spring lobsters or salt-water crawfish found in warmer waters. These are caught in traps and by hand or can be purchased from bait and tackle dealers. The tail sections of these crustaceans are used after the hard covering has been removed. This bait will catch bonefish, groupers, grunts, snappers, and many other fish found in the same waters as the lobsters.

The far-flung shrimp and prawn—from the jumbo, or edible shrimp down to the tiny sand shrimp—is perhaps the most popular of natural foods for almost every kind of salt-water fish. If you canvass the tidal creeks and bay shores of the coastline, you can scoop up tender young shrimps with a long-handled, fine-meshed dip net. These crustaceans sneak under the edges of creek banks, crawl along sandy coves, and sometimes get stranded in holes of the marshlands at low tide. They can also often be purchased at fish or bait dealers.

Shrimps should be kept alive in a bait box containing damp seaweed or sawdust when shore fishing, and in a live-bait pail (wire cage) submerged in the water when angling from a boat, being careful always to keep them in shade.

The larger shrimps are usually removed from their shells and the meat of the tail is threaded on the hook. The smaller shrimps are used whole and are hooked through the tail or body segments. They take weakfish, flounders, striped bass, channel bass, blackfish, bonefish, snook, grunts, snappers, groupers, pompano, sheepshead, and a multitude of other game and bottom species.

The small grass shrimp, or common prawn, is well known to weak-fishermen who use them for chum and bait. But many anglers do not know that these small, almost translucent shrimp can also be used to lure and catch blackfish, flounders, porgies, striped bass, and many others. They can be bought from some bait dealers; but since several quarts are needed in chumming, it often pays to catch your own. They frequent shores, coves, flats, and tidal creeks. A small dip net or small seine made of fine wire mesh or cloth will trap them. Keep them in large cages suspended in water. For immediate use put them in containers filled with damp seaweed or sawdust over a layer of ice. Common prawns can be used alone on a small fine-wire hook for small salt-water fish.

Sand bugs which are found in the sand where ocean waves break on the beaches along both the Atlantic and Pacific are dug out of the sand or caught in special scoop traps. They are used for such fish as bonefish, blackfish, pompano, sheepshead, and striped bass along the East Coast and for croakers and corbina along the West Coast.

Baitfish

There is a long list of these fish which are used for bait. They can be bought from tackle stores, bait dealers, fish markets and from commercial

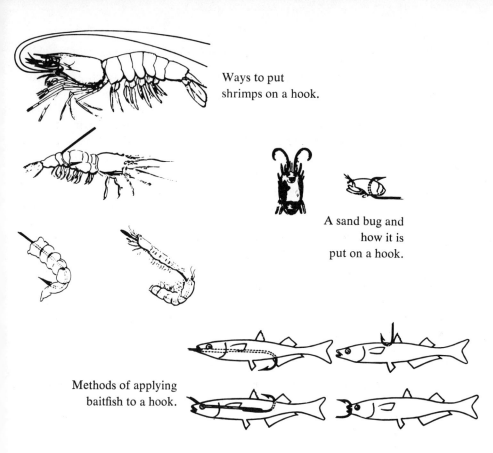

Ways to put
shrimps on a hook.

A sand bug and
how it is
put on a hook.

Methods of applying
baitfish to a hook.

fishermen. They can also be caught with seines, funnel-type traps, cast nets and with drop or umbrella nets. Most of these baitfish are rather delicate, and to keep them alive for any length of time they must be held in live boxes submerged in the water. But some of them, such as the common eel and killifishes, are quite hardy and they can be kept alive for hours in camp seaweed in cool spots. When using baitfish it's important to remember to keep them alive or use only fresh ones.

The mullet is a baitfish which most salt-water gamefish like to eat but can't always catch. The silvery mullets are the most common; two species, the white mullet and the striped mullet, are equally good for bait. These small fish travel in huge schools along the surf and in the inlets and bays. In the North look for them in the fall of the year, but down South they are present all year round. Whole small mullet are hooked through the back or lips and used for channel bass, bluefish, striped bass, and weakfish. The larger ones can be scaled, filleted, and cut into strips or chunks to attract the same fish.

The menhaden, or mossbunker, is a very popular baitfish because of its abundance and because of its oily flesh which attracts most salt-water fishes. Called "bunker" for short, it is caught by the millions for commercial uses, and tons are used for chum and bait. Small bunkers can be used whole, while the larger ones are filleted or cut into chunks. Channel bass, bluefish, sharks, striped bass, weakfish all like this bait. Bunker chum will attract albacore, blues, bonito, striped bass, tuna, and many other fishes. Other members of the varied and prolific herring family, such as the common herring, Pacific herring, pilchard, alewife, and sardine are widely used. Anchovies make good bait, especially in the Pacific Ocean where they are used as chum and bait for albacore, barracuda, halibut, and yellowtail.

Another baitfish which is plentiful is the spearing or silversides. They are almost always around in inlets, bays, and surf, and furnish food for many fishes, including bluefish, albacore, bonito, fluke, mackerel, sea bass, striped bass, and whiting. When using spearing, run the hook through the mouth, out the gill, and into the body. Another good bait found in the bays and inlets, along the beaches, and offshore is the sand launce or sand eel. This fish attracts bluefish, fluke, striped bass, mackerel, weakfish, and whiting. You also can rig them on a couple of hooks behind a spinner for trolling.

The killifish or mummichog is the top bait for fluke. It can be purchased inexpensively from bait dealers; or you can capture your own in a minnow trap baited with crushed clams, mussels, or crabs. Killies, as they are better known, live a long time when hooked through the back or both lips. The medium-sized killies are best for fluke, while the small ones are a favorite bait with the young angler when fishing for blue snappers (baby bluefish).

If you see a wide expanse of the ocean surface sprinkled with slim, wriggling objects about half a foot long, these are probably sand eels. They are "sweets" to game fish and sea gulls alike, and both vie to clean up the crop first. When trolled behind a spinner in shallow water, a sand eel, whether alive or dead, will soon get nabbed—but quick, if striped bass are around. Blues, pollack, and weakfish will not be bashful either.

The system here is to pay out a nickel spinner which has a sand eel right behind it clamped to a double-hook rig. The first hook is inserted in the head of the eel while the second hook, about three inches in the rear, is run through the body in a way to make the bait twirl. This is a fetching setup, and induces many greedy fish to take their final bite.

The common eel is also occasionally used for bottom fishing, alive or cut up into chunks. But it is more commonly rigged whole with two hooks (see page 123), giving it a motion like an artificial lure, and used for striped bass. Eelskins, attached to eelskin lures, are also used for bluefish, weakfish, striped bass and others.

There are many other fishes which are used as bait, such as the albacore, balao, barracuda, bonefish, bonito, butterfish, catfish, dolphin, flying fish, halfbeak, grunt, common mackerel, Spanish mackerel, and whiting. Most of these are used offshore for salt-water fish like marlins, sailfish, swordfish, and the tunas. These baitfish are rigged in various ways depending on the fish sought, methods and tackle used, and the area being fished. For still-fishing or drifting, the bait is usually hooked through the back or lips. In trolling, to give the bait a natural wriggling movement, the backbone is either broken in several places or removed. The hook can be hidden entirely inside the bait or it can protrude from the belly, side or back. The hooks should be sewn in, and if the fish has been slit open, the belly cavity should also be sewn up. The mouth and gills can be sewn up to keep the water out and prevent the bait from revolving when trolled.

Many of these same fishes are also used for strip baits that are trolled through the water in offshore fishing. For details on the preparation of strip baits, see page 142.

ARTIFICIAL LURES

The first actual information regarding the use of artificial lures to take salt-water fish was recorded by Captain James Cook in his notes on Hawaii in 1772. The natives, he reported, used with good results a spoon-type lure made from a shell. Today, however, the surf angler has a great variety of block tin squids, rigged eelskins, and heavy plugs from which to make a selection. The offshore troller can use spoons, rigged eelskins, spinners, or feathered jigs, while the salt-water fly fisherman has an assortment of large streamer flies.

Metal Squids

One of the oldest artificial lures used in surf fishing is the metal squid. These come in various sizes, shapes, and weights ranging from one to four ounces. Some are molded with fixed hooks set rigidly in the squid, while others have swinging hooks held by a ring or pin. The swinging-hook models tend to ride higher in the water and are less readily thrown by a hooked fish. The swinging hook is usually wrapped with colored feathers or bucktails; the most effective colors are usually white, red, yellow, or combinations of these. The fixed-hook squid often has a swinging hook slipped over the stationary hook. A strip of pork rind is sometimes added to the fixed hook to increase the lure's effectiveness. Some squids even have a treble hook arrangement. (For use of squids in surf-fishing and an illustration of the types of squid, see page 121.)

Metal squids weighing from one to two ounces are used with a light outfit, while those from two to four ounces are best with the medium or heavy rod. The lighter squids usually have more action than the heavier models. Most metal squids imitate such broad, fat fish as mullet, herring, and sardines. Or they try to imitate such long, slim baitfish as spearing and sand eels. The best metal squids are made of block tin which can be polished with fine steel wool. (Some are also painted white, yellow, blue, or any other color.) All metal squids should have a wire attached to the eye.

While the metal squid is primarily used in surf fishing, it is also excellent when cast or trolled from a boat. Then it will take such fish as albacore, bluefish, bonito, mackerel, pollack, striped bass, and weakfish.

For maximum action, metal squids should be bent in the center. Wide squids with shallow keels generally ride higher in the water than narrow squids with deep keels. Yet almost any squid can be manipulated and regulated to ride deep or high according to the way the rod tip is held and the speed of reeling or trolling. To make a squid ride deep, the rod tip should be dropped, and the reeling or trolling should be slow; conversely, the squid will ride high when the rod tip is held as high as possible in an upright position and reeling or trolling is fast. In surf casting, when a wave overtakes the squid and the line becomes slack, the reeling in should be speeded up. When a wave recedes and the undertow catches the squid, creating a drag, the reeling in should be slowed down.

The speed at which you reel or troll your metal squid is a very important factor when seeking certain species of fish, too. Striped bass usually hit a fast-moving squid fished over rocky bottoms. Over sandy bottoms, reeling at a moderate speed is best. The smaller striped bass usually prefer a faster-moving metal squid than the big ones. In fact, most of the stripers caught on metal squids will range from one to twenty-five pounds. Striped bass over that size are only occasionally caught on metal squids, and then usually on a slow or moderate retrieve.

Other fish that like a fast-moving metal squid are albacore, bluefish, bonito, and mackerel. For some of these fish, such as bluefish or bonito, you have to reel in as fast as you can turn the handle, or troll in a boat moving from five to ten miles per hour. Fish that prefer a slow-moving metal squid include channel bass, pollack and weakfish. If you reel or troll very slowly and deep you many even catch summer flounders or fluke on metal squids.

Plugs

This is a lure of wood or plastic, having one or more hooks or sets of hooks. There is no greater thrill than to see a big bluefish, striped bass, tarpon, or some other salt-water gamester come up and take a whack at a plug. Salt-water fishermen now have a choice of a wide variety of plugs made of wood or plastic. You will find that there are almost as many varieties and types used in salt water as in fresh. Actually, almost every popular fresh-water plug has an oversize salt-water counterpart. Many salt-water anglers use standard fresh-water plugs, particularly for bay and river stripers.

While there are still many wooden plugs on the market, the plastic models are replacing them in popularity. Plastic plugs are more durable and have permanent colors. Since most salt-water baitfish are colored green, blue, white or silver, these are good colors for a plug. Yellow, red

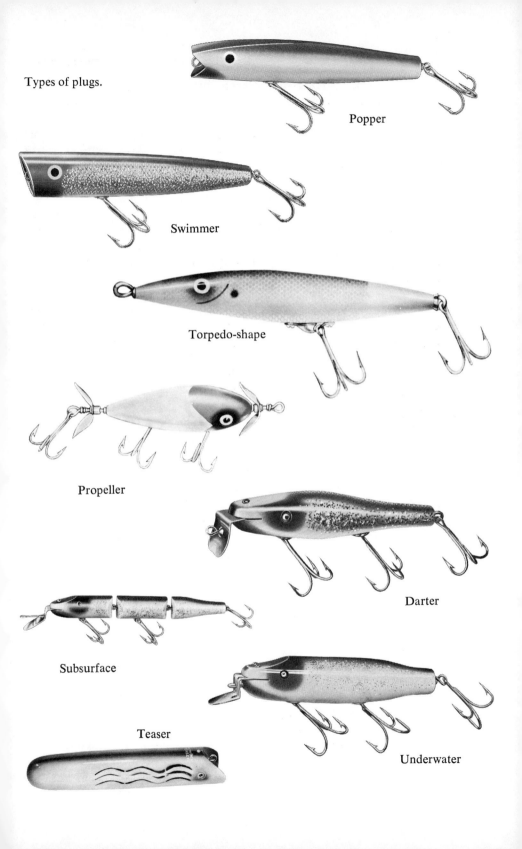

Types of plugs.

Popper

Swimmer

Torpedo-shape

Propeller

Darter

Subsurface

Teaser

Underwater

and white, or silver colors are also productive. Actually, it is best to use dark shades and natural-colored scales in calm, clear water, and bright shades at night.

Plugs come in varying sizes from three-inch models for light spinning gear to big, heavy 12-inch plugs suitable only for heavy surf outfits or trolling. They weigh from ½ to 4 ounces. But, regardless of the size and weight of the plug, be sure that the hooks are of strong, heavy wire. Weak hooks are quickly straightened by big fish.

Every salt-water plug angler should carry an assortment of plugs in surface, semisurface, and underwater models. Some surface types are poppers, swimmers, and torpedo-shapes; many of them are equipped with revolving trails or propellers. Most plugs of this type are built to create a splash, spray, or ripple on top of the water to attract fish. The trick in using surface lures is to make them act like crippled or sluggish baitfish such as herring, menhaden, mullet, sardines, or spearing—or like a terrified baitfish trying to escape the jaws of big fish. When the poppers are jerked, they throw a big spray of water which looks like a game fish chasing a baitfish. No doubt game fish in the vicinity are attracted by this splash, and feeling that they must catch the baitfish before the other fish gets it, strike at the surface plug. For best results when using the popper type, use the "jerk, turn" technique—that is, jerk it, stop it, and skip it. Retrieve at a fairly fast rate.

The swimming type generally has a metal lip and, when reeled fast and jerked, this lure, too, can be made to throw a splash like a popper. It's very effective for big striped bass when used in this manner. At other times it should be reeled slowly or at a moderate speed so that it swims in a snaky action on top, creating a ripple or wake behind it. Some plugs of this type come in long, double-jointed models and resemble eels or big baitfish floundering on top of the water.

Another surface plug is the torpedo-shaped type which is a very deadly lure in southern waters. It is a favorite lure in Florida for such fish as jack crevallé, snook, tarpon, and other surface feeders. The torpedo-shaped plug is worked fast on top, with long jerks or sweeps of the rod tip to make it skip along the surface.

The "flattail" plug is still another surface teaser. This lure is equipped with a propellerlike tail which turns as the lure is retrieved, creating a miniature wake as it moves along. These plugs are intended to simulate a herring, mullet, squid, or another fish swimming at the surface.

Another plug which isn't exactly a surface model, since it rides a few inches below surface when reeled fast, is the darter type. This was long a fresh-water favorite, and has been widely used for snook and tarpon in Florida waters. Stronger and larger models have now become popular with surf fishermen for bluefish and striped bass. The darter plugs have notched heads which cause them to dart or swim from side to side. They are often worked in a series of snappy rod whips with fairly fast reeling in between, especially in Florida. This plug can also be worked on top for short distances by holding the rod tip up, then a few inches below the surface by lowering the rod tip and reeling fast. Surf anglers also use the darter for striped bass at night by working it very slowly—barely reeling in and twitching it as it lies on the surface.

The subsurface or semisurface plugs usually wobble and slash or dive when in motion, float when not retrieved. They generally have a cut-away front of about 45 degrees which causes them to dive when reeled in. This type works best about a foot or two below the surface, when the water is slightly clouded or at night. Slow or moderate reeling usually produces the best results.

The underwater plugs may or may not float when at rest. Some float and dive to varying depths on the retrieve. Others sink and dive deeper or travel on the same level when reeled in or trolled. They usually have metal lips or heads cut at an angle to cause them to dive and give them action, usually a dart or a side-to-side wriggle. However, some plugs have pointed or blunt heads and little built-in action. These must be worked with the rod tip to give them a lifelike look.

When using underwater plugs you must have that feeling of motion which travels up the line and indicates that the plug is working properly. The key to the problem is to change the speed of the retrieve so that you always feel the plug working. When the tide or a wave pushes the plug in your direction, you have to speed up the retrieve. As a general rule, calm, clear water calls for somewhat faster reeling than rough or dirty water— if you want strikes. Likewise, daytime fishing means a faster retrieve than nighttime fishing.

Although most underwater plugs have a built-in wriggle, these are often better if they are jerked at intervals, stopped or slowed down, then speeded up to create an erratic action. On the underwater type, the depth at which the plug travels can be varied by bending the lip. Bending the lip down will cause it to ride near the surface, while bending the lip up will cause it to dive. If more weight is needed to cast an underwater plug, a clincher sinker on the leader a few inches in front of the plug will provide the weight without hindering the action of the plug.

Accurate casting is important when you spot fish such as channel bass, snook, or tarpon in low clear water. A plug which lands in the right spot stands a good chance of being hit—but if it is off by a few feet it may fail to bring a strike or, worse yet, frighten the fish away.

Jigs

If there is any salt-water lure which can be called an all-around fish-getter it's the jig. Also known as bucktail, barracuda, bugeye and bullhead, this lure is the deadliest fishing device made when in the hands of a man who knows how to use it.

Jigs come in different weights, sizes, dressings, and colors. Most of them have heads of heavy lead or other metal, with hooks wrapped in bucktail, feathers, hair, or nylon, rubber, or plastic skirts. The metal head is plated, chromed, or painted in various colors. White, red and yellow are the most popular colors for painted jig heads and for jig feathers and hair. The single hook, molded into the head, ranges in size from 1/0 to 8/0. Generally, there is a hole bored through the head in which the wire leader is run.

The original Japanese feather types, very popular for years both abroad and in this country, weigh up to 12 ounces. These lures are still used, with great success, in trolling for such surface feeders as albacore, bluefish, bonito, mackerel, and tuna. But, with the advent of spin casting, smaller jigs, ranging from ⅛ to 2 ounces, have become very popular. It's amazing how many different species of fish can be caught on these jigs. Almost every type of game fish, as well as some so-called bottom fish, will strike such lures.

As previously stated, jigs are highly versatile lures and can be trolled, cast, and bounced on the bottom. They are trolled fast for such speedsters as albacore, bluefish, barracuda, bonito, mackerel, and small tuna. For other fish a moderate or slow speed is better. Jerk the rod at regular intervals while trolling.

When fishing from the surf, small boats, piers, and bridges, jigs can be easily adapted to all conditions. When fish are feeding on baitfish at the surface, the jig is cast out and immediately reeled in at a moderate speed or fairly fast. On other occasions, the jig is cast out, allowed to sink a few feet, then jerked, allowed to sink, jerked again, and so on. We have used a variation of this for albacore and bonito when they refused a hook baited with butterfish or menhaden. Then the fish appeared in the chum slick and we could see them darting at chunks of the bunker. So we dropped black and white bucktail jigs with silver heads and worked them up and down quickly in the chum. The albacore and bonito took these at regular intervals.

The jig is one of the few lures which sinks deep in a strong current and is highly effective in tidal rips, canals, and rivers. Here you cast upcurrent or upstream and let the jig drift and sink with the tide. If the current is very strong you can let out slack line to permit the lure to sink still deeper. When the jig hits bottom you start reeling back with regular jerks. This "jigging" procedure is a favorite method of catching blues and pollack, and often catches cod, blackfish, and other bottom species. Fish take the jigs on the way up—just off bottom.

Another way to use a jig when you are anchored or drifting in a boat is to let it down to the bottom. Then make it dance up and down by jerking the rod tip up. Now let the jig settle, and keep repeating this until a strike is had. This way you'll hook many bottom fish rarely taken on artificial lures.

Salt-water anglers looking for the ultimate in sport use a fly rod for many of the smaller species (see page 215). Bucktails, popper bugs, and streamers are the main types of lures used. Surface-feeding fish such as bluefish, snook, bonefish, striped bass, and small tarpon go for the popping bugs, especially when the water is fairly calm or when they are chasing small baitfish. For best results the popping bugs should be jerked hard to create a lot of commotion. Bucktails and streamers are retrieved in foot-long jerks with pauses either down deep or near the surface. Fished down deep they will catch many bottom varieties. Near the surface they will take almost any game species that will strike artificials.

Spoons

This lure usually consists of a long, oval-shaped disk made of metal or plastic. While they are widely used in salt-water fishing, there are not very many sizes and shapes of spoons on the market for this purpose. The ones made for salt-water use are usually gold-, chrome-, or nickel-plated, or of stainless steel. Some are equipped with treble hooks, but for the greatest strength large single hooks are usually used. Many spoons have a bucktail wound around the hook. White, yellow, or red-and-white bucktail is generally used.

For fishing in bays, inlets, tidal rivers, and flats, the smaller spoons of 2 to 4 inches are best. (They come even smaller for spinning.) They usually run up to an ounce in weight. These spoons are good for most salt-water game fish that feed on smaller fish. The bright flash and wobbling action of a spoon will attract fish in most waters. When using the smaller spoons with a bait-casting or spinning outfit a slow or moderate retrieve is best. The minute you feel the spoon working on the end of the line, maintain that speed. As you reel, jerk the rod tip to make the spoon dart forward and rise, then drop the rod tip and make a few turns. This causes the spoon to rise, then flutter and sink—it imitates a helpless, crippled baitfish. Channel bass, snook, striped bass, tarpon, weakfish, and several others will go for it.

When trolling from a boat with a spoon, a moderate or slow speed is considered best. Here it is important to find the depth at which fish are feeding. As a general rule, such fish as albacore, bonito, bluefish, channel bass, mackerel, striped bass, and tarpon will strike spoons trolled near the surface. However, there are times when you have to go down for them. Then you must add heavy trolling sinkers above the spoon or use wire or lead-core lines.

Giant size "bunker" spoons, up to 12 inches long and equipped with heavy-duty 10/0 hooks, have been successful for big striped bass. Some of these big spoons come with lead keels which can be adjusted to control the depth at which the lure travels. For best results the big spoons should have a wobbling, swaying motion and shouldn't revolve or spin.

The line should be trolled as slowly as possible or just fast enough to bring out the action.

Since spoons offer quite a bit of wind resistance, you can't cast them as far as some lures and so they are seldom used for surf angling.

Spinners

These lures also take their share of salt-water fish, especially when trolling for the smaller species found in inlets, bays, and tidal rivers. Spinners, like spoons, depend on flash and motion to attract fish. They are made of the same materials and in the same finishes as spoons, and are used in the same general way. They are constructed with one or two round, oval, or leaf-shaped blades that revolve on shafts or swivels for action. The revolving blade may also give off vibrations which attract fish. But, because of their revolving blades, spinners are difficult to cast any distance and are used mainly in trolling.

Although spinners will catch fish when used alone or with feather or bucktail hooks, they are generally combined with various natural baits, such as strips of squid, pork rind, small, whole baitfish, or sea worms. For example, the popular June bug and Cape Cod spinners, when trolled with bloodworms or sandworms on gang hooks, are good in bays, rivers, and quiet beach waters during the spring and summer, particularly at night. They are fine for small stripers, but get their share of the big fellows, too. For best results spinners should be trolled deep and slow with at least 60 to 80 feet of line out.

The two-bladed "fluke" spinners, with live killies or worms, are almost standard for fluke. Similar smaller sizes, used bare or with spearing, are good on fly or other light rods for snappers, small blues, and mackerel. Such a lure is attached above a sinker and is bounced off the bottom while the boat drifts.

Other Lures

Other lures are used in salt water in various areas, such as the rigged eels and eelskin lures popular on the East Coast for bluefish and striped bass. These also work at times in southern waters for snook, cobia, and other fish. For details see Chapter 6.

Finally we have such lures as the rubber surgical tube and the plastic tube. Here the hook is run through the hole and one end of the tube rests against the bend of the hook. When trolled these lures leave a trail of bubbles and have a twisting action which is especially effective for bluefish, but will also catch albacore, bonito, striped bass, and other fish. There are also quite a few rubber lures on the market. These are made to imitate natural baits, such as baitfish, eels, sea worms, squid, and shrimp. Since these lures have no built-in action, it is up to you to provide the proper manipulations.

The spin fisherman can use any of the lures just described, but generally prefer lighter models. They can also use ultralight lures, too. These lures are available in plug (all types), spinners, spoons, squids, jigs, and flies.

FISHERMEN'S KNOTS

Knots may be the weakest link in your terminal gear. There are several special knots used mostly by salt-water anglers to attach lines, hooks, or lures to leaders. The most commonly used ones are described and illustrated here (see illustrations on pages 68 and 69).

Blood Knot

This is used for joining two strands of leaders or line. It is well known to most fishermen. First, lap the ends of the strands to be joined, and twist one around the other, making at least three turns. This drawing shows only three and a half turns, to avoid complexity. Count the turns made. Place the end between the strands, following the arrow. Then hold the end against the turns already made, between the thumb and forefinger, at point marked "X", to keep from unwinding. Now wind the other short end around the other strand for the same number of turns, but in the opposite direction. When this is completed, pull on both ends of the leader or line. As you continue pulling on the ends, the knot becomes tightened. (The short ends may be worked backward, if desired, wasting too much material). When the knot has been pulled together tightly, the last thing to do is to cut off the short ends, close to the knot.

Leader Knot

This is used for tying two strands of nylon together. It is easier to tie than the blood knot. First lap the ends of the strands, holding with the thumb and forefinger where indicated. Then loop the end around both strands three times, and pull the end through all three loops as indicated by the arrow. Then pull up slowly and evenly until this part of the knot takes the form of an "A". Now loop the other short end around the other strand in a way similar to what you did previously. When both sections of the knot have been pulled up, take the long ends and pull the two sections together slowly, and then pull them up tight. Cut off the short ends close to the knot.

Perfection Loop

This is used for tying a loop on the end of a leader. It is a safe knot to use with nylon, and as in all tying, the knot should be pulled up very tightly and securely. First take one turn around the leader, and hold the crossing between thumb and forefinger. Then take a second turn around the crossing and bring the end around again between the turns.

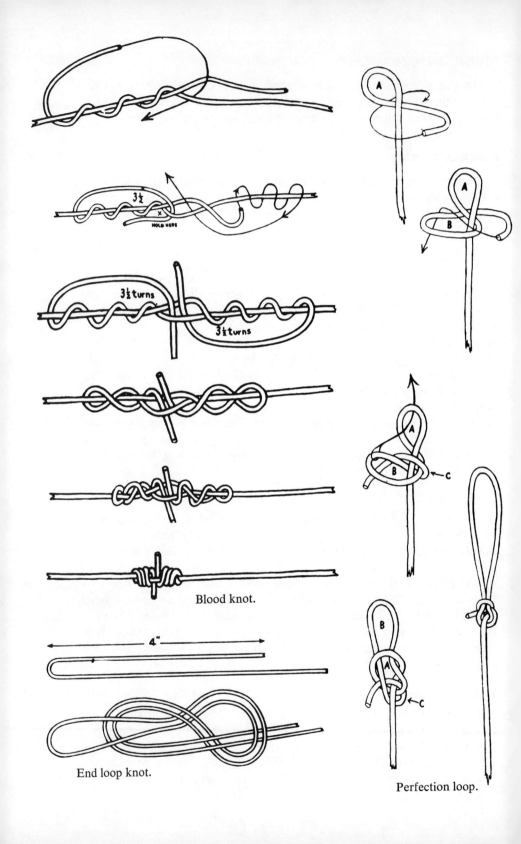

Blood knot.

End loop knot.

Perfection loop.

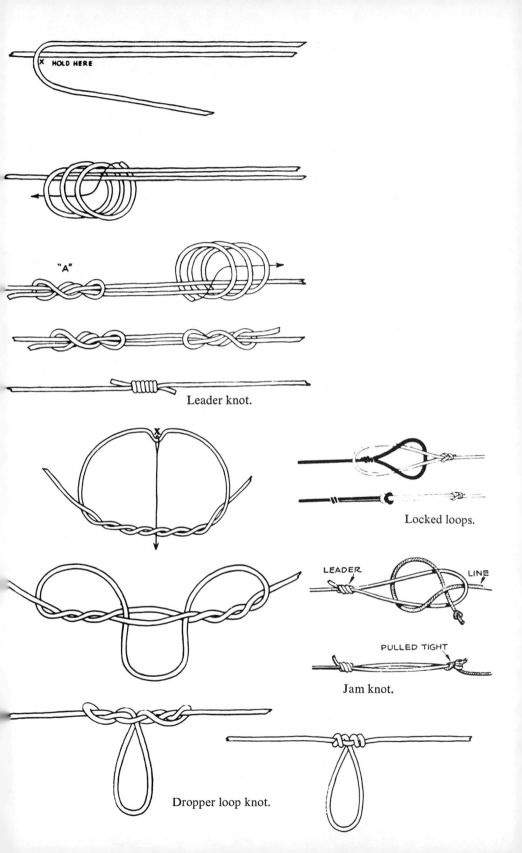

X HOLD HERE

"A"

Leader knot.

X

Locked loops.

LEADER   LINE

PULLED TIGHT

Jam knot.

Dropper loop knot.

End Loop Knot

This is used for tying leader or line loops too. While bulky, this loop knot is exceptionally strong and can be used for joining leader to line, or can be used for attaching snelled hooks to the leader and line, or to any other form of eye or loop. First bend over the nylon strand or line about 4 inches from the end of the length, so that you have a U-bend. Then bend the U-bend through the opening made by its backward turn, and pull it up tight.

Dropper Loop Knot

This is used for tying dropper loops. It is highly recommended for use with nylon leaders. First make a multiple fold overhand in the strand where desired. Pinch a small loop at point marked "X" and thrust it between the turns as shown by the arrow. Then place a pencil or your finger through the loop, to keep it from pulling out again, and pull on both ends of the leader. Finally, the knot should be drawn up tight.

Locked Loops

These are so simple that they scarcely need describing, but they should be mentioned here. You merely make two perfection knots and join them together as shown, passing each one over and through the other.

Jam Knot

This is used for joining a line or leader. First tie a simple overhand knot in the end of your line, then thread this under the leader loop, over one strand and across and under both strands, over the strand and under the loop. Pull the knot up tight so that the overhand knot tied in the line pulls up snug against the loop. This is a very practical method of joining line to leader when going after small fish, but the angler must be certain to renew the overhand knot tied in the line when the line point begins to show signs of wear.

Tucked Sheet Bend Knot

For joining a line to leader, this is the safest and easiest knot to tie. In this knot the end of the line is brought back and "tucked" through the loop on the end of the leader. The illustration shows the method of tying this knot. The one thing you have to watch out for is to see that the line doesn't slip through the loop at the butt end of the leader before it is jammed. Many anglers tie a regular knot at the end of the line to prevent this. If it does slip through, it will still hold, and it won't be a tucked sheet bend, but a figure eight. The figure eight knot is also secure, but it isn't as neat, it does not have a straight pull, and it introduces a lump on the leader which has a tendency to foul.

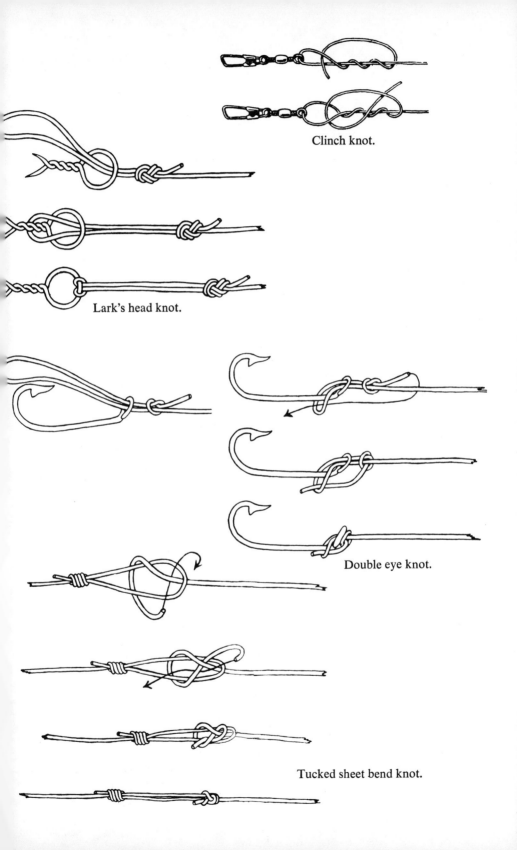

Clinch knot.

Lark's head knot.

Double eye knot.

Tucked sheet bend knot.

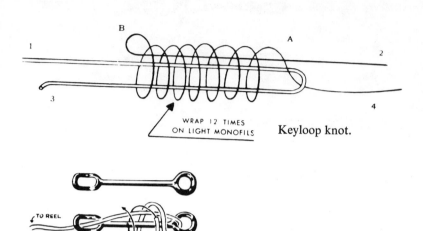

WRAP 12 TIMES
ON LIGHT MONOFILS

Keyloop knot.

TO REEL

HALF HITCHES

TO REEL   LINE-SAVER   12" WIRE OR FILAMENT

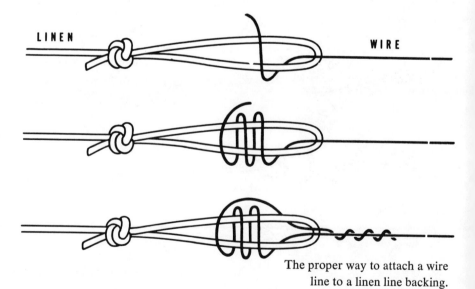

SWIVEL AND SNAP

TO TERMINAL TACKLE

Method of rigging a line-saver.

LINEN   WIRE

The proper way to attach a wire
line to a linen line backing.

Clinch Knot

This knot is used for tying a lure to a leader. It is also highly recommended for bait hooks and swivels. To tie the clinch knot, put the end of the material through the eye of the swivel, lure, or hook, and double it back against itself, making two or more twists (two are shown in the illustration); then pass the end between the eye and the coils. Next slip it through the loop and slowly pull it tight.

Lark's Head Knot

This is used for tying a leader to a lure or swivel that has a ring. It is formed on a swivel or ringed hook, with a loop on the end of the leader. First make a loop of any kind which is secured on the end of the leader. Pass it through the ring or swivel, and over the lure. Then draw the leader back to the ring until it upsets the loop around the ring.

Double Eye Knot

This is used for tying a hook to a leader or line. For bait hooks without tackle and feathers, when a strong holding knot is desired, the double eye knot has been found most satisfactory. First, tie a single running knot on the end of the leader and push it through the eye of the hook. Then pass this loop over the bend of the hook and draw it up to the eye. Finally, take the short end of the single running knot, push it under the loop against the shank, and draw it up tight.

Keyloop Knot

The keyloop knot is used to tie nylon braid to monofilament, and monofilament to monofilament. To make this knot, hold lines at position *B* and position *A*. Retaining position *A* firmly with thumb and forefinger, pull line 3 tight. Retaining position *B,* pull line 2. Holding lines 1 and 3, jerk knot tight. Trim off 3 and 4 close to knot.

Line-Saver Rig

Line-savers are cleverly designed attaching devices for rigging all types of terminal tackle to lines with almost no loss of the line's original strength. In tying the line-saver, the line from the reel should lie straight along the shank before the wraps are made. When half-hitches are applied, a noticeable gap must remain between the last wrapping and the first half-hitch.

The arrangement illustrated is the recommended rigging for a line-saver. A 12- to 18-inch wire or filament connector leader should always be used to separate the line-saver from the bright swivel and snap. This is particularly important when fishing for school fish. In their feeding frenzy they will strike at anything bright and attractive. By separating the swivel and snap from the line by a wire or filament leader, the likelihood of the line being cut by the fish is greatly reduced. It also provides easy means of changing terminal tackle.

Splicing Wire Lines

A splice in a single stranded line is made by wrapping two interlocking eyelets, making the wraps tight, each turn right up against the former one. A wrapped splice will generally hold in a twisted line unless the material is too springy to make a tight wrap. But if there is any doubt about the security of the wrap, you should make the splice in the manner recommended for braided wire. With the splice, you overlap the ends and overwrap them with the whip finish used in wrapping line guides (see page 254). Do not solder wire lines together; the stiff solder joint will almost always break from the flexing of the line.

OTHER GEAR

Other gear is necessary for certain types of salt-water fishing. This equipment is discussed in detail in Chapters 5 through 7. For example, gaffs are important. A long-handled or long-pole gaff is used to facilitate the landing of the fish. Such a gaff is also handy to have around jetties where it is difficult and dangerous to go after played-out fish. Large hooks of stainless or galvanized steel are attached to a wooden handle, usually from 1½ to 9 feet long. The size and design of the gaff hook varies according to the type fish for which it will be used. Smaller fish may be gaffed with a 3-foot pole of ½-inch diameter using a 12/0 to 16/0 hook, while big-game fish require a gaff hook with a spread of four to nine inches between hook-point and shank. In the latter the handle is usually from ½ to ¾ inch in diameter. The larger gaff is 5 to 7 feet long and of wood stock approximately 1½ inch thick.

The "flying head" gaff, which is detachable from the pole, is the best for real big-game fishing. This type has a ring on the hook's shank to which a gaff line or cable is attached so that after the fish is struck you can detach the pole and hold the fish on a line.

A landing net is very handy in landing small fish and may be used in place of a gaff.

Tackle boxes for onshore and offshore work are another must. The size of these will depend upon the amount of gear you possess, but they should be easily stowable in the trunk of your automobile or in your boat. Such boxes may be purchased from your tackle dealer or, if you are a do-it-yourself fan, you can easily make a box.

CHAPTER 4
_____

What Every Salt-Water
Fisherman Should Know

IT IS SELDOM that you associate fishing with gambling, yet fishing definitely is a gamble. You gamble your time and money against the pleasure you hope to get. Fortunately, too, the odds favor the fisherman's raking in a big recreational pot, as proved by the millions of anglers scattered along both coasts and the Gulf of Mexico.

You also gamble your casting ability, your choice of tackle, lures, and baits, and even your knowledge of a good fishing spot, against the I.Q. of finny gamesters; and the odds are not always in your favor in this competition. Whatever the latest investigations on fish intelligence disclose, Mother Nature certainly has endowed a large percentage of the marine population with a sixth sense that puts the odds in their favor. An old-time fishing captain once told me, "To be a good fisherman, you got to think like a fish." Well, that seemed to be a crude way of putting it, but to catch fish you must know their habits and what influences their behavior.

TIDES AND THEIR EFFECTS ON FISHING

Tides are possibly the most important influence on the more common types of salt-water fish. To be a successful salt-water angler, one must therefore understand how the tides behave. This is just as important as the tackle you select; it will actually affect the size of the catch. The fisherman must plan for the tides, especially if he wants successful inshore still-fishing, bait and surf casting, or inshore trolling. Tide has little effect on big-game fishing in the "blue water" far offshore where oceanic currents, rather than tidal currents, prevail.

Fish move from one place to another chiefly in search of food. But they must remain in water compatible to their own cold-blooded body temperature. Even in relatively small areas billions of tons of water are moved daily by tidal action. These movements cause drastic water temperature changes, flood beaches and banks with food for fish, and form currents that trap baitfish and carry them within easy reach of bigger species.

Tides are caused by the gravitational forces, or "pull," of the moon and sun. The moon, being closer to the earth, exerts the greater influence. Twice each twenty-four hours the tide pours out of the bays and away from the coast, pauses for a short time, and then rushes back. Because the moon rises approximately fifty minutes later each day, the tide is that much later each twenty-four hours. There are local variances, particularly in bays, which may make a difference of thirty minutes or more. For all practical purposes, however, you can estimate the tide at a given location as being one hour later each day.

The incoming tide at its crest is known as high tide, and the outgoing tide becomes low tide when it has reached its maximum retreat. The tide is said to be "flooding" on the way in; at "half tide" three hours later; and at "high water slack" after six hours when it reaches its peak. The tide is said to be "ebbing" on the way out, and reaches "low water slack" just before the "turn of the tide" starts the flood on its way back. "Dead water" occurs at both high water and low water slacks, when the tidal current stops and the water is apparently at a standstill. There are exceptions when tides ebb from bays through narrow inlets. Great amounts of water, almost landlocked, continue to ebb through the inlets long after the turn of the tide. The result, choppy water where both currents meet, is dangerous for small boats and inexperienced boatmen. The tidefall at one point may be one or two feet but seven or eight feet just a few miles away. Oceanographers attribute this to contours of the ocean floor. Near the equator the tidefall is less—often just a few inches less—but becomes greater toward the poles. In the Aleutians or the Bay of Fundy it is normally forty to sixty feet, and sometimes more.

The relationship of the moon and sun also influences the tide. For example, "spring tides," unrelated to the season, occur twice each month at full and new moons when the moon and the sun are in direct line with the earth and exert together their greatest force. These tides are abnormally high and often reach flood stage. "Perigee tides," which occur when the moon is closest to the earth, are exceptionally high tides. "Neap tides" are abnormally low and occur at the first and last quarter of the moon, when the moon, earth, and sun are at right angles and the gravitational pull is weak. "Apogee tides" occur when the moon is farthest from the earth and also are exceptionally low. All these tide variations must be known if you are to be on hand when the tides are at their most advantageous stages and the fish are in their best moods. Time and tide, you know. . . .

The hours of the tides may be learned by reading the daily tide tables published in leading newspapers along the seaboard and in some almanacs. The wise salt-water angler will follow them.

Unfortunately, there is no rule of thumb by which one phase of the tide can be judged ideal for all fishing, under all conditions. Also, different species of fish react in different ways. Surf fishermen know that a flood tide may be good at one location, while the ebb, slack, or any other phase may produce better results just a few hundred yards away. But in general, the beginning of the flood, or rising, tide generally provides the best fishing for the surf fisherman, particularly from dusk to dawn when traffic is light and there is no beach commotion. Why? The surf churns up crabs, sea worms, sand fleas, anchovies, clams, sand eels, and other food from the outlying sandbars that are bare at low tide. Baitfish also gather in the quiet pools inside the bars, where they are easy prey for bluefish, striped bass, kingfish, weakfish, fluke, channel bass, corbina, yellowfin, spotfin croakers, and pompano.

On a flood tide the fish usually swim inshore into the bays to feed on bottoms, and in banks that they are unable to reach at low water. Beach areas which may be entirely out of water at low tide frequently provide the best feeding grounds at high tide, with the surf or high tide churning up the bottom and uncovering mussels, clams, and other marine food. Weakfish, corbina, and striped bass follow the channels and come within reach of jetty and bridge anglers, and also work so close to shore—especially at night—that they can often be seen finning. Summer flounders (fluke) and other bottom fish may be heard splashing as they chase baitfish right up on sandy banks. Frequently, then, the best action takes place from approximately an hour before full tide to an hour after. When tide is on the ebb, the fish retreat to deeper water at the outer reaches of sandbars, or to channels that furrow the bays and inlets.

When the tide reverses itself, the change in the flow of water disturbs tiny plant growth and animal life on the bottom, sets the baitfish in motion, and encourages larger species to come in and have a banquet. You should be on hand then, for the fishing will be fast and furious.

Remember that a good fisherman is a keen observer. If you have good luck at a given location and phase of the tide, you should mark it as a hot spot to be fished one hour later on the following day. Unless there is a drastic change in the temperature, wind, or weather, you should have good luck there again.

CURRENTS AND THEIR EFFECTS ON FISHING

There are two types of currents that we must consider: the tidal currents and the oceanic currents. The former affect inshore fishing, while the latter concern the deep-sea angler.

Tidal currents, as the name implies, are caused by the rise and fall of the tide, and they affect inshore marine life greatly. For instance, during slack tides, small baitfish usually keep close to beaches and bars, generally out of the range of the bigger fish. As the strong flood and ebb-tide currents pick up speed, the baitfish are carried along, which makes fine fishing in channels leading to inlets and bays and just outside these spots, at either phase of the tide. Best fishing at such locations is during the first two hours of the flood or ebb tide.

As you mingle with veteran anglers, you will learn that the direction in which the tidal current flows is termed the "set," while the speed at which it moves is the "drift." Where two tidal currents collide, the water boils up into ripples and strong eddies, known as a "tide rip." Your angling efforts at such a place should be well rewarded, for the rips stir up food, which brings bluefish, striped bass, pollack, and many other fish to the supermarket.

These rips, cross currents, or other turbulences can be predicted fairly closely since they occur approximately at the same "tide time" every day. The experienced fisherman will know almost to the minute when to get his lines overboard—and when to move on and fish other rips, as the current slows down and allows the bait to escape from the spot he is fishing.

The rowboat angler who knows the tidal currents can drift over an entire bay or inlet on one tide and return on the turn of the tide, using his oars or outboard to choose his position of drift. This technique is particularly good for weakfishing and fluking (see page 104). The wise angler also knows that flounders and other bottom fish use these tidal currents to carry them from one feeding area to another, and that fishing is usually good along the channel ledges when the tide is moving in either direction. At slack tide, and when the tide slows down, the fisherman should find such a feeding spot and stay there, because the fish will remain pretty well put until they take another free ride on the tidal currents.

Tidal currents also often remodel the physical features of a beach— filling in some hollows, digging other holes and sloughs, and creating passages between bars. You should know where these places are in order to locate fish in the shallows. You will note that fish cluster around the downcurrent end of a shoal or bar, since food is more plentiful there.

Along both sea coasts, oceanic currents—the Gulf Stream, the Humboldt Current, the Florida Current, the North Equatorial Current, the California Current, the Equatorial Current, etc.—have an effect on offshore fishing. Marine biologists believe that only migrating or spawning fish frequent these currents, which are almost completely devoid of fish interested in taking a lure. But it is along these currents' edges where the mighty marlin, the sailfish, the leaping dolphin, and other big-game fishes are most frequently taken. A fine example of this is Cabo Blanco, Peru, where almost every major Pacific game fish is found in abundance. Here the unique blending of the cold Humboldt (or Peru) Current from the south and the warm Equatorial Current from the north has created an outstanding area for year-round fishing. The converging currents act as a gigantic force pushing game fish, along with the fish on which they feed, into the area.

WEATHER AND ITS EFFECTS ON FISHING

Weather does not have as great an effect on salt-water fishing conditions as it does on fresh-water angling, although it does have some. For example, you will find that the trend of the barometer can be a deciding factor. Generally, just before (a falling barometer) and after a storm (rising barometer) are good fishing occasions—unless the water is so dirty or roiled up that it looks brown, in which case you may have to wait a day or two for the bottom to clear up. During a storm, high seas and strong winds may make surf fishing very unpleasant and difficult, but many excellent striped bass catches have been made under such adverse conditions.

Water that is either too warm or too cold will make the quarry torpid. Temperature also governs the depth at which some fish will feed, and stimulates their daily travels to and from shore and their seasonal coastwise migrations.

Winds also play a part in the fishing scheme. For example, observations along the northern portion of the Atlantic Coast have shown that cold waters may be driven inshore by a persistent southerly wind, sending weakfish, croakers, cod, kingfish, and others into deeper areas. A northeast wind may bring warmer waters close in, while a long siege of stiff west wind usually forces the warm surface water out to sea and lets cold undercurrents wash the bars.

Offshore winds blowing from land to sea make surf casting much easier and they tend to calm the water. During an offshore wind, fishing conditions are generally poor for striped bass. (Onshore winds usually drive the baitfish close to the shore where the bass can easily feed on them.) However, bluefish, channel bass, and other species prefer calm water for feeding in the surf. In the late fall of the year when striped bass are schooled up and feeding heavily, calm water often produces many excellent catches. But in general you will find that it is easier to fool the striper in rough seas than in clear, calm water.

HOW TO LOCATE FISH

For the angler who has not too much time for his fishing and lacks knowledge of nearby waters, there are several methods of finding productive locations. Most local seacoast newspapers carry salt-water fishing columns with the latest information on what fish are running and where.

Another good method is to watch for the bait and tackle shops that dot our coast line. Wherever you see them, good fishing is usually nearby. Stop at one of these places, tell the man who runs it that you are new to the area and wish to do some fishing. He will gladly tell you where to fish, what bait to use, how to rig your line properly for the given section and tide conditions. If you do not have your own tackle, he will also be glad to rent you whatever is required, for a fair price. There are, besides, other reliable ways of selecting productive waters in any given stretch of shore line.

Here are some points to look for: On a coast line that is mostly rocky, try to find a short stretch that is smooth and sandy. Usually any fish in the vicinity that prefer this type of bottom will congregate there. On a long stretch of smooth, sandy beach, try to find a section where the breakers occur consistently twenty-five to fifty yards offshore, and where there is one fair-sized breaker rather than a series of little ones. Many game fish will lie just beyond that big breaker feeding on the baitfish and food released by an incoming tide. (See Chapter 6 for more information on locating fish in the surf.)

Where the shore line is quite rocky and unbroken by any smooth, sandy areas, try to find a location where you can get beyond the breakers into deeper water. Such a spot may be a jetty, breakwater, sea wall, pier, or even a natural ledge that extends beyond the surrounding surf line. Watch for any small estuaries where fresh-water rivers or streams empty into the salt water. Fish where the two waters blend and you may have very good success. If you own a boat or rent one, you can, of course, try your luck in spots that are not accessible from shore. (More data on this type of fishing will be found in the next chapter.)

It is sometimes possible to sight your prey on calm days when the water is clear. In southern and Gulf waters, tarpon reveal their presence by rolling over in the water. Feeding sea trout (spotted weakfish) can often be located by the characteristic popping of their surface strikes. Bonefish can often be spotted by their ghostly shadow, as they stalk the shallow flats with the incoming tide, or by the mud they stir up—or they may be seen "tailing" or "finning" as they feed on the bottom. The slashing entrance of salmon into a herring school can be detected from a considerable distance, frequently rolling—especially the big specimens. (Further techniques on spotting fish will be found in Chapters 7 and 8.) With some practice, it doesn't take long to learn how to locate fish by sight. For this, polaroid glasses are a decided help—and the darker the glasses, the more they shield your eyes against the hot sun's glare, the better.

To the observant salt-water angler, there are also several surface indications that disclose the presence of fish. Terns and gulls are always on

Sea birds, swooping and diving for baitfish stirred up by feeding game fish, indicate the presence of a school to the observant angler. Trolling or casting through the hungry fish often sets your line to humming.

the lookout for fish. When you see them wheel, dive, and make more noise than usual, it is a good indication that they are over a school of fish. If you want to share in their spoils, particularly if bluefish are running, hurry and get your boat under the gulls when they dive and scream. With these rapacious fish on the feed, the action may not last long. If you spot a tiny shower of spray in the distance, close to the surface, move that way—it may be caused by a leaping school of baitfish trying desperately to escape the slashing, raiding game fish underneath. On calm days, when the water is generally quiet, the school may just look like ripples caused by a gentle breeze. The sport can be terrific if you get alongside such a school. Just run the boat slowly around the school and cast or troll your bait or lure into it.

Remember, most salt-water fish have a preference for the type of bottom over which they settle—coral, sandy, rocky, muddy, weedy, almost anything except slimy sections. Learning where these stretches are, and at what depths, will greatly improve your catches. You can observe mud and sand flats when they are out of water during low tide; they'll be excellent market places in high tide.

The shoals that dot our coast lines are teeming with a variety of fish. Many of the shoals have caused shipwrecks during storms. These hulks of these wrecks, together with relatively shallow water, provide protection for baitfish and make the shoals centers of fish activity. The development of sonar equipment during World War II has been a boon to charter boat owners; this device makes it possible to locate the exact position of reefs where black sea bass, red snappers, porgies, yellowtails, and an endless variety of other fish abound. Wrecked ships are also being located and marked with buoys—both as navigational warnings and as beacons to the angler to come and get his sport. Therefore, regardless of the type of fishing you are planning to do, you should know thoroughly the sections you plan to fish regularly.

A good plan is to obtain a standard United States Coast and Geodetic Survey Chart of each region you expect to visit. This may be done by writing for the free catalogue of charts to the Superintendent of Documents, Government Printing Office, Washington 25, D.C., or to one of the following offices of the United States Coast and Geodetic Survey:

Northeastern District: Tenth Floor, Custom House Building, State Street, Boston 9, Massachusetts.

Eastern District: Room 602, Federal Office Building, 90 Church Street, New York 7, New York.

Southeastern District: 418 Post Office Building, Norfolk 10, Virginia.

Southern District: 315 Custom House Building, 423 Canal Street, New Orleans 16, Louisiana.

Southwestern District: Room 1434, Post Office and Courthouse Building, Los Angeles 12, California.

Western District: 114 Custom House Building, San Francisco 26, California.

Mid-Western District: 502 Panama Building, 534 S.W. Third Avenue, Portland 4, Oregon.

Northwestern District: 705 Federal Office Building, Seattle 4, Washington.

Pacific District: 244 Federal Office Building, Honolulu, Hawaii 96812.

Charts are also available at some tackle, boat, and map stores. Most charts cost from 50¢ to $1.00.

These charts were designed primarily for navigation, but they also offer a wealth of information for anglers. Soundings and depths are given that indicate channels, drop-offs, sloughs, shoals, bars, and complete contours of the bottoms. Symbols indicate rocks, wrecks, underwater piling, and other obstructions, as well as landmarks such as buildings and towers that are helpful in fixing shore ranges when good fishing is located. Other symbols indicate type of bottom, such as coral, mud, sand, gravel, rock. All of these, as we have said, are closely related to the lives, feeding habits, and movements of fish. Generally, best results come from fishing just beyond the edge of a shoal or a bank. Knowledge of these formations is especially useful when you angle for the many bottom-feeding species (see Chapter 5 for more details).

While prospecting the shallows, take careful note of the underwater vegetation. Plant life provides succulent "chow" for the finsters, and variations in feed mean differences in the game fish to be taken. Rockweed, for instance, is one of the most prevalent of all seaweeds along both the Atlantic and Pacific shore lines, and its thick growth is a rich haven for all kinds of tiny aquatic animals. This attracts schools of hungry pollack, common cod, and cunners to feast in these beds. Kelp and eelgrass are found along sandy bottoms, or attached to rocks. Countless small fish seek refuge in kelp and eelgrass, but tautog, striped bass, and others ferret them out.

Salt-water anglers who take the trouble to observe tides and their effects, plant growth, and how these relate to bottom formation and contours, will find their time richly rewarded.

CHAPTER **5**

Inshore Fishing

A LARGE PART of the fish that journey up and down the Atlantic, Pacific, and Gulf coasts remain in the shallower, food-bearing inshore areas. Very likely your own salt-water fishing began by hooking some member of the inshore tribe. Or if you have yet to become a salt-water fisherman, here is a good way to begin. Once you tangle with these nomadic creatures, you will be drawn back time and again. There is always a different fish to conquer, some new mystery to fathom, an experiment to try, or a tempting spot to investigate.

Inshore fishing means fishing either from the shore or not far from shore. It is done by still-fishing the sea bottom or trolling in bays or inlets, or just off the surf.

Surf casters, big-game fishermen, and other ocean anglers often refer disparagingly to inshore anglers as "lead bouncers," "sinker bouncers," and "line jerkers." They are trying to perpetuate the belief that inshore, or bottom, fishing requires little skill. It's true that less skill is needed in this type of angling compared to surf casting or even deep-sea trolling. Yet there are plenty of tricks and skills in inshore fishing. The habits of the various species of fish that live in our inlets, bays and sounds are a lifetime study. Day after day and year after year, old-timers and expert anglers make good catches consistently while other inshore fishermen go without, or get only an occasional fish.

Another common misconception is that inshore fish are poor fighters and furnish little sport. Sure, some of these fish are sluggish, but the vast majority are fine scrappers, especially if caught on light tackle and under the right conditions. Besides, bottom fish are not the only ones taken in inshore waters with bait. Many of the so-called game fish like natural baits, too. Striped bass up to forty or fifty pounds have been taken within a few yards of the breaking surf. Even larger channel bass feed along the inshore bars and holes. Sharks of a hundred pounds or more may hit your hook.

In fact, one of the thrills of inshore fishing is that you never know what may hit next. Fishermen after half-pound flounders with a hand line have sometimes hooked and landed 15-pound striped bass. You may be bobbing around in a boat in a rocky area just a few yards offshore, trying for sea perch, when there will be a hard yank on your line and you will land a 6-pound tautog. There are so many different fish haunting our shore waters that you cannot always guess what fish has struck.

Finally, inshore fishing is inexpensive, healthful, plenty of fun, and more productive of fine eating fish (most species taken in inshore waters can be eaten) than any other kind of salt-water fishing.

KINDS OF INSHORE FISHING

Bottom fishermen are fortunate because they can practice their sport almost anywhere. From most large seashore areas, open party boats leave daily for bottom-fishing trips. They generally charge $3 to $10 per person, often with bait included. Some of the boats will even rent you tackle and sell you soft drinks, coffee, and sandwiches. No reservations are usually required. You just step aboard and find a spot to fish. Some of these boats can also be rented for the day by organizations, firms, or groups (see page 242 for complete details on party boats).

Most inshore fishermen go out in rowboats or skiffs, either their own or rented from one of the many boat stations that line our bays and inlets. Many of the bigger fishing stations may have more than a hundred boats and a choice of two or three sizes. These rent anywhere from $1.50 to $8 a day without a motor. In many spots you can fish a short distance from the fishing station and can row out in a short time. In some places they will tow you out to the fishing spot and bring you back at no extra cost. If you want to rent an outboard motor, this will cost an additional $5 to $15, depending on the size and condition of the motor. Most of the boat liveries also sell bait and tackle and some have refreshments and restaurants. The rowboats and skiffs, ranging from twelve to sixteen feet, will hold three or four anglers safely. Don't forget that it's dangerous to overload the boat and also difficult to fish in comfort when too many are aboard.

A recent trend has been the renting of large inboard boats known as "U-Drives." These range from sixteen to twenty-eight feet and are powered by engines of up to 115 hp. These inboards are larger, safer, and will accommodate up to five or six persons. They are popular with families who want to combine a day's outing with a fishing trip. When a gang from the

Inshore fishing can result in some big fellows, too. This young man caught this 225-pound grouper off the Florida Keys.

office or neighborhood get together and want to go out fishing for a day, they rent these larger boats. Many are equipped with cabin, toilet, bunks, rod holders, and fish or bait box. They rent for $30 or $50 a day with extra charge for gas and bait. The boat can be used for both inshore and offshore fishing.

Piers, docks, and bulkheads are favorite locations for inshore fishing. Some of these are located in inlets and bays, while others extend into the ocean. Many piers offer free fishing, but others charge you anywhere from 25 cents to a couple of dollars for the right to fish. Tackle can be rented or bought, and on many of the piers you can get food and coffee. Barges along the California coast offer a similar type of fishing (see page 244).

Causeways and bridges offer good fishing in many sections of both coasts and the Gulf of Mexico. These are particularly good locations because many species make it a habit of gathering around the piles or lingering in the strong currents beneath bridges. But you must make sure that fishing is not prohibited on the roadway you locate.

Breakwaters and jetties offer excellent inshore fishing since the rocks attract marine life and small baitfish which in turn draw the larger fish. Some of the wider, higher rock piles are safe and easy to navigate. Others which are broken up, low, or slippery, are dangerous under many conditions such as high tides and big waves. (Be sure to follow the safety precautions described on page 135 when fishing on breakwaters and jetties.)

Finally, in inshore fishing, you can fish in many spots right from shore, especially in rocky areas where you have deep water at your feet, or along many of the beaches where you can fish in the surf (see Chapter 6.)

INSHORE FISHING EQUIPMENT

The tackle you use in bottom fishing varies and includes anything from hand lines to elaborate and expensive surf rods or even trolling or big-game tackle. While a complete description of rods, reels, lines, and terminal tackle used for inshore fishing is given in Chapters 2 and 3, here is a summary of the equipment that you generally employ.

Hand Lines

Many years ago, hand lines were very popular for almost every type of bottom fishing. Today they are still used to a certain extent, from shore, rowboats, piers, bridges, or party boats. For hand-line still-fishing, braided or twisted cotton line or a tarred line is recommended. The line should be wound around a wood or plastic frame or stick.

A few hooks, some sinkers, and bait are all you need to start your fishing operation. You may buy these in any tackle store, all rigged with two hooks and a sinker. Usually, however, the sinker is located above the hooks. To my way of thinking this is wrong. Since you want to be sure to feel the slightest tug on the line, why be handicapped by having the sinker between you and the fish?

Hand-lining is of course a bottom fishing proposition in most cases. Always rig hand lines, no matter for what fish, with the two hooks a foot or two above the sinker, keeping the latter on the very end of the line. In this way you can let the sinker rest on the bottom, slack up just a bit, and feel even the slightest touch. And in order to impart a more animated appearance to the bait, you should raise and lower your arm frequently, until a bite occurs. By doing so, you also reduce the chances of having the bait robbed by fish that are too small to keep. When baiting with clams, shrimps, crabs, or minnows, lower the line gently from the gunwale or edge of the dock—do not fling it out as far as you can, or the bait will come off. Be alert to every tug, and set the hook promptly.

If a fish struggles hard, let him calm down before reaching the surface, and bring him to the top by drawing up line with one hand as it slips through the thumb and forefinger of your other hand. In this manner you maintain a steady pressure, lessening the danger of losing your prize. If the fish makes little resistance, though, pull him up hand over hand. Sometimes you have to try different levels to find just where the schools are circulating. Pollack, for example, may cruise about the middle depths rather than along the bottom. When you have located these fish, you mark the proper depth by tying a piece of twine to the line.

One of the major advantages of hand lines is that you can easily carry and use several lines at the same time. And when the fish are running, you can haul them in fairly quickly with little fuss. Of course, this limits the sport. But there is a lot of fun dropping your line and hook down into the unknown and wondering what you may catch next.

Rods

The most popular rod for bottom fishing is the "boat rod," usually in two sections but sometimes in a single piece. At one time, these rods were of solid wood and split bamboo, but now glass rods (hollow or solid), have taken over. They usually run five to eight feet in over-all length. (A short rod has some advantages: it enables you to lift a fish into a small boat or over the side of a party boat without a net. However, it is usually stiff and unyielding.) The average boat rod weighs nine to twelve ounces (some as much as twenty ounces). If you are after black drum, jewfish, and similar heavyweights which simply drag on the line, you should use a strong rod. Also, a stronger rod is justified where the bottom is rocky, and you may hang up frequently. It is not possible to recommend exact weights for boat rods, since conditions vary greatly around our eastern and western coast lines and the Gulf of Mexico. But, in general, better pick the lightest instead of the heaviest on the dealer's rack unless you positively need a strong rod. You will get more sport from bottom fish on a light rod.

The average boat rod is less effective in open bays. For these shallower waters and for protected water in general, the rods known as bay, weakfish, or flounder rods are best. These have a one-piece tip section of four to nine ounces in weight and a short detachable butt. The over-all length of these rods usually runs about five to seven feet, but they are often much more limber than the boat types.

Surf rods are used by some bottom anglers from shore, piers, or boats. These rods are especially good where long casts are required and for bottom fishing in the surf. The big-game or heavier trolling rods are also used occasionally in bottom fishing for such big fish as amberjack, jewfish, rays, and shark. Even fresh-water bait-casting and fly rods are sometimes used in bottom fishing for smaller fish (see Chapter 9). And in recent years, spinning rods have become popular with many bottom anglers. Because spin rods use mostly light, monofilament lines, you can use lighter sinkers. These are therefore excellent for the warier salt-water species in clear water.

The most inexpensive and simple bottom fishing outfit is the ordinary cane pole. It can run anywhere from eight to eighteen feet long. A line long enough to reach the bottom, a hook, and sometimes a small sinker or float are the only other things you need. Such poles are used mostly from shore, piers, docks, jetties, and low bridges where the water is fairly shallow. Here, you just pull or haul in the fish one after another, but your sport is limited because you do not get a chance to play the fish. Nowadays, anglers would rather catch fewer fish but have more fun and sport in fighting a fish.

Reels

The reels used in bottom or inshore fishing should match the rods and lines used. For most boat and bay rods, reels holding fifty to two hundred yards of line (1/0 to 4/0) are used, depending on the kind of fishing. (Further information on proper size of inshore reels can be found on pages 9, 16 and 21.) Neither star drag nor free spool is necessary on a boat-rod reel, since the drag serves to prevent line breakage from heavy fish (which is unlikely) and the free spool is a casting aid (only short casts are made from a boat). Most novices, however, seem to prefer a free-spool, star-drag model because they believe it is easier to handle than a single-action reel. For light rods, small fish, and shallow water, the smaller boat reels (1/0 or the small service-type reels—these have star drag, but usually no free spool—made by a number of companies) are best. For heavy rods, big fish, and deep water, the larger or big-game reels (4/0 to 6/0) are used. For surf rods the regular surf reels can be used. With spinning rods the same reels used with the rods for casting will serve.

Lines

Synthetic lines have almost completely replaced linen for inshore fishing today. A few diehards still employ linen lines in the 18- to 54-pound test class for this popular phase of salt-water fishing. In nylon, dacron, and monofilament, lines testing 12, 20, 27, 36, and 45 pounds are used. The best size depends mostly on the size of the fish you are after, the weight of sinkers used, the depth of water, and the obstructions in the area. Remember, the lighter your line, the less weight (sinker) required to hold the bottom in a moving tide. Too many inshore fishermen use heavy ropes that would do for hand lines. 20-pound test should be sufficient for most inshore angling; 27- or 36-pound test for the heaviest possible kind or around obstructions on which your rig might hang up and have to be pulled free.

In some deep spots with strong currents, metal lines of 26- or 35-pound test are sometimes practical. Where there are obstructions, such as barnacles, coral, mussels, piles, oysters, or rocks, monofilament lines stand more chafing than either braided dacron and nylon. Actually, the new ultra-limp monofilament lines have become very popular with inshore fishermen.

Terminal Tackle

Sinkers are essential in inshore fishing because they get the bait down to the proper depth—usually right on the bottom—and hold it there despite tides and currents. As described on page 43, many types of sinkers can be used for this type of fishing. The lightest sinkers are the split-shot and clincher types, which you squeeze on anywhere along your leader or line.

These are good when used with bobbers or floats to keep the bait down in a light current or tide. The oval-shaped, almond-shaped, or egg-shaped sinkers, which have a hole through the center, are good for wary fish. The line or leader slides through this hole when a fish bites and you can feel the lightest nibble. The pear-shaped or dipsy sinkers are also fine light outfits in shallow water.

The most commonly used sinker for bottom fishing is the bank type. Depending on its size, it can be used in deep or shallow water and most types of bottoms. Another type commonly used for all-purpose bottoms is the diamond-shaped sinker, which comes in big sizes for strong current and deep-water fishing. In rocky areas, round sinkers are often used because their shape tends to prevent their being caught in the rocks. In fishing over sandy bottoms, pyramid sinkers hold best. The weight of the sinker you use will of course depend on the strength of the current or tide and depth of the water. In general, for light tackle and shallow water, a 1- or 2-ounce sinker will often serve, but for deep water, heavy tackle and lines, and strong currents you may need sinkers up to twelve ounces. Remember, use just enough weight to hold your bait where you want it.

For your inshore rigs (page 93) you can use several three-way swivels of various sizes. The 3/0 is about the largest you will ever need. For light-tackle angling, the No. 4 swivel is the most used size. In-between sizes such as the 2, 1, 1/0, and 2/0 should also be on hand. Some barrel swivels in sizes 4, 2, 1/0, and 3/0 should also be available.

Synthetic leader material—either braided or monofilament—testing 10, 15, 20, 30, and 40 pounds will be needed for most forms of bottom or inshore fishing. Nylon can be obtained in coils of 10- to 100-yard lengths. If you are after sharp-toothed fish such as sheepshead, channel bass, bluefish, barracuda, and pollack, you can use cable-wire leader material (see page 38) instead of nylon.

Hooks are also a very important item of the terminal tackle in inshore fishing. You can often purchase them on short or long leaders in a tackle shop. If you wish to tie or snell your own, loose hooks bought by the dozen or by the box are best. Buy those with eyes for tying on the nylon leader material, or without eyes for wrapping with fine nylon thread to make snelled hooks. Eyed hooks, however, will save time and are preferred by most novice anglers when they do not buy ready-made ones. The proper types for the various inshore fish are given later in this chapter.

Tackle Bag

In addition to the basic tools—the rod, the reel, the line, and the terminal tackle—a host of gadgets are available which are really essential. While the following items were selected for inshore use, this list can serve as a guide in equipping yourself for most types of salt-water fishing:

A pair of good sun-glasses (not the cheap type) that will really protect your eyes from exposure to both sun and water glare

A pair of long-nosed pliers with a wire-cutting device for making up leaders

Extra swivels, sinkers, hooks, and lures

A fish knife

A fish scaler (sometimes combined with the knife)

A hook hone or stone to keep the points sharp

A hook disgorger

Ferrule cement and high-grade reel oil

A coil of hand line

A flat piece of wood on which to cut bait

Small screwdriver

An extra cork in case you want to drift a bait downtide at a certain depth (see page 98)

Roll of tire tape

A cloth for wiping your hands after cutting bait or cleaning fish

Scissors; needles and thread for sewing bait fish

A first-aid kit for quick protection of hand cuts or punctures made by hooks, fish fins, or a slip of the knife

Landing net or gaff, or both

And if you are tender of skin, you'd better have a small bottle of suntan oil. If you are fishing a marshy section where gnats and mosquitoes abound, a small bottle of insect repellent is very important.

Pair of white workman's gloves

This is a résumé of what you might find in any well-equipped salt-water angler's bag. We use the word "bag" advisedly because the best way to carry necessities is in a surf bag (page 120) or a tackle box (page 74). It may sound like stretching the budget, yet all these items are small but important when you are away from "civilization."

PROPER DRESS FOR INSHORE FISHING

The average inshore angler prides himself, if he is at all enthusiastic about his hobby, on the care of his tackle and on the selection of his location and rig. He will argue these points with all comers, yet he will often be uncomfortable during the course of a day if the weather changes. This needn't be, because it is so easy to dress correctly and enjoy yourself in all kinds of weather.

Perhaps the most miserable weather an inshore fisherman regularly meets is during the codfishing season along the Atlantic Coast north of Virginia. This is a late fall and early winter sport. Nevertheless many fishermen brave the elements in inadequate clothing, going more or less on pure intestinal fortitude rather than common sense.

The two major points to keep in mind when selecting your clothing for cold-weather fishing are (1) that it must break the bone-chilling wind and (2) that it must allow you to keep warm with a minimum of weight and restriction. It stands to reason that you are going to be splashed before the day is over. In the summer, this is not very serious; but when you become wet, even just a little bit, during near or below freezing weather, this becomes a very important consideration. Therefore it is wise to remember that your clothing must not only hold body heat and break the wind, but it also must keep you dry.

Commercial fishermen have licked, to a great degree, the problem of keeping both dry and warm. They wear rubber overalls, held up high across the chest by suspenders. On their feet they wear short rubber boots. Covering the upper body is a rubber parka, preferably with a hood. With this rig on, only the hands and face are exposed. Add a pair of rubber gloves and staying dry ceases to become a problem.

To know the proper way to dress for cold weather inshore fishing, let us start at the skin and go on from there. Several types of "insulated underwear" are available today. These are good for two reasons. First, they are light in weight because they are manufacturered from the new "miracle" fabrics. Second, because they are based on the thermos principle, the air spaces hold warmth in rather than keep the cold out. With this air space principle, developed during the Korean conflict, underwear has done away with the skin-tight, binding effect known in grandfather's day of red long-johns. It has been proved that constriction of any part of the body invites cold rather than repels it. Therefore, dressing loosely is a good idea.

Wear a lightweight wool shirt over the underwear, and over this a heavyweight wool shirt. Put on a pair of wool trousers, then an oversize jacket, preferably lined, and you will stay warm under your parka and rubber coveralls. Top this with a wool cap having ear flaps and you will be comfortable regardless of the cold.

In spring the temperature in the North will often change as much as 35 degrees. The water is still cold when the winter flounders begin their run, and fishermen wind up as chilled as their codfishing brethren if they do not take steps to prevent this. Here again, the main thing is to keep dry. In a boat, wear either a pair of commercial fisherman's rubber coveralls or a lightweight plastic raincoat. Your underclothing should be proper for the weather, and remember that it is always colder near or on the water.

In warmer climates or during the summer months, many of us overestimate our ability to withstand excessive exposure to the sun. Off comes the shirt and we fish happily until that familiar tightening across the shoulder blades is felt. Then it is too late. So unless you are out in the sun constantly, you should be prepared to cover yourself, particularly in summer weather. Nothing in the fishing world makes as little sense as a short-sleeved fishing shirt.

On the market today are all kinds of lightweight poplin shirts. The long-sleeved varieties are ideal. If the day is excessively warm, it is a simple matter to roll up your sleeves. But remember to roll them back in time.

Always wear a lightweight cap or hat during the summer months. This allows you not only the extra protection from the sun, but also serves as a shade to hold early morning and late afternoon rays from your eyes.

Being wet in warm weather isn't much of a problem. But if you get wet, you want to be able to dry off in fair time. For that reason, stay away from tight dungarees and levis and stick to loose, comfortable pants of cotton or khaki. College boys have recently been wearing pants called "chinos," which are fine for warm-weather fishing. Comfortable and lightweight, they dry very quickly.

In a boat, it is hard to beat the heat. Do not forget to take along plenty of drinking water, and watch out for sunburn. The average inshore angler uses a small boat devoid of shade. Some fisherman brace open umbrellas over the seats and are thus protected; others use homemade or commercial boat tops on a metal framework. Every salt-water angler planning a summer excursion should pack a bottle of salt tablets in his tackle bag. Take them as directed on hot days. Heat exhaustion is caused by the depletion of body salt. The victim's skin turns pale and clammy, and he may even lose consciousness. If salt tablets are not available, take a teaspoon of salt in a glass of water.

In warm weather, footwear is designed mainly for balance and footing aboard boats rather than for protection. Boat shoes, available at sporting goods stores, serve this purpose well. Wearing leather or smooth rubber soles is asking for trouble, particularly on a wet deck. For winter wear, stick to the short commercial fisherman's boots—worn by men who make their living from the sea. These are designed to be warm and stable on wet surfaces. In addition, they are relatively light in weight, and when worn with two pairs of wool socks are as comfortable as any insulated pac, at half the price. For a discussion of proper footwear and clothing when fishing from the surf and jetties or other rocky areas, see page 120.

INSHORE FISHING RIGS

The kind of fish you want to catch, and where, determine what type of rig to select. The basic bottom rig consists of a sinker tied onto the end of the line and hooks tied to the line *above the sinker*. Some bottom fishermen merely tie the loop of a snelled hook into the line itself a few inches above the sinker and let it go at that. But this arrangement often causes the hook and the leader to wrap around the line. To overcome this difficulty, tie a three-way swivel on the line, which allows the hook to stay clear of the line.

The standard blackfish (or tautog) rig has become increasingly popular for winter flounder, northern whiting (kingfish), eels, and any other species that picks or sucks its food on the bottom. It consists of a nylon leader twelve to sixteen inches in length, tied a few inches above the sinker.

Then another hook on a shorter nylon snell (six to ten inches in length) is tied near the center of the longer leader. Notice that no swivels are used, since they would increase chances of snagging in the blackfish's cluttered abode. For this same reason, many expert blackfish hunters use only one hook.

The old standby of the party-boater is the deep-sea rig. This rig is fine when fishing the offshore banks and wrecks. It makes use of two hooks, one tied just above the sinker and the other just high enough above the first to clear it. For tautog, ling, porgies, sea bass, and similar fish, use small, short-snelled hooks. Longer leaders and larger hooks may be employed when using this rig for pollack, codfish, halibut, and haddock. For smelt, whiting, silver hake, and herring, three hooks are often tied one above the other. Using more than three hooks is unwise because it increases the chance of tangles and has no advantages. The bank-style sinker should vary in weight from four to twelve ounces, depending upon the current, tide, and depth of water. At certain times, the currents and tide may be working in opposite directions, and it becomes very difficult to keep your

Inshore fishing rigs. (*A*) Basic bottom rig. (*B*) Deep-sea rig. (*C*) Blackfish rig. (*D*) Spreader-type rig. (*E*) Fluke rig. (*F*) High leader rig. (*G*) Sliding-egg sinker rig.

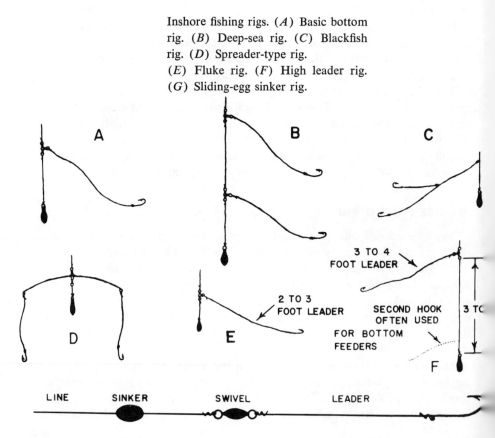

line taut enough to feel a strike. This is one occasion when you will be more successful if you move your bait around by raising and lowering your rod tip.

Another good old-timer is the spreader-type winter flounder rig. The sinker is tied in the center of this heavy wire spreader and two hooks on short leaders or sneels are attached on the ends. This rig, however, is giving way to the same type of arrangement as is used for tautog, since it is hard to feel a feeble flounder bite because of the spreader, and the weight and resistance of this rig slows down the fight of the flatfish.

The high leader rig is primarily a weakfish layout, but it will take striped bass, bluefish, and similar active feeders. A 3- or 4-foot leader is tied an equal distance above the sinker, which is heavy enough to reach the bottom. The hook is baited with a baitfish, a strip of squid, a sea worm, or a piece of crab. The high leader rig is sometimes used with another hook on a shorter leader or snell tied just a few inches above the sinker. This lower hook is for the bottom feeders.

The fluke (or summer flounder) rig is the same as the high-leader setup just described, except that the leader (two to three feet in length) is attached only a few inches above the sinker. To attract fish, a double-bladed fluke spinner is often used in front of the hook. The spinner arrangement works best in a fast tide or when the boat is drifting and the sinker is bouncing along the bottom (see page 104).

The sliding-egg sinker rig is the bottom fisher's counterpart of the surfman's fish-finder rig (page 126). It is a light tackle rig and is effective in protected waters where tides and currents are gentle.

The rigs described here are those most commonly used for inshore fishing, but there are some variations in certain sections and for certain species of fish. It is wise to watch closely how the experienced or successful fisherman makes up and uses his rig. Pay particular attention to such details as the length and thickness of the leaders or snells; how high above the sinker they are tied; the size and style of the hooks; and the weight and type of the·sinker. All these items play a very important part in presenting the bait properly to the fish. (Further information on this subject will be found later in this chapter.

It should be noted that the best rig would be worthless if the wrong bait is used and if it is not fresh. Try to find out in advance which bait the fish have been taking best (your bait dealer generally knows this). If you cannot find out what bait is best, it is a good idea to take along three or four different types. Then you will have at least one that will prove successful. Always buy the freshest bait available and change it often on the hook.

LOCATING INSHORE FISH

Inshore fish are fairly easy to find once you know the type of bottom, depth of water, and food they prefer (see Chapter 4). Unlike the high-speed, wandering game fish, inshore bottom fish usually stay in one area for long periods of time. And unlike game fish, which usually chase baitfish, the bottom fish feed mostly on clams, crabs, shrimp, sea worms, and other similar slow-moving sea creatures which tend to gather in a small area.

When you drop your line and rig overboard into salt water, you never know what you will catch. Mixed bags are common in inshore fishing. But generally you'll get the best results if you aim at a single species. Whenever possible, consult some experienced fisherman in your locality about hook sizes, best rigs, kind of bait, and method of fishing for the various species. The method that works on the north Atlantic Coast will not always take the same fish in the Gulf. So any general advice here is intended only as a guide and not as the final word. Also, do not be afraid to experiment, because we know from experience that the standard, accepted method of taking a species in one locality is often not the only way it can be caught. But do your experimenting after you have caught a few.

TECHNIQUES OF CATCHING INSHORE FISH

As indicated in Appendix D, there are several methods used to catch inshore fishes. The most common are still-fishing, casting (both bait and surf), trolling, drifting, and jigging. To be successful at inshore fishing, you should know and use all of these methods at various times.

Still-fishing

There is much more to still-fishing than just casting or dangling your line overboard and waiting for a strike. While fishing for many inshore species around rocks, pilings, and other obstructions there are times when you want your bait to stay put in one place. But after dropping your baited hook overboard, bounce your sinker by raising your line or pole every once in a while to make sure that it is right on the bottom where it should be. If the current moves it away or lifts it from the bottom, add a little more lead. Check your bait occasionally, too, just to be certain that some bait thief or crab has not stolen it and left you with a naked hook. Needless to say, bare hooks do not catch fish. Do not be impatient. The prime virtue of any angler is patience. But if after a reasonable time you have had no promising bites, pull up anchor and move to another spot a few hundred feet away. On a pier, dock, or bridge, moving a few feet from your original location may change your luck. Fish are unpredictable creatures; sometimes you have to offer them their food right at their doorstep. Some days you can make a good catch without moving from one spot; other times you may have to shift your location several times.

A fairly strong tide or current is helpful in moving your bait around. For example, when you let your line down, wait until you feel it strike bottom, and let it lie there for a short while. Then raise your rod tip and lower it, letting out some line. The tide should carry your bait and sinker farther away from your location. Then, after allowing the bait to remain still a few minutes, raise and lower your rod tip again, letting out more line. Repeat this procedure until your bait and sinker have been taken a good distance off. Then reel in, check your bait, and do the same thing over again. For best results, use the lightest sinker that will hold bottom. Should the tide start to run faster and you cannot hold the bottom, change to a heavier sinker. But if the tide slackens, change back to a lighter one. The advantages in making your bait move with the tide are that it makes the bait appear alive and prevents crabs from getting your bait. Besides, this way you cover more territory.

Another way of accomplishing the same purpose while anchored or fishing from a beach, dock, or pier, is to make a long cast and then reel in your bait and sinker slowly, letting it remain in a new spot a few minutes; then reel, rest—continuing this maneuver until you have your bait and sinker back at your original position. Keep trying until you get a strike, and if this occurs, fish that spot heavily. This is the method surf fishermen use when bottom fishing behind the breakers.

"Live Line" Angling

"Live-line" angling is suitable for areas having fairly strong currents, such as tideways or places where rivers enter; it is used primarily for fish that cruise the middle or upper depths rather than along the bottom. From a bridge, bank, or anchored boat, you drop your baited hook to the surface and let the current take the leader and line out. When fifty to a hundred feet of line have uncoiled from the reel, you hold the rod steady until a fish

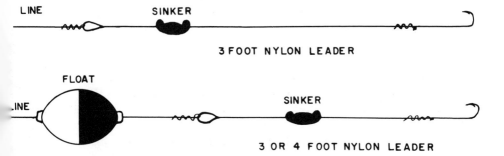

The proper rig for live-line angling (*top*) and float
fishing (*bottom*).

bites. If the flow is too strong, add a small sinker to improve results. The swirling water gives your bait the right life and movement, and it is a tricky way of tantalizing such fish as striped bass, weakfish, mackerel, white sea bass, bluefish, yellowtail, and pollack.

"Float" Fishing

Where the current is moderate, you can try "float" fishing for the smaller fish of these species. A large float is tied to your line, with a short length of line, a wire leader, and a hook dangling below the bobber. When the hook is baited, this rig is allowed to drift with the current a way, then is held until some nibbler ducks your float. The distance your line hangs below the float will depend on the species you are after. For example, when fishing for snapper blues (small bluefish), make your rig so that the bait is offered at three to five feet below the water surface. The prime purpose of the float or bobber, which is made of cork, plastic, or some other very buoyant material available at any tackle store, is to keep the hook at the desired level below the surface. It also serves to indicate a bite, for when a fish seizes the hook he carries the bob under.

Setting the Hook

Setting the hook in a bottom fish requires a certain knack which comes only with experience and practice. Some species—those that grab the bait, swallow it, and run—are easy to hook. Others, which suck it in and lie still or nibble nervously, are often a problem. The sucking fish, such as flounders, require lifting the rod tip at regular intervals to find out if they have taken the bait. The nibblers require a lot of patience and self-control. Many anglers cannot wait, and as soon as they feel a series of light pecks, they strike back. This jerks the hook away from the fish and loses the bait. It is much better to wait until you feel a strong tug or feel the fish move away with your bait. Then a sharp lift of the rod tip will usually set the hook. A good rule to follow when the fish takes your bait is not to try to set the hook until he attempts to run with it. Give him his head, but keep the line taut.

Blackfish, or tautog, is one fish that requires a great deal of patience. This is due to the fish's habit of chewing food in two stages. First he nibbles with his front teeth. This feels like the bergall (a great bait stealer and companion of the black), but it is a bit more solid. Sticking or reeling in at this time usually results in a clean miss, or at least a lightly hooked fish. The black then passes the bait back to the crushing teeth. This is a very solid bite, and if the angler strikes quickly and vigorously, it's almost sure to mean a hooked fish and fast action. Remember that a hooked black and a landed black are two very different things. The tautog bores steadily for the bottom, and can apply plenty of leverage with his compact build and big fins. Down to the sharp barnacles and rocks he goes, and unless stopped with steady rod pressure, a fouled and cut line is the sure result.

The California sheepshead's bite and method of play are similar. The fighting style of this fish, as well as its habitat, makes plenty of spare rigging a must.

Many fish follow a regular striking pattern. For instance, a channel bass will give a few light taps. For about a half minute there is no action at all. Then the line starts to go out in earnest, which is the time the fish must be struck. Striking too soon will pull the bait from the fish's mouth, and waiting a little too long will result in a spit-out.

Location also has some effect on how a fish acts. For example, you will find the fish of the inshore bays and those of the deep approach the bait in different ways. When in a bay, the sea bass, while not loath to take a hook, sometimes tests the angler's patience by nibbling at the bait before mouthing it. He might even seize one end of it and move away a few feet, still ticking away at the morsel, so that it becomes necessary to play along with him, carefully feeding him a little line. There won't be any real pull on the line while he toys with the bait in this manner, and you won't be able to set the hook until he gets through nibbling on the bait and takes it into his mouth. Keep your line as taut as you can without pulling the bait away from him—keep in contact with the fish all the time. When he finally mouths the bait and feels the hook he will start his resistance, and a short, smart upward movement of your rod tip will plant the point. However, when these fish are in open ocean water, they usually hit the bait with real enthusiasm and then exhibit a violent desire to go elsewhere.

Inshore anglers are often troubled by bait stealers such as blowfish, bergalls, sea robins, oyster crackers, small sharks, and rays. These are small fish which nibble at the bait and usually succeed in cleaning the hooks. It does not pay to strike and try to hook these bait thieves. One possible exception is the blowfish, ugly-looking but considered a delicacy and sold under such names as fish fingers, sea squab, chicken leg, and the like. But catching blowfish endlessly is no fun when you are bottom fishing.

To stop bait stealing, use bigger baits so that it takes longer to clean the hook, or use tougher baits which are not stolen so readily. Baits such as conchs, crabs, sea snails, and whelks are tough and stay on the hook longer. Another trick is to use the softer and more attractive baits in combination with the tougher baits. Thus, if the softer bait is stolen, you still have some bait left on the hook and will not have to reel in your line quite so often.

Playing the Fish

The longer you play a fish the more fun you will have, and the more tired the fish will become and therefore easier to land. Once he is hooked, you should stop him short only if it looks as though he is about to hang you up in an underwater tangle. If you want to stop him, bring the rod tip down, even to the point of dipping it into the water. With the pull more in a downward direction, the fish will fight under water. Keep the line tight at all times and reel in only when the fish is coming toward you or after the fish is completely tired out.

If you are playing a fish in a rip or a strong tide, try to keep him fighting against the tide as much as possible. Battling the current as well as the rod, he will tire much sooner. If he goes downstream, go after him. You can lose even a small, completely played-out fish if you try to drag him against the current.

Sometimes a fish will drop down to the bottom and sulk. If you try to haul him in, the line will break and you'll lose your fish. You must "sweat it out" by slacking off your line to let the fish think he is free. In a few minutes he will move, and you can start battling him again. Or you can try rapping the rod butt, at the same time moving the rod from side to side. This may disturb him enough to provoke more fight.

A different technique may be needed for the larger inshore fish. It is known as "pumping," and it is the only way to make some of the larger fish budge and to gain line on them. After the hook is set, you raise the rod tip, lower it quickly and at the same time wind in those three to four feet of line you have gained. Doing this repeatedly will gradually work your fish up to the boat. Make the spring of the rod do most of the work for you, and have your star drag set to keep him constantly tired.

Inshore salt-water fish may be picked out of the water by a net, a gaff, or by hand—depending on their size. Since many of these fish have sharp teeth or equally sharp gill covers, the hand method is not the safest. When using a landing net, place it so that the hoop is about three-fourths underwater, lead the fish headfirst into it, and then swing the net into the boat. If the fish is too big for your net and you have a gaff handy, sock the hook-like point into him while he is swimming away from you. Thus, his efforts to escape will keep him on the point of the gaff. But regardless of the method you use in landing a fish, be sure to keep the line taut and hold the rod tip high. If you do not plan to use the fish for food, release him. Of course, do not gaff a fish you plan to release.

Use a good disgorger to free the hook so that you will not injure your hands or the fish. Beware of the sharp spines on the dorsal and anal fins of many of the inshore fish. A dry rag, to hold the fish with while he is being de-hooked or cleaned, will prevent painful cuts and possible infection.

Fishing over rocks and shellfish and around wrecks, you will lose hooks and sinkers, because they often snag. Therefore be sure to have extra terminal tackle with you. There is a little trick which you can use to minimize hook losses due to snagging. When you attach the sinker to your line, tie it on with ordinary string instead of fish line—be sure that the string is strong enough to hold the sinker, yet weak enough so that if the lead gets caught on an obstruction the string will break. That way you stand to lose only the sinker, not the sinker and hooks, plus some line. There will be

Three ways to remove inshore fish from the water: net (*left*), gaff (*lower right*), or by hand (*right*).

times, of course, when the hook itself gets fouled up on something down below and cannot be freed. In such a case the only thing to do is to cut the line with as little loss as possible and rig up again.

Chumming

Closely associated with still-fishing, especially the live-line and float-fishing methods, the practice of chumming has good uses. Inshore chumming is really an art and something that you learn best only from experience. However, here are some principles which are helpful:

Chum is baitfish ground into a hash—usually prepared by putting the baitfish through a meat grinder. Since the more popular baitfish, such as shrimp, anchovies, sardines, clams, smelts, menhaden, mossbunker, and herring, may weigh up to a pound, and can be frozen, a sturdy hand-driven, hotel-size meat grinder generally is employed, rather than the smaller kitchen type. The chum then is ladled or thrown overboard in small gobs from an anchored boat at regular intervals, according to the strength of the current or tide, forming a chum line or chum streak, which is the unbroken line of ground chum particles leading from the boat. This induces fish to work up the current toward the source of supply, bringing them within hooking distance. Just so long as you keep them interested, and keep your bait in the chum stream, you can take your share of bluefish, mackerel, weakfish, sea bass, yellowtail, California corbina, tautog, and croaker.

A chum line or chum streak must be unbroken to have maximum effectiveness. If the line is interrupted or broken for any distance, fast-moving fish coming up on the outside end of the line will follow it to the break, then lose interest. That's why chumming should be a steady process; it is also why it is not desirable to chum in a place where the line will be crossed and recrossed by other boats. The quantity ladled overboard each time is generally a matter of convenience. Many chummers use an ordinary kitchen soup ladle, scooping out one ladleful of chum at a time and dropping it over. With a few preliminary ladlings, observe how the current carries the chum away. This will help you determine how often you should chum—less often if the current is slow, more rapidly if it is fast. Anyhow, you should always have plenty of chum on hand.

Chumming can be done from the stern, but it is probably better from the side and a little toward the bow, when the tide is strong. Though chumming technique presents no problem on a calm day with a skiff laying at anchor, you cannot keep chum floating steadily when a boat yaws—that is, swings in the grip of wind and tide working against each other. Knowing that such a wind-sea problem requires stable anchorage, the forewarned chum fisherman usually carries two anchors. One is set in the bottom in the normal manner, with care that it holds securely, after which the helmsman runs the outboard to one side and ahead of the spot where the first anchor is firm in its mooring. Dumping the second anchor over the side, letting the boat drift backward, you end up with a triangle effect—the two anchors at the corners of the base, the anchor lines forming the sides, and the boat itself at the apex of the triangle. This rig is a bridle, guaranteed to hold a skiff firmly, bow into the current. It allows the angler to chum over the transom and keep a steady bait streak.

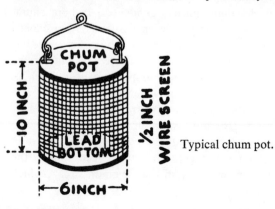

Typical chum pot.

Suppose you are in a swift tideway without a wind problem, and there are enough people aboard to tangle the tackle if everyone fishes over the stern. Drop one anchor over the stern, run dead ahead, perpendicular to the current, till the anchor line comes taut, then heave the second anchor over the bow. The bow will drift downstream till it holds broadside, at the apex of a "V" mooring. You will be able to chum and fish directly over the gunwale. If you have only one anchor aboard, you can use the impromptu "Y." mooring shown in the illustration.

After you have anchored properly and have your chum line started, you allow your baited hook to drift out with the chum (according to the live-line method, page 97), keeping your rig as much as possible in the chum. The hook of your chumming rig may be baited with a full-size piece of the same material used for chumming or any other proper bait for the fish you are after. It is usually best to keep your rig a hundred or more feet astern. It helps, therefore, to cast your baited rig a good distance out into the chum line, then pay the line out freely as the current takes it. A fish will usually strike while your bait is in motion, drifting along with the chum. If you get no fish on your first try, reel the rig in and let it drift out again.

Chum is sold ready for use, and is kept under refrigeration until then. It spoils quickly in warm weather. Sometimes refrigeration forms ice crystals in the chum. These crystals not only make the chum more difficult to handle but also keep it afloat and prevent it from diffusing properly in the water. So let it thaw a bit before using.

By cutting up menhaden, or mossbunker, into tiny oily bits and ladling these overboard, you can create a "slick" on the surface that will attract any bluefish within "smelling" range. You can hold them near the boat for a long time in this fashion. Mackerel will also come a-swimming when scraps of menhaden, herring, mullet, or squid are being drifted out. Anchovies and sardines (pilchards) are the favor chums for yellowtail and white sea bass.

Most weakfish are caught by chumming with live grass shrimp. Drop your shrimp over in clusters of four or five at a time, spacing each cluster a foot or so apart (frequency of clusters will depend on the current). Fewer shrimp are used after the fish arrive. From four to six quarts are enough for a day's fishing; they are expensive, but the cost narrows down when shared by the fishing party. If shrimp are scarce, porgies, sea robins, or other fish can be run through a meat grinder and used as chum—sparingly, however, and only in a good flow of the tide, or the chum will sink to the bottom and attract crabs, sea robin, small porgies, dogfish, and other undesirables. With a shrimp chum line, a top-fishing rig is used, with or without small weights or with or without a cork float-all, depending on the strength of the current. Baits used in top fishing for weakfish include shrimp, sand worms, and bloodworms, according to the feeding fancy of the fish on a given day. Also good in top-fishing for weakfish is a small pearl squid, the hook of which can be baited with shrimp or a piece of worm. Another lure, one which is used when the current is strong, is a mackerel jig, its hook baited with a sea worm. No additional weight is needed with a mackerel jig.

While chumming for bottom feeders like flounders, sea bass, corbina, tautog, and fluke, it is a good idea to use a chum bag or chum pot. This consists of a burlap sack (bags that oranges and onions come in are fine as long as the mesh is fairly small) or a fine mesh wire basket filled with ground chum or crushed bait fish. Although sea bass will go for most types of chum, it is best to use crushed mussels for California corbinas and flounders, ground mossbunkers for fluke, and ground clams for tautog and

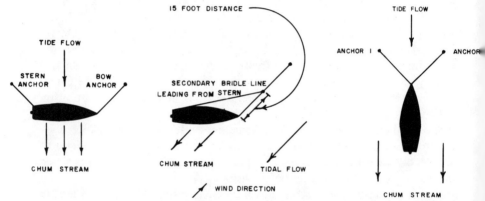

Typical chumming mooring arrangements. (*Left*) "V" mooring—no wind. (*Center*) "Y" mooring—one anchor. (*Right*) Conventional bridle—two anchors.

California sheepshead. Close the neck of the container and tie on a fairly long piece of cord or rope, then lower the chum pot over the side to the bottom and tie its line to an oarlock or bitt on the gunwale. Every so often you can bounce this chum pot on the bottom, so that small fragments of meat and flavorsome juices will seep into the water and attract fish.

If you locate a particular spot that yields day after day, and you mark it with a buoy, you can ensure continued success by maintaining a chum bag at that point. Fill a burlap bag with crushed clams or mussels or pieces of mullet, pilchards, or menhaden, adding rocks for weight. The game fish are attracted to this potent sack just as catfish are lured by a bag loaded with overripe meat.

Inshore Drifting

Drifting in your boat is a favorite and highly successful method of inshore fishing for tautog, fluke, weakfish, mackerel, bluefish, barracuda, bonefish, tarpon, porgies, salmon, and others. There are good reasons for the success of drifting as an inshore technique: a drifting bait is more natural in appearance than one anchored in place by a sinker; a drifting bait covers a great deal of territory and sooner or later is bound to pass near some hungry fish; drifting is silent—boat noises make some fish, such as mackerel, disappear like a flash.

The first consideration in drift fishing is the "set" of the tide and the wind. Locate your starting point very carefully so that you can get the maximum amount of fishing out of a given stretch of water. This means that you should strive for the longest possible drift over a large section of productive bottom or, in smaller holes, pinpoint your drift over the center of a good spot. Having located the best starting point by trial and error, get precise ranges on it so that you may return each time you complete a pass. In other words, be sure to take cross bearings of the spot where you have had luck, since where there is one fish there will almost certainly be more.

Use a simple triangulation method. Line up two shore objects, say, a telegraph pole in front of a tree; then, looking farther along the shore, line up two other objects. You, of course, are at the point where lines projected through your ranges would intersect. If you are a careful type of angler, write these points down instead of trusting to memory and you will be able to return to the hot spot again and again. Tides change in strength or direction, or the wind diminishes or picks up, which will necessitate slight adjustments in your drift starting point. Experience will soon show you how to make up for these basic variations.

In general, try to fish as close to your boat as possible, especially when working over a rocky bottom—for drifting is very apt to result in bottom snagging of your rig. With the line close to the boat and hanging virtually straight down, a quick pull-up of your rod tip usually will break you loose. It is very important to note that lighter sinkers than would be ordinarily used are practical when drift angling, as the lift of the current and tide on the line is minimized. Use only weight enough to "feel" bottom. The lighter the sinker, the less bottom fouling. Over mud or sand bottom you sometimes can improve your luck by substituting a fish attractor such as a small block squid or a simple spinner for a sinker. In cases where a spinner will not get down and hold bottom, pinch light leads ahead of the flasher.

Sea bass, tautog, winter flounder, and whiting prefer the offered bait to drift slowly and steadily across the water's bottom. The less motion imparted to the bait, the better your results will be. Hold your rod well above the gunwale so that the action of the craft will not bounce your rig on the bottom. On the other hand, summer flounders (fluke), porgies, and many Pacific Coast fish go for a bouncing bait in a big way. Let your rig hit bottom, then bounce it a foot or so by raising the rod's tip. It will not take too many bounces to produce fish. In fact, if you make more than a dozen bounces without a strike, you have either drifted out of the productive area or lost your bait.

Another way of teasing fluke is to drift-fish with a cork float. You can manage this from a boat, from the top of a jetty where you can walk along as your cork drifts in the current, or from shore where there is a long, deep channel. You sound with a lead to find the depth of the water, then tie the float at the proper length of line so that the live killy or spearing (you need a live bait for float fishing), which you have hooked through the lips, will move just above the bottom. A 2/0 to 6/0 hook is used, together with a thin wire leader and pinch-on sinker. This system lets you cover a good deal of productive territory and makes for plenty of action when a sizable flounder takes hold.

It is always important in drifting to get the "feel" of different types of bottom, for, with changes in bottom conditions you may expect different species—and a matching change in fishing technique may spell success. One way of finding the bottom types is to ask someone who knows, or check navigation charts and try your dead reckoning. Sometimes that is easier said than done. If you want to do as the old-timers did, take a standard sounding lead and put a blob of soap in the indentation in the bottom. Keep on sounding, and when the soap does not pick up anything off the bottom—mud, sand, gravel, etc.—you can take it for granted that you hit rock.

In drifting for subsurface feeders, it is general practice to cast a moderate distance to get the bait away from the boat. Casts of more than twenty or twenty-five feet should be avoided, however, since drifting with such a rig generally results in some slack which causes difficulty when setting the hook on a strike.

When drifting for surface gamesters like bluefish, weakfish, striped bass, and yellowtail, the technique is a cast-and-retrieve process. When a school of feeding fish is sighted, the most successful method is to drift past the school—not through it—casting well beyond and reeling the bait or lure through the center of the school.

Regardless of drifting method, wait until you are well past the hot spot before starting your motor for the uptide trip and be careful to circle the productive water, rather than going right through it, particularly if the water is shallow. Many species of fish will shy at motor noises, even going so far as to leave their feeding grounds for the rest of the tide if they are so disturbed.

Inshore Jigging

Jigging is a time-honored method of fishing for weakfish inshore. It also takes some other species of fish—mackerel, striped bass, ling, and bluefish. Actually, jigging for blues in fast rips is one of the most productive forms of bluefishing. But regardless of the species, in this method you go to the fish by drifting your boat over deep holes and channels. In inlets and shallow water, small metal jigs (one ounce or less) with a high shine are baited with worms or a strip of squid, or are left bare. In deeper waters, a heavy diamond jig is required. The line is stripped off the reel until the bait reaches the bottom. Then, with the boat drifting, the lure is "jigged" so that it bounces or dances through the water in a skipping motion a few feet off the bottom. This is accomplished by raising and lowering your rod's tip.

If you get no strikes at this level, repeat the procedure, but this time do the jigging a few feet higher—and then even higher still. Jigging is usually a blind operation, with no signs of fish present, diving gulls and terns often point out schools offshore, but the inshore fisherman must find his fish. You will ultimately locate your quarry, at whatever level they are feeding. Mark the spot where the first fish hits, and remember how much line was out. Return to the spot and anchor (this is a good idea whenever you are drifting), jig at the same depth, and the chances are you will be working in a school. Where there is one fish there are usually plenty more.

Inshore Trolling

Sometimes conditions are not favorable for drifting. The tide might be too strong, or the wind might be blowing in the wrong direction, or perhaps there is too much boat traffic. On such occasions, trolling may be a better fishing technique.

You can troll with a hand line, but a rod and reel is preferable. You can do light trolling with a bay-fishing outfit, but this outfit is too light for many inshore or near-shore species. So it is better to use a boat-fishing outfit which will handle anything likely to strike. Remember that some of those inshore fish put on real weight—tarpon rather frequently weigh more than a hundred pounds; and 40- and 50-pound striped bass and channel bass are fairly common. Also, you need equipment heavy enough to stand up under the fast trolling of fairly heavy lures, a strain that would be too much for bay equipment.

For this heavier trolling, your leader can be stainless steel wire in the smaller diameters, which will have all the test that you need. If you want nylon leaders, probably fifteen pounds will be as low as you can safely go if you are after a big fish, with 30- and 45-pound test the best if you are trolling fast and expecting to take fish of twenty-five pounds or more. Length of the leader should be at least four feet, but many fishermen prefer to use a 6-foot leader to make a wider gap between the line and the lure. Of course, the end of the leader next to the line must have a single-barrel swivel; those Monel snap swivels are good, placed next to the lure so that you can change lures quickly and lose less fishing time. Don't make the leader so long that you can't reel your fish near enough to the boat to net or gaff it.

Trolling lures are legion. Spoons, spinners, feather jigs, barracudas, plugs, strip baits, etc.—these probably make up most of what you will troll. One of the most killing ways to take striped bass is with a smooth-running spinner whose trailing hook is baited with sea worms. Trolled slowly this is hard to beat. This spinner will take weakfish, too, and blues, and many others. If you cannot get worms, use a piece of pork rind or a thin strip of cut fresh squid. In fact, when trolling for mackerel with mackerel jigs, you can step up your catch by hooking on a small (1½ inches long and ½ inch wide) V-shaped piece of cloth cut from a shirt-tail or handkerchief. Incidentally, a bit of pork rind—you can get the bottled variety with a hook inset—attached to a metal jig or feather jig gives an extra wiggle which sometimes makes the difference between catching and not catching fish. If you are using metal spoons or jigs, keep them polished. A bit of fine emery cloth is good for this job. And keep those hook points sharp; regular hook hones, no bigger than your forefinger, can be bought for about 25 cents at most hardware or sporting goods stores.

The rate of speed that you troll should conform to the lure you use. You will note that each lure has its own best speed which gives it a more lifelike action than when trolled faster or slower. As a rule, you should troll fast (five to six miles per hour) for eelskin rigs and nylon or feather jigs—you'll need that speed to make the lure wiggle in the water. Even then, working your rod tip up and down continually will give the lure extra dive and flutter. A good strip of cut bait will wiggle more slowly (three to five miles per hour) and is especially popular on the Florida inshore reefs. Many spoons like those used for fluke give their best action at slow speeds (1½ to 3 miles per hour).

Typical feather jig trolling rig.

Deep trolling rig with releasing pin. This rig should be trolled about two feet from bottom. More information on deep trolling can be found on page 146.

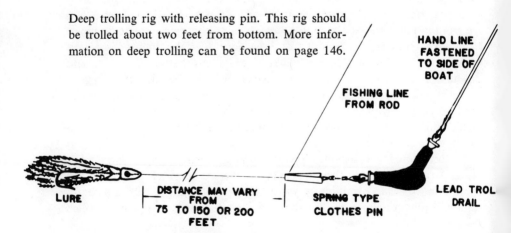

HAND LINE FASTENED TO SIDE OF BOAT

FISHING LINE FROM ROD

LURE

DISTANCE MAY VARY FROM 75 TO 150 OR 200 FEET

SPRING TYPE CLOTHES PIN

LEAD TROL DRAIL

When trolling for bottom fish, such as fluke, the lure must be brought down to a level (on or close to the bottom) where the fish are feeding. Use a drail of appropriate weight. As the boat moves slowly along, the lure is allowed to sink; then, when it is felt to hit bottom, it is lifted a foot or two, and this is the level at which it is trolled. The best distance above the bottom is variable; you should experiment by moving your lure a few inches either way. Keep it reasonably close to the bottom, however. A little extra attraction can be given to the lure by jigging it at intervals.

Frequently, when trolling in shallow water, you will need to pay out a longer line (100 to 150 feet) than when covering deeper inshore water. This depends upon the kind of fish, of course, since some are more wary than others, or customarily stay at the surface or far below. While waiting for a strike, your rod should be held with the tip extending slightly upward, toward the stern of the boat; never at a right angle. If you wish to rest and place your rod in the boat's rod holder, tighten the star drag on the reel just enough so that if a fish grabs hold the hook will pierce his jaws.

Most fish will hook themselves securely when they strike on a trolling outfit, since they have to seize the bait quickly. In most cases, all you have to do is clamp your thumb down on the leather thumbstall on your reel for a few moments, or raise the rod's tip quickly, and the hook will become imbedded. Be careful, though, not to screw the brake drag too tightly, or you will either cause the line to break when a fish hits suddenly or force the hook out of his mouth.

After you have connected with a fish, it may be necessary to slow the boat or even stop while fighting your opponent. If you are a novice, in your excitement after the hook is set you are apt to "freeze up" on the reel and not give the fish sufficient line to run his full course. This is a risky practice even when inshore trolling. Your prey should be given plenty of line with which to work off his steam on that first long violent rush, and you should not hurry him toward the boat. An exception to this, however, is when you troll in shallow water near rocks or over coral reefs, and your fish fights along the bottom. Here you must exert enough strain to prevent him from wrapping the line around a rock, or from darting into a cavern in the coral.

Wear out your catch until he is ready to gently submit before bringing him too close, and be sure to keep your rod tip elevated while playing him. Do not point the tip directly toward the fish; the rod must carry its share of the burden. If possible, never let a fish get under or ahead of the boat. Above everything else, almost, do your best never to allow the line to go slack. If you do, in most cases you are sunk—or at least the fish sinks and you are left holding the empty hook.

When the fish is near the boat on his last leg of his trip to your frying pan, always be wary of a last-moment plunge. Lift your quarry over the stern, or near it, by means of a net or gaff. Do not ever try to raise a fish by the line. If the fish is heavy and hooked solidly, your partner can pull it over the side by the leader. (Further data on trolling will be found in Chapters 7 and 8.)

Fishing Inshore Reefs

So popular and important is inshore fishing along the coral and rock reefs of the Florida, Lower California, Gulf Coast and Bahama Islands regions that it has become a class of fishing of its own (see Chapters 7 and 9), but it deserves a brief description here. Among the species that frequently come from the reef beds are albacore, amberjack, barracuda, bonito, bonefish, flounder, grouper, kingfish, mackerel, muttonfish, pompano, porgies, sea bass, snook, tarpon, yellow jack, and wahoo. Many of these are caught during late fall and winter, but the spring months also yield fine strings. Usually the tide makes no difference, for these fish bite throughout the day or night.

A silver king tarpon is being hauled on dock to keep company with two fighting darts of dynamite, the vicious barracuda, as these anglers haul in three prized catches from inshore reef fishing.

There are two leading methods of angling over the reefs: trolling slowly with feathered jigs or strip baits and drift fishing. In the latter, the boat is allowed to coast along with the tide or wind, while the bait—a small fish hooked just beneath the dorsal fin—is trailed behind the boat close to the bottom. When a number of strikes occur in one locality the anchor is put over and the place fished carefully. Most reef fish hook themselves by the speed and force of their strike. You must keep a tight line and give as little as possible, holding the fish away from the disastrous sharp edges of the coral and rocks. For this reason heavier tackle is required for reef fishing than for smooth bottom fishing, for as soon as a victim is hooked he heads for a cavern where the line may be slashed in two.

Many of the larger bottom reef fish are partial to a mullet that has been split from head to tail along the backbone, rigged on the hook so that the tail extends beyond the bend of the hook, fastened by its head to the hook's eye. The object is to impale the split mullet so it will have a weaving motion when drawn through the water.

Spoons, big plugs, brightly polished squids, and feathered jigs also appeal to the reef fish. These should be separated from your line by means of a wire leader about six feet long. Always tie on one or two swivels between the line and leader so the line will not become untwisted. After you have trolled for a long time with a revolving lure, your line will probably become somewhat untwisted and kinked despite the use of swivels. In this case you remove the lure and tie on a line-twister, which resembles a spoon. You troll this gadget on a long line, and presently the trouble will become remedied. An untwisted or kinked line is greatly weakened, and this must be guarded against in all salt-water fishing.

The reel should be equipped with a leather thumb-drag so that you can stem the run of a fish toward the coral or rocks without burning your unprotected thumb. A race-crazed fish must be checked, and thumb control is the best method when fishing inshore reefs.

Spinning and Mooching

Spinning and mooching are almost sure-fire methods for garnering West Coast salmon. This system is not spinning in the sense which the word usually has, meaning the use of a spinning rod, a fixed spool reel, a thread line, and small artificial lures, together with a particular style of casting and retrieving (see page 221). In the sense in which we are now using it, "spinning" means a form of salmon fishing based on the use of a specially cut slice (called a "spinner") taken from the side of a bait fish, attached to a certain type of rig, and worked in the water according to ways that have developed from experience over many years.

As practiced on the West Coast, spinning is especially alluring to the feeding king (blackmouth) and silver salmon found in tidal eddies and similar spots. For spinning, the rod should be of lightweight glass, from

9 to 10½ feet in length, with a flexible tip section that has enough back bone to set the hook in a striking king salmon.

For this kind of fishing you'll want a fast-retrieving level-wind free-spool sea reel that accommodates 600 to 750 feet of line. No star drag should be used, for the line is light and all you need do is apply tension with your leather-protected thumb, plus the ordinary click-drag of the reel. You may fish with a 12- or 15-pound test braided nylon. By means of a brass barrel swivel, you attach a crescent-shaped sinker to the line—or a common ringed sinker from one to four ounces in weight, depending upon the size of your line, the force of the current, and the fish you are after.

If you are going to spin for silver salmon, then put on a 1-ounce sinker, since these fish are usually close to the surface. If small blackmouths are at hand, then use an 8- or 10-pound test line and a 2-ounce sinker; but if the larger blackmouths are feeding, a 4-ounce sinker is best, for these fish will be deeper. To the end of the sinker you connect two swivels having a split ring in between, and to these you tie a 4-, 6-, or 8-pound test nylon leader six or seven feet long.

To obtain the best action, you'll use only one ringed hook when you're after kings. When spinning for silvers, though, with either regular cut spinners or small herring minnows, you may find that two hooks are more of an advantage, since these fish have a habit of pulling at a bait. Kings, on the other hand, customarily mouth the bait from the head—like lake trout seizing a minnow and "processing" it for swallowing so as to avoid injury from the spiny fins. Try O'Shaughnessy hooks, sizes 1/0 or 2/0. You tie the leader to the hook by pushing the nylon through the eye of the hook, making two loops over the hook, extending the end of the nylon through these loops, and pulling tight. Tuck the protruding end of the nylon through the eye and snip off. Be sure to tie the leader carefully to the sinker swivel as well as to the hook, so the nylon won't break at these vital points.

With this work accomplished, you reach the most important phase of the deal—cutting and preparing the "spinner." For this purpose, you bring along two or three dozen medium-sized herring, which will be sufficient for a good day's sport. These fish must be kept cool and firm; otherwise they turn soft in a short while and become difficult to cut properly. You place them in a pail of salt water, in the shade, and change the water frequently. In doing so, take care not to rub off any of the scales.

The method
of making a
cut spinner.

For the cutting job, you'll need a thick, smooth slab, like a meat board, and a knife with a razor-sharp, three-inch blade of quality steel. With these, you are ready to begin the delicate, precise process of carving out a perfect spinner from the side of a plump herring. If the fish is still frozen you won't have any trouble cutting through the scales, but if it has thawed much, or you have a fresh herring, you should scale the fish with the back of the knife blade. The edge of the blade is used for cutting only, and should not be dulled by the scales. Now, with the fish resting on the board, you place the knife blade beside the gill cover, up near the back, and make a cut crosswise and downward, following the shape of the gill cover, so that the front edge of the spinner will have an arc. Simultaneously the blade is tilted at a 45-degree angle, with the knife handle slanted towards the tail, to form the all-important beveled front edge on the spinner. Next, make a beveled cut from the top point of your first incision in a backward stroke to a spot near the tail, in a slightly curved line. Then from the bottom point of the first, crosswise cut make another beveled slice towards the tail in a rather straight line, meeting the previous cut and creating a tapered, triangular-shaped bait. Finally, work the blade with care under the lip of the head end of the spinner until it reaches the bones, turn it so the blade is flat and the edge is pointing towards the tail, and slice under the flesh. As the blade moves along, turn it upward a trifle so that the rear part of the strip will be thinner than the forward portion. With the head thicker, this makes the bait act like a crippled minnow. Sever the spinner from the fish, and scrape off the dark brown film that tinges the meat side next to the herring bones.

Flip the fish over and cut another spinner from that side, using the same procedure. After stringing one on the hook, you'll have to test its actions before casting it to the salmon. If it's a "dead" bait, or twirls in a corkscrew fashion, it shouldn't be used. In the first case it will arouse no interest, and in the latter instance the spinner will probably alarm the salmon. An inactive spinner results from cutting it too narrow, or possibly too pointed or too broad at the head. A corkscrew movement comes from slicing the spinner too thin, or too straight, at the head. The size that trials have shown to be most suitable is a spinner about an inch wide at the head and around 4½ inches long. You may have to nip off the sharp pointed corner at the upper, forward end in order to make the spinner swim enticingly. But, as suggested, you'll quickly find out if the bait is cut right or wrong by testing it in the water before the actual fishing. A little practice will soon have you in mass production of suitable spinners.

With one of these baits in hand, take your 1/0 size hook and press the barb (pointing tailwards as it starts) into the skin surface at the upper corner near the beveled front edge. The hook should enter from the side at a spot about an eighth of an inch below the top. Run it entirely through, then—at a point almost the length of the hook's shaft back from the first hole, and about ¼ of an inch in from the thick edge—turn the hook, pierce the meat surface with the barb, and come out at the skin side, completing a loop. Now pull on the leader until the eye of the hook disappears into the opening made by the first puncture, leaving the point of the hook protruding from the skin side. Conceal the shank by tamping the meat down around it. With this final touch you are ready to make the cast.

Seated in your boat, you face the incoming tide—unless a strong wind is blowing in the opposite direction—and make ready to cast the spinner you have cut and rigged. If the morning is dark, the fish will be feeding near the surface, so at first you won't be needing as much line as later when the fish go deeper. However, it is sometimes well to explore from the bottom up—especially during the summer when the water temperature is high—to cover all the productive levels for stray fish. Some fine salmon are picked up in this manner. You strip around sixty feet of line from the reel and lay it in wide, loose coils on the floor boards. Then (perhaps from a standing position, as is often done) you cast the sinker and spinner out against the current. The coiled line passes easily through your hand as the sinker carries it outward and down.

If you are anchored in forty feet of water you let the sinker reach bottom, then reel in just enough so that the bait hangs about six feet above the rocks, sand, or gravel. But if the depth is eighty or a hundred feet, you still let out only forty or fifty feet of line at first, to try the higher levels where the greater number of salmon will be at that time of day; then, if nothing happens, you may try the deeper areas.

With your bait at the depth desired, you let it remain there for several minutes to await a possible strike. The rod tip extends over the gunwale about three feet, in case a silver salmon grabs hold and jerks downward sharply; this is to protect the tip, and also helps set the hook by the spring of the bamboo. After five or ten minutes have elapsed without any response, you begin stripping in line. This is done in easy spurts, to make the bait dart like a frightened minnow or resemble a wounded one in motion. You strip in a little, pause, then strip in some more; and repeat this until the lure is at the surface for another cast.

Having landed a few salmon as described, you have learned the rudiments of spinning. You must practice this to develop your skill in cutting and maneuvering the spinner if you want the best catches. If you are a person who doesn't like to stay put for long, and want the added sport of covering more ground, then you'll combine the technique of spinning with the movements of trolling, and thereby carry on what in Puget Sound is known as "mooching."

In order to mooch effectively, you use much the same tackle and bait as for regular spinning, but you row the boat slowly. You control the action of the spinner by how fast you move, by weaving the rod back and forth gently, and by stripping in and releasing line as you stop at intervals to let the bait sink. Where the bottom is free from snags and jagged rocks, it is sometimes profitable to let your bait go as deep as possible, then draw in twelve or fifteen feet of line so the spinner will twirl along just over the resting salmon. You have to experiment carefully for type of bottom and different depths, in a certain area, before you can mooch to the best advantage. By the weight of the sinker and swivel you attach, and by the speed with which you row, you can get down to any level desired. As mentioned previously, if you use a line of small diameter it doesn't take as heavy a sinker to reach bottom as with a thicker line. There are moochers who employ a 6- or 8-pound test braided nylon line—the same kind adapted for the standard form of spinning—since this type of line sinks readily. However, remember that the weight of lead and size of line you should use are largely influenced by the level at which you fish. You'll be fishing near the top in early morning and late afternoon, and near the bottom at other times. When mooching at the surface on a dark morning, you may use a 7-foot nylon leader of 8- to 20-pound test, but if the day is bright and sunny you would want a 6- to 10-pound test leader of the same length. This also applies when the salmon are deeper during the day, for a light leader will hold nearly any fish under cautious handling unless you are at a place where the tide is strong.

The bait for mooching may be a large cut spinner, a medium-sized dead herring rigged so it will twirl, or a small live herring. If the live minnow is used, insert your single 1/0 size hook into the flesh between the head and the back fin without piercing the spinal column. In this case don't fasten on a sinker, for it's better to let the minnow work down to the right depth in a natural manner. It's necessary to give a salmon sufficient time to grab a live herring, swim off a short distance, and begin to swallow it before you try to set the hook. When the second, firm pull is felt, then give a short, moderate jerk.

On many occasions, it's possible to chum the salmon to your hook, as with other salt-water species, by dribbling ground fish overboard or by towing a cage filled with small herring so that the scales will loosen and drift back. As these sink they prompt the salmon to look for the source, and thus the kings and silvers come upon your trailing hooked minnow.

CHAPTER **6**

Surf Fishing

Ever rolling, tumbling, surging over the hard-packed beaches, there is something about the billowing combers that holds a magnetic attraction for thousands of salt-water fishermen. The music of the splashing, foaming breakers is like a stimulant to those who are drawn again and again to the seashore with rod and reel. Enthusiastically, they yield to the song of the surf.

Surf fishermen are considered by some a strange breed. They wander the 4,840 miles of United States coast, hopeful of catching fish, but generally much more interested in *how* they catch their fish than in *how many* they catch. They have more blank days (or should we say nights, since most surf fishing is done during the nocturnal hours) than full ones; but when a fish is on, there is fast, exciting action unlike anything experienced in boat fishing.

Surf fishing is probably the most rapidly growing branch of salt-water angling. Every season sees more men and women (girls are now taking to this sport, once the special domain of males) flocking to the beaches to enjoy this truly sporting method of fishing.

Let's take a closer look at surf fishing and see what it has to offer. First, it's one of the least expensive forms of salt-water fishing, once the tackle is bought. You can go out any time you like. You have plenty of shore line to choose from. Second, surf fishing is the nearest thing in salt-water fishing to trout fishing in fresh water. The surf angler and trout angler have a great deal in common. Both are individualists who depend on their own knowledge and skill to be successful. They both must know their casting, gear, lures, water, weather, and habits of fish. Both like plenty of elbow room and enjoy their surroundings almost as much as the actual fishing itself. And no matter how long one has fished, he never knows it all and he learns something new almost every time he goes out surf fishing or trout fishing. There's no such thing as a bored surf or trout fisherman.

Fish of every kind can be taken with a surf-casting outfit, whether you live on the East, West, or Gulf coasts. To name them all would be listing a "Who's Who" of the finny family, but you will quickly recognize such well-known varieties as striped bass, weakfish, channel bass, corbina, bluefish, barred surf perch, salmon, yellowfin croakers, yellowtail, spotfin croakers, white sea bass, sharks, tautog, pompano, kingfish (northern whiting), flounders, fluke, and even "berry," better known in southern waters as barracuda.

Surf angling is also more exacting then most salt-water fishing; it's a game well worth learning and playing. As a surf angler, you are strictly on your own. You have no captain, mate, or guide to help find your fish and catch them. It's a challenge in which you and the fish match wits at even odds. Actually, surf conditions favor the fish. Shifting sand provides uneasy footing for the angler. Many surf fish feed around rocks, which often slash the line. The surge of seas against a shore and the resulting back currents add power to a lunker's rushes. A smart fish will dive into a breaking sea and, as the wave throws him forward, use the slack to toss the hook. By riding the undertow, he will pull back to deep water. In other words, every fish, large or small, fights harder and longer when caught in the surf. But when the battle is over and you survey your catch, your joy is all the greater since you know that your own knowledge and skill are responsible for your victory.

There are, however, prerequisites to success: proper equipment and the ability to use it proficiently, knowledge of the fish and the waters where you fish, observation and patience.

SURF-CASTING TACKLE AND ACCESSORIES

In order to enjoy the greatest sport and success from surf casting, there are certain articles of equipment and special items of tackle you should possess. Select good equipment, take care of it, and it will last a lifetime.

A complete discussion of the proper rod, reel, and line for surf fishing can be found in Chapter 2. But in selecting your surf-casting outfit, be sure that it is "balanced": size of rod, capacity of reel, diameter of line, and weight of the lure should all be in correct proportion.

Recommended Surf Tackle

Light Standard Tackle: 6- to 8-foot rod; 150-yard reel; 12- to 27-pound test line. Casts to 2½-ounce lures.

Medium Spinning Tackle: 9-foot rod; reel spooling 200 yards 12-pound test line. Casts ¾- to 2-ounce lures.

Heavy Spinning Tackle: 10- to 11-foot rod; reel spooling 250 yards 18-pound test line. Casts 2- to 3½-ounce lures.

Medium Spinning Tackle: 9-foot rod; reel spooling 200 yards 10-pound test line. Casts ¾- to 2-ounce lures.

Heavy Spinning Tackle: 10- to 11-foot rod; reel spooling 250 yards 15-pound test line. Casts 2- to 3½-ounce lures.

Light tackle is designed for small surf fish, women surf anglers, and "light tackle" specialists who want the most sport. This weight is not practical for use in medium or heavy surf, but it is ideal for casting light lures and baits from piers and jetties which are adjacent to relatively quiet water.

Medium tackle is the best for all-around use and is the most widely used outfit. It is suitable for the average-sized or even the shorter-than-average person. With proper lures or sinkers, this outfit can pinch-hit for the light or heavy outfits, if necessary. In other words, if you use a lure of over 3 ounces or a heavier sinker, the outfit could be considered as a heavy rig; with a lure of 2 ounces or a lighter sinker, it could be considered as a light outfit.

The heavy tackle layout is the "heavy artillery" of the surf-fishing outfit. Naturally it is for big fellows with strong arms. It is ideal for extra long casts in heavy surf and strong tides, but it requires more skill to handle it. This tackle is usually too heavy for most men casting continually with artificial lures.

Locality must also be considered when selecting the outfit. For example, on the Pacific Coast, the distances from the sandy shores to the breakers are usually rather long—appreciably longer than at most Atlantic Coast waterfronts—and this is somewhat of a handicap for the beginner. The average casts have to be extended more than is normally the case along the eastern seaboard, and this means that longer and heavier surf outfits are advisable for Pacific beaches. The longer the rod, the farther you can swing into the surf.

Spin outfits have claimed many followers of standard surf equipment, and while this ultralight tackle group of surf casters increase rapidly every season, there is another group that has discarded spinning for monofilament surf equipment. A large number of West Coast surf fishermen are using monofilament lines on long, slender surf rods with a surprising success. This overcomes the difficulty of heavy tackle but gives a rod that can cast over the breakers, so necessary on the Pacific Coast. When using monofilament lines for surf casting, you must employ a reel especially designed for the purpose (see page 16); these lines are somewhat more difficult to control than the braided types (see page 26).

Specialized Gear

In addition to your rod, reel and line, you need other specialized gear. For instance, a surf belt is considered a must by many surf fishermen. It is simply a leather belt, with a heavy leather cup in front, into which the end of the rod butt is dropped to give support (and comfort to the angler) while reeling in or while a fish is being played. Without a rod-butt rest your abdomen can easily be injured by pressure of the rod against it when tussling with a really heavy customer. In rocky fishing areas, however, surf rod holders are rarely used because in such locations it is easier to hand control your rod.

The sand spike or rod holder—the item has numerous names among surf fishermen in various sections—is another very valuable piece of equipment for fishing on beaches. This device, a hollow pipe that is pointed at one end so it may be jammed into the sand, holds the rod while hooks are rebaited or lures changed. Never place your rod and reel directly on the beach since they will soon become fouled with grit and sand particles. Many surf anglers use a sand spike when still-fishing with bait. In other words, after they cast, the rod is slipped into the spike. This allows them to rest from gripping the rod constantly. I'm not of this school, however, since I don't like to leave a line in the water unattended. Unless the fish swallows the bait, he will not hook himself. That's your job. If you must rest or eat, stand near the rod and be ready to grab it as soon as you get a bite. By watching the rod tip, you can tell the instant a strike comes. Immediately slip the rod out of the holder, set the hook, drop the butt into your belt cup, and begin the business of wearing out your fish. A big fish striking on an unattended line can pull your rod over into the sand, or worse yet, drag it out into the water. Sand spikes may be purchased at most tackle dealers.

In the absence of a sand spike, a quart milk bottle makes a fine holder for keeping your surf rod upright and out of the sand while you are rigging lures, baiting hooks or removing fish. It should not, however, be used for still or bottom fishing. Just bury the bottle in the sand up to its neck and insert the rod butt in the open top.

When casting for large fish from a rock jetty or rocky coast line, special equipment is generally needed to land the fish. You will need an 18- to 36-inch gaff. Some surf anglers prefer a "pick" to the conventional gaff. These homemade affairs are about 15 inches long; but the steel head, instead of being shaped like a fishhook, like the conventional gaffs, is bent at slightly less than a 90-degree angle to the handle. Anglers who use this device claim that it is almost impossible to gaff a fish in a rolling surf, but the pick solves the problem. Instead of catching the fish from underneath (in the normal gaffing fashion) the pick is driven in from above. To make the pick easier to drive home, several ounces of lead are encased in the top of its handle. This extra weight also converts the pick into a handy billy for killing fish just landed. Whether you use a gaff or a pick, it should be carried on your belt, with the point covered by a length of rubber tubing for safety. The tubing is slipped off when the fish is brought in.

A fish chain, approximately 10 feet long, may also be attached to your belt. This saves a great deal of time when fishing is fast, because the wading angler can string his catch and continue casting, instead of walking up to the beach to deposit the fish.

A plug box, with plastic compartments to prevent triple-hooked plugs from tangling, is a worthwhile investment for a surf fisherman who likes to carry as many as six plugs. The container may be slung from a shoulder strap or carried on your belt. Squids can also be carried in the plug box, or they may be put in a special squid bag strung from your belt.

There are several small objects which you will find valuable (but not essential) on your trips. These include pliers, knife, screwdriver, insect repellent, a bottle of reel oil, sharpening stone, leather thongs, a stick of rod cement and an extra leader wire, hooks, swivels, squids, and pyramid and bank sinkers. These may be carried in a surf kit—a canvas bag, or a wooden bucket with metal compartments for receiving your equipment and iced bait.

The seasons and weather conditions require additional equipment. For daytime fishing on sandy beaches, you need a pair of colored sun glasses and a long-visored swordfisherman's cap; without these, the terrific glare of the sun on the water and sand will hurt your eyes intensely.

During the day, if the weather is warm, you may be able to wade into the surf barefooted (popular in southern waters); otherwise you should wear either waders or hip boots. In making your selection between waders and boots, you should consider the local conditions where you fish. Chest-high waders offer more protection, allow the angler to venture into deeper water than with boots. In many locations, it is often necessary to wade out into the surf in waist-deep water to reach favorable fishing spots. Under such conditions hip boots are not practical. Hip boots are cooler to wear during midsummer and can be used for jetties and very calm beaches. The addition of a foul-weather suit or a pair of oilskin overalls pulled over the hip boots makes a dry outfit, but naturally, one can't wade beyond thigh-deep water. Remember that there is no saving with inexpensive boots of light rubber or plastic material. Anything other than sturdy rubber waders or boots is quickly torn or punctured. Moreover, the rubber types can be quickly patched on the beach with little loss in fishing time.

When surf casting from ordinary beaches, waders or boots make your footing sure. But on jetties or other rocky areas you need special footwear to keep your grip on mossy boulders. Ice creepers—the old standard—are now giving way to felt sandals or soles glued on the bottoms of your waders or boots. Both provide good footing, but the felt makes easier walking.

In colder weather or when night fishing, even in the summer, you must keep warm and dry. To make a waterproof ensemble, you'll need, in addition to your waders or boots, a surf hood: a waterproof parka with elastic cuffs, zippered throat, and drawstringed hood and waist (no buttons). It covers your head, arms, and body, and fastens about and over the tops of your waders. This surf hood, won't dam out the flood if you go over the top of your waders, but it will bounce back spray and give you protection against the wind. Although there are several types of surf hoods on the market, the best are made of a synthetic material called Neoprene. Because the hood envelops your shoulders and arms and is subject to all the strains from casting, a poorly made one soon gives out. Rubberized cloth, for example, gets stiff in cold weather. An army surplus gun belt, worn snugly, will also help to keep splashing water from rising inside your parka. The belt can hold the gaff or pick and it may also hold the plug bag too. For the proper underclothing to keep warm, see page 92. Heavy wool socks may be worn underneath your boots or waders.

For night fishing under any weather conditions, a head lamp is another essential. The searchlight type which has a head—a head lamp connected to batteries by an extension cord in the pocket—is considered best. The switch should be on the lamp, not at the batteries where it would be inaccessible. A hand searchlight is not advisable because it soon gets lost or wet and is always in the way.

Squids and Plugs

You will find "purists" among surf fishermen who believe that the only sporting way to fish is with an artificial lure (see page 59). Squidding, as this method is called, was originally done with a block tin squid, or drail, weighing about 3 ounces. But today these squids and their chrome-plated counterparts come in a variety of weights, shapes, and sizes, each designed to simulate the shape and action of some item of the fish's natural diet—generally sand eels or mullet. Such metal squids will take striped bass, weakfish, channel bass, pollack, mackerel, and some other salt-water fish. (See Chapter 3 for further information on types of squids and their applications). You can regulate the depth of your squid, no matter what its design and its action, by the way you retrieve it. If you want a metal squid to ride high, hold up the tip of your rod, and reel in at a moderate or fast speed. When the fish are not showing, or if they are not hitting a fast-moving squid near the surface, you can try slow reeling to allow the squid to sink. In fact, there are times when weakfish and striped bass prefer a metal squid that is barely moving along or merely sinking to the bottom. Here you cast out and, as the squid sinks, you must turn the reel handle enough to keep a taut line. The squid will have plenty of action as it flutters toward the bottom. Of course, when it does reach the bottom, you reel just fast enough to keep it moving without resting it on the bottom. Sometimes a combination of slow and fast reeling, alternately making the squid ride low, then high, and so on, may be more effective than either of the other techniques.

To get the best action from a metal squid in the surf, wait until a wave breaks, then cast your lure behind it, If you do not cast at this time, the incoming wave will pick up your squid and bring it toward you faster than you can take up the slack. A slack line will stop the action of your lure and cause it to sink. On the other hand, after a wave breaks, the water rushes back to the sea, creating a pull against your squid. Then you have to slow down, since reeling fast at this time will cause your lure to spin and rise to the surface. The same principle holds true in a strong current—you have to reel slowly to get the best action out of a squid. A fast current or tide will give the squid action even if you barely turn the handle. After a while you will develop a certain "feel" for the way the lure is working and you will be able to change the speed of the retrieve to suit the waves and currents.

One of the more popular types of lures used today in surf fishing is the plastic or wooden plug described on page 60.

The surface plugs create a commotion or ripple on the water which attracts nearby game fish. Two popular types are the "popper" and the "flaptail." The former, which measure 4 to 6 or 7 inches in length, are retrieved in jerks and starts, causing the plug to "pop," or throw a shower of water. After it pops, let the plug settle for a second or two—this is when the fish will strike. The purpose of these plugs is to create an illusion of an injured sea creature trying to elude its enemies. They are best used during the day. The swimming type which is similar to the popper in action, is excellent for big striped bass. While effective at any time, a "flaptail" plug is especially good after dark.

The subsurface or semisurface plugs float when at rest and dive and dart or wriggle when retrieved. While there are several types, the wrigglers and

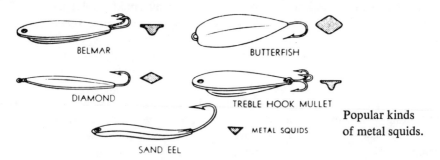

BELMAR

BUTTERFISH

DIAMOND

TREBLE HOOK MULLET

SAND EEL

METAL SQUIDS

Popular kinds
of metal squids.

darting plugs are the most popular and effective in the surf. They are retrieved slowly to impart a fishlike action and are best used at night. The darting plug is retrieved fairly rapidly in still water during the day to bring out its characteristic erratic action. In "rips," these plugs are most effective after dark, when they are retrieved very slowly.

The underwater plugs generally have metal lips which cause them to dive and wriggle in lively fashion when retrieved. When using these plugs you must get that "feel" which travels up the line and indicates that the plug is working properly. The key to the whole problem is to change the speed of the retrieve so that you always feel the plug working. When the tide or a wave pushes the plug in your direction, you will have to speed up the retrieve. If the current or backwash pulls the plug away from you, then slow down your reeling. As a general rule, clear, calm water calls for somewhat faster reeling to produce strikes than rough or dirty water. Likewise, daytime fishing means a faster retrieve than nighttime fishing.

Although most underwater plugs have a built-in wriggle, these often work better if they are jerked at intervals, stopped or slowed down, then speeded up to create an erratic action. The "jerk-turn" technique brings them raging, whereas the steady retrieve goes for hours without being noticed. The illustration shows the progress of the popular West Coast "shrimp plug" in action through the water when fished with the "jerk-turn" method.

Most plugs are too light or bulky for easy casting and therefore are ordinarily used from rocky shores, jetties, bridges, or other locations where long casts are not required. But some of the heavier models can be cast a good distance and may be used from beaches with good results. In general, poppers and darters cast best. Flaptail, underwater, and wriggling plugs do not cast as well because their nose plates increase wind-resistance. All types of plugs are best in light and medium wave action. They cannot be manipulated in heavy surf.

Rigged Eels

Though technically not an artificial lure, since eels are natural foods for surf fish, the methods for working eels put them into the lure classification. The eel is rigged by using a long baiting needle, drawing one hook with a short length of heavy line up through the anus and bringing it out through the mouth. The second hook is then attached and sewed through the lips. Strong linen, nylon, or chain is used for the tying. Most effective of this group are whole eels (9 to 14 inches in length) and they are available in tackle shops, in jars or frozen.

The best time to use an eel rig is generally after the migration of small baitfish, in the spring and early summer. From then until late fall, eels will give a good account of themselves in taking fish. Eels begin to feed about dusk and on throughout the night, so eel rigs work best after dark. Under most conditions, rigged eels should be retrieved very slowly— usually on or near bottom and close to every natural hiding place, such as rocks, piling, breakwaters, and wharfs. But rigged eels are hard to cast any distance and very difficult to use against a strong wind. You can add sinkers to make casting easier, but this will cause the lure to run poorly.

When casting, allow the rig to sink near the bottom, then retrieve a few turns and jerk, retrieve a few turns and jerk, and continue the procedure until the lure comes back to you. Though you may find rigged eels somewhat of a nuisance to use, they pay off in big fish.

Almost as effective for striped bass and bluefish as the whole eel are the eelskin lures.While they vary in design, most of them use pretty much the same principle. They have a weighted head with a hole in the center to allow water to pass through and fill out the eelskin. Attached to this head is a short length of chain or wire to which two hooks are fastened. The eelskin is tied to the weighted head, and the hooks are pushed through the skin so that only the points and barbs protrude. These hooks may be arranged so that both emerge from the top of the skin, or both through the underside, or so that the forward hook emerges from the top and the tail hook comes out on the underside. When the eelskin lure is retrieved, the

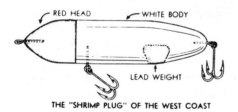

THE "SHRIMP PLUG" OF THE WEST COAST

DIAGRAM SHOWING THE PROGRESS OF THE "SHRIMP PLUG" THROUGH THE WATER WHEN FISHED WITH THE "JERK-TURN" METHOD.

The popular West Coast "shrimp plug" in action when fished with the "jerk-turn" method.

Popular eel rigs and eelskin lures.

water runs through the hole or ring in the weighted head, inflating the skin and causing it to flutter conspicuously.

A variation of the eelskin lure is a ring soldered on a metal squid. With the eelskin pulled over the ring, and tandem hooks inserted through, it is effective in the surf. Or the skin may be pulled over the entire metal squid and tied around the head. In other words, the eelskin squids have the action of a metal squid, with the appearance of a live eel. The lure should be reeled in at a moderate speed, with slight twitches, and is especially effective at night.

Natural Bait for Surf Fishing

Surf fishing with artificial lures requires plenty of energy on your part since you generally must cast hour after hour with a rod and reel, which are not exactly light. With natural bait, you can fish on the bottom where the main requirement is patience. Actually, most of the fish that swim in the surf can be taken on natural bait, often more readily than on artificial lures. Even a few of the surf fish (fluke, tautog, and flounders) can only be taken by means of bottom fishing and natural bait. To make surf fishing more interesting and productive, many anglers use both natural bait and artificial lures alternately. The one unpleasant aspect of using natural bait is that you will continually tangle with bait robbers. More information on the kinds of natural baits and how to use them will be found in Chapter 3.

Surf-fishing Rigs

Surf anglers are rather fussy about their terminal rigs—and rightly so. While an elaborate and costly surf rod and reel may be a joy to use, the best gear isn't worth its salt unless the terminal part of the equipment is serviceable and correct for both surf fishing in general and the species of fish at hand. From a fish's view, the rod and reel are nonexistent. What the fish sees is the lure or bait and, if he's in the mood and if the lure or bait is presented properly, there's a chance he'll strike.

The basic function of the surf rig, like the rig in the other types of fishing, is to offer the bait or lure attractively, keep the fish in action well off the line, and place the bait in full vision of the fish. The size of hooks depends somewhat upon the fish; this is discussed in Chapter 3. For leaders, many surf fishermen prefer nylon or snelled hooks (3-ply for weakfish and kingfish and 6-ply for stripers), except when bluefish are likely to be encountered. But the sharp teeth of the blue devil is unable to sever the leader if it is made of wire. It can be either a short casting trace or a solid piece of stainless steel or Monel wire at least 12 inches long.

The shape and weight of the sinker has just as much effect on your success in surf fishing with natural baits (surf bottom fishing—page 132) as the size and pattern of fly has on trout fishing. You should choose your sinkers to go with the tide and with the type of bottom. A pyramid sinker should be cast where the bottom is sandy or muddy, and a bank or oval-shaped sinker where rocks abound. The latter shape is also good in light surf conditions or at slack tide, since it tends to move with the current and allows greater bottom coverage without constantly moving the bait.

The 4-ounce sinker is best for all-around use; the 5- and 6-ounce sizes are used only occasionally with heavy rods and in a rough surf.

In surf fishing with natural baits, fish generally take time to inspect by nibbling, nudging, or just taking the bait lightly before making the final gulp. All fish are naturally suspicious and line-shy. Baits should conceal the hooks, should be rigged so they look and act alive, and should be kept well off the line with light leaders. The "standard rig" and the "fish finder" (see illustration) are excellent for natural baits in surf casting. Either rig will take most of the fish that feed in the white water. Both rigs are also often used for many species in deep-sea fishing.

The standard bait rig for surf fishing makes use of a three-way swivel. The swivel has three loops: the leader and hook are tied to one, the other holds the sinker, while the third is attached to the line. Crabs are often a nuisance when you are bait fishing in the surf, so put a small cork on the leader to keep the bait off the bottom and away from crabs. The cork will also help to keep the bait active and in full sight—out of weeds and away from rocks. If nuisance fish—sand sharks, blow-fish, sea robins, skates, etc.—are stealing your bait, tie it on with a few turns of fine wire or thread. Pyramid sinkers minimize rolling on hard sand bottoms; or a bank sinker may be used when it's desirable for the rig to drift.

The fish-finder rig makes use of a gadget which has a ring on one end and a snap on the other. The snap holds the sinker, while the line runs through the ring and is tied to a rawhide thong which is, in turn, attached to the leader and hook. With this contraption, your sinker is free to slide along the line, yet after a cast is made it will stay down near the bait, where it belongs. The momentum of the cast forces the sinker to keep close to the leader, yet when a fish grabs your bait the line can ease through the fish-finder ring without being held back by the sinker. This gives the fish a chance to pick up the bait and take off with it unhampered (you

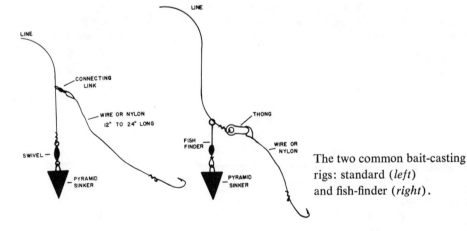

The two common bait-casting rigs: standard (*left*) and fish-finder (*right*).

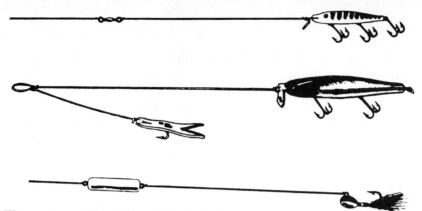

Three common lure casting rigs: standard or common rig (*top*), Massachusetts striped-bass rig (*center*), and bucktail fly rig.

can notice the line moving), and not until you give the hook-setting jerk does he become aware of the sinker.

The line that goes with this device can also be fed through the ring, into the current, by manipulating the rod. This makes it possible to cover a lot of territory on just a single cast. When there are plenty of fish in the surf they do not toy with the bait, but strike hard and fast. When fish are not plentiful and only an occasional fish is taken, then it is best to use the fish-finder rig. In fishing with such a rig, it's important to remember to keep your reel in free spool until you have hooked your fish.

The surf-casting rigs shown in the diagram are the more common ones used for metal squids and plugs. The "working part" of the rig is a leader of nylon or wire—12 to 36 inches long, depending on personal preference and the size of fish being hunted. When using wire to avoid kinking, many surf fishermen prefer the shorter lengths. The leader can be tied into the line directly or by a swivel (a must in the case of wire). To the other end of the leader is attached a swivel snap or similar connector, to permit easy changing of lures. Rigged eels are attached in the same manner as metal squids and plugs.

A few years ago several Massachusetts surf anglers developed an excellent striped-bass rig that has given fine results. Instead of placing the pork rind on the rear hooks of a plug, they place it about 3 feet ahead, using a single 4/0 or 5/0 hook tied on a 6-inch nylon leader dropper of about 20 to 30 pounds test. Bass that formerly followed plugs without hitting seem to pass the plugs with a burst of speed and grab the pork rind. It looks as if they nab the rind to beat the plug to it.

The latest method of rigging a squid is to use about 18 inches of 40-pound nylon leader attached to the lure, and a yellow or yellow-and-white bucktail fly fastened to a short piece of nylon at the upper end. It is surprising what you can catch on this upper hook when the blues and weakfish are in the surf. Flounders, weakfish, bluefish, and even kingfish have been known to strike this fly.

Where very big fish are expected, or for rocky spots, a more durable squid or plug rig should be used. To convert your rig, a swivel is tied to the line, and an 18-inch length of 45-pound test braided monofilament is tied to the other end of the swivel. At the end of the monofilament, a 75-pound test stainless steel snap is tied. Each of your lures has a 5-inch length of #8 stainless steel or Monel leader wire attached, with a loop on the end. The snap is attached to the loop.

HOW TO SURF CAST

When linen line was used for surf casting it had to be thoroughly soaked before it was casted to reduce backlashes and to add to its tensile strength. The use of synthetic lines—dacron, nylon, or monofilament—makes this unnecessary. I still like to take two or three short practice casts before taking any serious ones. It seems to give me a "feel" of my tackle. Speaking of tackle, before applying your terminal rig, cut off a few feet of line. Chafing of the sand and the pressure of casting wear a line quite rapidly and therefore the line should be cut before each fishing trip. After your bait or artificial lure rig is securely fastened to the line, you're ready to start casting for the big ones.

In order to attain proficiency in surf casting, coordination of body movements must be patiently learned. Physical vigor is necessary, but brute strength is not. In learning to cast, it's well not to aim for distance; you should concentrate rather on coordination, on acquiring the proper form. After the fundamentals have been mastered, distance will follow naturally.

The Overhead Cast

To place yourself in the overhead casting position (see illustration), put your left foot forward toward the spot you want to cast, toe set a bit to the right. The right foot is a normal step to the rear and right. You are facing to the right of the target, at an angle of about 45 degrees. Place the right hand up under the reel, with your thumb on the spool. Put the reel in free spool, let out about three or four feet of the line with about a 4-ounce sinker or lure, and grasp the lower end of the butt with your left hand. Now twist your body at the hips and, facing backward, bring your rod back as far as possible by extending your right arm and bending your right knee. Your left hand is near the chin, and the tip low to the ground. The left side plate of the reel is facing upward by a slight twist of your right wrist to the right. From this position, the cast is started by bringing your right hand near the shoulder and your left hand forward.

Up to now, the butt is higher than the tip. The power is put into the cast by the simultaneous upward and forward thrust of your right arm and the downward and backward pull of your left arm. During the cast, the body is pivoted, and the weight shifted from the right foot to the left foot as the cast progresses. The rod swings in an arc of about 45 degrees. When the rod is near the vertical, you ease off on the spool with your thumb so the line and lure can start to fly out on a high curve, and from then on apply only enough thumb pressure to prevent the overrunning of the spool.

The split second when you are exerting the impetus with your wrists to send the lure leaping out and just before the rod reaches the zenith of its arc, is the vital point of the cast where perfect timing—and therefore practice—counts very heavily. If you relax your thumb too quickly the lure will shoot up straight and not land where you want it to. If you are too slow at relieving the pressure, then the rod moves too far forward and the lure dives into the water only a few feet from shore. Proper timing will come only with experience, but proper thumbing can be mastered by watching *not* the sinker or lure but the reel spool, and thumbing lightly as soon as loose coils of line develop on the spool. The thumb action will eliminate backlash. To complete the cast, follow through with your rod until the tip is in line with the flight of the lure or sinker. You are now facing the target with your body leaning forward and your left knee bent. Your right arm is well extended and your left hand near the left thigh. Hold the rod in this position until the sinker drops or the lure hits the water, at which time stop the spool completely to prevent overrunning. Take the reel out of freespool by shifting it in gear, and reel in all slack line. Then place the rod in a comfortable position between your legs or into the cup of your surf belt, and move the left hand up the rod just in front of the reel.

Remember that even the experts backlash occasionally, so don't be dismayed by a few bird's nests. We are all bound to slip up on one once in a while. Should a backlash occur, perhaps you forced the cast too much. Straighten out your line and try again with less force. You can cast almost as far with half your total strength. Antibacklash devices (see page 12) are available to help you during the early days of surf casting, but are not recommended after you have the technique mastered because they do generally cut down your distance.

Variations in Casting

Once you have learned the overhead cast, you can easily master the other casts used in surf fishing, such as the side cast and the snap cast. In the side cast the rod travels low, parallel to the ground; this is very useful against a strong wind. The snap cast is used for artificial lures. In this cast the rod moves faster and in a shorter arc than in the overhead cast; it comes three-quarters overhead rather than directly overhead.

The principle involved in surf spin casting is approximately the same as the method just described with the conventional revolving spool reel, but it is not necessary to thumb the spool since it does not turn during the cast. It cannot overrun, therefore, and cause a backlash. (The casting and retrieving methods are described fully on page 223.)

Regardless of your casting method, there should never be a jerk in your motion. This is especially important when using live bait, since jerky casting may shake the bait loose from the hook—and this, of course, means no fish. Surf anglers often exclaim, "Robbed by the crabs!" when they reel in and find their hooks, clean of bait—but the truth of the matter may be that the bait was lost during its flight through the air, or so weakened by jerky casting that it was stripped from the hook upon impact with the water.

The only way a novice surf man can become proficient in casting is to practice. Most beginners learn to cast on the beach while actually fishing. But you will get faster results if you concentrate first on mastering the techniques of casting and forget about catching fish for the time being. Dry-land practice in an open field will help a great deal, too. But when using a conventional spool reel in dry-land casting, you should put a thumbstall or a piece of adhesive tape over your thumb to prevent burns, because you do not have the water to cool your line. However, no matter where you practice, do the casting the right way first and you won't have to break bad habits later.

A. START OF CAST

B RAISE ROD

C. ROD PASSES VERTICAL POSITION

D END OF CAST

Steps in making the overhead cast.

When you are squidding or plugging, retrieve the lure immediately and vary the speed of your retrieve (see pages 60 and 121); often the fish will strike a fast-moving lure after having refused it when it was reeled in slowly. If you are surf bottom fishing, strip out several feet of line so the bait will settle to the bottom. When you are retrieving in either type of surf fishing, level-wind the line, because long and smooth casts depend a great deal on the proper spooling of the line on the reel. The thumb and forefinger of your left hand, which is gripping the rod just above the reel, should work back and forth spreading the line evenly on the spool. If the line happens to spread unevenly, to avoid trouble the next cast should be short and easy.

PLAYING AND LANDING SURF FISH

Fish are often lost due to the angler's bad handling of the fish. The novice usually gets excited, freezes to the rod and reel, and thinks only of bringing in the fish as fast as possible. He fails to-remember that a big fish has a lot of power on the initial run and must be allowed to run freely with only enough tension to prevent a slack line.

Always hold the rod tip fairly high, so that the shock of a jolting strike and the strain of a fighting fish are borne by the line and rod together. The spring of the rod also lessens the possibility of the line's breaking from a stiff jerk, or of the hook tearing away from a hard pulling catch. To some degree the resiliency of the rod will also take up some of the slack should the fish change direction suddenly, or should the force of a wave or breaker grip him momentarily. But you must be prepared to reel in fast if an appreciable amount of slack develops in the line. A surf fish can throw a hook easily enough anyhow; no need giving him a helping hand.

The experienced surf man sets the drag on his reel just enough so that he can set the hook in a fish, but at the same time he allows the fish to take line under a tension which doesn't strain the line or the rod. Setting the drag too tight will cost you a fish through a snapped line. Not setting it tightly enough defeats the purpose of the drag, which is to offer resistance to the fish and thereby help tire him. Experience—perhaps some of the heartbreaking variety—will soon teach you just how much drag tension should be applied with your particular reel.

Let your catch go the full length of his initial dash under only ordinary restraint. This will help to tire him, because the more line the fish unwinds and hauls around, the sooner he will "capitulate," as one Long Island beach fisherman, Ken Johnson, used to say. After this run you may want to tighten the drag, or bear on the thumbstall a bit, but do not try to hurry matters. As the fish is brought closer to shore the drag can be tightened slightly. (While casting, you should always test your drag at regular intervals to see if it has accidentally become loosened or tightened.)

When you hook a fish on an open beach it should be allowed to run freely. Do not retreat onto the beach, but either stay where you are or move along with him if he is an old lunker chugging through the surf parallel to the shore. As the fish weakens you can reel him in slowly, but you should be prepared for a surprise run. Give him all the line he wants, but strive to keep it taut every movement, especially since many surf sojourners have a trick of shaking their heads from side to side in an effort to eject the hook.

As you bring the fish in, let the surf give you a hand. Use the incoming waves to help sweep in the fish—retrieving your line as each breaker seizes the fish and moves him bodily toward the shore. But as soon as the wave starts to recede, let him drift back into the trough between waves or just try to hold him still, if the strain on the line and rod tip is not too great. On the next incoming breaker you should speed up your reeling again. This procedure should be continued until he is finally swept up high and dry on the beach.

Sometimes just before you can grab the fish, he will make a last desperate lunge oceanward as the air sears his gills. When this happens—you haven't played him enough—let him go, but keep your line taut and rod tip high, and work him in again with the aid of the surf. A gaff or pick is seldom required in beach fishing in ordinary surf, except for landing sharks or rays. Just seize the leader and haul him on the beach by grasping him by his flaring gill covers. Setting your rod into the sand spike (never lay the rod and reel on the sand), you can remove the hook with a disgorger and then place the fish under a heap of dampened seaweed to shield him from the blazing sun. If you have landed a fish on a plug, make sure he is perfectly still before you attempt to remove the hooks. Otherwise the swing trebles in a bouncing fish may rip open your hand. Some surf anglers carry a small club to stun the fish before removing the hooks.

On the sand bars, many surf fishermen, in order not to make the long trip back to shore with each fish, carry stringers and tie the fish to their belts. This is fine as long as you guard against puncturing your waders or boots by the dorsal fins of big fish. A long stringer helps, and do not try to hold too many fish on it. But the added weight of a stringer may pull you off your feet when a good-sized wave comes in.

When fighting a fish from a rock jetty or a breakwater, take care to prevent the fish from fouling or weakening your line on the rocks. If you are some distance away from the end of the jetty and the fish tries to take your line around the point, you should follow him to the tip of the rocks. If that is impossible because walking is difficult or waves are breaking dangerously, then the only alternative is to try to hold the fish until he moves off in another direction. Where your fish has to be killed quickly in a small, snag-free area, the drag must be set tight and your outfit must stand up under the terrific strain. A gaff or pick is almost a must when fishing from rock jetties or breakwaters, especially when the water is rough. During calm water conditions you can often climb down and reach a fish with your hands.

On a rocky coastline where there are ledges, submerged boulders, rocks, etc., you will often have difficulty in fighting a striped bass because the fish invariably heads for the nearest rock and tries to run behind it. The smaller fish can often be turned or held, but the larger ones will usually run around a rock or over a ledge and sulk there. Sometimes the fish can be fooled into leaving its position by allowing some slack line. But under no circumstances should you try to move the fish by sheer force. The taut line will easily be cut by rocks, barnacles, or mussels. If you are on a high boulder above the water, you should always have a prearranged plan for landing the fish in some cove or on a rock which slopes into the water. (For further information on fishing from rocks, jetties, or breakwaters, see pages 81 and 86.)

Bottom Surf Fishing

Regardless of where you are, there are times when fish are present in the surf but refuse to strike artificial lures. Then you may have to resort to bottom surf fishing with live bait to catch them. This very popular phase of surf casting is accomplished in the same manner as we have described for inshore fishing (Chapter 5). In other words, when you cast out your line, let your bait lie in one spot for five to ten minutes, then reel it in a few feet. Let it lie there for approximately the same amount of time, and then reel in a short distance. Repeat this procedure until the bait is almost on shore. After fishing one spot for about an hour without results, move to another spot a few hundred feet away and try there.

If the line is slack after the sinker smacks the bottom, you should reel in just enough to make it tight, but take care not to pull the sinker any nearer because the push of the surf may do that all too obligingly. Should you encounter difficulty in holding the bottom in a rough surf and find that the rig keeps getting washed in, a heavier sinker should be used. If the water is really rough, it is a good idea to avoid the sand bars where the breakers are strong and concentrate on protected waters in holes inside the sand bars. Or perhaps a jetty will be nearby, and you may be able to walk out on it past the spot where the waves break, and thus have less trouble holding bottom.

In bottom surf fishing, as in any kind of fishing, always be sure to keep your line taut. Slack does not make much difference with fish that slam into the bait and impale themselves on the hook—but usually the bait is picked up and mouthed cautiously. With this kind of fish, it is necessary to set the hook beyond the barb. This is particularly true with game fish like striped bass, yellowtail, bluefish, channel bass, corbina, northern kingfish, surf perch, and weakfish. When a bite is felt you can lower the tip of your rod slightly, then after a few seconds you can raise it to take out the slack. When a fish starts to tug violently or moves off strongly, you should set the hook by coming back sharply with your rod. With slack in your line, a wary fish may pick up the bait, feel the pull of the sinker or the slack line, and drop it before the angler even knows that he's had a serve-yourself customer at the other end.

It is also usually a poor idea to cast, set the drag, and use a sand spike to hold your rod while waiting for the strike. Few game fish can be taken this way and many, if not most, will be lost. Another disadvantage in using the hand spike is that your line will become all the more chafed on the sea's bottom than if you hold the rod and are responsive to each strike.

If the fish are not hitting actively, or are beyond reach, here is a stunt that will work when everything else fails: chum the waterfront where you stand. You will be amazed at the good luck you can induce by cutting up anchovies, pilchards, smelt, mullet, or menhaden into fine pieces and dribbling them into the water where the receding waves will work it out to the tide and cause a slick to form. When the fish—striped bass in particular— get wise to this chum, their appetites are kindled and they come close to investigate the source. This is when you slip in your bait-hidden hook and "go to town."

A lot of anglers are unaware that chumming can be successful as an adjunct to surf fishing. The use of chum is so strongly associated with the method of trolling, and to some extent with still-fishing, that comparatively few anglers think of it as a means of getting reluctant fish to strike from the surf areas. But it is a useful trick, especially in the bays, coves, and inlets where there are rocky shoals and channels.

SAFETY AND SURF ANGLERS

Unfortunately, some of the best surf fishing comes on stormy nights when the sea is boiling. At other times you may have to crawl out on slippery rock jetties to reach the fish. Now this doesn't mean that all surf fishermen should start fishing on dark nights, or wade out up to their necks on a shifting sand bar, or crawl out on rock jetties that even a mountain goat would avoid. You know your own limitations and it is only sensible to play safe. For instance, if your eyesight is poor, it would be foolish to fish on dark nights. A man who cannot swim should not venture too far out on a sand bar. Likewise, if your footing and balance are not up to par, the rock jetties are good places to stay away from. But by knowing the pitfalls and taking the proper precautions you can fish under all average surf conditions with a considerable degree of safety.

Number one on the list of dangers in all surf fishing is, of course, the water itself. Most surf fishermen study the ocean's waves and tides in order to find out how it affects their fishing. An understanding of the waves and tides is even more vital from the standpoint of safety.

Winds are possibly the greatest single factor responsible for producing waves. Your veteran surf angler can tell you what kind of surf to expect before he even sees the ocean, by studying the wind's direction and velocity and the phase of the tide. He knows that on the Atlantic Coast a strong onshore wind from the northeast, east, or southeast will usually produce a heave or swell within twenty-four to forty-eight hours. (On the Pacific Coast, northwest, west, or southwest winds cause rough seas.) If the wind continues to blow strongly from these quarters for two or more days, the heavy ground swells will make surf fishing hazardous and nearly impossible. Then, even if the wind shifts to an offshore breeze, it will take some time for the surf to calm down.

A moderate or strong south or southwest wind (south or southeast on the West Coast) will also cause a heavy surf, but generally the water quiets down as soon as the wind dies or shifts. Storms, squalls, and hurricanes which begin far out to sea often cause ground breakers and swells when you least expect them. As a regular surfman, you will notice several of these unpredictable and unexplainable swells during the fishing season. Therefore, the only safe rule is to stay off breakwaters and jetties on an incoming or flood tide if there is the slightest chance of being trapped.

Jetties Are Dangerous

As previously mentioned, some of the most productive surf-fishing spots are rock jetties, but jetties also have the reputation of being the most dangerous locations for fishing. They are usually moss-covered and extremely slippery. When the tide is near the low mark, the best footing on rock jetties will usually be found near the lower rocks if the water is not too rough. These rocks are covered with barnacles or mussels, so you must wear shoes that hold well—ice creepers or felt sandals (see page 121). Rocks that are covered with black or green moss are especially treacherous.

Sometimes rocks have fallen apart on older jetties so that you may have to jump from one point or rock to another, or crawl on your hands and knees. If you are crossing breaks on jetties of this kind, the safest procedure is to wait for a lull in the waves before making your move. You will notice that the largest waves come in groups of three or four at a time. Then there is an interval when the waves are somewhat smaller. That is the time to cross. The same precaution should be followed when you select a rock to cast from. Stop about twenty-five feet short of the rock you have chosen and carefully study it for a few minutes. Notice how the waves break when they are at their highest. If they don't wash over the rock, then it will be safe, unless an unusually large wave rushes in. No matter how careful you are, sooner or later you are bound to slip and take a fall. If you find yourself falling, double up quickly and try to break the impact with your arms or hands. Doubling up helps to protect your head and you will not hit the rocks as hard as you would when falling from your full height.

It is much harder to judge your footing when you are fishing from rock jetties at night. While a headlight or flashlight helps, the moss on a rock seems to change color under the light and it becomes very easy to make a mistake. Moonlight is also deceiving, with reflections and shadows making it hard to judge depth of water and distances. For these reasons, move slowly at night and do not be tempted to jump from rock to rock.

Those low wooden jetties, which are nothing more than a catwalk supported by piles on both sides, are also by no means safe as fishing spots. If you must fish from a wooden jetty, either stay close to the shore away from any breaking waves, or go out past them toward the very end of the structure. Waves have more height and force just as they start to curl over to break. Brace yourself with feet slightly apart and with legs bent at the knees, and you can take almost any wave up to your hips without being washed overboard; but you must have ice-creepers on—and also make sure you use a different pair for wooden jetties. The points of creepers that are worn on rocks become dulled and will not hold on wood.

When fishing from the beach you need not worry about rocks, but you encounter something nearly as dangerous: sand. Sand bars are especially treacherous, since they may change from day to day. A storm, for example, can alter a familiar sand bar so radically that you will have to learn the location of each hole and slough all over again. It is never safe to fish a sand bar at night unless you have studied its conformation the day before.

In beach fishing you will always have to contend with the undertow, which can be very strong at times. The worst areas are those where the beach drops off sharply and the oncoming waves don't break up until they are almost on the beach. Here the angler should stay out of the water. If you are in the water when a strong wave breaks, turn your body sideways and take the force of it against your shoulder. Never turn your back on a wave. You won't see it coming; it may knock you over, and then the undertow can sweep you out to sea.

Should you accidentally step into a deep hole or fall off a jetty with heavy surf gear on, here are some points to remember:

1. Remain in as nearly a horizontal position as possible.
2. Keep both feet up, so the air trapped in your waders or boots will provide buoyancy.
3. Be careful in breathing so as not to choke.
4. Take it easy and don't become panicky. A person will not sink to the bottom like a rock. It is possible to swim out.

The easiest method to swim with heavy footwear on is side stroke—or simply lie on your back and scull along. If you are caught in an undertow, don't fight it. Allow the current to carry you, and swim in a diagonal line toward shore. You will be carried into water where there is no undertow. Remember to swim fairly vigorously with the waves, and rest while you are in the troughs between waves.

In recent years surf fishing has grown tremendously in popularity and many of our fishing spots have become congested. In some places anglers stand no more than five feet apart and cast squids and plugs over each other's heads. In addition to the lack of sportsmanship in such conditions there is the awful possibility of getting a hook in your face or, even worse, in your eye. It isn't worth it. Move away where you can have more room—and, as often as not, you'll have more fish, too. Surf fish are naturally active, and they cruise up and down the beach looking for food.

No matter where you fish you should always study the formation of the beach and rocks around you so that you have a prearranged plan for landing a fish. If you wait until a fish is hooked, you may take a nasty spill during the excitement that follows.

BEACH BUGGIES

The surf angler who consistently enjoys the best fishing along our beaches is the energetic fellow who covers plenty of ground. To cover the most territory, many surf fishermen are equipping themselves with "beach buggies."

A beach buggy is an automobile rigged to run on soft sandy beaches. Its chief function is to carry the owner, his fishing cronies, and their gear along the miles of beach open to them. Beach buggies are, however, far more than mere sand taxis. They have evolved into self-propelled camps with galleys, full-length beds, numerous compartments for stowage, and abundant water supply. The extent of these facilities is limited only by your ability to fit your requirements for comfort into the restricted space. The automobile itself may be anything from an old Model A Ford to a brand-new station wagon, depending on the whim and financial standing of the owner; but, whatever the make and vintage of the car, it must meet certain fixed requirements before it will plow through soft, windblown sand.

First, it must be mechanically sound, with the transmission, engine, clutch, and rear end in A-1 condition. The radiator should be clean and should hold sufficient water, since beach buggies overheat on long runs, especially when driven in hot weather and in second gear. Some beach-buggy operators have substituted fans with extra blades or have installed surge tanks to hold the water, which would otherwise be lost when the engine overheats.

What is most important on the beach are the tires. They must be wide and flexible enough to support the vehicle and to provide good traction on the soft sand. For the lighter cars, the 8.20×15 super-cushion tire works well. For heavier cars, the 9.00×13 tires are best, and they should be no more than 4-ply. Heavier ones are not flexible enough for the soft sand. One money-saving point: there is no need to purchase new tires, since partly worn or even bald tires perform better on soft sand than do those with deep treads. All tires should be deflated to a pressure of 8 to 10 pounds while on the beach. To mount these special-sized tires, most cars demand 13- or 15-inch wheels. For some makes, you can pick up the wheels ready to mount; but for others a change of hubs and brake drums, or even specially made wheels, may be required. Light vehicles with a short wheel base seem to go somewhat easier than the larger models.

Well-equipped beach buggies resemble miniature trailers. They have compartments for fishing tackle, clothes, dishes, silverware, stoves, water, and other odds and ends needed for fishing and beach camping. Rod racks or holders on the sides, top, or front of the buggy are also essential. The buggy itself must have a tow rope or chain, an auto jack, a tire pump, a pressure gauge, and a complete set of tools. Extra cans of gasoline and water are comforting to have along, too.

The most expert driver will find driving on sand quite different from driving on hard-surfaced roads. Usually, when driving on sand, it is best to follow the ruts made by other beach buggies, and these ruts should be approached at a gradual angle, and left in the same way. All turns on sand should be gentle and sweeping; an abrupt swing of the wheel usually results in trouble. If you have a four-wheel drive, you can of course make your own tracks. If you "break trail," here is a word of caution: watch for partially exposed or buried driftwood and other rubbish which may give you a flat tire or damage the car.

Where the sand is soft and the ruts curve back and forth, you usually have to travel in low or second gear a good portion of the time. Where the ruts are straight and on a hard beach, you can often stay in high gear. Even at low tide, most "beach jockeys" run their buggies above the high-water mark, where the sand is softer, rather than below it. True, the sand below the high-water mark is generally packed down and you can make good speed. But if there are soft spots, you are in more trouble than you thought possible. Especially if the buggy bogs down in front of an incoming tide!

When your beach buggy slows down in a soft spot and starts to labor, shift to low, and hope that this will pull the buggy over onto a firmer base. But if the wheels continue to sink, the gear should quickly be thrown into neutral—speeding the engine only causes the spinning wheels to dig themselves in deeper. Should your buggy bog down, you will usually find that the front wheels are turned too sharply. Straighten them out before you try moving again. Piles of sand in front of the tires should be scooped away. Then, with a helping push by two or three men, you can usually break free and be on your way. If you're alone, try moving the buggy back and forth a few inches at a time. Keep rocking back and forth until you can move a couple of feet. Finally, back up as far as you can go. With the tracks cleared a few feet ahead, you can make a good start and keep going.

In the event you bog down so deep that the buggy's frame rests on the sand or your wheel is buried, you will have to jack the car up, fill in the hole under the sunken wheel, and put a board under it. Stones and beach grass will also help to provide fill and traction if no boards are available. Then, with a helping push or by moving ahead slowly but steadily in low gear, you can usually get out of the hole.

Beach buggies are used along most of the wilder stretches of sand on the Atlantic and Pacific coasts and Gulf of Mexico. On many beaches near the large cities, however, beach buggies are not allowed because of the many bathers. Even the more remote beaches may be crowded with bathers during the daytime. But at night, or before or after the bathing season, these beaches are deserted and then the beach buggies roll.

CHAPTER 7

Surface and Deep Trolling

Trolling is a method of angling whereby the lure or bait is trailed behind a slow-moving boat. There are two types of trolling: surface and deep. Market fishermen use both types with equal facility, choosing whichever method will put the bait in the midst of feeding fish. Sportsmen—who are not faced with monetary considerations in their angling activities—devote their efforts almost exclusively to working the surface. Regardless of which method is employed, if a check were made on the type of angling used in catching the world's record fish (listed in Appendix A) probably trolling has caught the most. And there is good reason why trolling is so successful.

First, you cover more territory by trolling than by any other method.

Second, your lure is always in the water and works full time. No pauses while the lure is cast or reeled through shallow or unproductive water, as in surf fishing. The action is also continuous. Many fish are likely to follow a lure a long distance before striking. A cast lure is likely to be plucked from the water just as the fish decides to hit. The lure theoretically can be seen by more fish than can a still-fished bait. And only by trolling can you reach all depths of the water.

Third, trolling saves the physical exertion of bottom fishing, where an anchor has to be lowered and raised with each change of location.

TROLLING TACKLE

This brings us to the question of what tackle and types of rigs are suitable for general trolling conditions rather than for specific kinds of trolling.

A few notations may be of service to many who want an over-all picture of this fishing method.

Most of the rods used for trolling today are made of fiberglass, with a tip section that measures five to six feet in length, and a butt from eighteen to twenty-four inches. A 6-ounce tip will bear up under the drag of nearly all the lighter fish, in the hands of a seasoned angler. The beginner might feel safer with a 9-ounce tip. As you can see, trolling—except for deep trolling—enables you to use lighter tackle than is practical in still-fishing, where a vertical strain is imposed on the rod and often the fish must be yanked out from under a rock without waste of time.

The reel and line are chosen to balance the rod with which they will be used (see page 260). The tip should not be overloaded by a heavy line. The 20-, 27-, and 36-pound test synthetic or monofilament lines are adequate for taking fish up to about 150 pounds. When trolling around coral or rocks, though, a 54 or 72 test line is more practical, to guard against chafing.

The size of your reel will vary from 2/0 to 6/0 for the majority of requirements. By and large, a 3/0 reel will be employed with 18 test line, a 4/0 reel with 27 test line, and a 6/0 reel with 36 test line. A special wire line reel (page 29) with one hundred yards of Monel or plastic-covered lead core line, backed up with sufficient linen or nylon, is usually a satisfactory deep-trolling rig. The reel used in trolling should have a star drag, a leather thumbstall, and a free spool device. Salt-water trolling puts a reel through extremely tough paces, so it pays to purchase as good a one as you can afford.

The size of reel to employ, together with the corresponding amount of line, depends a great deal on the kind and average weight of fish to be caught. Specific tackle data for the different species taken by trolling will be found later in this chapter and in Chapter 8. The beginner would do well to use the heaviest recommended line until he has acquired the feel of his gear and has learned to fight the fish with the tackle rather than with his emotions and brute strength. Information on the proper selection of reels, lines, and rods for trolling will be found in Chapter 2.

A leader is always used in trolling. The line should never be tied directly to the lure; to do so would court defeat, for many of the ocean prowlers have teeth, gill covers, or fins sharp enough to chop even a heavy line in two. Wire or braided nylon leaders are used, except for leaping fish—marlin, sailfish, swordfish—for which a cable leader is used. Tinned or stainless steel leaders in size Nos. 6, 7, and 8 are popular with lines of 20 to 36 test. A tinned wire leader is considered by some anglers to be better than a braided or twisted cable leader for most trolling situations.

The length of the leader depends on the kind of fish you are after, and on the depth and bottom conditions. For average requirements, a leader six to twelve feet in length is practical. The usual advice is to tie on a leader that is longer than the fish you plan to catch, although the accepted limit for most purposes is fifteen feet. At any rate, you will want a long, strong wire leader when trolling for bluefish, bonito, barracuda, or any other fish armed with knifelike teeth. A 6-foot tinned wire leader is suggested for taking tuna of the "school" size, for under normal light tackle trolling conditions this length serves better than one of three feet.

Swivels are always attached to the line end of the leader. They are essential with any revolving lure, to prevent the line from becoming untwisted, or "unlaid" and weakening. The ordinary box or barrel swivel works well up to a point, but it will frequently jam under a heavy load, and adding more swivels to the line will hardly remedy the situation. The bead-chain type of swivel will keep revolving under a much heavier load than will a box or barrel swivel. And at the top of the list is the ball-bearing swivel, which is practically jamproof. It is more expensive than the other types but is worth what it costs, especially for the big fish. A trolling "fin" will also keep the swivel revolving continuously.

A Saranac or keel sinker—pinched or fastened to the line an inch or two ahead of the swivel—greatly inhibits the tendency of the line to twist. The important thing is to have the keel large enough for the job it has to do.

The trolling triangle—a three-sided wire device with a sinker attached to one corner, the main line to another, and the leader extending to the lure to the third—is an effective preventer of line twisting. It is somewhat more awkward on the line than the other devices. To make the trolling triangle simpler and less bulky, a three-way swivel with a sinker attached

Popular trolling weights. (*Top, left to right*) Ringed sinker, clincher sinker, and trolling lead with chain swivels and snaps. (*Center left*) Heart-shaped sinker flat and folded on line. (*Center right*) Keel sinker with swivels and snap. (*Lower left*) Depth glider trolling aid and (*lower right*) drail. (Courtesy of Horrocks-Ibbotson Company)

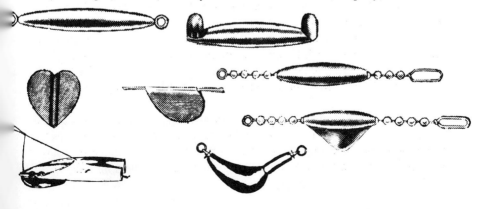

to one of the eyelets is often employed. The "cross line" swivel type with
the third eyelet at right angles to the line of the other two is more efficient
than the standard type that consists of a metal ring with three eyelets pro-
jecting at equal intervals; but it is harder to find in tackle stores.

These devices will keep line twisting to a minimum or even prevent it.
But if you are going to do a lot of trolling besides a great deal of surf
or bait casting, you should have a separate line for trolling. Good casting
calls for a line in fine condition, and it is difficult to keep it in top shape
if you do a great deal of trolling with it.

If light swivels are used, do not tie on a heavy wire leader, or the swivels
may stop functioning; and if you have heavy swivels on, steer clear of
using a light wire leader, or the wire may buckle or coil. Your whole outfit, you should remember, must balance to work efficiently.

In joining the line to the leader, remember that a knot impairs the
strength of a line. Experienced fishermen resort to the use of a short
leather thong with a loop at each end. Their method is to run the thong
through the eye of the swivel, pass the line through the loop at each end
of the thong, then jab the line down through each loop at the ends of the
thong. With a series of half hitches, which you probably learned to make
as a Boy Scout, you pull it tight and have a binding link without putting a
knot in the line. If you don't have a leather thong, you will use one of the
knots described in Chapter 3.

TROLLING RIGS

The offshore rigs shown in the illustration are usually provided by the
charter boat operators for use when trolling for such game fish as albacore,
bluefish, bonito, wahoo, school tuna, king mackerel, and many big fellows
such as broadbill swordfish, blue or black marlin, mako shark, and bluefin
tuna. The strip bait rig is baited with a carefully shaped strip from a fresh
squid or from the sides of small bait or food fishes. It should be widest
near the middle, tapering gradually to a sharp point at the head and tail.
Two holes are punched or slit in the strip, one at the head, the other at a
point where the hook is to pass through the bait. The point of the hook is
passed through the strip. A short length of free leader, which remains
after you bend the leader through the eye of the hook, is passed through
the bait and wrapped with a one-half or full-turn around the leader ahead
of the bait. Thus it acts as a safety pin, securing the hook to the bait and
preventing the bait from curling back on the point of the hook under pressure of the water.

The whole fish rig may be baited with anything from a small mullet or
mossbunker (menhaden) to a whole bonito, and is used for marlin, swordfish, school and giant tuna, and other big fellows. The backbone is removed
from an incision in the side, which makes the bait flexible so it will "swim"

naturally when trolled. A wire leader is inserted through the mouth and attached to one, two, or three hooks that are sewed in and allowed to protrude from the belly or side. Gills are also sewed up with light nylon thread. When using fresh squid for trolling, impale it on two or three hooks, and allow it to drift in the current. This arrangement generally does a good job with striped bass, and usually takes big ones.

A quick way to make a tandem hook is to bend down the barbs on two hooks and put them through the eyes of the preceding hooks as shown in the illustration.

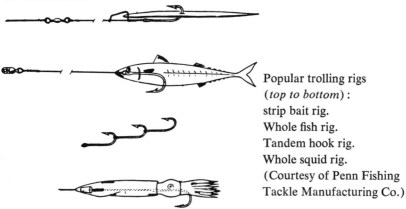

Popular trolling rigs
(*top to bottom*):
strip bait rig.
Whole fish rig.
Tandem hook rig.
Whole squid rig.
(Courtesy of Penn Fishing
Tackle Manufacturing Co.)

For white marlin and sailfish, a wire leader is run through the body of the squid and attached to a hook buried in its tentacles. The tail is held in position by a cork and clamp sinker previously strung on the leader, as shown in the illustration.

Since one of the prime objectives in trolling is to sink the lure to where the fish are feeding, your interest is in finding that depth as quickly as possible. One of the best ways of doing this, when you skirt the deep edges of bars and banks, is to make use of the competent fresh-water Seth Green hand-line rig. (This is frequently put into service while trolling for trout in very deep lakes, such as the Finger Lakes, and can be used to excellent advantage for many salt-water species.)

This rig consists of a heavy line six hundred feet or more in length, with a triangle (a salt-water "cross-line swivel" will also serve) tied to the end. Leading from another corner of the triangle is a line of the same strength, fifteen or twenty feet long, holding a leader and the lure. Extending down from the remaining corner of the triangle is a weaker line about ten feet in length, bearing a heavy sinker. Above the triangle are four other leader-and-lure lines of equal length (and of the same strength as the main gear) running out from the trunk line at regular intervals (ten or fifteen feet apart) by means of three-way swivels. In this manner you troll at several levels simultaneously, and thus discover where the fish are. Likewise you can learn their food desires by offering five different kinds of baits and lures. If either the sinker or lower hook becomes snagged, you can break it off and save the rest of your tackle.

There are many artificial lures which can be used in place of the so-called natural baits. Definite recommendations will be given later in this chapter and in Chapter 8, but here are a few general suggestions.

By and large, one of the best trolling lures is the Japanese feather nickel-headed or the nylon type jig. There are various sizes, shapes, colors, and weights (½ to 1½ ounces are the most popular) in the tackle shops to satisfy the most pernickety fish, and several of these merit a workout. Color is a matter of personal preference. One day fish will strike a yellow-and-green combination and the next day a white or a red-and-white lure. So it is a good idea to have feather and nylon jigs in various weights and colors. When you need additional weight you can use two lures together, or put a ½- or 1-ounce egg sinker on the wire leader just ahead of the lure. These jigs are excellent for bluefish, school tuna, bonito, and false albacore. Baited with two or three sea worms, this jig is an outstanding tempter for striped bass.

One difficulty with a feather jig is that any fish with keen-edged teeth will tear the feathers to shreds. For this reason the jig is not trolled as extensively as some other types of lure where such fish predominate. The practice in Florida waters, for example, is to use a strip of mullet, bonito, or

Popular feather and nylon jigs. (*Left*) Strip bait trailing from a feather. (*Right*) Nylon jig with a double-hook arrangement.

 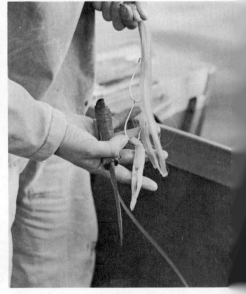

barracuda on a double- or triple-hook or tandem rig, fixed so it will not twirl but will weave along gently. For the best results, a strip bait should be strung on so that it stretches out flat from where the safety-pin catch or snap is mounted above the eye of the hook and runs through the bait. It is hard to fool certain game fish, so this detail should not be overlooked in preparing a strip bait for trolling.

Before the Japanese feather lure was used along our Atlantic Coast, the block-tin squids or jigs were quite popular. The 3- and 4-ounce ones were used for trolling and jigging. The heavy "heave and haul" chrome-plated jigs, weighing 1 to 1½ pounds are excellent for jigging (see page 106) in very deep water. A pearl-luster spoon-shaped lure, a favorite on the West Coast, is fast becoming popular in our eastern waters for striped bass and bluefish.

On the whole, you will have better luck with a smooth-working lure than a jerky one. Ordinarily, spoons and spinners get more cooperation from the fish than wobblers, for action of the fast revolving type draws attention and interest more readily. However, pearl wobblers, and the nickel Del Rey wobbler, have accounted for many great catches. Your spinners and spoons should be kept brightly polished to be most effective. Large solid plugs frequently take their share of salt-water fish when trolled.

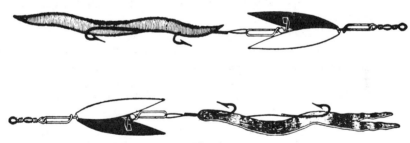

Cape Cod spinner with sea worm on hooks (*top*) and with pork rind on hooks (*bottom*).

A spinner garnished with sea worms whets the greed of numerous in-shore and channel-ranging fish, under almost every condition. The Cape Cod, Fishkill, and Montauk spinners are tops, and so is the June Bug. A hammered brass spinner that spins red salmon-egg beads is very fetching, and the same is true of a plain nickel spinner with a strip of pork rind trailing behind. This last teaser is the downfall of pollack in particular.

When trolling with one of these spinners, your safest plan is to tie on a leader of tinned wire at least three feet long, testing about twenty pounds, with one or two box swivels at the line end, and a lock snap swivel at the lure end. Sometimes the fish will strike short of your spinner or spoon. To remedy this vexing habit, behind the spinner connect a gang of three separate hooks, each fastened to a length of light cable wire. The gang has a medium-sized hook at the top (next to the spinner), followed by a larger hook six inches below, then a third hook of the same size after a two or three inches below that. You impale a large bloodworm on the first hook, with its end free to wriggle, but leave the other two hooks bare. (A pork rind strip is equally tempting.) This rig, trolled slowly, causes striped bass, pollack, weakfish, and others to make their last mistake by nipping at the worm.

TROLLING TECHNIQUES

Most trolling is done from charter boats whose operators have the knowledge and skill necessary to practice this method of angling, so the angler need only follow their instructions. The following information is for those who fish from small skiffs, outboards, or their own inboards.

Surface-trolled lures and baits can be handled in three different ways: a straight line (or "flat"), outriggers, and kites. Until anglers adopted outriggers and kites, all trolling was straight or flat. In this method, the angler sits in the stern of the craft and fishes over the transom, the line running directly from the rod to the water. Actually, flat is the most common way of trolling, especially in small boats, and it is ideal for the smaller species both offshore and inshore.

This manner of trolling, however, has several disadvantages. First, it is tiring to hold a rod hour after hour against the drag of the line and bait. (Although a good rod holder will help to overcome this problem.) Second, the number of anglers who can fish at the same time is limited by the width of the beam of the boat; in skiffs and other small craft, only one or two fishermen can troll comfortably. Third, flat trolling is very hard on natural baits, particularly if they have not been properly prepared. The continual pressure of the water soon reduces the bait to ragged pieces, especially when the line is in the wake of the boat. If the bait has not been properly trimmed, this disintegration is sudden, and, once this starts, the bait will spin and soon ruin the line. Finally, when fish are exceedingly nervous, the disturbance caused by the craft arouses their suspicion. The fish associate such baits with churned-up waters and noise and allow them to go by without striking.

In spite of its many disadvantages, straight trolling is the most popular for inshore and offshore small game fish. A great deal of this type of fishing is done with artificial lures which are not as difficult to troll as live baits. Kites and outriggers, while they do overcome some of the disadvantages of flat line trolling, are fairly expensive to install and require room to make full use of their capacities.

The kite is an eccentric device, hard to control and to raise aloft. It restricts fishing to one person, requires favorable weather conditions for complete utilization, and holds the boat to a course favorable to the kite's operation. Most well-equipped charter boats carry one in their locker since there are times when no other means will do except a kite. For example, schools of feeding fish are sometimes so nervous that sound scatters them before the boat can present the baits to them. They will not re-form and commence feeding until after the boat has traveled a considerable distance away. There is nothing more discouraging or annoying than to spend the entire day chasing such fish all over the ocean and never get within striking distance. Then, under favorable conditions, the kite may be used.

The kite is usually square in shape and constructed of light crosspieces with balloon silk or nylon as covering. Kites vary in size, from small ones 12 inches wide for use in heavy weather to large ones of 36 inches wide employed in light air. The device can be raised and flown well away from the boat, maneuvering it so that the skipping bait will be placed carefully along the surface of the water on the outer edge of the area where the fish are feeding and will not disturb or scare them away. But the kite's operation requires a great deal of skill and is seldom used by the average deep-sea angler.

Outriggers are the best of all the various means of presenting baits to big-game fish such as marlin, sailfish, and swordfish. This is because the interval between the strike—when the line drops out of its clothespin holder and floats slackly toward the surface—and the tautening of the line—gives a big fish a chance to get the bait well into his mouth, thus greatly increasing the opportunity of setting the hook. Outriggers also may be used to take smaller game fish.

Outriggers can be simple or elaborate and can be used on small outboard cruisers as well as larger inboard charter boats. They are long cane poles or slender spars of wood or metal, ten to forty feet long, held in tubes of Monel metal, galvanized iron, or aluminum, which in turn are held by brackets fastened to the deck or strapped to the wheelhouse stanchions. The bracket is hinged so that the pole can be lowered outward to approximately 45 degrees from the water. The poles or spars are strengthened by crosspieces which are securely guyed to distribute the strain when the outriggers are dropped into working position.

The primary purpose of an outrigger when angled out in fishing position is to troll a bait along the surface of the water, perhaps trailing a strip of pork rind, or making a dead baitfish "swim" just below the surface or skipping it over the surface to simulate a flying fish (a favorite food of the big fellows). Artificial lures are seldom used on outriggers. The outrigger bait is trolled well off to the side of the wake. The bait is held at the desired trolling position by an arrangement on the outrigger consisting of a trolley line with a common snap-type clothespin on it. The trolley

Cruisers with outriggers.

line runs from a metal or glass ring at the top of the outrigger to the gunwale. After a bait has been let out to the desired distance, the clothespin is then clipped to the fishing line where it comes off the rod tip, and then pulled to the outrigger tip while the reel is in free spool, allowing sufficient slack in the fishing line. While the bait is being trolled, the rod may be placed in a rod holder, or held by the angler. When a fish strikes the bait, the fishing line is automatically pulled out of the clothespin and the fish is then fought on the rod.

Another advantage in the use of outriggers on average-sized fishing boats is that they allow four to six men to fish at the same time. Many charter boats carry three 'riggers, one on either side and one in the center. Three anglers fish the outriggers and two or three fish flat lines. It is possible to fish for marlin, sailfish, and other big fellows from the outrigger, and for wahoo, kingfish, bonito, albacore, and dolphin from the flat lines. The anglers can take turns tending the heavy outfits, rotating their positions every now and then.

The salt-water angler who is usually successful in fishing the blue offshore waters depends not so much on luck as on his knowledge of the habits of the fish he is seeking and the location of the various fishing grounds. The best way to locate fish is by sight. They can often be seen swimming just under the surface, finning or chasing bait. Wheeling and diving terns or gulls mark the places where fish are feeding. When birds are in large groups, sitting on the surface, there are probably fish below— the birds know it and are just waiting for them to start feeding. This is a good spot to watch for action. A good pair of binoculars is helpful, both in finding active birds and fish that are breaking the surface as they chase bait.

Customs in fishing are hard to change. An angler may troll a lure over the surface of the sea for hours without a strike just because this is the usual practice in fishing for school tuna, bonito, albacore, dolphin, and bluefish. But when we consider the vast depth of the water and the variety of depths where baitfish are found, our chances of catching fish only from the surface are about 100 to 1. The experienced angler will try various trolling depths by using the Seth Green rig (page 143), a lead drail, or a trolling sinker. These sinkers weigh a few ounces to one or two pounds, depending upon the depth of water and the speed of travel.

When you have received a strike, or have hauled in a fish, it is advisable to troll again past that spot in the same direction as you were going when the fish was encountered. The chances are that other specimens are nearby and they will be headed in the direction in which the baitfish are moving, the way your lure was traveling when the gamester struck. A good way to mark a productive spot is to open a newspaper and spread it flat on the surface of the water. Its thinness will minimize drifting from the spot because of wind or tide. Some charter boat captains use semianchored kegs as markers, or blown-up paper bags; but if there is any breeze, bags are blown from the spot too quickly.

The wooden teaser, jumping and diving with its erratic action twenty or thirty feet back of the boat, will raise many species of game fish to strike trolling surface lures. Chumming (see page 101) is also another excellent method of bringing fish up from deep water and at the same time keeping fish feeding within a small area. But if too many boats are chumming over a fishing ground, the fish may soon stuff themselves and lose interest in anything you offer. The small commercial fishermen often use this knowledge to their advantage, letting the fish rest until very early in the morning and bringing in a boatload of fish taken just before daybreak.

When fish have been driven down (usually because too many boats are trolling over the same area) it becomes necessary to fish deep. You can get your line down low by several methods: by using additional lead attached to the swivel on the leader, by using a plastic lead-core line or a Monel wire line, or by using a trolling planer. The Monel and plastic-covered wire lines are preferred by many anglers who use medium-weight rods. Trolling drails and round cigar-shaped leads are used when additional weight is needed. The planers will take fish when all other methods fail, but on light tackle these metal plates cause a severe vibrating strain on the rod, so use a rod with a 12- to 16-ounce tip for this kind of fishing.

Trolling is done at three to ten miles per hour (lure speed), depending upon the species of fish being hunted, the type of lure used, and also the wind or tide. Slower speeds are maintained when trolling against a tide that will keep the lure working well. When you are deep trolling, slower speeds are better, especially if you are using an underwater outrigger. This prevents the trolling weight or sinker from working back toward the surface. Strong currents will affect the trolling, carrying the bait or lure off to one side or the other.

Short lines keep the bait or lures high, whereas longer lines let them sink. Long lines are used in clear or shallow water where fish may be shy. It is, for example, advantageous to use long lines when trolling for bluefish. Although some fish are taken on lines of twenty to thirty feet, you will have greater success with lines of seventy-five to a hundred feet. These keep the line away from the white waters of the wake.

Some fish, such as school tuna, bonito, and albacore, take lures fifteen to thirty feet from the stern and propeller, because they are attracted by the churning. Sailfish and marlin also come close in to see what is causing the disturbance. Short lines are also a must where there is heavy traffic and boats are crisscrossing as they work a hot spot. Except when extra-long lines are out for swordfish, most trolling is done with the line thirty to a hundred feet off the stern.

When trolling for school tuna, striped bass, albacore, bluefish, and bonito, you will find that the fish usually strike and hook themselves. It is difficult to resist the impulse to strike back when a fish grabs the bait. This is not necessary, and it can even be bad if the tip of the rod is brought past the 90-degree angle. With a rod tip pointing toward the bow of the boat most of the strain is put on the top section of the rod. If more people would remember that the rod tip acts like a spring between the angler and his prey fewer fish would be lost because of the hook's pulling out. (The method of playing or landing of smaller game fish taken by trolling is described on page 109.)

The most practical way to retrieve line when the heavy fellows are attached is to "pump" it in. After a fish has made his first two or three strenuous runs, and is apparently weakening or has gone to the depths to sulk, you raise the rod tip just past the perpendicular, then quickly lower it and reel in furiously at the same instant in order to keep the line taut. Then you strain upward on the rod again and go through the same performance, keeping up this pumping process until your fish comes to the boat or speeds away on another rampage. If you want to get credit in fishing contests or "rodeos," or to compete for world records, you must manage the fish yourself, although after the fish reaches the boat, someone else can bring him aboard.

Handling a boat that has two or three big fish hooked on that number of lines, is a difficult art. The skipper moves his craft away from the school as the fish are played, so as not to panic other fish. The boat must "follow" exceptionally large fish, to recover line that may be getting thin on the reel spool. When a fish gets coy and charges toward the boat, the skipper must help his passenger keep a tight line by opening his throttle. He must also keep his eye on the lines at all times, altering his course and changing his speed so as to keep the lines straight and moving in the same plane as the boat. He must also watch out for other boats and their lines.

In trolling, then, some of your main considerations are: be familiar with the physical features of the bottom, watch the sea gulls and terns for signs of feeding fish, adapt your outfit to the depth of water and species sought, employ only balanced tackle, and let your fish run and fight until completely spent. You should also guard against slack line, keep your bait or lure moving to impart lifelike action, skirt the edges of surfacing fish, and hit for the shore when high winds, strong currents, or lashing waves make your course too dangerous for reasonable safety.

TROLLING FOR SPECIFIC KINDS OF FISH

Successful trolling depends on the fisherman's knowing the habits of fish, the signs of where they are, how to prepare and offer baits, what lures are required, and what trolling methods will catch particular fish. Various methods of trolling are employed in bays, sounds and inlets, over reefs, in the ocean offshore areas, and way out in the "blue water," far from shore.

Inshore Species

Several of the bottom and inshore species described in Chapter 5 can sometimes be taken by trolling. In that chapter we have also mentioned some of the general techniques of inshore trolling. Now let's discuss ways of catching specific kinds of inshore fish by trolling.

Striped Bass

While the vast majority of striped bass are taken from the surf, the best way of catching them is by trolling near shore: past rocky coastline in harbors, bays, and inlets; in wide rivers; in marsh streams; and along the outer edge of the surf. This is a particularly telling method during July, August, and September in the region from the Chesapeake Bay to the York River in Maine, when nearly every bay and inlet has a good crop of striped bass in its confines. The Pacific Coast striped bass is taken the year around, principally from Coos Bay to Monterey Bay. The best trolling for stripers is from sunset to sunrise when the sea is calm.

For long-line angling, you may put a 3/6 or 4/6 tackle outfit into service, or a regulation boat rod with short butt and a reel holding 250 yards of 36 or 45 test line. The choice of lures includes a smooth-working spinner with one or two bloodworms or strip of a mullet (trolled slowly), plugs with three-hook gangs, a feather jig with two or three sea worms hooked through the middle, a metal squid tipped with pork rind, a spinner-and-streamer fly combination, drone spoon, an eelskin rig, and live minnows. The hook sizes may range from 7/0 to 10/0, since in trolling you are likely to tangle with the larger bass.

On a day when the stripers seem to be striking short, you may be able to solve the problem by trying a contrivance made up of a 6-foot heavy nylon leader testing 15 pounds, to which is tied an elongated spinner with both ends pointed and revolving about its own stem and with a double-hook rig fastened below the spinner by means of a swivel. On the hook nearest the spinner impale a large bloodworm by its head, but don't thread the worm on the second hook. The spinner will entice the fish within close distance, and the lower hook will prove fatal to the short-snapping bass.

If the fish are at or near the surface, use lures that ride on the top or just beneath; and when the fish are deep, heavy trolling lures, with trolling sinkers and wire lines. Big stripers are often lazy and won't move far for a lure nor chase it. When they are down deep the lure has to move slowly and close to the fish, which makes slow trolling most productive. While trolling you can also improve your luck by chumming with pieces of squid, menhaden, mackerel, sardines, or herring to create a slick on the water and bring the fish up the current. This is especially necessary when the stripers are slow to cooperate.

Channel Bass

These fish, too, are primarily for the surf caster, but channel bass—both small and large—are taken in salt-water and brackish bays, sounds, and creeks by trolling. The favorite trolling rig is a large spoon, but feather and nylon jigs and underwater lures are also used with success. Big bass have been caught on extremely light tackle, but the average equipment is a standard, medium-weight trolling rod with a line about 45-pound test. Hook sizes range from 6/0 to 10/0 in the O'Shaughnessy pattern. Natural baits—mullet, bunker and crab—are favored by dedicated channel bass fishermen. The mullet is filleted and a whole side used to bait a hook. A wire leader is not necessary, as channel bass do not have teeth, but most anglers prefer to use a short leader of No. 9 wire, 18 to 24 inches long, in case bluefish or shark are encountered.

Big channel bass are seldom caught on low tide. Pilots whose business it is to locate schools of fish for commercial boats report that channel bass lie in deep water off inlets and sloughs at slack or low water. Usually the fish move in to feed with the rising water and the best fishing time is during half-rise, full, and half-slack tides. Winds, too, are important to the anglers who fish channel bass. The fish do not bite often in rough water—even what is called "bluefish water" is too rough for channel bass—and they rarely move in a millpond surface. A light to moderate breeze that is not directly alongshore is best because it will not create a current that makes it difficult to keep bait in likely spots—in the surf, inlets, and behind bars.

Once hooked, the channel bass is no longer the slow-moving fish he is while feeding. Channel bass are fast and powerful. Although they aren't as tricky as stripers, they have more strength and endurance. A big one, snubbed on a tight drag, can break a heavy line as though it were a kite string. It's much safer to play the fish slowly on a light drag.

Black drum are taken in much the same waters (the Gulf of Mexico to Maine) as channel bass (red drum), although they are less often caught by trolling. But those that are, are taken in the same manner as their smaller cousin—the channel bass.

Pollack

The pollack is distributed along the north Atlantic Coast but is never found south of Chesapeake Bay and seldom south of Long Island. Its center of abundance is along the Maine coast. While pollack are caught on the bottom in the cold months, they are on the top in spring and fall (summer in northern New England) and are caught trolling with feather lures, spoons, metal squids, and nylon jigs. Strips of squid or pork-rind flags are sometimes added. Hook sizes 1/0 to 3/0 cover average trolling needs, for the smaller pollack that wander inshore usually weigh two to fifteen pounds.

Pollack trolling is an exciting pastime, for the fish strike forcefully and tug briskly, making you work for each one you finally bring aboard. If you are a novice, a 6- or 9-ounce boat rod is advised, with a standard 2/0 reel and 36-pound test line, but for the seasoned angler a 3/6 tackle outfit is adequate. Many expert fishermen prefer to use wire line because it keeps the lure twenty to thirty feet deep, which they consider the best depth for pollack.

California Yellowtail

The California yellowtail is one of the finest game fish of the Pacific. It should not be confused with the yellowtail snapper of the Florida Keys, which is a much smaller fish. The Pacific yellowtail's average weight is ten to fifteen pounds, with some individuals sagging the scales at eighty pounds or more.

While California yellowtail are taken by surf casting, and at times by bait casting, the most popular ways of fishing for them are trolling and still-fishing. In their efforts to find their preferred food (sardines, anchovies, herring, soft-shelled crabs, and shrimps), yellowtail spread over rocky and sandy bays, gather in coves and inlets, loiter around buoys and islands, and at times even chase baitfish right up into the surf. They probe every kelp patch for eatables, and advance over the shoals in formation.

The tackle that a novice might handle to his advantage while trolling may be a two-piece boat rod 5½ feet long over-all, weighing about fifteen ounces, with locking reel seat, equipped with a 3/0 or 4/0 free-spool reel having a star drag, 250 yards of 36-pound test, and a 15-foot leader of piano wire. Lures, having hooks in sizes from 4/0 to 6/0, may consist of cut baits (herring, sardines, or smelt), spoons, metal squids, feather jigs, or bone jigs with pork rinds trailing from tail hooks; these lures often work best in the order named.

An expert angler would probably find greater sport in using the 3/6 tackle outfit, with a 2/0 reel and 18 test line; or perhaps he would care to wield the 6/9 outfit, with a 3/0 or 4/0 reel holding 300 yards of 27-pound test line.

Pacific Rockfish

Prominent among the swarms of salt-water pan fish scattered from Alaska to Mexico is the rockfish family. Numbering nearly sixty species in all, at least fifty occur off the shores of California, where anglers catch around half a million pounds annually. Heavy fishing is done from such places as Eureka, San Francisco, Monterey, and Santa Barbara, and many rockfish are also landed from Puget Sound and lower British Columbia.

As a group, these fish are commonly taken by hand-lining or still-fishing as they huddle in the rocky shallows close to shore. In deeper water—they are known to go as deep as eight hundred fathoms—fine specimens are brought to net or gaff by trolling with small jigs and spoons.

When trolling, the regulation 6/9 tackle outfit is satisfactory for any of the heavier rockfish. A light single or double swivel is advisable, together with a leader of No. 6 stainless-steel wire or nylon, three feet long. The hook size should be 1/0 to 4/0.

Foremost of the rockfish family in value and popularity, at least in California, is a slant-jawed, pugnacious-looking fellow called bocaccio. This species roams from San Diego to San Francisco in generous quantities, some straggling up to Queen Charlotte Sound, south of Moresby Island, British Columbia. Small fish make up much of their diet, and at places like Howe Sound, British Columbia, herring-skin lures are generally used with great success while deep trolling with light tackle. These are swift-moving, vigorous-tugging customers that may reach a length of three feet and a weight of eighteen pounds.

The priestfish deserves respectful mention because it is one of the leading sport species of rockfish in the California area, and also makes itself known off Alaska. These fish are ready to accommodate you throughout the year, in both shallow and deep water, by seizing baits and lures that are still-fished or trolled.

Dominating the catch at Eureka, the orange rockfish are found with their cousins all along the California waterfront, as well as up in British Columbia. The youngsters stay mainly inshore, but the adults like to settle in deep holes. Specimens 2½ feet in length are secured at depths of a hundred fathoms when trolling shiny jigs baited with live herring.

Cabezon

A scaleless, wrinkled-looking creature, the cabezon is a curious member of the sculpin family. There are several sculpins; the cabezon, one of the commonest, is found along the West Coast in tidal pools, shallow shore waters, and deep basins. This fish runs anywhere from 1 to 2½ feet in length, weighing around twenty pounds. It spreads out over an area from southern California (off San Diego) to Alaska, and is an especially important game species off central and northern California, where in some seasons the sport catch exceeds the commercial haul.

Inshore cabezon are generally taken by still-fishing on live baits such as sea worms, crabs, mussels, and shrimps. In the deeper waters, where large specimens hang out, it is advisable to troll with a rod having a medium to heavy tip section, and use 27 to 45 test line. They will strike a jig, plug, or flashing spinner. Because of the cabezon's sharp teeth, a No. 6 stainless-steel wire leader three to six feet long, with a light swivel, is necessary. O'Shaughnessy hooks in tinned finish, of sizes 4/0 and 5/0, are recommended for taking the bigger cabezon by any method.

Pacific Salmon

Outshining all other fish along the Pacific Coastal region from the standpoints of both sport and market value are the five species of salmon—king, silver, sockeye, humpback, and dog. It is estimated that there is an annual yield of around 600 million pounds, of which the rod and reel catch runs into several millions. Complete details as to where and what seasons to catch salmon can be found on pages 331 to 342.

Due to the importance of knowing where to troll, as well as when and how, the wisest plan is to hire a guide, at least until through careful observation and many trials you become acquainted with the local depths, types of bottom, feeding stations, positions of the salmon on incoming and outgoing tides, and similar factors. The areas over which to troll are those harboring natural food, and these you should explore yourself or learn from an experienced guide.

However, in searching for good spots, there are certain signs which will help you. Sea gulls may lead you to where salmon are attacking candlefish or herring at the surface, or baitfish may be moving in schools along the shores of islands or the mainland. You may locate eddies formed by the tide sweeping past rocky or sandy points, where minnows lurk and salmon come in to stuff themselves. At these headlands you troll close to where the ledges and bars drop off into deep water. You might also come upon kelp beds near shore, in which baitfish hide and salmon take refuge. Kings and silvers like the swift, well-aerated stretches where food is plentiful, and for this reason you look closely along the banks, beaches, inlets, and bays where strong currents back up or tide rips occur. You troll parallel to a tide rip so that your lure will come into the area where the baitfish are held by the current.

Stretching across the mouth of nearly every river you will find a sand bar, and it is here that salmon tarry while waiting for the right time to start upstream for the spawning beds. When the tide is flooding you will usually find them on the inside of the bar, facing oceanward, and on the ebbing tide they are on the outside of the bar, facing landward. The greatest number and the largest fish will be near the eddy created by the tide and bar.

If you wish to profit fully from the salmon's feeding sprees, you should be on hand before daybreak or at dusk. The baitfish are customarily at the surface before dawn and this makes for better success at this time. As the sun rises, if the day is clear and bright, the schools of herring and candlefish seek lower levels, and the salmon can close in on them without having to come near the top. This causes you more difficulty in locating the salmon. But if the morning is dark, then the baitfish are apt to remain close to the surface, to your definite advantage.

During the day, if it is sunny and warm, the salmon stay in the depths and do most of their gadding about after dark. In Puget Sound many anglers have their best luck trolling in the dark of the moon, in summer. When it rains, however, with fresh water rushing down the rivers into the sound or coastal inlets, the fish are more active over a longer period. At the mouths of rivers that are fed by snow waters throughout the summer, salmon strike baits and lures with greater abandon.

It has been observed in some areas that, in spring, salmon apparently follow a schedule of feeding from around 10 o'clock in the morning until 1:30 in the afternoon, and again from about 5 P.M. until dusk. As summer advances, when the days are bright and warm, salmon forage much earlier in the morning and later in the evening. Like other fish, they are not as responsive to lures in hot weather as when the temperature is cold. On sunny days in the fall, salmon often strike readily if the nights have been frosty. When you begin trolling as the first streaks of dawn appear, you use only a 4- or 6-ounce sinker and let out about a hundred feet of line, inasmuch as the baitfish are at the surface. Then as the day continues, with the minnows leaving the shore and going deeper, you put on 8-, 12-, or

16-ounce sinkers—as necessary—and lengthen the line to two hundred feet or more. In these circumstances, it is very important to maintain the proper trolling speed.

Due to the average trolling rate and force of the current, a large share of the salmon become hooked upon grasping the lure, but at times an added jerk is required to set the hook solidly. You hold the rod at an angle so that, when a fish strikes, the spring of the tip will help to drive the hook home and relieve the sudden strain on the line. For greater assurance, you inspect the hook points frequently to see that they are sharp.

After the connection is made, a salmon will start on a long, swift run, and you've got to give him line. Keep the rod tip elevated all during the skirmish, and when the fish turns toward the boat you reel furiously to take up the slack. A king salmon is apt to fight deeper and sulk more than a silver salmon. If your prey is big and swims fast, you may have to chase him with the outboard motor in order to retrieve him.

Play your salmon until his energies are completely spent, before trying to land him. And never let him rest! If he sounds and lies quiet, do something to stir him into action again—twitch the rod tip, pull ahead a bit faster, or rap on the handle above the reel seat with a jackknife. Pump him up as you would a tuna, and adjust the drag tension so that the tip section will bend and help bring the fish surfaceward by its leverage.

If you have been drawn into a strong tideway or current, or are close to a kelp bed, watch out for a calmer or less obstructed place in which to play and boat your fish. Lead him into the shallows, if possible, so you can reclaim more line and tire him quicker. Be careful when your salmon is at the top, for he may get a notion to roll, dart off on another stiff run, or plunge for the depths. If he begins rolling, you'll have to ease up a trifle, yet be certain not to allow a bit of slack. This is a difficult situation to control, and it is often hard to avoid a disastrous outcome.

A big salmon is not licked until he reaches the surface and comes meekly to the boat on his side or belly up. Only then should you feel safe in attempting to bring him over the gunwale. If not too large, he can be lifted aboard by his gill cover, or by leading him—always head-on—into a deep, wide-mouthed landing net. For a really large salmon, you must rely on a gaff. In doing so, try to place its point beneath the salmon's head and lift quickly and steadily. If possible, avoid gaffing a salmon through the edible portion of his body, for this tends to ruin sound flesh by tearing it badly or causing bacteria to infect the tissues. These fish begin spoiling soon after being killed, so you should dress and clean them while you are still out in the boat, or as soon as you have returned to the dock. Wash away all slime and blood in clear water, and wipe dry.

If you want to handle 40- to 60-pounders, your trolling tackle must be equal to the task. The rod must be capable of lifting and managing a fairly heavy line, and its tip must have evenly distributed power in order to con-

trol the bait or lure efficiently. For average conditions, many anglers like a
6½- to 7½-foot rod having a flexible tip section and straight butt. With
a rod of this sort you are able to hook more fish on the strike, and can
determine if the trolling speed is correct by watching the vibrations of the
rod tip. The rod should bend evenly under the pull of the salmon; it must
not be too light in the tip or it will be difficult to handle large fish. When
trolling in the tidal portions of rivers, some fishermen use a 6-foot steel
rod.

Your rod should have a sturdy sea reel with star drag. The reel should
hold 150 to 200 yards of waterproof braided nylon or dacron, having a
test ranging from 36 to 54 pounds. You may also use 150 yards of copper
or Monel metal wire line.

In certain areas there is a practice of adding a length of line directly to
the spool, as a backing line, then attaching about three hundred feet of
wire, and to this tying twenty or twenty-five feet of 45-pound test nylon
or dacron line. At the end of this is tied a swivel, connected by a double
loop to a 6-foot No. 4, 5, or 6 stainless-steel wire leader—about 45-pound
test being the popular size and strength—followed by a snap swivel or a
double loop and the lure. For the braided synthetic line rig, you will need
slip sinkers two to sixteen ounces in weight. The size of the sinkers to be
added varies according to the water depth, the force of the current, and the
time of day. Where the tide is strong, fasten your sinker ten or twelve feet
ahead of the lure, especially if it is a plug, for this aids in steadying it.
Under normal currents, though, the sinker should be fifteen to eighteen feet
ahead of the plug.

The type of lure to be tried depends on the current, the depth of the
water, and the species of salmon you are seeking. As a case in point, both
young and adult kings seem to favor attractors that move slowly, while
silvers prefer those that are fast-twirling. For this reason, the "spinner"
type of spoon is often used when trolling for silvers, and the wobbler model
for kings. In many regions, among the best salmon getters are spoons or
wobblers in nickel, chrome, and brass finishes; and combinations of these
with copper work well on certain occasions. You should tuck a can of
metal polish and a piece of soft cloth into the tackle kit so that these metal
lures may be brightened whenever they begin to tarnish.

Some of the consistent winners in plugs of solid and jointed construction are those of large sizes that are white or red-and-white in color. Where
the water is clear the white plugs seem to excel, but for cloudy waters the
best plugs are often those with frog or herring-scale finishes. Besides the
ordinary herring, spoon, and plug lures, special adaptations are frequently
employed for greater eye-catching appeal. These are known as flashers and
dodgers, and are put to good account chiefly in Puget Sound. Their purpose
is to draw attention, thereby inciting the salmon into striking the bait or
lure which trails behind.

The flasher is a small piece of bright metal that is rigged together with a spoon or plug, and gets attention by its glittering effect as it whirls. It must be attached correctly so that it swings freely, or it will impair the action of the lure in spite of any speed at which you may troll.

A dodger is a rectangular strip of metal which entices salmon by its lively motion; it is shaped so that when towed rapidly it darts from side to side, yet does not turn over. The dodger is joined to the line by a swivel, and from the rear of this device there extends a stainless-steel leader (eighteen to thirty inches in length, depending on the size of your dodger) which connects with the herring bait. The herring is strung on a three-hook tandem rig, or a triple gang hook, so that it curves slightly, making the fish revolve when trolled. To prevent briny corrosion, a new leader should be attached at the outset of almost every trip, unless braided nylon material is used.

Considerable care must be taken to clamp your slip sinker at the proper distance up the line, for this determines the degree the flasher or dodger will swing and sway. You move the sinker back and forth until you've hit upon the exact spot for the amount of movement desired. This is usually about six feet up the line if you intend to troll at a fast pace, and a couple of feet ahead of the flasher or dodger if you plan to move slowly.

If you place the sinker near the dodger, it will dart faster than when you put the lead farther away. But with a flasher, you move the sinker closer if it is lurching too widely, so as to reduce the span of its orbit.

When you reach the fishing grounds and start to pay out line, hold the dodger and herring nearby for a minute or so and watch them as the boat slips along. You can guage by their movements of each, in relation to the oscillation of your rod tip, just how fast you should troll. Then let the lure drop back to the distance and depth desired, and keep watch on the rod tip to maintain the right speed. Since the rapidity with which you troll greatly affects the success of your efforts, you should pay particular attention to this factor when using either spoon or plug. By and large, a plug (suitably joined to the leader) brings better luck when it weaves along at a fair clip, while a spoon should turn at a moderate rate only, and a wobbler should just wobble—not revolve. You hold steady to the speed required by observing the vibrations of the rod tip—counting the beats per minute, if necessary—and by rowing or operating the outboard motor accordingly.

During the time that spawning-bent kings and silvers are in the shallower water by the river mouths, most anglers find it more expedient to troll a spoon, plug, or herring without benefit of flasher or dodger. In this case, they fasten the slip sinker fifteen feet or more up the line from the leader, to lessen interference with the bait or lure and ensure smoother action.

California White Sea Bass

The white sea bass rank high on the list of the more important game fish of the Pacific Coast. They can be found from Vancouver Island to Lower California and are one of the major game species from Santa Barbara to Mexico. Their average size is twenty to thirty pounds. It is best to fish for them early in the morning, toward evening, or at night. At night they feed near the surface, while during the daytime you often have to fish deep for them.

Though California white sea bass are taken by a number of different fishing methods, trolling around inshore kelp fields or offshore island seaweed areas is the most popular method, since these fish live in and under these beds. For this type of fishing, a very sporty outfit is the 6/9; or you may choose a boat rod with a 9-ounce tip and 4/0 free-spool reel filled with three hundred yards of 45-pound test. Hooks of sizes 4/0 to 6/0 will meet average trolling requirements. Also use a 3-foot wire leader; it gives better results than synthetic.

Long-line trolling should be done at a slow speed (about three miles per hour or less) while skirting kelp beds and islands. Fish can be coaxed into a striking mood by being chummed heavily with sardines and anchovies. White sea bass are reluctant to attack objects that move swiftly, so the most effective lures are spoons, metal squids, feather jigs, underwater plugs, and strip baits that travel at a leisurely pace, a foot or two above the bottom. Some of these lures, particularly jigs and plugs, are trolled at night with good success. Anglers have often taken sizable white sea bass on June and July nights, under the full moon, trolling from skiffs out of Avalon. Their baits have usually been small flying fish or large sardines.

California corbina are found from the Gulf of California to Point Conception, and at times as far north as San Francisco. They are available all year, but summer offers the greatest inducement for gathering up your tackle and forsaking the household. When trolling for this fish, use the same technique and tackle as for the California white sea bass.

Tarpon

Although he may roam as far north as Nova Scotia, the tarpon (or silver king and sabalo, as he is also called) is a warm-water fish that is more plentiful off Cape Hatteras, and most abundant on both coasts of Florida, on the Gulf of Mexico, and among the West Indies. They prefer shallow waters where there are channels, passes, tideways, bays, coves, and rivers. These fish have coarse and unsavory flesh, but their renowned fighting spirit more than makes up for what they lack in flavor. Most fish are returned to the water, unless they are to be kept for mounting or to be photographed, or have been badly injured. Tarpon average sixty to seventy pounds, but there are portly ones going better than two hundred pounds. To figure out the weight of your captive in pounds, here is the formula: Multiply the square of the girth at the thickest point (in inches) by the length (in inches) from point of mouth to crotch of tail, and divide by 800.

Tarpon are strange and interesting fish in several respects. They can remain a long time in fresh water, far up tidal rivers, where they move in schools and approach bait in a sideways roll that makes it difficult for anglers to catch them unless a fast-sinking lure is rested on the bottom and inched along at frequent intervals. However, if the tarpon are gathering up small fish close to the surface, they may be induced to accept surface or shallow-running lures.

Night and early morning are the best times to be out with rod and reel. From the turn of low tide to the crest of the flood tarpon slip through the shallow areas tracking down their food. They often feed when the surface is lit by the moon (you will see this from new to full moon), but for the most part they are attracted to lures when the nights are dark. Indeed, in almost any place where these fish roam they may be captured by more different methods than any other of the big-game ocean nomads. You can plug and fly cast, troll with live or artificial baits, still-fish on the bottom with dead or live baits, drift-fish, or troll a short distance below the surface with dead baits or deep-running plugs.

One of the most popular ways of dealing with tarpon is trolling from a power boat at a comparatively slow speed (two to four miles per hour), with about 150 feet of line out. Cut mullet, a whole baitfish, a spoon, or a feathered jig is generally used. Some anglers, however, have found that it may be better to troll a spoon at only about thirty to forty feet from the boat, moving slightly faster than the normal rate when towing fresh bait. Remember that tarpon are slow strikers, and for this reason slow trolling is generally better.

Tarpon have hard, bony mouths, making it essential to give a powerful jerk to drive the hook home. They may hook themselves by the force of their strike, but usually a stiff yank is required. Your rod is held almost parallel to the water so that on the first strike you will have enough upward swing to set the hook, and can also resist the fish's frequent jumps by pulling hard and keeping the line taut. Be sure that the line is tight every moment.

As soon as a tarpon feels the barb he darts for the surface and springs into the air, shaking his head violently. It is a fairly safe bet that he'll throw the hook after the first or second leap, but if he is still connected on the third bound you have a chance of winning. At times he slides along the surface in his impulsive rushes, head fluttering briskly, and you hold on for all you're worth. It's fast and furious work, and you don't dare relax for a second. When hooked inside the mouth with a plug, a tarpon will "blow his top," making several rapid-fire leaps in the same spot in his frenzied efforts to snap the lure out. His gill covers may even rattle, and his sides will quiver in a blur of motion. A tarpon is never licked until he has made his last wiggle after a long and tiring struggle. You should not risk bringing a large one to the boat unless he is whipped into meek submission.

If possible haul him over the gunwale without resorting to a gaff, for you will want to release him.

Skilled trollers often use the 6/9 outfit, or a light rig made up of a 5-foot rod with 6-ounce tip, and 27- or 36-pound line, for the average-sized fish; or a medium outfit consisting of a rod with 9-ounce tip and 54-pound test line for the larger tarpon. The novice would be wise to employ the so-called "heavy" gear that includes a 12- or 16-ounce rod tip and 72-pound line. The reel should be size 2/0 to 6/0, balancing the particular rod to which it will be attached, and be capable of holding 250 to 400 yards of line. You will want a leader of No. 9 stainless-steel wire six feet or more in length, to make allowances for the tarpon's habit of rolling. This wire protects the line from fraying when in contact with the tarpon's large scales. A 1/0 or 2/0 barrel swivel should be fastened to the leader. For trolling with live bait or strip bait, and for still-fishing, you can use O'Shaughnessy hooks of sizes 7/0 to 11/0, in tinned finish.

Snook (*Robalo*)

Snook wage a truly rough battle. They will seize nearly any trolled lure with a viciousness that shakes you, then speed off on rip-roaring runs, making fancy leaps and savage lunges until you wonder if they'll ever quit. Generally, the best times to have an argument with these fish are at just about daylight and again in late evening. Many are caught after dark, when they are especially agreeable about snatching trolled lures.

These temperamental rascals patrol the entire coast of Florida, but are most abundant in the southern portion. The Ten Thousand Island region is particularly noted for snook. Snook also are captured all along the Gulf of Mexico shore line, and are one of the most important sport fishes in this part of their realm. In the Port Isabel section of Texas they are taken in good numbers in summer and winter alike. You will connect with them wherever there are beaches, coves, and inlets. Often they invade the tidal rivers of the Gulf, but seldom go above brackish water. Averaging about five pounds, there are hefty fellows weighing up to fifty pounds, so you always have the possibility of sparring with an old-timer who'll give you a real workout. Large snook often come inshore, where much of the fishing is done.

For trolling, your rate of speed should be very slow and you may use either the light 3/6 tackle outfit, or a stiff-action salt-water casting rod 5½ feet in length. If your weapon is the casting rod, fit it with a level winding bait casting reel of 100-yard line capacity and 18-pound-test casting line, or a reel of 150-yard capacity and 27- to 36-pound-test line. Even though snook lack teeth, you should always tie on a light wire leader twelve inches long for trolling because their sharp-edged gill covers can sever a line quickly. You might round out this gear with 3/0 or 4/0 hooks of O'Shaughnessy style, or 5/0 or 6/0 Carlisle hooks, with shrimps, crabs, or small fish for live bait. Both deep-running plugs and surface plugs, as well as spoons, feathered jigs, and spinners, may also be used.

Offshore Species

The term inshore fishing implies that the angler is fishing a reasonable distance from the shore (generally in bays, inlets, and sounds). Offshore fishing means that the angler is fishing a mile or more away from the shore. But it's impossible to make a hard-and-fast distinction between inshore and offshore fish. Many of the fish described as inshore species can be found offshore, and the opposite also holds true. The fish we call offshore species are merely those generally found offshore.

School Tuna

While the giant tuna make the headlines, it is the school tuna, five to seventy pounds in weight, that are the average angler's fare. These bluefins and yellowfins give thousands of sportsmen a scaled-down version of big-game fishing. Except in size, school tuna lack none of the qualities of their parents, the giant tuna. They are found in the same spots as their parents (page 180), but usually arrive a month or so earlier than the big fellows.

Finding tuna is no cinch. They are constantly on the go, and travel far and fast. Some days they may be close to shore, at other times well beyond the horizon. In the old days a skipper would find the fish and keep it a secret. Now there is more cooperation; a skipper lets other boats know about his find over a ship-to-ship radiophone, and everyone nearby gets in on the kill.

One of the most reliable indicators of the presence of school tuna are the pigeon-sized birds known as Mother Carey's chickens. These little birds can be seen fluttering over schools of tuna, picking up scraps of baitfish. At other times the school tuna will be seen leaping from wave to wave, like so many tinsel Christmas tree ornaments. Other indications of the presence of school tuna are large red jellyfish and floating sargassum weed. Tuna prefer water temperature from 63 to 68 degrees.

Trolling is the method for taking these "junior torpedoes," but there are

special techniques. The boat must be run considerably faster than for most species—seven to ten miles per hour is right. An extremely important point is to troll the lure very close to the boat. The schoolies are attracted by the commotion of the wake and the flashing prop. The usual plan is to troll four lines. Two are fifteen to eighteen feet behind the boat. The third is about twenty-five feet, and the "long" line trails fifty feet behind. The short lines usually see most action. If three or four lures are struck simultaneously, the last fish should be played, and not boated, because tuna will follow a hooked fish right to the boat, and a hooked tuna in the water serves as a living decoy.

These lusty fellows will hit with a jolt and probably will hook themselves, but usually it is wise to lean back quickly to make certain the fish is connected. The star drag should be set on the light side and not "pressured" until the fish has had its first run. It is not unusual for a big one—a 40-pounder—to run off four hundred yards of line in a few seconds. Novices often get "tuna fever" and jam their drags on hard when the fish strikes—which means the end of the fish lure, some line, and maybe a rod tip.

You will have a rough fight, for after going on a long race the fish will sound and put up a stiff resistance in the depths. Keep the rod tip fairly high while the tuna is peeling off line; then when he begins to rest you must start the pumping and reeling process at once. Apply pressure with the star drag gently but firmly. When finally you have him near the boat he will make another powerful run and head for the deep, although not going as far down this time. When his run is ended, pump him to the surface again and bring him close to the stern. When he turns on his side you know he is beaten. Reel him in gingerly until one of the boatmen can grab hold of your leader, then ease up on the drag in case the fish makes a sudden recovery and lunges before he is gaffed.

In selecting tackle for school tuna, experience indicates that normal requirements are adequately met by: a trolling rod with a 5- or 5½-foot tip weighing nine to fourteen ounces. The expert may use a 6- or 8-ounce tip, but the novice should rely on a 12- or 14-ounce rod tip for greater safety. The rod butt may measure twenty-one to twenty-four inches. For a reel, the beginner may equip himself with a size 4/0 or 6/0, filled with about five hundred yards of 45 or 50 test line or three hundred yards of 63 or 72 test line. The seasoned angler may prefer a real holding three hundred yards of 27 or 36 test line. Tuna fishing with lines lighter than 27-pound test is "stunt" fishing. It is loads of fun, but unless the entire party uses ultralight gear, the boat will be tied up with one fish for as long as an hour. The other anglers will just be standing by while the fish is fought and landed because trolling cannot be continued while a fish is being caught.

In trolling for school tuna, only the last ten feet of the line need be doubled; your leader may be ten to fifteen feet of piano wire. You should have a supply of these leaders, brass box swivels, O'Shaughnessy hooks in sizes 6/0 to 8/0, and a wire cutter. For lures you may try metal or wooden squids with pork rind attached, spoons, eelskin mounted on the regular two-hook rig, or cut bait such as strips of menhaden or herring. Two old-time lures, however, still lead the list for school tuna: the Japanese feather and the cedar jig. The jig is generally unpainted. White or red-and-white are the most popular colors in feather jigs. Nylon jigs are also now widely used. With your choice of this gear, you may troll along the offshore banks and treat yourself to the very finest sport which light tackle and vigorous school tuna can afford.

Bluefish

Bluefish can be taken offshore as well as inshore (see Chapter 5) and from the surf (Chapter 6). These strong, swift-running rogues beleaguer the baitfish all the way from the Gulf of Mexico (where bait casting, trolling, and still-fishing are done with plugs, spoons, and live shrimps from about March or April into September) to the vicinity of Penobscot Bay, Maine. In the fall they gather in mass formations off New Jersey, Virginia, and the Carolinas, and swarm over the coastal waters of Florida.

In fishing for bluefish, which are known to have a ravenous appetite and a lust to kill, observe the gulls that gather over the water where blues are feeding. They are watching for the small particles of herring, mullet, butterfish, sand eels, and other baitfish that will float to the surface. These bits of slaughtered baitfish create an oily slick that signifies fish feeding in that vicinity. Actually one of the best methods of attracting bluefish when either trolling or still-fishing for them offshore is to create an oily slick by chumming with ground-up menhaden or herring. You dribble this oily mess over the stern of your boat until a slick has resulted, then you put a piece of menhaden on the hook and "float fish" it back in the slick. When the bluefish strikes, you must avoid letting any slack line occur, even for an instant. The fish will break water and jump repeatedly, giving you all the ruction you can manage, so any slack line will be fatal. Keep him on the prod, and tire him out before you try to haul your prize over the gunwale.

If you troll toward a school of blues that doesn't need to be chummed to incite action, stay along the edges of the school. If you frighten them by powering through the milling fish, they will sound. After boating a few of these savory cutthroats, you will notice that fish of practically the same size travel together in each school. Offshore you may snag into 10- and 15-pounders, or even up to twenty-five pounds, but inshore their average weight is two to five pounds. When trolling, it is best to use long lines—seventy-five to a hundred feet from the boat.

A 6/9 tackle outfit is satisfactory for trolling. For either trolling or still-fishing, however, many anglers like a boat rod having a 4-ounce tip section, together with a 2/0 or 3/0 multiplying reel holding 150 yards of 27 or 36 test line, and O'Shaughnessy hooks of 3/0 to 6/0 sizes in the tinned finish. A wire leader from one to three feet in length, in about No. 7 size, is a requisite for any method of fishing for blues. Artificial lures such as metal squids, Japanese feather or nylon jigs, small plugs, and spoons are very effective when trolling. Natural baits such as sand eels, whole or cut mullet, strips from menhaden, and pork chunks are also good.

When school bluefish have been forced down by having boats cutting through their schools, a good method is to drop a cup of oil on the surface of the water where the fish were last seen and wait until the other boats seek a more productive area. The oil will cover a very large area and will mark the spot where the fish should be. Start up your motors and head into the wind to the outer edge of the spot you have marked. Cut the motors and drift over this area. This is where jigging (page 106) pays off. Use a hand line and a heavy bright metal squid. This lure is allowed to strike the bottom and, as the drifting boat takes up the slack in the line, the lure is retrieved by a hand-over-hand method. Usually when the squid moves five or six feet from the bottom the bluefish will strike. Jigging may also be done from an anchored boat if you know where the fish are.

Mackerel

Mackerel and their kin are easily recognized by their deeply forked tail, which narrows greatly as it joins the body. Both dorsal and anal fins have small finlets behind them; and, finally, mackerel all have a sleek, streamlined form with smooth, almost scaleless skin. Their irridescence makes them more attractive than many other species. These swift fish usually travel in schools, which migrate widely. They live along shore and far out at sea. For the offshore angler, the more important species are: Atlantic mackerel, chub mackerel, king mackerel, Pacific mackerel, and Spanish mackerel.

Averaging about two pounds, but occasionally reaching eight pounds, the Atlantic mackerel are speedy swimmers that travel in large schools on forays for minnows to appease their ravenous appetite. At times the surface of the water may boil up violently as a great horde of mackerel sweeps through a cluster of baitfish and riddles their numbers. Small menhaden, herring, and mullet are particular favorites, but squids, crabs, and shrimps will also not escape them.

You will find the Atlantic mackerel off Cape Hatteras around the middle of March or in April, and they steer a northern course along the offshore pathways to appear in New England waters during May. Huge schools of them spend much of their time in deep water from Long Island to the Gulf of Saint Lawrence, and may be taken on most any tide. Your best catches will be made from July to late September.

Since Atlantic mackerel keep much to the offshore waters, trolling is the surest way of taking them. The tackle for this job comprises a salt-water trolling rod with a 5-foot tip section weighing four ounces, a 2/0 or 3/0 free-spool reel, 350 yards of 20-pound test monofilament line (mackerel are line-shy, as evidenced by the fact that fine monofilament will outfish more visible lines), No. 5 wire or monofilament leader three feet in length, and feathered jigs, metal squids, and plugs with 2/0 to 4/0 hooks. Chumming with ground bunker not only keeps the school around but makes the fish less choosy. Long-line trolling is a good idea when trolling for mackerel.

When the Atlantic mackerel come inshore for a change of diet, you may have a lot of sport with them in the bays and at the edges of bars by casting out small bright plugs, feathered jigs, spoons, or metal squids. You use a regular 5- or 5½-foot fresh-water bait-casting rod, a level-winding reel holding one hundred yards of line, a leader of thin wire, braided gut, or monofilament one foot long, and a lure. A spinning or fly rod will also give fine sport. If you are spin or bait casting from a boat, don't let your craft move over a school of mackerel, but circle the fish and cast in among them. It doesn't take much disturbance to send these streamlined sleuths hightailing for the depths.

Mackerel will clamp down hard on the lure and start off on a long swift run, and you must play them cautiously—giving and taking line quickly—until they are fagged out and come meekly to your net.

The chub mackerel weighs on the average somewhat less than the Atlantic mackerel and is found from the Gulf of Saint Lawrence to New Jersey—occasionally as far south as Virginia. The "chub" is often found with Atlantic mackerel and is taken in the same manner.

The Spanish mackerel is, like others of this family, a superior food fish, a smashing striker, and a great fighter. They will rush for almost any bait that is trolled or cast, being voracious eaters and living close to the surface. Moving in schools offshore, they may be spotted while chasing food by their leaps from the surface and by the excited cries of the terns. Mullet, menhaden, and silversides form the bulk of the rations consumed by the Spanish mackerel. Occasionally they come close inshore and at such times offer good sport for the jetty and pier angler.

In the spring their northern migration brings them to North Carolina during April, and to the lower Chesapeake Bay by May or June. They may be seen as far north as Maine with favorable water temperatures, but their principal habitat is the warmer climes of the south. Fine specimens are taken from New Jersey to Texas, with most being caught around Florida from November through March. They range from one to three pounds on the average, but some reach twenty pounds.

Trolling and bait casting, with the tackle mentioned for the Atlantic mackerel, are the two most popular methods of hanging up the spotted Spanish warrior. Black-tin squids, small spoons, feathered jigs, plugs, and bucktail flies are successful artificials to use, with shrimps and small fish the best in live baits. Whenever you come upon a group of Spanish mackerel feeding at the surface, spin casting with plugs or flies into their midst will afford some fast fishing. You must remember that these fish are speedy strikers, so your lure should be worked through the water in a rapid fashion. Playing one of these fellows on a light casting outfit is a thrill, for he is swifter than a redfish and gives a spectacular initial run.

The Pacific mackerel is the only representative of the mackerel family in the Pacific. They are found from northwestern Alaska to Cape San Lucas and the Gulf of California. They spawn chiefly in the area from San Diego to Santa Barbara. The Pacific mackerel is slightly heavier than its eastern cousin—the Atlantic mackerel—and is caught by casting, trolling, and still-fishing, using live or cut bait, shrimps, clams, or pile worms on the same tackle as for the Atlantic species. They also may be taken on metal squids, small spoons, feathered jigs, bucktail flies, and plugs, either trolled or cast.

The biggest of this species is the king mackerel—also known as cero, cavalla, and kingfish. They are prized as a food delicacy, and average around ten pounds in weight. They travel in extensive schools hunting for bloodworms, sand worms, sardines, mullet, clams, squids, and menhaden. Generally king mackerel prefer to pause in the deeper water just beyond the bars and reefs. You will meet them from Texas to Cape Cod, but they congregate in vast numbers off the coasts of North Carolina, South Carolina, Georgia, and Florida. In this region you can make fine catches from November to March.

For the most part, this mackerel is brought to terms by trolling. Live minnows, strip bait, metal squids, drone-type spoons, feathered jigs, and giant plugs, with 6/0 or 7/0 hooks, are all good lures. An expert angler would likely be satisfied with the 4/6 tackle outfit, but the inexperienced fisherman would do better using a 6/9 outfit, or a trolling rod with 6-ounce tip, 2/0 or 3/0 reel, 27- or 36-pound test line, and a steel wire leader six or nine feet long. Troll at moderate speed, and sink the barb solidly when a king strikes. Often, though, the very force of his rush will set the hook, leaving you with the difficult problem of taming a wild actor. In striking a trolled lure, a king mackerel will frequently leap fifteen or more feet into the air.

Wahoo

Angling authorities place the wahoo among the world's top ten marine game fish, Two outstanding characteristics account for this rating. One is the shoulder-jarring power of the wahoo's strike; the second is the sizzling speed of its runs. It has been said of this fish that it packs the wallop of a heavyweight fighter and the shifty speed of a featherweight boxer. Anglers equipped with a timing device have clocked the wahoo at speeds in excess of forty miles an hour.

If you are using a small baitfish, strip bait, a feathered jig, a spoon, or a large plug, it is likely to be nabbed by a wahoo. You will have to keep a fairly stiff drag, yet let him race at random. Averaging about twenty pounds in weight, the wahoo sometimes goes over a hundred pounds, and is considered to be very fine food. The wahoo is a lone traveler, and is most in evidence during the winter and spring.

Wahoo lurk in the deep water of the warm Gulf Stream from the Florida Keys and up the eastern coast to North Carolina, and are taken at various points offshore from the west coast of Florida. In the region of the Keys they are often hooked from January through July, and they are present in good numbers off Bermuda and in the West Indies. Generally they move along the outer edges of the reefs where drop-offs occur, in search of small fish. The natural baits that prove tempting to sailfish will take the wahoo, for these two species compete for food in the same areas; both may be caught trolling with either baitfish or spoons and feathered jigs.

Your sailfish tackle is also entirely suitable for fetching the wahoo aboard by long-line angling. A 5-foot rod with 9-ounce tip, fitted with a 6/0 reel and four hundred yards of 54-pound test line, meets the favor of many sportsmen. A 10-foot stainless-steel wire leader must always be used as a safeguard against the knifelike teeth of the wahoo.

Bonito and Albacore

These speedy fish—like the wahoo—are large members of the mackerel family. Several species of bonito and albacore are found in United States waters. Atlantic bonito make the coastal stretch between Cape Ann, Massachusetts, and Florida their principal parade grounds, but sometimes a few straggle up to Nova Scotia. The California bonito, the Pacific member of the family, ranges from Mexican waters to Vancouver Island, but is not common north of Point Conception. The skipjack or oceanic bonito prefer the warmer waters along both the Atlantic and Pacific coasts. The Pacific albacore is found from Alaska to lower California, while the false albacore (blackfin tuna) frequents the Atlantic from Cape Cod south to tropical waters. Other closely related species are seen in other parts of the world.

These fish roam the offshore waters in large groups, coming close to shore only for spawning or chasing baitfish. While bonito and albacore are not generally fished, they are often caught while trolling or chumming for other offshore species. Many are caught by trollers seeking school tuna, since small jigs and high trolling speed are ideal for them. Very much like tuna in habits, they are also attracted by the wake of the boat. Marlin fishermen cuss them out for ruining expensive and hard-to-make marlin whole fish or squid baits.

Most of your clashes with albacore and bonito will occur when you troll along the deeper side of the shelf marking the inshore shallows where other and larger game fish abound. For this reason you should handle tackle that is heavier than that necessary for fighting bonito alone; you many snag a portly, vicious battler such as a tuna. A 6/9 tackle outfit is recommended under most conditions.

Remember that bonito are especially fast and make diagonal runs along the surface. Frequently, when a school shows up, all lines will be filled at once, and the excited anglers are hard pressed to keep lines from crossing. These fish don't jump, but they know all the other tricks. Albacore fight much like tuna, making a long run and then sounding at the end of it.

However, if you are an experienced salt-water fisherman, and make a point of dealing only with a foraging school of bonito and albacore, then you'll have much greater satisfaction in bucking the rugged performance of these fish on the lighter 4/6 outfit. In either case, the lures to offer include feathered jigs, metal squids, spoons, giant deep-running plugs, wobblers, and strip baits cut from baitfish. They also take whole or cut mullet, menhaden, butterfish, herring, sardines, anchovies, and silversides. Live sardines and anchovies are also used. For most fishing, hooks from 2/0 to 9/0 are used, but when fishing in clear water with live baits, small No. 2 or 3 hooks may be needed. Since bonito and albacore have sharp, strong teeth, you must tie on a No. 8 or 9 stainless-steel wire leader of six to nine feet in length.

Bonito and albacore like fast-moving lures. Average trolling speed is seven to eight miles per hour and lures should be offered close to the stern—from twenty to thirty feet. Many anglers swear by the crest of the second wave in the wake as exactly the right spot. If spoons are used, which many sport fishermen prefer, slow down to five or six miles to minimize the whirling action of the spoon. The double-tapered squid spoon is popular for these fish—and do not fail to use swivels or your line will tie in knots.

Both species are often seen jumping clear of the water as they chase bait, at which time they are reluctant to take a hook. When they "push water"—cruise just under the surface with their fins showing—that's when they'll take hold. The spin fisherman gets his fish by casting a spoon from the bow or cabin roof, and letting it drift back into the school. A bright spoon will do. As the boat passes, the "pushing" fish will sink, and then the action starts. They take the lure with a lunge and keep right on going at top speed.

In the Atlantic bonito and albacore can also be taken by chumming with ground bunker. When they come close to the anchored boat, a hook baited with a piece of bunker, or butterfish or a whole silversides is drifted out in the chum slick. Occasionally, albacore will appear in the chum slick and refuse the bait, although they can be seen feeding on loose chum. One trick that may work is to bait a small hook with several bunker hearts. The fish seem to prefer this to other portions of the bait. For Pacific albacore, live sardines or anchovies are thrown into the water for chum, and hooks baited with these same live baitfish are used.

Cobia, in some localities called the black bonito, are taken from May to November in the lower Chesapeake Bay, and in Florida during the winter. These fish run up to fifty pounds. While primarily bottom-dwelling fish, they will strike at deeply trolled metal squid, plug, or feather lure. When still-fishing, use crabs or shrimp and the bottom rig described in Chapter 5. A 6-ounce tip, 27 test line, a 6-foot wire leader, and a 6/0 hook make a good outfit for this fish.

Dolphin

Among the game fish that slip through the Gulf of Mexico and along the Atlantic Coast, dolphin are one of the most prized and beautiful. They are characterized by a steep facial profile, a long ventral fin, and a very long dorsal fin that begins on top of the head and ends near the base of the deeply forked tail. The dolphin can change color quickly, but there are always flashes of green, yellow, and purplish blue, together with dark spots lining his sides. They are fleet-finned swimmers, bold fighters, and amazing leapers, and travel both alone and in schools.

These fine-flavored streamlined fish are an oceanic wonder, widely distributed, abundant from Texas to North Carolina. From June through September, in particular, many are caught from such places as Port Isabel, Velasco, Matagorda, Biloxi, and Pascagoula in the deeper waters, although in early summer large schools of young dolphin may be seen a short distance from land. Dolphin parade along both coasts of Florida, and sometimes they reach the New England coasts, but they perfer the warmer waters and seldom stray north of Virginia. They are occasionally reported along the Pacific Coast, too, especially in the Catalina Island area. The largest specimens weigh around sixty pounds, but the average size runs three to ten pounds. The big fellows usually are lone wolves or go in pairs, while the young ones travel in gangs. Sometimes the schools stretch out for miles.

Wherever flying fish are plentiful you'll find dolphin, for they are avaricious for this choice food. Balaos, mullets, and other small fish make up the rest of their diet. Offshore trolling catches most dolphins. They are brought to a "photo" finish by means of live baits of the fish mentioned, or by offering feather lures, spoons, plugs, jigs, metal squids, and strip baits.

While they are not particular about what they hit, dolphin prefer a fast-trolled bait. Like albacore and bonito, they are attracted by the commotion of a propeller and come right up into the churn. That is where lures or baits are offered—from fifteen to thirty feet off the boat. In the more northern waters, these colorful "dorados" are usually caught by anglers trolling for school tuna. In the region of Florida where dolphin are caught the year around, fisherman frequently take them while trolling for sailfish.

Like tuna, albacore, and bonito, dolphin follow a fish being played, then disappear when the fish is boated. Apparently they are curious to see what is causing the unusual behavior of their kinsman and to learn if there is something good to eat in the offing. By playing a hooked dolphin for some time before pulling him in, others are encouraged to hang around long enough so that every angler in the boat has a chance to snag into some fun. The strategy is to tussle with your fish, or hitch him behind the boat, until someone hooks another, then land him and get your trolling gear right back in the water. Often several sizable beauties are hung up in this manner. At the same time, while the fish are in a cluster near the boat, it is possible to have some rare sport by using a bait-casting or fly-fishing rig and sending plugs, spoons, or streamer flies into their midst. If you are jigging strip baits, then it's advisable to give a short drop-back before setting the hook.

Since most dolphin are caught by anglers trolling for bigger game fish with comparatively heavy tackle, too few sportsmen know the thrills they are missing by not using really light tackle. A 4/6 tackle outfit is satisfactory for even the larger specimens, with about four hundred yards of 18-pound test line on a size 2/0 or 3/0 reel. A 27 test line is sufficient to cope with the heaviest dolphin. Many of these fish have been landed on spinning gear. This tackle is especially appropriate when the fish are milling around one of their hooked brethren. Any lure with a short wire leader will do. On spinning tackle, dolphin run and leap wildly, but they do not go straight off in one direction. For this reason, there is little danger of running out of line. Often, when a leaping dolphin throws the lure, another will seize it the instant it hits the water, and the fight begins anew. Action may continue for hours.

Jack crevallé

The common jack crevallé are good food fish that stray as far north as Massachusetts and Oregon, but make their chief sea sites from Georgia and the Gulf of California south through the tropics, the West Indies, and the Gulf of Mexico. In these southern regions they are most in evidence during the winter months, although they will grab live baits or artificial lures at almost any time of the year. Around Texas, jack crevallé are usually caught from about mid-April into September. You can fish them from jetties or in the open Gulf, using shrimps, spoons, and plugs.

Crevallé crave mullet and smaller fish for their regular diet, as well as crabs and the ubiquitous shrimp. You can also get their ready cooperation by trolling or casting feathered jigs, metal squids, plugs, and spoons. When hooked, they give you a rigorous, stubborn battle punctuated with sharp lunges and swift runs. There is no horsing around with even an average-sized 2 or 3 pound crevallé, and these fellows sometimes go better than 20 pounds. If you should snag into an ordinary jack on a bait-casting rig, you'll be amazed at the long, tough fight that such a small fish can wage. The encounter may last for more than fifteen minutes, leaving you with a decidedly sound respect for the artful crevallé. He just will not quit until the last flicker of strength has been spent. You can use the same casting tackle as suggested for pompano on page 219.

The crevallé wiggles his way around docks, pilings, and bridges, and pokes about sheltered coves and inlets; but he also ventures into the deeper waters offshore. The larger specimens tour outward in small groups, and these will be yours by trolling. For these bigger fish, you will need tackle that is heavier than the bait-casting rig mentioned above, for a sizable crevallé can quickly wreck such light gear. To meet all situations successfully, your safest plan would be to use the regular 6/9 trolling outfit. By doing so, you would be prepared to subdue the most obstreperous crevallé, or any other fighting fish that you might hook along the drop-offs. For this sport, your lures should be giant plugs, feather jigs, or strip bait.

Roosterfish

Except for the long, almost filamentlike spines protruding from its dorsal fins (somewhat resembling a rooster's comb) the roosterfish would probably be grouped with the crevallé, so similar are they in other characteristics. Found only on the lower Pacific Coast, they attain their greatest size (up to eighty pounds in weight) in and around the Gulf of California. They are usually taken between July and December.

Swimming close inshore or by offshore islands or bars, the roosterfish is quick to strike a feather lure, spoon, or cut bait that is trolled slowly over a sandy bottom. When linked to an 18 or 27 test line (200 to 250 feet in length) and a 6-ounce rod tip, he speeds off on a run similar to that of a dolphin.

Occasionally he makes a jump, but for the most part his fight is beneath the surface, with many great sweeps and powerful rushes. When he comes within sight of the boat he really cuts loose, and must be allowed to race against a tight line until his energies have been sapped. One of the roosterfish's traits is that on some days they are in a feverish striking mood, and you never lack for action, and then there are other days when the roosterfish seem apathetic or are off their feed.

Amberjack

These sizable, powerful fish also are part of the crevallé family. They have a reputation for making long, sweeping runs, for tugging strenuously, and for shooting bottomward when clinched by the hook. Their average weight is around fifteen pounds, but overstuffed characters sag the scales at about one hundred pounds. They revel in the warm waters around Florida and the West Indies, but some of them check in at the Carolinas and a few fin their way farther north. They may mingle with other migrants off North Carolina from about June until early autumn.

When moving along the offshore reefs at a depth of twenty-five or thirty feet, they go singly or in small groups, and may be enticed to the surface by distributing small fish in the water. As soon as amberjack appear, you hook on the same kind of bait and cast it into the midst of the festivities. This is almost certain to stir up results. A big jack will surge forward, clamp his jaws over your bait, and make a beeline for the protection of the rocks. You let him race twenty or thirty feet, then give the hook-setting jerk that spurs him to frenzied efforts to break loose. For several minutes he will give you a hard time, for you have to be ever alert to guide him where he can't chafe your line or duck into some coral cavern. When at length he grows tired and you pull him near the boat, watch out for a final burst of action.

Winter and spring see the finest catches, and since these fish strike at various times throughout the day, the tides have little effect on your luck. Most amberjacks are brought to terms by means of trolling. You should use fairly heavy lines to counteract chafing, and to hold up against the pressure of steering large fish from dangerous rocky crevices. Their rushes and deep-sounding runs must be restrained deftly and promptly once they are hooked.

There is, of course, some latitude in the choice of tackle suitable for taking these fish. Your rod might well be a 6½-footer, with a tip section weighing nine to twelve ounces. This may be held by a leather rod butt rest, to ease your arms in gripping the rod for long intervals. You will want the best reel you can afford, of 4/0 to 6/0, holding 250 to 350 yards of 54- to 72-pound test line. A piano wire leader, or a No. 8 stainless-steel wire leader, nine feet in length, and O'Shaughnessy hooks in sizes 7/0 to 9/0 in the tinned finish, will also be needed. With this trolling outfit you may tease the amberjacks by tying on a feathered jig, a metal squid, a large spoon, a giant plug, or cut strip bait. However, live baits, such as small grunts or yellowtail snappers, are usually much more effective.

Barracuda

The great barracuda are the largest members of the barracuda family, which contains a dozen or so species. They are one of the most barbarous and feared of coastal fish since they attack nearly anything that moves in the water. In some respects they are considered more dangerous than shark, though the average weight only runs five to fifteen pounds. In the Atlantic, the range of the barracuda is from Brazil north to South Carolina, although a smaller species is found north of there. On the Pacific Coast is found the California barracuda which ranges from San Francisco down to Panama.

Along the outside reefs of Florida, specimens are usually bigger than those found around the inlets and bays, so that heavier tackle is required for deeper trolling. They swim close to the bottom, and frequently hide in

Barracuda, whether big or small, have mighty efficient dentures. They strike hard and have a bag of tricks which makes them worthy adversaries.

holes from where they dart out swiftly to attack small fish or baited hooks. The incoming tide is a good time to be out trolling, and you can use the same outfit and bait suggested for amberjack trolling.

Known in some places as "scooters," the slender, racy Pacific barracuda bully their way through the hordes of luckless baitfish from the Gulf of California up to Alaska. They seldom migrate to any great extent above Monterey Bay, but fair numbers occasionally besiege the shores of British Columbia from Juan de Fuca Strait to the Queen Charlotte Island and vicinity of Prince Rupert. For these and the small great 'cudas wandering inshore over the shoals, a rod with a 6-ounce tip is sturdy enough, together with a 4/0 reel holding two hundred yards of 36-pound test line. A No. 8 wire leader six to nine feet long, with a 1/0 barrel swivel at one end and a 7/0 or 8/0 O'Shaughnessy hook at the other—if you intend to troll with a strip of baitfish in back of a feather lure—will complete your needs.

There are several other species of fish that are occasionally taken by trolling—snappers, groupers, grunts, weakfish, pompano, permit (palometa), croakers, hakes, and jewfish. But since most of these fish are more often caught by other means, they are discussed in Chapters 5, 6 and 9. The big-game species are described in the next chapter.

CHAPTER 8

Big-Game Salt-Water Fishing

THE SEVERAL SPECIES which are considered as marine "big game" are fish of the open oceans. They require considerable expense in tackle and guide service to take successfully, but to those who have the opportunity and like to pit themselves against the most powerful of hook-and-line fishes, they provide the thrill of a lifetime.

While going after these big fellows is definitely luxury fishing, there is no reason to consider it exclusively a "rich man's sport." With the modern charter boat setup (see Chapter 10 for details), the captain will furnish the bait and will either loan or rent all the necessary tackle. With three or four anglers splitting the tab, the average angler can afford to splurge a few times a season. Try it and see.

Most big-game fishermen rent rather than own their tackle for this phase of angling. But if you desire to purchase big-game fish tackle, check the general recommendations in Chapter 2 and the specific information later in this chapter. As with any salt-water tackle, purchase the best you can afford. For example, it is highly important to have a reel of the finest quality, for the line can be torn off so swiftly on the strike that an inferior reel may readily be ruined. The size of the reel you use will determine, of course, the amount of line it can hold, according to the thickness of the line. However, from 500 to 1,000 yards of line is advisable. Line of 108 to 162 may be utilized with a 36-ounce rod tip, and 84 test line with a 23-ounce rod tip. Some anglers prefer a happy medium, and wind a 108 test line on a 12/0 or 14/0 reel with a 30-ounce rod tip. The 108 test line is a good size for most requirements. For the heaviest fish, in the 800- to

1,000-pound division, a 162 test line is considered by experienced anglers to be strong enough to battle the monarchs to submission when the playing and pumping is done with adequate care—and 108 test subdues 900-pounders in the Wedgeport tuna cup matches.

Be sure that any tackle you purchase meets with IGFA requirements just in case you land a record fish. Also be sure that your rig meets IGFA requirements (page 4). For instance, the leader and the double line on all weights of tackle up to and including the 50-pound line class must be limited to 15 feet of double line and 15 feet of leader. For heavier tackle, the line must not be double at the trace (leader) end for more than thirty feet and the trace must not exceed thirty feet. This doubling of line is "standard operating procedure" when dealing with all big-game species, particularly when trolling—the method generally used to take them. Make sure that the connecting hitch made to the eye of the leader swivel cannot slip. In attaching your line to the swivel, avoid tying a knot, for this will weaken the power of the line. The end of the line should be wrapped around the swivel ring three or four times, looped around the mainstem of the line several turns, and then passed back through the loops and drawn tight.

Double line at the end not only adds necessary strength, but also lets the angler and guide know when the fish is close and about ready for the gaff. It's always a thrill to see that double end come speeding to the rod tip, and a relief to feel that the long, exhausting conflict is over. That is, it's over unless the fish, frightened at sight of the boat, shows a sudden spurt of life and plunges for the depths again. In which event you would like to heave the whole outfit into the ocean!

To fight a big-game fish you will need some type of rod harness. This device is worn in order to transmit more muscular power to the rod and to absorb strain. And unless he is wearing a harness, an angler cannot let go of the rod or reel, even momentarily. The rod harness allows the angler to rest his arms when tired. It is made of canvas or leather and has adjustable straps with snaps that can be fastened to the rod or reel.

There are two acceptable kinds of harness used by most big-game anglers, the shoulder and the kidney types. The former resembles a vest and enables the angler to use his back and shoulders to better advantage when pumping a fish. The shoulder harness pulls from a point about two feet above the fishing chair. It is suitable for the smaller types of big-game fish. The kidney harness is roughly oval-shaped, approximately 3 feet long and 10 to 15 inches wide at the back, and is usually padded with sponge rubber. It fits against the small of the back and is worn like a belt. The kidney harness absorbs the strain at a point about halfway between the shoulders and the chair. While this type may not be as helpful to the angler in pumping a fish, it is less tiring to his shoulders and upper back muscles, and holds the rod and reel in position in the chair gimbal equally as well

The two most popular big-game fishing harnesses: kidney (*above*) and shoulder (*below*).

Successful game fishing begins with proper dockside preparations. Here the captain tests the heavy tackle and the girdle gimbal, or rod belt harness, before leaving the dock.

as a shoulder harness. The kidney type is often recommended for anglers below average weight, for women, and for those using tackle heavier than 108-pound test line.

When fishing for smaller-game fish, many anglers wear a girdle gimbal or rod belt in place of a harness. This device has a rod butt gimbal mounted in a sponge rubber padded belt-type waist harness and allows the angler to move around the cockpit of the boat, rather than remain seated in the fishing chair, when fighting a fish. It is extensively used by light tackle enthusiasts when fishing for game fish.

Most boats equipped to do big-game fishing have a "fighting" chair. This chair is generally used only after a fish is hooked, the anglers sitting in ordinary yacht chairs at the sides and forward end of the boat's cockpit until they receive a strike. When a big fish is hooked, the angler takes the chair, wearing his harness, and places the rod in the chair's gimbal or rod holder. All other anglers take in their lines so that the captain can devote his complete attention and boat-handling skill to the man in the fighting chair. This chair should be as comfortable as possible and be equipped with a solid foot brace. To avoid chair cramping, the chair should be so designed that the rod gimbal turns on or over the same center as the chair. The rod holder, in other words, should be directly above the center of the chair post. The chair post, in turn, should be mounted along the center line of the boat with sufficient room behind so the crew can help you land a big fish safely.

When battling any big-game fish, it is advisable to wear a pair of heavy cotton workman's gloves for protection against friction from handling the rod for hours. The gloves are also necessary in "bulldogging" a big fish. In this technique, you not only hold the fish by means of the star drag, but also by gripping the line with one gloved hand and pulling it outward between the reel and the first butt guide. This stunt is often done by big-game anglers when wrestling with huge bluefin tuna, marlin, or swordfish. Do not let your victim rest when doing any big-game fishing (actually this is true for any angling), but keep him on the prod. And get him thoroughly tired out before reeling him close enough to be boated.

There are not many species of big-game fish, but the few with which the sport fisherman does big business are the very best of what the world's marine heavyweight class has to offer. Descriptions of them, and the most popular methods of fishing them, follow:

TUNA

Among the tunas in the Atlantic and Pacific there are at least seven defined species. They are the bluefin, the yellowfin (Allison), the Atlantic big-eyed, the Pacific big-eyed, the blackfin, the albacore, and the false albacore. (The latter two species are described in Chapter 7.) Of all the species, the bluefin stands out as the largest of all and the most exciting to take on rod and reel. Fighting this big fish to the finish is the dream of many a rodman, for it is an achievement worth bragging about to master a fish, on appropriate tackle, that weighs four, five, or six times more than you do. Some will not dare attempt to handle such a mammoth fish; but the timid-hearted may be encouraged to know that a girl only eleven years of age fought and reeled to the boat, unaided, a tuna that weighed nearly 400 pounds. Each season finds more women going in pursuit of these giants, and they are landing specimens that tip the scales at well over 700 pounds.

The bluefin, known also as horse mackerel and great albacore, is the largest member of the mackerel family, and moves in big schools. Generally they leave the vicinity of Bimini, in the Bahamas, late in the spring and migrate as far as Labrador if the water temperature is warm enough there. These fish are caught most frequently during the summer and early fall from New Jersey to Nova Scotia. Some of the best "hot spots" are the Wedgeport-Liverpool area of Nova Scotia, Casco Bay, Maine, Ipswich and Massachusetts bays, Block Island off Rhode Island, Montauk Point and Freeport, Long Island, and Seabright, New Jersey. On the West Coast, the bluefin move northward from Guadalupe Island, off Mexico, to northern Oregon, with the best spots being around the Catalina Islands, Santa Barbara Islands, and Coronado Islands. These fish are taken on the West Coast most frequently during June, July, and August, with an over-all season lasting from May to November. While the bluefin frequent the open seas of both oceans, they are also found in channels and the tide rips flowing in and out of bays along both coasts. Many times during a migration, bluefins are within a few hundred yards of shore.

Though giant tuna generally prefer meat, they can be sometimes taken on artificial lures. Feather jigs seem to be best for these large fish, with cedar and metal squids also scoring. The location of the tuna determines the kind of fresh bait to offer, since the species of small fish vary at different places and times of the season. Along the New England coast good luck is had by using mackerel, whiting, whole bunkers, or hake for bait, and trolling deep. Off Long Island, New Jersey, and the West Coast, the system is to pour over a stream of ground chum and use a whole herring or menhaden for the tempter. The big fish often come right up to the stern in the chum and look many times their actual size as they grab the chunks.

A big tuna usually takes the bait gently and swims off a bit before making the big swallow. When he has clamped his jaws over the bait, you lean back, brace your feet, and throw all the force you can muster against the fish, striking hard several times to imbed the hook solidly. You will, of course, be wearing a leather shoulder harness for leverage. Don't tighten the drag on your reel too much at first, or the hook may pull out. Give the tuna a chance to make his first run. After that he will sound deeply, unless you are lucky enough to prevent it. It's important not to let him get directly beneath the boat, or he'll rest and you can't readily bring him surfaceward. Keep to one side of him, and let out 100 yards or more of line. Then apply all the pressure necessary with the reel drag.

Your next problem will be to begin the long performance of pumping and reeling, pumping and reeling, until at length your catch is at the top where you can really gain some headway at breaking down his resistance. When he reaches the surface he'll probably shoot off on another long race, so you must crank in as much line as you can while pumping him from the depths. You have to keep him coming constantly toward the boat and do not give him an opportunity to rest, or you'll spend extra hours tussling with the big brute—unless, that is, your own endurance collapses first. Whenever he wants to "take off," let him! The more line he pulls out the heavier is the burden he must buck against.

Boating a giant bluefin is a tricky art calling for a flying gaff, a tail loop, and a lot of running around the cockpit. When this exciting process starts (just as soon as the mate's gloved hand gets hold of the leader), loosen your drag so a surprise lunge by the fish doesn't shatter your expensive rod against the gunwale. Be prepared for the unexpected! You can always tighten up and pump the fish back, but the reverse process will not work. Plan your actions in advance and you are more likely to emerge the winner.

Getting the big fish into the boat is another difficult job, but here under IGFA rules, the captain and his crew can help you. The illustration shows the four most common methods used when boating any large game fish.

Because of their boat's design, some captains and crews just haul a big bluefin over the side. This is the method generally used off Wedgeport, Nova Scotia. On both Atlantic and Pacific coasts, the gin pole is popular. This device is a stout, short mast fitted with a block and tackle at the upper end and is used to "derrick" the fish aboard. In southern waters, a roller on the side or stern, or an open door arrangement in the boat's transom, is generally used to bring big fellows aboard.

Spit-outs are a tuna fisherman's nightmare. Bluefins will often toy with your offering enough to mangle the bait completely, then reject it. To prevent this, anglers out Catalina way rig their mackerel bait so that the hook is folded back along the baitfish's flank and held in place with a piece of light line. This arrangement allows the barb to point away from a tuna's throat as he takes the mackerel headfirst. If a tuna cannot feel the hook, he is far more likely to swallow the bait. You are less likely to have a bad day if you use colored wire for leader material instead of a shiny surface. Bluefins are apt to shy away from brass hardware and bright swivels if they see them before the hook can be set in their mouths. Color camouflage can be the difference between catching or missing a tuna.

Before you start still-fishing or trolling, you should pay out about 50 yards of line to wet it thoroughly so it may be controlled better if a strike comes shortly after the bait or lure has been put overboard. You'll soon

Methods of bringing a big fish aboard.

Crew pulls the tuna over the side or gunwale of the boat.

The bluefin is hauled in with gin-pole, block and tackle and plenty of brawn.

learn how much strain you can safely put on your rod and line, and how to regulate the drag of your reel to best advantage. This is a knack that each angler must acquire for himself through actual experience. It is always the object of anglers to use light tackle for the high sport it gives and to let the fish have an even break for freedom, but you have to become accustomed to the "feel" of both the rod and the lunging fish in order to handle the lighter equipment successfully.

Although still-fishing accounts for some fine bluefins, the favorite method throughout the realm of the tuna is trolling. Because of the movement of a trolled bait, the big fellow has no time to inspect the bait, and thus he must take it immediately rather than toying with it as he prefers. When trolled, the hook is often set right away. But two or three stiff jerks should be used to set the hook solidly. While trolling, keep the bait close to the boat— perhaps only 50 feet away—so when a bluefin starts on his first run, and then sounds, you have plenty of line to give him.

Tuna are particularly fond of flying fish, so any bait or lure that skips over the water like a frightened flying fish gets attention. Therefore outriggers are often employed to make the baited hook act like a flying fish. An outrigger is of course a metal or bamboo pole, ordinarily extending outward 12 or 15 feet from the side of the boat, for keeping the bait free from the wake of the boat and for making it jump and skip along the sur-

This tuna brought aboard through a hinged door in the boat's transom.

A roller mounted on the stern of a boat can also be used to bring aboard a big fish.

face of the waves (see Chapter 7 for more details about outriggers).

A variety of gear may be used in trolling for tuna, depending on the average size of the fish and the skill of the angler. Heavy-duty tackle (page 36) should be put into action to cope with the struggles of the giants and provide the great length of line that is taken out when the fish settle into the depths. But above all, the outfit must be balanced.

For the medium-sized bluefins, an ordinary salt-water boat rod of split bamboo, glass, or hickory with a tip of 16 ounces is adequate; an expert fisherman may be able to use this rod for even the big ones. The 23-ounce tip satisfies many anglers for general needs.

For the big tuna, a deep-sea trolling rod is appropriate. The 30- or 36-ounce tip is favored by most seasoned rodmen for fish of this class. The reel will range from 10/0 to 16/0 in size, with star drag. A novice might employ a 14/0 reel with adjustable drag of the star or lever type. The leader may be of No. 7 to No. 12 steel, or braided wire cable, depending upon the size of the fish you expect and the test of line used. For example, when using a synthetic line which tests 162 pounds when wet, you generally employ a No. 12 single-strand wire leader which tests at 174 pounds. Some boat captains, when going after real big tuna, prefer twisted cable testing about 500 pounds because they believe the leader pound test should be close to the weight of the fish. Hooks that will cover general needs in taking the giants of the sea are O'Shaughnessy and Mustad in sizes 7/0 to 14/0, with the 10/0 and 12/0 satisfying most anglers.

The tackle just described is generally used for the bluefins taken in the Atlantic. Unlike the giants of the Atlantic Coast, the bluefin tuna of Pacific waters seem to reach a top weight of about 250 pounds, with the average around 60 to 125 pounds according to the locality. But their vigor, plus the fact they may be captured on lighter tackle than the Atlantic bluefins, make them tough adversaries to conquer.

Guides estimate tuna weights at sea. Formula is: length times square of girth; results divided by 800.

The natural foods of the Pacific bluefin include mackerel, herring, flying fish, and squids. For trolling, one of these fish, or a feather jig, makes an excellent lure. If a flying fish is used, insert the 6/0 to 8/0 size hook under the chin and bring the point up through the head and in line with the eyes; or rig the bait with two hooks, one through the mouth and the other imbedded in the skin at the base of the tail. With a boat rod having a 5-foot tip section weighing 9 to 12 ounces, a 6/0 to 9/0 reel, 350 to 500 yards of 72 test line, and 12- to 15-foot light tuna cable leader, you are prepared to manage the bluefins of the Pacific.

The yellowfin tuna likes warm seas and does not go into lower-temperature waters as much as the bluefin. Within its range along the Atlantic Coast, from Maryland to Florida the yellowfin is not a common fish. It is taken off the east coast of Florida and in the West Indies in winter and early spring, and some are taken at Bermuda. It is much more abundant in the Pacific, especially from Point Conception southward. While the tasty yellowfin may be caught all year in the warm waters off Lower California, the best season for boats putting out from the Los Angeles and San Diego areas extends from June to October. Yellowfin up to 450 pounds have been known, although a fish over 125 pounds is rather rare.

These fish are taken with the same trolling tactics, using outriggers, as bluefins (page 183). The yellowfins will often strike swiftly moving lures—like feather and bone jigs, metal squids, and plugs—as well as natural squids, shrimps, whole mackerel, herring, and flying fish.

The yellowfins are ready to smash into bait or lure on any tide. To compensate for their hard-hitting and tough fighting qualities, you should be equipped with sturdy tackle. This can be a regular deep-sea boat rod, having an over-all length of 5½ feet and weighing 16 or 18 ounces. With this rod you might use a 9/0 to 14/0 size reel with star drag, made from the finest-quality materials; 500 to 1,000 yards of 72 to 108 test line (which should balance with the rod), the last 15 feet of which should be double; No. 7 or 9 stainless steel wire, or braided wire cable leader 15 feet long; and 8/0 to 10/0 size hooks.

The Atlantic big-eyed tuna, the Pacific big-eyed tuna, the blackfin tuna are taken in the same general area as the yellowfins and on the same tackle outfit.

SWORDFISH

The swordfish (until recently known as the broadbill swordfish—the prefix has been officially dropped) is considered by big-game anglers to be the world's greatest game fish and well does it deserve such honor. He has tenacity, pluck, cleverness, speed, and size—and provides "steaks" that fairly melt in your mouth. The swordfish is also one of the most difficult fish to catch on rod and reel. Zane Grey, one of our pioneer big-game fishermen, tells of fighting a huge broadbill for more than 11½ hours while fishing the Pacific, off Catalina Island, only to have the hooked fish start feeding on a school of passing flying fish and break the line. Another time, he and his brother fished for 93 days, during which they sighted 140 swordfish, were able to get the bait to 94 fish, had some 11 strikes, and boated only one fish.

The swordfish is easily distinguished from the marlin and sailfish, which resemble it superficially, by the lack of pelvic fins and scales. The sword is long, broad, and flattened, a shape very different from the round spike of the marlin; the sword is also longer relative to the fish's body than the marlin's spike. In one 11-foot swordfish the sword measured 42 inches from the tip to the anterior eye. In many specimens it is approximately one-third of the total length.

The fish's sword is more battering ram than foil. A few men have experienced the attack of an enraged broadbill, an attack that ended with the spear shattering the solid planking of a boat's hull. If the bill breaks off, the fish is helpless. The sword will not regenerate.

Swordfish are distributed throughout the warm waters of the world and in the eastern Atlantic are found from the Newfoundland Banks and Cape Breton southward to beyond the Tropic of Capricorn. Most of those caught along our eastern shores are taken north of New Jersey, off Montauk Point and Block Island, New York. The swordfish run off Block Island sometimes begins as early as June, and the peak of the season off Nova Scotia is in August or sometimes in September. Choice grounds off California are between San Pedro and Avalon. In this area a swordfish may be found nearly any time from May to December, with the best period lasting from July to October. Some are taken off Mexico and in recent years the cold waters of the Humboldt Current off Chile and Peru, especially the areas off Cabo Blanco, Tocopilla, and Talora, have become known as perhaps the finest swordfishing grounds. Swordfish are seen off the coasts of Cuba but not many are caught there.

Swordfish generally follow the deep-water edges of offshore banks, or the continental shelf, feeding on menhaden, mackerel, herring, mullets, flying fish, bonitos, and squids. When gorged with food, they sleep in the sun with their tail and dorsal fin showing—resembling a pair of sharks cruising close together, as sharks often do.

It's not hard to get within harpoon range of a swordfish. This is all right for the market man—or, as a last resort, for the angler, if the fish refuse bait. But it's not much sport. The dart is sunk deep into the fish, the harpoon is thrown overboard attached to a keg, and after the fish fights the keg for a time, it is hauled in. This is no fun, but broadbills do bring a high price when laid on the dock. You can never tell when your broadbill is going to show up, so it's always a good idea to have swordfish tackle aboard any time you go out for big fellows.

Rod-and-reel fishing for these monsters is a true sportsmen's sport. The commonest technique is to wear your eyes red-rimmed trying to spot them. Broadbill loll on top, fins protruding—a sharp, distinct silhouette in calm weather. In a running swell, they often ride the crests. Since the bronze bulk and wide black tail may be partly under the water, a swordfisherman has a better chance of seeing his quarry from a flying bridge. A boat equipped especially for broadbill has a crow's nest, a perch high in the superstructure from which fish are spotted. When these huge fellows are sighted—some running close to 900 pounds, with the average being from 250 to 400 pounds—the lookout man shouts excitedly, "Swordfish ahead!" and you get ready for action. The system is to discover in which direction they are moving, then swing around behind and, with a rather long line, troll in a half-circle, coming across their pathway in front.

The bait should be skipped along as you troll past the basking swordfish. This is the best means of inducing them to strike when they are not particularly hungry. (Occasionally they will swat at it out of annoyance, and become foul hooked, which makes them tough to play.) A whole squid, 12 to 18 inches in length, makes good bait. Mackerel and skipjack are commonly used, but some skippers swear by a five-pound bluefish. The guide first removes the innards of the baitfish, then reams out the backbone by twisting a hollow instrument along the spinal column, and finally sews two Mustad hooks, from 10/0 to 14/0 in size, inside the fish. These two hooks aid in keeping the mackerel, shipjack, or bluefish intact, and in gripping a swordfish solidly. If a squid is used, then only one hook is needed.

Swordfish are also known to be partial to a large rigged eel. The secret of getting them to strike is part scent, part the lifelike quality of the rig, part the presentation, part luck. Scent is an important factor in swordfishing. Trolling a bait for an hour may cause it to deteriorate or lose its smell. Broadbills like a fresh, preferably a live, offering. So take a variety of baits, all of healthy size, and keep them alive or in an icebox. Remember that the swordfish, being a big fish, likes a man-sized meal. Make the offering on the rod, not the outriggers. Outriggers are too cumbersome and clumsy for the delicate touch that may spell the difference between hooking or missing a fish. Swordfish do not favor artificial lures.

The rod should be kept as high as possible while baiting the fish. Holding the rod in your hands, the reel on free spool, try jiggling the bait slightly as it floats in front of the fish. You can make an eel undulate like a champion burlesque dancer, but do this only if your fish seems disinterested in a straight pass. Try the easy way first. If you fail, follow with refinements. Try switching baits. You can break your heart offering swordfish baits. Some fish tantalize you by following; others ignore everything you have to offer. It's a rare broadbill that strikes immediately. I have seen them disdain three, six, and even ten passes only to be tempted on the 11th.

Perhaps three out of twenty are hooked and most of these are lost far short of the gaff.

If a swordfish disappears, it probably means he has spotted the bait and is about to attack. If he is suspicious or has become frightened, he'll stay down. But let's suppose he aims to oblige. His first act is to tap the bait with his bill to kill it, so you must throw off the reel drag and give him time to get the bait in his mouth. You wait until he stops, swallows again, and moves off with some speed. Be careful to keep your thumbs off the line. The slightest resistance and the broadbill may spit out the bait.

When about 100 yards of line is out, clamp on the drag and give a firm upward heave of the rod tip. If the hook has reached its mark, strike two or three times more to drive it in securely. With the connection made, you're in for a rough fight. The great black bill will rise and smash! You will be yanked forward by the force of each of his blows. You should remember, however, that a swordfish has a fairly tender mouth, so caution in playing is necessary. Let the fish strain against a moderate drag, keep the rod tip elevated and the line snug. A broadbill must be given leeway to race and thrash about, and shouldn't be forced. Wear him down by the tension of the reel, and keep him on the move whenever he pauses to rest. Retrieve line when possible, but don't try it when he sets off at full steam. It may take you several hours to land him, so you must conserve your strength without easing up on the fish.

Another system of trolling calls for a teaser—an artificial, gyrating hookless plug of immense size designed to interest deep, unseen fish. The swordfish is attracted by the antics of the lure, enraged as it is maneuvered out of reach. With its caution dulled by anger, the incensed broadbill takes a hooked bait substituted for the teaser. The teaser is towed 50 or 60 feet behind a boat, sometimes even closer. However, it works better on marlin and sailfish than the swordfish.

Swordfish are heavy tackle boys. The rod used in catching swordfish should have a 21-inch butt with a 5-foot tip weighing between 16 and 30 ounces. There is a combination of rod tip and line for every kind of angler and size of fish; a 16-ounce tip with 72 test line for taking the average swordfish, or for use by the seasoned angler; a 22-ounce tip and a 108 test line for the larger fish; and a 26- to 30-ounce tip with a 108 to 162 test line for the novice angler, or the heaviest fish. The size of reel will vary according to the line used; it should accommodate at least 500 yards of line. The size should range between 10/0 and 15/0. For example, a 14/0 reel holding about 1,000 yards of 108 test line is practical for catching swordfish if the angler is a beginner or is aiming to take the biggest fish. With the 16-ounce rod tip and 72 test, a 10/0 reel holding 600 yards would be adequate.

For average situations, the leader may be of stainless steel cable 15 feet in length; for the largest swordfish, perhaps 25 feet long. Hook sizes should be from 10/0 to 14/0, with the 12/0 answering most needs. But, unhappily, swordfish breach. They make wild, awesome, towering leaps that carry their great bodies entirely clear of the water. To hold that kind of acrobat, you need a hook with maximum distance between point and barb. Thus the hook should have a long point running parallel to the shank. All you can do is compromise. A good way is to insert the hook in the bait so that the barb comes out of the vent, point facing the tail. Lash the leader around the caudal fin, doubling the wire backward along the belly. Tie the wire to the bait's mouth with a piece of light thread, stitching the mouth in the process. The bait will troll head first when you put it overboard. It will swim like a normal fish. Once the broadbill strikes, the thread will break allowing the bait to sink headfirst. Once the swordfish picks it up, swallowing headfirst, he will not be disturbed by the wire and will miss feeling the hook since the point will face away from the throat. It is a trifle complicated. The advantage lies in the fact that it takes more swordfish.

You'll need a flying gaff with a detachable head. After bringing a broadbill within reach, strike behind the dorsal fin, and lift the fish to raise the tail clear of the water. Despite all the commotion of a death flurry, a big fish is helpless with his tail out of water. Of course you'll also want auxiliary straight gaffs to help to bring the big fellow close to the boat, and a tail loop to complete the lashing process. A block and tackle or a gin pole will help you haul the fish aboard.

MARLIN

Anglers who heed the mysterious call of the deep-blue offshore waters where swim the giant fish will likely agree that the spectacular surface fight of a marlin, with its tail-walking, greyhounding, and head-shaking battle, is one of the most thrilling episodes of salt-water fishing. The strenuous period between the time the marlin feels the cold steel of the barbed hook and the time it lies ready for the gaff is a backbreaking struggle that is the pinnacle of angling achievement.

There are five prominent species of marlin: the blue and the white marlin, inhabiting the Atlantic; and the black, the silver, and the striped marlin of Pacific waters. The flesh of most marlin is flaky and not tasty, so sportsmen usually release them when the battle is over. In recent years more deep-sea anglers have "come of age" and recognize the childishness of bringing billfish to docks merely to be seen and photographed with them. Many fishing ports give silver pins and certificates for billfish returned to the sea. However, anglers getting a marlin for the first time generally keep the fish for mounting; on the average, a taxidermist charges about $100 to do the job.

Blue Marlin

These fish, sometimes called the Cuban black marlin, are some of the mightiest game fishes roving the ocean depths. They have become the special target of hardy, adventure-seeking salt-water anglers. Boats are chartered and taken into the Gulf Stream for the express purpose of hooking and mastering these enormous brutes with their fixed bayonets.

The blue marlin usually strikes the bait with his bill before grabbing it. Unless slack is offered immediately, he will become suspicious because the bait does not drift freely as though "dead." The experienced fisherman thumbs his reel as the bait is dropped back, and waits for the marlin to turn and pick it up. He does not strike until the marlin swims away with the bait and has had time to "mouth" it. An early strike, while the fish has the bait clamped between the lower mandible and the bill, will be useless. For this reason, fishermen count to ten before striking. Then you clamp on the reel, drag and sock it to him. A marlin has a hard-cased mouth, so you must put strength behind your jerks, bringing up on him two or three times with all the power your rod and line will stand. Actually, setting the hook is one of the more difficult phases of marlin fishing. For many years, until fishermen learned the trick of hooking marlin, it was thought they could not be caught.

With the hook set, the marlin dives and shoots off on a run that whisks the line from your reel in a twinkling. The reel drag shouldn't be set too tightly at the outset because then the line may break or the hook may pull out. When a marlin decides to go places, don't try to sidetrack him— just let him go. But care must be taken to keep the marlin from getting slack line. Very often they will throw the hook if given a bit of loose line. Also the boat must be kept as close to the hooked fish as possible. If the blue marlin gets too far away, the resultant "belly," or slack, in the line may let the fish get away.

When a blue marlin sounds for the depths, you should race away from him a few hundred yards so that the line forms an angle with the water instead of going straight down. It is important to raise the fish to the surface as quickly as possible, because he may sound until the pressure becomes too great and he will die. If this should occur, it is difficult or impossible to raise him to the surface. (The only possible way is to pump and reel, pump and reel to bring up a dead weight!)

You fight the fish until finally he grows weary (you have passed that condition ages before). The sooner you get your fish over the gunwale, the surer you will be of having a whole specimen. Sharks populate the waters where marlins live, especially on the east side of the Gulf Stream, and when a marlin is struggling for freedom the sharks follow and bite off huge chunks at the slightest opportunity. Some anglers have hauled in merely the head and skeleton of a marlin.

For this reason many fishermen use tackle that is on the heavy side, so as to wear down the resistance of a marlin quicker and bring him to gaff before a shark subtracts a few pounds. A glass rod is good, with the tip weighing from 30 to 42 ounces, together with a 12/0 to 14/0 reel holding about 600 yards of 108 to 162 test line. The heaviest line is frequently put into service.

Where there is little danger of sharks, and a marlin can be played for a longer interval, lighter tackle is in order. This may be a rod tip weighing from 16 to 26 ounces, and a 10/0 to 12/0 reel filled with 600 yards of 72 to 108 test line. With the heavy tackle suggested above you should use a 25-foot leader of piano wire or stainless steel, testing over 250 pounds; with the lighter gear use the same kind of leader in 15-foot length. Hook sizes range from 10/0 to 14/0, with the 12/0 size in common use.

The average blue marlin tips the scales anywhere from 200 to 400 pounds, with a top weight exceeding 700 pounds. Generally marlin are lone voyagers that like the warm waters. They feed both the surface and in the depths, and during June and July many are hooked by trolling in the region of Cuba, Bimini, and Miami. Along the Florida Coast they are mainly encountered from Fort Pierce to Key Largo; they are fairly common from Bimini to Cay Sal Bank in the Bahamas. The best season is from May through July although good catches are made in the winter months. Occasionally blue marlin go as far north as Montauk Point, and they are sometimes taken off Texas.

To give the bait the skipping movements necessary to attract attention and to insure the proper drop-back of the bait before setting the hook, outriggers are used; they are standard equipment on charter boats. The outriggers cause the bait to skitter across the surface like a frightened baitfish. The jolt of the strike knocks the line from the outrigger, providing necessary slack while the line drops to the water. This system also allows from two to four anglers to troll at the same time, minimizing the chances of getting the lines entangled. In some cases mackerel, mullets, or bonefish are trailed in the wake of the launches to lend additional attraction. To add to the commotion, wooden plugs without hooks are dragged on short stern lines as extra "teasers." The trolled tempter will not only attract marlin that are frolicking on the surface, but also helps to bring those that are below up from the depths.

Marlin like any smaller fish, and good natural baits are mullets, dolphins, barracudas, and mackerel, with bonefish being the best by far. But a great deal of skill is required (the boat captain generally does the job) to prepare marlin baits; this knowledge is usually acquired from years of fishing for these big fellows. There are many ways of rigging a skipping bait for billfish, and you will find each locality has its own favorite method. Much, of course, depends upon the kind of bait used. For example, the customary method employed in rigging a flying fish for bait at Bimini is to tie the long pectoral fins to the fish's sides, sew the mouth closed, and tie the nose of the bait to the bend of the hook with a short length of line. You might think that a rig of this kind wouldn't attract a marlin, but results prove otherwise. Some guides break the backbone in several places in a skip bait so that it will have more freedom of action. Others will employ a deboner (a metal tube with one end sharpened to a knifelike edge) to remove most of the spinal column so the bait will have a lifelike movement.

White Marlin

These fish are somewhat smaller than blue marlin, averaging around 60 pounds with a top size of about 160 pounds. But their fight is fast and strong, punctuated with jumps and scudding leaps called "greyhounding." Few fish, if any, can greyhound so effortlessly or fast as the white marlin. Actually, the captain's handling of his boat has as much to do with the capture of a marlin as an angler's ability to "pump and reel."

If you wish to stretch a point (and most anglers do), white marlin are in a way responsible for this book. While I had the normal boyish interests in salt-water fishing, it wasn't until, at the age of fourteen, I hooked into a 79-pound white marlin off Freeport, Long Island, that I became devoted for life to this hobby.

White marlin travel singly, in pairs, and in groups; they are caught in great abundance from the West Indies and Florida up the Atlantic Coast to Cape Cod. Many are taken in summer from Martha's Vineyard to the Carolinas. Usually white marlin are reported to be especially plentiful in the Ocean City, Maryland, area during July and August, and fine catches of these great leapers are made on light tackle. From around Vero Beach, Florida, down to the Keys, and at Bimini and Cat Cay, these marlin battle furiously from January to July, with March and April being the best months.

You should curb the impulse to strike too quickly in setting the hook on a white marlin; but as soon as the line straightens out after being pulled from the outrigger, you can give a stiff jerk. If your fish has missed the bait, skip it along the surface towards the boat and keep your rod tip raised slightly. Have your reel on free spool so that if the marlin makes another attack and taps your bait, you can let it drop back for a few seconds. If the line begins to leave the reel swiftly, engage the gear and strike hard. It may take three or four drop-backs of the bait before the marlin is hooked, especially if you have failed to wait long enough each time for the fish to grab hold firmly. On each occasion as you skip the bait ahead, the marlin thinks it has recovered from being stunned and is trying to escape, so once more he attacks. If done crudely, though, the marlin may become suspicious after the first or second attempt and vanish. Sometimes three, four, or a few dozen white marlins may come to the baits at once.

White marlin feed on mullets, mackerel, menhaden, flying fish, squids, and similar baits. When they are working along the surface they are easily detected by both anglers and seagulls. Then is the time to circle them, skipping a bait, or to troll across the front of their advance. White marlin are believed to be able to travel at over 60 mph, so fast trolling is the way to take them. In northern waters one of the most popular trolling baits for white marlin is a whole squid. Since the natural motion of this bait when alive is backward through the water, it must be trolled in the same position. The weak part of a squid is its head and, unless a tandem hook rig is used, with the tail hook placed through the head of the squid, the action of the water will quickly slap the head off.

A great deal of skill is needed in preparing the various marlin strip baits (dolphin, mackerel, bonito, and bluefish), and this knowledge is usually acquired from years of fishing. One of the most difficult baits to make is a strip cut from the belly of a mackerel. First, after cutting out the slab of flesh, you must determine how the grain or layers run so the head of the bait can be determined. If you troll a cut bait against the fleshy layers, the action of the water will quickly rip it apart. The layers lie upon each other like a shingled roof, and the water must run off the grain, not against it. The edges of the bait should be beveled with a very sharp knife, and the entire bait tapered toward the tail. The head of the bait should be the thickest part.

Although you follow the same procedure in hooking and playing a white marlin as for his blue cousin, the tackle is somewhat different (in the northern range, at least, where few sharks are encountered) because the white marlin is a lighter fish. The seasoned angler can manage the situation with a 6/9 outfit, and this meets with general favor. The inexperienced fisherman, however, is advised to employ a 5- or 5½-foot boat rod having a tip weighing 9 to 12 ounces; a 6/0 reel; and about 400 yards of 45 to 72 test line. The last 15 feet of the line may be doubled, and a No. 8 stainless steel or piano wire leader 15 feet long attached. Hooks of sizes 7/0 to 9/0 are suitable for trolling with strip baits. Occasionally white marlin have a pleasing tendency to grab feathered jigs or large plugs that are being trolled for school tuna, dolphin, and bonitos; but small baitfish, squids and strip baits make the best enticers.

Black Marlin

This Pacific marlin, a close relative of the white and the blue species, is the world's largest game fish, excluding sharks. Black marlin have been taken weighing up to 1,600 pounds. While native fishermen from Cuba believe that blue marlin grow to at least that size, none as large as the black has, at this writing, been taken on rod and reel. But fewer black marlin have been caught than other marlin. They are the masterminds of the marlins and, in their efforts to escape the angler, resort to every trick known to marlins anywhere in the world. The majority of them hit a bait with lightning speed. There is no dillydallying. They know what they want, and when they spot it they go in to kill and take it. Run after run follows the strike, interspersed with frenzied leaping. Jumping, tail-walking, greyhounding, and surface-rushing are just a few of the exercises performed by these giants of the sea—and if the angler is not on the alert, they will sound when their surface fight is over.

These fish have tremendous bills, as big around as a baseball bat. They taper down to a sharp point and are much broader and slightly shorter than the bills of other varieties of marlin. Once you have seen a black marlin bill, you will never mistake it for the bill of another marlin. In relation to its great girth, the head and shoulders of a black marlin are shorter and blunter, and the dorsal fins shorter, than those of the blue, white, and striped varieties. When hooked, most black marlin show a deep blue on their backs, with a gorgeous light silver on their bellies; but as they die, the top half turns a very dark and dirty blue. They have no stripes at any time. There is one sure way to distinguish a black marlin: the pectoral fins of a black marlin do not and cannot be folded or pushed back flush with its sides and flanks, as can those of the other marlin. Instead, the fins project rigidly outward like a pair of stabilizers—and quite obviously that is just what they are.

Black marlin are found from the west coast of Mexico near Guaymas to Australia, and especially off Peru, Tahiti, New Zealand, and Panama. There are probably as many black marlin off Panama in the summer months as anywhere in the world. Most of the fishing there is done over week ends and there are not many boats available to the angler. Ecuador and northern Peru have also yielded many large black marlin especially off Cabo Blanco, a few have been taken off Tocopilla, Chile, and several a year are also taken in Acapulco, Mexico, waters. Off Mexico the season for these fish is January to November.

The proper black marlin tackle is the same as the heavy outfit recommended for the blue species. Whole fish bait should be used, such as dolphin, barracuda, albacore, or bonito. Slabs or strips taken from the bellies of tunas are also excellent bait. The most successful anglers fishing off Panama always say, "The bigger the bait the better." A 15-pound fish is common when trolling for black marlin.

Silver Marlin

These fish are the principal marlin caught in the Hawaiian Islands and they appear to be the most common marlin in the central Pacific—at least more silver marlin are caught in those waters than any other kind. Probably these marlin were the kind commonly taken by members of the armed forces in the Caroline, Mariana, Marshall, the Gilbert Islands during the war. They are also the marlin found around Tahiti. Most of the silver marlin caught off the Hawaiian Islands by rod and reel fishermen run between 150 and 300 pounds, although they have been taken over 1,600 pounds by commercial fishermen with flag lines.

The silver marlin is the Pacific counterpart of the blue marlin. Actually, some experts believe the silver marlin is the same fish as the blue marlin. In some specimens the dorsal of the silver marlin may be a trifle lower and the bill a trifle longer and more rugged. It may look more silvery than the blue marlin, but the real difference, if there is any, lies in the number of spines in the dorsal fins. The fighting quality of the blue and the silver, however, is the same. Both are marvelous fish and both rank right after the black marlin as the greatest prize to be caught among marlin. The silver marlin knows every trick of the blue, and the tackle requirements for this species is the same as for the blue.

Striped Marlin

These marlin are the most common of all the five species and have been caught in many places thousands of miles apart in the Pacific Ocean. They range from Japan to California, as far north as Balboa and Avalon, and southward to Chile. The season usually extends from June to December off southern California, with the best action occurring in August and September. In Mexican waters, vast schools of striped marlin invade the Gulf of California in March and migrate northward. By the first of May they are plentiful off Guaymas, Mexico, and until October or November they afford marvelous opportunities to the many sportsmen who visit these famous grounds to exercise their skill on marlin. Another popular site is Guadaloupe Island, and excellent fish are caught in this vicinity as they move offshore along the coast towards Point Conception, California. Blue marlin hooked in the Atlantic may have some of the color traits of the striped marlin, which misleads a few anglers into believing striped marlin inhabit the Atlantic. They don't. Striped marlin average 250 pounds, but occasionally run as high as 400 pounds.

The great thing about striped marlin is they can be caught by almost any angler since they do not fight as hard or as long as the blue, black, and silver species. These fish are easier to take than their cousins because they jump a great deal more, which tends to tire them out faster. They are fast swimmers, but not as fast as the other varieties. Most of the time striped marlin rove the blue waters solitarily, but when breeding they may be seen in pairs or school. Even when not battling to break loose from a hook, they occasionally spring and plunge.

Striped marlin respond to the same fishing techniques used for all marlins and spearfish. The favorite marlin trolling baits—a flying fish, Sierra mackerel, or the belly strip from a bonito—may be employed. The flying fish is usually chosen because it lasts a long time before getting soft, and it trolls well. Often two baits are let out, one about sixty feet astern and the other about seventy-five feet, and this system works admirably. If using a whole fish, run a 9/0 or 10/0 size hook through the lips and secure it with thread. Most marlin are caught in the mouth, although some are hooked in the gills. This rig is attached to a 15-foot leader of small stainless steel cable wire testing about 250 pounds.

If you are an inexperienced hand at mauling the marlin, your gear might well consist of a trolling rod having a 16-ounce tip, a 10/0 size reel, and 500 yards of 72 test line. However, if you have some practice in managing big-game fighters, you can safely take striped marlin on a 10-ounce rod tip, a 6/0 reel, and 600 yards of 45 test line, and enjoy snappier sport. An expert would be more satisfied with the regulation 6/9 or even the 3/6 tackle outfit, especially where the marlin are of medium size (175 pounds).

With the first rig recommended, you can bring a sizable marlin to terms much more easily and in less time than with a lighter line and rod tip. So take your choice whether you want speed or sport—except in places where sharks are apt to bite large chunks out of your catch. Then speed in getting the marlin to the gaff is essential, particularly if you are out to make a record.

SAILFISH

Sometimes called the spikefish, sailfish are members of the spearfish family, as are the swordfish and the marlin. There are two varieties of this species—the Atlantic sailfish and the Pacific sailfish. Both varieties have approximately the same color: dark blue on the back and silvery on the sides and belly. The sail of the sailfish is really a dorsal fin. The sailfish can fold it down into a groove along its back, or extend it—which he does when he jumps. The sail extends about three-quarters of the length of the body. The spear is about a foot long in the larger specimens. The Pacific variety runs forty to ninety pounds, about twice as heavy as the Atlantic sailfish.

Atlantic Sailfish

Far offshore, in the Gulf Stream, your strip of mullet skips along the surface a few yards behind the power boat. Your trolling line runs from the rod to a clip holding it at the tip of an outrigger, and from there it trails in the wake where your bait is given an especially animated motion. All of a sudden there is a severe jar as a long-billed fish tops your mullet and jerks the line from the clip. Immediately you throw the reel on free spool and let fifty or sixty yards of line slip into the ocean, giving the fish a chance to seize and swallow the bait. When you think enough time has elapsed—a few seconds in all—you re-engage the drag to take up the slack, then heave upward and backward as hard as your line and rod will stand. Then you strike a second time to make doubly sure the hook has gripped its target. From the water there bursts a huge sailfish with his wide dorsal fin or "sail" unfurled to the wind, his mouth open, and his head wagging furiously. Down he plunges, off he goes on a long run, then up into the air once more. He is putting on a great show, and his performance is highlighted by his "walk" over the surface on his tail for some distance.

Time and again he gives terrific jumps, and flings himself in every direction to work the hook loose—and if there's a moment's slack line, he is apt to succeed. It's a spine-tingling, spectacular, high-rearing combat, like that waged by a big tarpon. You cling to the rod with all your might, letting the shoulder harness take much of the strain from your arms and wrists. The tip is held high so the rod and line together will share the pressure, and you crank away at the reel whenever there is the slightest chance. Gradually the tail-walking and head-shaking leaps cease—and the runs become short and less vigorous. But you must wear him out completely before bringing him close, for when he sees the boat he may spurt off on another wild charge. At length his energies are spent, and you reel him in so the captain or mate can grab the leader. At that instant you ease up on the reel drag a trifle, to prevent damage to your rod tip if the fish should give a sudden lurch. But soon the big blue and silver fellow is over the side, and you have won a Silver Sailfish Button—a coveted token of your accomplishment.

If he is not your first sailfish or close to record size, the chances are the skipper will either make an outright release or tag the fish, since the sailfish has little food value compared to his sporting ability. For the last ten years or so, most Florida boatmen have been carrying a supply of rubber rings (called tags) which are fitted onto the fish's bill. Nothing painful about it. These rings carry a number and a lot of other piscatorial stuff supposed to be interesting to everyone except the fish. So your boat captain will either tag or fin-clip your fish, and then he'll gently remove the hook from his mouth and let the fish swim away. You'll still have the credit for the catch.

Atlantic sailfish inhabit the tropical seas. They are most plentiful among the Keys and along the East Coast of Florida—for example, near Stuart, Palm Beach, and Miami—but they also cruise about the Gulf of Mexico and the West Indies. In the spring and much of the summer, they are caught from Port Aransas, Freeport, Sabine Pass, and other Texas ports, sometimes as close as three miles offshore and other times from twenty to thirty miles out. They range along the entire coast of Florida, but on the Gulf side they are usually found some distance out. They are ready to fight at any time during the year in this region, but the most active season is generally from late December until about midsummer. Following the edge of the Gulf Stream, they may roam as far north as North Carolina in pairs or in schools spreading out for miles, but they are seldom taken above Florida. It is somewhat difficult to predict just when and where these fish will appear. The average size is close to forty pounds, with top weights usually around seventy-five pounds.

These spike-billed creatures sometimes seize feather jigs, but they go more for natural baits like flying fish, sand perch, blue runner, bonito, balao, kingfish, mackerel, mullet, and other small fish. You slit the belly of your baitfish, imbed the hook, run the leader out through the mouth, and sew up the stomach. Some anglers use a piece of bonito belly or slice of king mackerel, trolling at a fast pace to try and make the bait skip over the surface. It is also effective to use a long and wide strip of barracuda, but you must keep the hook concealed and fastened so that neither the skipping motions of the bait nor the sailfish's tap will tear the hook free. The bait should trail in such a way that it won't twirl and untwist your line. Most outrigger baits are trolled forty to sixty feet astern. Some captains prefer to fish one bait five or ten feet back of the other, while other captains believe they should be trolled evenly.

Florida Keys captains generally prefer live bait, and one of the best offerings is an eight- to ten-inch blue runner, small enough so a sailfish can get the bait in its mouth and swallow it. Sand perch are high on the list of favorite live baits, and occasionally grunts are used. Mullet are thought by many to be the only live bait better than blue runners. Live mullet are hard to catch, but most of the other baitfish can readily be taken by trolling small spoons over the reefs.

Live bait is usually fished from the outriggers. The baitfish swims unconcernedly along six or eight feet beneath the surface—unconcernedly, that is, until it spots an approaching sailfish. Then all tranquility vanishes. The baitfish dashes frantically about, seeking to escape, and often dashes for the boat and tries to hide under it. I saw one sail take a small sand perch not a dozen feet from our boat. The angler may begin to shake, too, as the bait scurries about below. Occasionally, if this keeps up but the sailfish does not strike, the captain will advise yanking the line free from the outrigger clothespin. This allows the baitfish to swim more freely and may tease the spike-bill into taking. Offshore trolling is the only practical method of capturing sailfish, and at the same time you are quite likely to snag a king mackerel, a bonito, a barracuda, a wahoo, or a dolphin. This makes for a thrill-filled day!

The tackle varies according to the skill of the individual. A great many sportsmen like the 6/9 outfit, which proves entirely adequate. Less experienced fishermen would feel safer with a regular boat rod having an 8- to 10-ounce tip, a 4/0 or 6/0 free-spool reel with star drag and leather thumbstall, and three hundred yards of 36 to 72 test line. A No. 8 or 10 stainless steel wire leader ten feet in length, with a swivel between line and leader, and O'Shaughnessy hooks in sizes 7/0 to 9/0, complete the needs.

Pacific Sailfish

Setting a hook into one of the Pacific's sailfish is like cutting a line that releases a tautly held and very strong spring. You have only one course of action open until the first leaping impulse subsides—to hold on and pray. Pacific sails are big—almost 100 pounds bigger on the average than their Atlantic counterpart. What's more, they are numerous. In Panama Bay, if you tie onto the first fish, you can make money betting the rods will respond to half a dozen more that day. Also, in these waters you are likely to bump heads with silver marlin, tuna, bonito, and bull dolphin. Take tackle to handle them—and also take along some spare gear. You may need it.

Pacific sailfish are sometimes to be seen as far north as Monterey Bay, but the great bulk of thése dark blue and bright silver long-speared leapers concentrates around Cape San Lucas and up into the Gulf of California. The grounds off Guaymas, Mexico, are very famous for marvelous catches of sailfish from May until late fall. Sailfish are also found off Balboa, Canal Zone, off Cabo Blanco, Peru, and near the Perlas Islands and other Pacific islands. Mystery shrouds the sailfish's life span, spawning habits, and other particulars. Although schools of young Atlantic sails turn up occasionally, Pacific sails of less than fifty pounds rarely appear. This may indicate that the Pacific variety spawn much farther from land than does the Atlantic species.

In sailfishing, as in fishing in general, the trend is to lighter tackle. Seasoned sailfishermen prefer rods with tips weighing 4 to 6 ounces, 4/0 or 6/0 reels, and 18 to 27 test lines. The amateur is better suited with an 8-ounce rod tip and 45 test line. A 15-foot leader of wire, and O'Shaughnessy hooks in sizes 9/0 and 10/0, are used.

For bait, there is a choice of whole mackerel, mullet, sardines, or flying fish, or the belly strip from a mackerel or bonito. These should be prepared as described for the Atlantic species. When trolling for Pacific sailfish, as with the other billfish previously mentioned, it should be remembered that they have the habit of first striking their prey to stun or kill it before they swallow the bait. Therefore you should never try to set the hook when you feel the initial tap; instead, release the reel drag and let several yards of line coast backward. This will cause the sailfish to think that your bait has been crippled by his blow and will give him time to snatch the lure. Then, as he starts off, slam it to him—hard! Give two or three stiff jerks to be certain the hook will cling. Keep the rod tip elevated and the line taut, and you'll have one of the pluckiest, most sensational encounters with a surface-beating fish that you've ever lived through.

Sailfish seldom go for artificial lures, but now and then they may be taken on feather jigs. These jigs seem to be most attractive when the sailfish are idly moving along the surface. When there comes the rap of a bill on your feather jig, the best plan is to lower the rod tip and then strike at once; do not let any line drift back, as you do when using natural baits. This will prevent the fish from getting wise to the deception by feeling the metal— if he did, he'd quickly toss out the jig. Two or three sharp jerks are needed, though, to make a solid connection.

Mangled evidence of why sharks are not popular with anglers. The lady angler fought this blue marlin for more than two hours before the marauders attacked. The remaining portion weighed 568 pounds and if the fish had not been mutilated would probably have set a new world record for the species.

Sharks can sense when a fish is hurt or in trouble, which is one reason they are a plague to anglers. As shown here they will even come into shallow water if prospects for grabbing a meal with little effort looks good.

To repeat, every sailfish should be released unless it is a record-making fish, or is wanted for mounting. If he is not too badly injured, a fish will live to produce thousands more of his kind. Care should be taken in bringing a sailfish aboard, so that he may be released uninjured.

SHARKS

Of all the vast numbers of fish inhabiting the waters of the world, man has a strong inherent dislike for one species: the shark. Perhaps this unfriendly feeling toward the stealthy gray monsters is related to our fear of land-crawling reptiles. The very name "shark" calls to mind a huge, dark-gray dorsal fin throwing a wake after it as the fish quietly cuts through the peaceful waters of some distant tropical sea.

While the warm waters of the tropics are more thickly populated with sharks than the colder seas of the north, sharks do follow other marine species—the herring and mackerel—north in the spring, and they move southward only when autumn storms cool the water and food becomes scarce. Some species of sharks are classed as man-eaters, while others are merciless, depraved scavengers, always ready to take advantage of any crippled or disabled fish. Few anglers are familiar with the terrific battle a shark can give on rod and reel, because sharks are not often thought of as game fish.

Why catch sharks? They are big, they are a challenge to man and tackle, and they give a lot of sport. They are plentiful and so there need be few blank days. Some sharks are edible; the texture and flavor of their meat is not unlike swordfish. Though not all sharks are "man-eaters" they all destroy a lot of game fish. If you want to go to the trouble of skinning your catch and of having its hide tanned (any tannery will do it at small cost), you can have traveling bags made that the most careless baggage handler cannot dent or scratch.

This large family of salt-water fish has some hundred different species, but the IGFA, at present, keeps records of only five: the mako, the white, the tiger, the porbeagle, and the thresher. The hammerhead shark and the blue shark may be added at some time in the near future.

Mako Shark

For many years mako shark fishing was popular only in New Zealand and Australia. But thanks to Zane Grey's writings about his adventures with these fish in the Pacific, many anglers throughout the world became interested in this species and have gone after them. Within the past few years, mako fishing in particular, and shark fishing in general, have become very popular for those who want 'em big and who do not have the time or wherewithal to hunt giant tuna, broadbills, or marlin.

Mako is apparently a New Zealand word (Maori) meaning mackerel; the mako shark was identified by the New Zealanders with the mackerel shark because of a superficial resemblance between the tails of the two fish. The color of the mako is a dark, iridescent blue, not unlike that of the marlin and tuna. They are among the most streamlined fish in the sea, and one of the fastest. But makos are unpredictable fighters. Many hooked makos fight sluggish underwater battles—though a few will leap and run at high speed on the surface. The leap of one of those active makos is probably the most spectacular sight in fishing. They can jump up to twenty feet into the air when hooked—higher than marlin.

A surface shark, makos are most numerous in the waters adjacent to New Zealand. But they are found in both the Atlantic and the Pacific, generally anywhere you find mackerel and herring. Most makos are caught while trolling whole fish or squid for marlin; but a more productive method is to chum for them at night with chunks of fish, and then offer a whole fish on a 10/0 big game hook. A wire leader at least fifteen feet long should be used, because of the mako's habit of rolling up the leader. Their rough skins will chafe the line if they come in contact with it. Fishing for makos with spinning or other ultralight tackle falls under the heading of stunt-fishing, but some very respectable-sized sharks have been killed on this tackle. Most often, heavy offshore gear, such as is used for giant tuna or swordfish, is employed.

Makos, like other large sharks, are dangerous when brought into the boat. They should be gaffed in the tail, or roped, to prevent them from jumping. The usual method is to shoot them with a powerful rifle, but fish landed this way are not recognized by the IGFA. Clubbing has very little effect on sharks. Remember, a shark that has been dead for a half hour or so has been known to snap at anything near its mouth, as a muscular reaction. So be careful even of a dead one—they are dangerous. The teeth of a shark are so constructed that it is difficult to tear loose, once these steel-traplike jaws are snapped shut on your hand.

White Shark

The largest fish on the IGFA record list is the white, or man-eater, shark with a weight of over 2,600 pounds. Whites get a lot bigger than that, as evidenced by reports of them over thirty feet long. They range the high seas in the tropics and warm temperate areas of all oceans, and are perhaps most common in Australian waters. They are occasionally found as far north as the coast of Maine in the summer, but they are more common from Cape Cod southward. A voracious feeder, the white shark will engulf whole such large prey as sea lions, tuna, sturgeon, other sharks, sea turtles, and other large sea animals.

The best fishing for whites is at night when they move close to shore where a boat can be anchored. If the water is calm and the tide not too fast, the boat can be drifted. A mixture of ground bunker, bunker oil, and beef blood works into a slick that will attract whites (and other sharks too) for a mile or more, and before long they will start milling off the stern. A newspaper dipped in blood, tossed over the side, will also attract them. Just by way of passing, if you are tuna fishing and want a shark, just slit a tuna, hang it over the side, and sharks will quickly pick up the blood scent.

The white shark is a strong swimmer that has been known with certainty to attack boats when hooked or harpooned. Despite his ferocity, and great strength and weight, he generally takes bait gently. The first warning that a fish is on is a gentle nodding of the rod. Line is then set on free spool for fully a minute before the hook is set. He sounds a hundred feet or more and heads straight away when he feels the hook. The white shark doesn't leap when hooked, but he puts up a prolonged resistance. He generally tugs, makes a long, determined run at great depth, settles down and refuses to be moved, and repeats those actions until he is boated.

Because of his weight, the tackle recommended is the same as for the heavier black marlin—and the same bait should also be used.

Tiger Shark

These sharks are characterized by a sharp tail and a short snout, and have a distinctive color pattern of spots or transverse bars on the sides and fins. Tiger shark attain a maximum length of thirty feet, although about twelve feet is the usual length. They weigh 1,000 to 1,300 pounds when thirteen to fourteen feet long.

They are widely distributed in the tropics and subtropics of all oceans and are found both inshore and offshore. Common off Florida, they are only a summer visitor along the north Atlantic Coast, and rarely reach Long Island and Rhode Island waters. They are often found off the California coast the year around. These sharks range the high seas as well as coastal waters and at times enter the mouths of rivers. They are voracious and omnivorous; their food includes sea birds, turtles, sea lions, crabs, and fish, both large and small, as well as other sharks and rays. Like many sharks they are also scavengers.

The fishing technique, tackle requirements, and bait for the tiger shark are the same as for the white shark. They are usually sluggish in action until aroused by the smell of blood.

Porbeagle Shark

These sharks resemble the great white shark except for size and teeth. The largest on record, caught on rod and reel, weighed 260 pounds and was taken off South Africa. They are found on both sides of the Atlantic, and are common off the coast of Maine. They are seldom found south of South Carolina. A closely related species inhabits the Pacific Coast as far north as Alaska. Porbeagle sharks like the surface in calm weather, but they are also taken at mid-depths and at the bottom (about 500 feet down) on cod lines.

Adult porbeagle feed on fish, especially valuable species such as mackerel, herring, cod, and flounder. They also, like most sharks, actively pursue and eat squid. Porbeagle are very sluggish when hooked; they neither jump nor make any attempt to escape, and so are easily landed. For this reason, you can use a 6/9 outfit, an 8/0 hook and a 15-foot wire leader. Employ the same fishing methods described for white sharks.

Thresher Shark

A very interesting and game shark is the thresher. The name comes from its unique manner of feeding. It sweeps through schools of small fish whipping its enormous tail like a farmer threshing wheat. Then it turns back and gobbles the stunned and mutilated fish. The upper lobe of a thresher's tail is as long at its body. The thresher has a stocky build, but it is well streamlined. Its mouth is small, with fairly weak teeth. None of the many stories of their killing porpoises or billed fish with their tails have been authenticated, and they are not considered dangerous. They are found near the surface in the subtropic and warmer temperate regions in both the Atlantic and Pacific. In the western Atlantic they range from Nova Scotia and the Gulf of St. Lawrence to northern Argentina. They are generally found offshore in the warmer months of the year.

Though generally taken on live bait, the thresher is one of the few sharks that will strike an artificial lure. Quite a few are caught on feather jigs. Tackle should be the same as used for white marlin, or possibly a bit heavier. In North American waters the thresher averages from 100 to 150 pounds.

Hammerhead Shark

These sharks have elongated heads with the eyes at the ends of these processes. There are five known species, which are plentiful in warm waters and one of which is widely distributed elsewhere. They are active and voracious and attain a length ranging from three to fifteen feet. The large hammerhead are generally taken in warm waters while the smaller ones (three to nine feet in length) are taken as far north as Cape Cod in the East and Washington in the West.

Natural foods of hammerheads include other fish (including their own kind), squid, and skates. Their sense of smell is very keen, and they are among the first sharks to arrive on a scene when other fish are injured or cut up. These sharks are generally only taken on live bait; the tackle requirements are the same as for white marlin or slightly heavier fish.

Blue Shark

This shark is distinguished by its long falcate pectoral fins, a long pointed snout, and the first dorsal fin which is situated far back on the body. Its color is indigo blue above and changes abruptly to snow white on his lower sides.

The blue shark prefer to swim near the surface, and reside in the open seas in all oceans from warm temperate regions to the tropics. They are the most common of the larger pelagic sharks seen and caught offshore in the Atlantic. They have been reported to attain lengths of twenty feet, but twelve feet is usually the maximum for this species. The body is slender and light, so that a 9-foot specimen weighs only 160 to 175 pounds. They can be taken on live bait such as herring, menhaden, and mackerel. The tackle, again, can be the same used for white marlin.

Other kinds of sharks—such as basking, blacknose, smooth dogfish, dusky, lemon, sand, sharpnose soupfin, blacktipped, brown, and nurse sharks—may be taken along with the above species. Sharks may also be caught by surf casting and inshore fishing (see Chapters 6 and 7).

CHAPTER 9

Light-Tackle Salt-Water Fishing

THE CHIEF TREND in salt-water fishing techniques today is toward lighter tackle. Although the time-honored heavy outfits still have a place, great numbers of salt-water anglers are finding that they have more fun—and catch as many fish—with outfits no heavier and scarcely different from those used in fresh-water. On light tackle, many small- to medium-sized inshore game fish—such as striped bass, bluefish, white sea bass, salmon, shad, yellowtail, mackerel, and croaker—provide thrills rivaling those of the big-game species. While you can use lighter conventional tackle (see Chapters 5 to 8), the term "light tackle" generally means the use of bait-casting, fly, or spinning tackle. Actually, all the casting described in Chapters 5 and 7 can be accomplished with any light tackle. The choice depends upon the size of fish sought and the amount of sport you desire.

BAIT CASTING

The first type of light tackle used in salt water was bait-casting equipment, and it is still very popular today, with good reason. Of all light tackle, bait-casting gear is best able to cope with large game fish; the short rod and relatively heavy lines, are deadly to big fish. This sporty form of salt-water fishing may be done from rowboats, river banks, shores of inlets and bays, lagoons, jetties, bridges, and piers. Wherever fish linger along the inshore lanes of migration—and there are many hundreds of worthy spots dotting the Gulf of Mexico and Pacific and Atlantic coasts—

plugs, spinners, spoons or baits hurled out by the short fresh-water (or special salt-water) casting rod may bring singular results.

When casting from a pier, jetty, or river bank, at times you will connect with large fish that put your tackle to severe tests. For this reason you need fairly heavy, sturdy bait-casting rods, and stronger lines than are normally utilized for sweet-water fishing. The bait-casting rod may be 4½ to 6 feet in length, but one measuring 5 or 5½ feet is best for most situations. The one-piece tip may be made of bamboo, beryllium copper, glass, or steel. Solid or tubular glass is best. For top performance, the rod should be of medium or stiff action, with the rear and forward hand grips made of cork, and should possess a stainless-steel locking reel seat. The guides should be chrome-plated stainless steel, and not agate or agatine material.

With the bait-casting rod suggested, your reel may be one of the standard quadruple multiplying level winders capable of holding 100 yards of line; but an oversized model taking 150 yards is more practical for fish whose initial charge is far-reaching. Many bait-casting reels are equipped with a device to cut down your backlashes. Backlashes are common for the beginner and veteran alike, and do not let any so-called expert tell you otherwise. When the fish are biting, there is the element of human frailty which means less control; and less control can mean backlashes even among the best of anglers. Where big fish are encountered, a drag arrangement is handy. And you can bet that you'll be up against a big fish quite often when you're bait casting along the coast.

Lines for bait casting may be either braided synthetic—nylon or dacron —or monofilament. Both cast easily and smooth. A 12- to 18-pound test braided line is sufficient for average conditions, but 25- to 30-pound test is more in order for the heavy or hard-fighting fish. Monofilament lines of 12- to 20-pound test are also popular. If monofilament lines are to be used, care must be exercised to select a reel with close tolerances between the spool and end plates, so that the fine diameter line cannot work behind the spool into the gears or shaft. Several of the newer bait-casting reels are being made especially for this line.

Many novices just tie their line onto a lure or hook and start fishing. Don't you do it; there should be a leader of some type between your line and your bait or lure. This leader, which may be 6 to 18 inches in length, should have a barrel swivel at the line end and a lock snap swivel at the lure or hook end. If the fish you are after are not a sharp-toothed species such as bluefish or barracuda, the leader can be either of nylon or gut; otherwise it should be of stainless-steel wire. Remember that your leader need not be stronger than your line.

This brings us to lures and hooks. For the most part, the diving and deep-running underwater plugs of solid construction are more effective than surface plugs. These must be given action, a spurty movement that simulates the darting behavior of a minnow. You twitch the rod tip, reel in the slack, then jerk again; and continue this until the pickup is made for another cast. The clothespin style of lure is a favorite in Florida and along the Gulf Coast, for it is a deep traveler that appeals to many kinds of fish. This does not mean, though, that top-water artificials should be ignored, for some of these can be jumped and popped in a manner to make any hungry fellow strike. The modes of retrieving are similar to those tried in fresh water, and the response to your efforts will often be more than gratifying.

Metal squids, feather jigs, spinners, and spoons are also good bait-casting lures. Wobbling spoons are generally to be preferred to the revolving type for this method. The speed and manner of reeling them lend greater interest-provoking action, and they are well adapted for close-in work. If seaweed is abundant, resort to wobblers having weed guards. Actually, any cannibalistic fish—those that live on other small fish, eels, and shrimps—are apt to take a cast-and-retrieved artificial lure, when they are in the mood, that is.

If you are after bottom, live-bait feeders such as sea bass, tautog, tomcod, porgies, halibut, cabezon, sheepshead, corbina, bocaccio, cunners, pompano, and kingfish, you will need the right terminal tackle, the proper live or cut bait, and the right weight (sinkers) to get down where the fish live. This information can be found in the chart on page 368. One general rule to follow is that the bottom-feeding fish that live mainly on shellfish will not take artificial lures very readily.

Bait casting, like surf casting (see Chapter 6) is the act of throwing a lure or bait where you want it to go. While bait casting is similar in technique to surf casting, it is a great deal easier since you do not need to

A king mackerel breaks water as he nears the boat. He was taken on a subsurface plug and a light tackle bait-casting outfit.

Steps in making the overhead cast.

throw the lure as far. There are, however, certain things to remember, some moves to become acquainted with, and definite positions to be assumed. Hard and fast rules do not belong in bait casting. When the caster becomes proficient he casts overhead, from the side, backhand, flip, with two hands, or in any one of many other positions that may not be orthodox but which meet local conditions.

The Overhead Cast

The overhead cast is the most important for the salt-water angler and should be mastered first. The illustrations show the proper arm and rod movement. When preparing for a cast, hold the rod with the reel handle up and carry through the cast with the reel in the same position. This will permit the reel to ride smoothly on its bearings.

Put the reel in "free spool." For the right-handed person, the rod is held in the right hand with the thumb pressed firmly on the reel spool. The bait rig should be about six inches from the tip of the rod. At the beginning, the arm should be close to the side with the forearm parallel with the ground, dock, or boat. (*Left*)

Then raise the rod upward and backward quickly enough to make the rod bend backward. The movement is straight over the right shoulder. Stop the rod when the handle is straight up and immediately begin the forward cast by snapping the wrist and bringing the forearm forward. (*Center*)

Release the thumb pressure on the line as the line goes out and stop the

rod motion when the tip is pointed at the target. Keep your eyes constantly on the target and hold the rod in alignment with the outgoing line. As soon as the rig or lure reaches the target, the thumb is again pressed on the reel spool to prevent backlash of the line. (*Right*)

Then quickly place the rod in the left hand with the reel plate resting in the palm and the tip still pointing at the target. Re-engage the spool, and bring the drag into play. With an artificial lure, start the line retrieve as soon as it hits the water. When using bait, reel in any slack line with the right hand when the rig settles to the bottom and then follow the technique previously mentioned on page 132.

Casting with the left hand is precisely the same as with the right hand— with one exception. The reel handle is down instead of up. There is one real advantage to left-hand casting. It is not necessary to shift the rod from the right hand to the left when starting the retrieve. The rod is kept in the left hand at all times, and the reel is operated with your right hand.

The Side Cast

In making the side cast the rod should go back on the back part of the cast as far as it goes in the overhead cast, but on the forward part of the cast it goes almost straight out before you, instead of at the usual 45-degree angle. In making this cast the handle of the reel should be down, with the spool perpendicular and facing to the right on the forward cast. It is carried from back to front in this position. Best results in making this cast are obtained by bending the body to the right at the waist and cocking the head to the right, as this brings you more in line with the plane or level of your cast.

The hand action of the
three steps of the overhead cast.

The Backhand Cast

In the horizontal side cast, the cast is made from the right toward the left side. In the backhand cast, however, the cast is made from the left side toward the right. The position of the reel here is with the handle pointing straight up, and the line spool facing toward you. The rod pauses at a position behind your left shoulder and about thirty degrees below horizontal, and then travels to a position almost straight in front of you. One of the advantages of this cast is that it can be used by the angler seated in the stern of the boat; with this cast, he won't have to cast over the heads of other anglers in the boat, provided, of course, that the length of the boat is at right angles to the line of casting.

The Flip Cast

In making the flip cast, the rod is held with the tip pointing down, rod butt straight up, reel spoon facing toward you, and your thumb lightly pressing on the spool. The cast is made with a light flip forward, so that, at the moment the reel spool is released, the rod is aimed at the point to which you wish to cast. This cast can very easily be used in lawn practice, using a casting weight. All practice casts should be no more than fifteen to thirty feet. After getting a thorough knowledge of this method of casting, the caster can strive for greater distances. For the longer casts the rod can be carried up to an angle of thirty degrees in front of you, and as the lure drops to the water the thumb presses down on the line spool, and the reel is turned up to reel in the lure in the usual manner.

Two-Hand Casting

Some of the salt-water bait casting reels, because of their greater line capacity, lend themselves to two-hand casting. When making this cast with a two-hand rod, the action of the rod is precisely the same as with a one-hand rod using the overhead method. The three photographs show how this action is imparted to the rod. Notice particularly that the reel handle is not held skyward, but the spool axle is in a horizontal position at the start of the cast.

Cast with a two-hand rod.

CASTING ARTIFICIAL SURFACE LURES

As stated previously, one of the most popular techniques of bait casting is to use an artificial surface lure. Because the way of playing a surface lure varies somewhat according to the fish, only experience teaches which retrieve to use for which fish at which time—and even then you can often count on being double crossed.

In general, a slowly played lure pays off, especially in quiet water. But when hits are few and far between, it is best to try new lure behavior. Make the lure walk across the top; make it swish just under the surface for a foot or two. Impart a saucy, sideways flip to the tail. Make the action so enticing that if there's a fish around he just has to come out and swat it.

The procedure for awakening a drowsy fish in the salt water is the same as the one used for large-mouth black bass in fresh water. You pick a spot where you think there is a fish, and start with a fairly slow retrieve just in case a wide-awake fish happens to be there. Play the lure very slowly, let it sit quietly for half a minute, then give it a slight twitch by lifting the rod tip, then let it lie doggo again. After about six hitless casts, start increasing the speed of the retrieve and the loudness of the pops. Sometimes you get a strike on the fifteenth cast and sometimes it takes forty. But providing the fish is there, you'll almost certainly get action eventually. Even when fish are hanging out in the shade, resting and waiting for the coolness of dusk before thinking about food, you can use a popper to make them mad enough to hit.

The snook is one salt-water fish that is driven to shelter by heat. They are willing night hitters, and good daytime strikers if the weather is not too warm. But extreme heat puts them down or sends them back to sit it out under a protective mantle of mangroves. Surface lures are made to order for much of the water they seek out at this time.

Though warm water of the midday heat will put some salt-water fish down, it is cold water that can really send them out of reach of a surface plug. I was given a vivid example of this once when I fished the Gulf of Mexico out of the Everglades for sea trout (spotted weakfish). That day those fish were hitting popping plugs as if they were gold-plated shrimp. But the very next morning, in the colder Atlantic waters off Cocoa Beach, Florida, I found that while the trout willingly took an underwater lure, they would not rise to the surface plug. Numerous other salt-water fish also go deep when the water cools off. Generally fish do not come in on southern flats and shallows where they can be reached with surface lures until the water temperature is above 68 degrees—and 70 degrees is still better for top-water fishing. Some anglers even go so far as to carry a thermometer along.

It is difficult to name a water depth that could be called "best," or even "right," for using surface lures. Tarpon cruise just under the surface, seldom more than four feet down. Jack crevallé in schools are right on top, but a solitary jack will rest along the drop-off of a channel in three or four feet of water. Striped bass often lurk near the bottom in six feet of water, yet a big striper weighing twenty-five pounds will lie in two or three feet of water. Snook seldom are deeper than four feet and ladyfish run at about the same level. All these fish can rise with a single flip of a fin to a surface plug.

Some fish which will flush from a popper on the shallow flats are willing takers when you offer them a surface lure in slightly deeper water. Channel bass, called redfish in Florida, are very scary when they feed on the shallow flats. But with three or four feet of water over the grassy beds they like, they will hit a popper without hesitation and they're actually easier to take with a noisemaker than with a silent lure. Redfish are as blind as bats, and when fishing a streamer it is necessary to drop it within a foot in front of them or they will not see it. A popper can be dropped a little farther away and retrieved very slowly, and the fish will be attracted by the noise it makes and hunt it down.

Sea trout like a good loud pop, too. Commercial fishermen who cane-pole for trout use a popping cork to which they tie a short length of leader, then the baited hook. The loud pop of the cork on the surface attracts the trout, and when they swim up to investigate they see and smell the shrimp —and take it, including the hook. Sometimes those hungry trout will even try to swallow the big popping cork. I have heard of one commercial fisher-man who made a popping cork out of lignum vitae. It must have had a special voice for those Florida sea trout because every time he used it, the trout would rise up and swat the popper instead of eating the shrimp that dangled below it.

Since all fish do not attack a surface lure in the same manner, different techniques apply on the strike. For instance, a big tarpon sucks in a lure while a barracuda clamps down on it with slotted teeth. After the fish takes the lure, the strike must be delayed until the lure has gone well down in-side him, or at least until the fish turns or starts down, so you will not pull the lure out. You have to wait before striking groupers, snappers, channel bass, and bigger tarpon, too. On the other hand, cruising fish, like blues, mackerel, and jacks, do not stop to swallow. They hit on the run and the strike must be instantaneous.

School fish like to chase a fast-moving lure. A plug dropped in front of them should move faster than the fish are traveling or they will pass it, thinking it is just something floating on the surface. And the lure should be dropped right in their path so that they don't have to move to the right or the left to grab it.

Striped bass are great takers of surface lures, and usually the bigger the better. Stripers weighing over 15 pounds can't be bothered with tidbits— they want a full-course dinner, and most light-tackle lures are too small even to tempt a striper that size. But the angler can overcome some of that indifference by the noise and commotion he stirs up with a popping bug or other surface lure. The hit of a huge striper to a surface lure is a hair-raising experience. And while a fast, steady retrieve will pick up the school stripers, these big boys are more temperamental. They like their plug retrieves mixed up. Some days they go all out for a fast-moving lure. Other days they want it slow, like you play it for largemouth bass: slow, with plenty of stops, for half a minute at a time.

I generally start my retrieve for big stripers with a single loud pop; let the plug rest a few seconds; then retrieve it by a combined action of raising the rod tip and pulling back on the line with my left hand so that I get a three- or four-foot strip of line. This maneuver gives enough power to pull the plug just under the surface, and it stirs up a terrific fuss. Bub-bles will fly all over and the gurgling noises will be heard for a long way.

Then at the end of this stunt, when the plug rises to the surface, give it another loud pop and let it sit still again. If that doesn't gather in all the striped bass nearby, nothing will.

FLY FISHING

While the fly rod was designed for a clear, fast-running trout or salmon stream, many light-tackle addicts recently discovered that they may enjoy remarkable catches and unmatched sport on the salty waters with a fly rod and an appropriate lure. Salt-water fly fishing is gaining thousands of enthusiastic fans each season as news spreads of its fun and success. Furthermore, this sport gives you another way to use your fresh-water fly rod and reel, widening the scope of your angling vacations.

Many shore-trailing fish along the Gulf, around Florida, and up the Atlantic Coast will rise for fly-rod lures at one time or another. Among these are such skill testers as tarpon, bonefish, striped bass, barracuda, bluefish, snook, ladyfish, channel bass, pompano, snapper, weakfish, grouper, and mackerel. Around islands, up rivers, along lagoons, and in inlets you won't lack for action. And of course the favorite light-tackle method of taking silver salmon in Pacific waters is with the fly rod and a hair fly imitating a candlefish.

One place noted for a variety of fly-fishing sport is the Florida Bay. Here along the southern coast of Florida and throughout the Keys, there are ideal land and water conditions, providing an abundance of natural food for the spirited fish that swarm through the Bay. You could spend weeks in a canoe or outboard motorboat among the sheltering islands, in the calm of the season, catching fish of all kinds to your heart's content. However, unless you are an old-timer in this region, don't go far into the maze of passageways without an experienced guide. It's easy to "get away from it all" there—but getting back again is sometimes a different matter!

Fly Tackle

Fly tackle for salt-water use should be rugged and corrosion-resistant. Rods should generally be 8½ to 9 feet long, and weigh 7 to 9 ounces. Choose a rod with plenty of backbone—a stiff one—because you will want to handle heavier lures than the average fresh-water fly angler. Rods having "bass bug," "light salmon," or "steelhead" action are suitable. Many such rods, made of tubular glass, come fitted with stainless-steel guides and a tip-top which will not rust.

A large "salmon" single-action fly reel is usually recommended, especially if you plan to do a lot of salt-water fly fishing for bonefish, tarpon, mackerel, striped bass, blues, and weakfish. The newer automatic fly reels are being employed more than ever for salt-water fishing, especially for taking the many penfish species on fly rods or live bait rods. This reel has the advantage that by a touch of your finger you can recall line rapidly enough to avoid slack—and a lost fish. But regardless of the type, make sure it will hold the usual thirty yards of level, double-tapered, or torpedo-tapered line—B, GBG, and GBF respectively—plus at least a hundred yards of backing or running line. Nylon fly lines, which do not rot in salt water as do silk lines, should always be used. The backing can be 15-pound nylon (braided), or perhaps you can get 125 yards of 12-pound on; if so, the longer yardage is preferable to the heavier test.

No matter how good your reel is, keep it clean and well oiled (see Chapter 11). In fresh-water fly fishing, the reel generally serves merely as a convenient holder of line—it has little to do with the actual playing of the fish. But in salt-water fly casting, in addition to being a line container, a big and hard-running fellow your reel must be able to take care of the first long rush when you hit a big, hard-running fellow. That rush will run out your 30 yards of fly line very quickly and you'll be glad that there is plenty of backing or running line and that your reel is in top-notch condition.

Your terminal gear may be size No. 2 or 3 stainless-steel wire leader three to six feet long, hitched to the line with a No. 8 or 10 barrel swivel. Good lures to try include bucktail and streamer flies tied on No. 1, 1/0, or 2/0 hooks of O'Shaughnessy style; salt-water flies made to resemble sand eels, sea worms, shrimps, or herring; bass bug floats; spinner and fly combinations; feather-minnows; small fly spoons; and midget plugs. Streamers and bucktail flies in brown and white, red, and white colors are held by many anglers to be the best lures in salt-water fly rod fishing. Regular salmon flies in popular patterns are also magnetic to ocean fish.

Steps to follow when fly casting in salt water.

Fly Casting

Fly casting is not exactly the same as surf or bait casting. But with practice you should be able to place the lure where you want and to make it behave the way you want. Study the following steps with the illustration:

A. Grasp the rod with your right hand, the reel down, the left foot forward.

B. Pull about twenty feet of line off the reel and loop the excess on your hand.

C. Raise the rod upward and backward, using a sharp snap of the wrist and forearm.

D. Watch the line go backward and when the loop straightens out, pause a moment and then cast forward, using the wrist and arm movement.

E. Stop the rod when it reaches about a 45-degree angle, and, as the forward loop begins to straighten out, release the line held by the left hand.

F. As the lure falls downward, raise the tip of the rod slightly so that the lure will settle naturally on the water.

Repeat the cast, pulling out more line with your left hand if necessary to lengthen the cast. With twenty or thirty feet of line out, you have a better chance to hook and land your fish than you have with a longer line since you have better control of the line. When enough line is out, press the line with your index finger to prevent it from unwinding while casting or when a fish strikes.

In all fly casts the left hand always holds the line; it should keep the line taut at all times to be sure of maximum-power delivery. During the cast the right and left hands move back and forth in a parallel path, just as your hands would move when swinging a two-handed ax. If the left hand remains stationary, the distance between the hands will of course vary, thus tightening the line on the back cast and slackening it on the forward cast just when you need maximum power. This is a very common mistake.

The left hand serves to (*a*) keep the line taut, (*b*) take up slack when necessary, and (*c*) add extra power and speed when needed. To accomplish these, the left hand must maintain an equal distance from the right hand.

With a surface lure, make as long a cast as possible (unless you are aiming at a rising fish), and let the lure sit for fifteen or twenty seconds before retrieving. The retrieve should be made in short, halting steps, giving the fish plenty of time to get off the bottom and look the lure over. Many anglers are inclined to work too fast. Often the slightest disturbance will put the big ones down. The subsurface lure should be fished in much the same manner, the only difference being that a longer time should be allowed before starting the retrieve so as to get the lure down to the depth desired. Then start your retrieve.

Here is a good trick in handling a hard-running fish on a fly reel that has no brake or star drag. Since the reel is under the rod with the handle on the right hand side, you will be holding the rod in your right hand. As the fish fights, you can exert thumb pressure as you desire on the inside of the spinning reel's spool. If you do not, your line may overrun and backlash. But watch out for your knuckles on that whirling reel handle.

If you are just starting salt-water fly fishing and happen to have a fresh-water fly fishing outfit, you can find use for it just as is. Go after mackerel for instance; your 4- or 5-ounce fly rod and regular reel, line, leader, and flies—streamers, preferably—are just right for these fish. You must tie on a fine, light-tinned wire leader about twelve or eighteen inches long, for mackerel have needlelike teeth and can slash a line or a soft leader in no time flat. A great deal of sport for the beginner comes from little blue-fish, also called snapper blues and skipjacks, which run into our tidal rivers and bays. While they may not be bigger than eight to twelve inches long, they're all dynamite on a fly rod and manna from heaven on the dinner table. Use small white, red-and-white, blue-and-white bucktails on long-shank No. 6 or No. 8 hooks.

In the Chesapeake Bay region, fine luck has been had with a yellow streamer fly linked to a chromium-plated spinner. This has been especially appetizing to striped bass. Striped bass have also taken bright fly and spinner rigs and bass bug floats. In these waters stripers are caught by casting in sheltered coves and along tidal rivers. When not feeding at the surface, they may be chummed up to the field of battle.

POPULAR LIGHT-TACKLE FISH

Bonefish

The number one fish to most light-tackle enthusiasts, and especially to fly anglers, is the bonefish. Swift as lightning, wild and strong in fighting, this silvery fish is one of the most difficult to hook and play that swims in the salty sea. But it's a prize worthy of your effort. Bonefish loiter in the warm waters all year, but they are noticeably abundant in the Florida area from about May until October. However, they may be taken with reason-able regularity in the Florida Keys and Bimini districts from December to April, and all year at the Dry Tortugas. In Pacific waters bonefish do not ordinarily venture very far up the California coast. Upon occasion they may appear as far north as Monterey Bay, but they are generally con-tent to stay around San Diego and southward.

In your efforts to hook and tame the bonefish, you may fortify your-self with such tackle as a 9- or 9½-foot trout fly rod weighing 5½ or 6 ounces, with a "salmon" single-action fly reel or one of the newer auto-matic fly reels with 150 yards of 18-pound test nylon fly line and 18-pound test braided nylon backing, a 6-foot monofilament leader, and trout flies of Professor, Silver Doctor, Parmacheene Belle, and similar patterns, tied on 1/0 hooks. Streamer flies are also excellent.

When you spot the bonefish feeding along the sand, you edge up close enough to cast your fly so it lands a bit beyond him and to one side, then you twitch it over the bottom, an inch at a time, at a spot where the fish will see it and strike. It's important to stay perfectly quiet and not cause any vibrations in the shallow water, so you hold your breath and rivet your attention on the lure. There comes a slight touch and you gingerly let out a mite of slack line. Perhaps the bonefish is mouthing the lure. Soon he turns to swim away with it. Instantly you clamp your thumb on the reel spool and swing the rod tip upward.

This bonefish was snapped just as it spotted the camera man and opened the throttle wide for a fast getaway.

Once the hook is set, you release the spool at once—or if not, you'll get a good thumb burn. The bonefish springs outward with lightning swiftness, and considerable line is claimed on that first run. The fight will be fast and furious, with several exciting charges, and it is up to you to be alert and avoid any slack line—or you will be lost pronto. You can never predict just what one of these crazy customers will do. He may dart straight away for thirty yards or more, then sweep around in a circle that makes the line slice the surface. Or he may tear off many yards from the reel on a dash for deeper water, then turn and head right for you with a spurt that makes you crank furiously. If you lick a big bonefish—and some run over fifteen pounds, with the average about four pounds—you are entitled to pat yourself on the back, for their sprightly and capricious tactics win their freedom more often than not.

A big pompano, or permit, is a hard fellow to tame on a fly rod, for he will go scooting, in among the coral formations, sponges, and weeds where he chafes the line and soon rends it apart. He has a habit of swimming at right angles to your line and then, after going the limit of his run, turning quickly and swimming broadside again. You have probably noticed this same trait when you've hooked one of the spirited panfish of lake and pond. With a pompano, you just have to apply easy pressure until he is fagged out and ready for the net. Snook like lures that splash and hop along the top, and have been partial to yellow-bodied bass bugs whose hooks are hidden in white or yellow feathers or bristles.

Shad

A new sport on the West Coast is catching shad on fly-casting tackle. These members of the herring family—they average around three or four pounds in weight, but may go as high as fourteen pounds and grow to a length of thirty inches—are plentiful from Monterey Bay to the Columbia River, but extend from Alaska to southern California. Some of the centers for shad fishing in California are the Pittsburg, San Francisco Bay, Sacramento River, and San Joaquin River areas; in Oregon and Washington, the Columbia River provides the best catches, Shad linger in brackish water of inlets for long periods. During the summer months, large numbers of these fish are caught off the west coast of Vancouver Island and in the Fraser River. Although widely distributed along the Atlantic seaboard, the shad is generally sought as a game fish in only a few areas. These include the Connecticut River, the Susquehanna River, the Potomac River, and the St. Johns River in Florida—the southernmost limit of their range. Near the mouths of all of these rivers, inshore salt water provides excellent fly-casting sport.

Shad move into rivers and streams for the purpose of spawning. This generally takes place along both coasts from March to June, after which they return to the oceans. As the water temperature lowers, the shad retreat into deeper nooks offshore; their migrations seem to be more in this manner than from north to south. There is no closed season on shad, but from about mid-June until mid-March there is a daily bag and possession limit of five shad per person in California waters. This affords the fish a measure of protection—which is well, for these popular fish furnish fine sport and tasty meals and deserve every consideration.

You can angle for them with a 5½-ounce, 9-foot fly rod, to which is fitted a single-action or upright model automatic fly reel of large capacity, and thirty yards of D level oil-impregnated nylon fly line backed with fifty yards of 12-pound test braided nylon or dacron casting line. A 6-foot level trout leader will also be needed, together with such lures as wet flies in popular trout patterns (bright colors predominating), streamer and bucktail flies on No. 6 hooks, small spoons, tiny feathered spinners, and plain spinners with their single hooks imbedded in small sea worms, shrimps, or minnows. With such an assortment of lures, you'll have plenty of interesting sport in taking shad.

Having assembled this rig, station yourself at a sheltered point in one of the ocean inlets, or along a river while the shad are running up, or returning to the sea. Cast to the edges of feeding schools and twitch the lures slowly along near the bottom, or at the level where the fish are cruising. Set the hook lightly, but solidly, when a shad grabs hold. The shad's mouth is none too tough, so you must play him gingerly until he is ready to call it quits.

Salmon

On the Pacific seaboard, fly-rod fishing for salmon in the coastal rivers, and far up some of the tributaries, is a major attraction whenever these regal fish invade fresh waters on their mission to perpetuate their race. For this method of salmon fishing, you might use a three-piece fly rod 9½ feet long, weighing about 7¼ ounces; or a two-piece fly rod 8 feet long. To either of these rods you could attach one of the upright models of the popular, free-stripping automatic fly reels weighing 8½ ounces, capable of holding 75 yards of size G level nylon fly line or 60 yards of heavier line; or a single-action fly reel with frame and spool of noncorroding aluminum alloy, weighing 5 ounces, with a line capacity of 100 yards. Nylon line of 18- to 30-pound test, with nylon leader material of 20-pound breaking strength, may be put into service. Among the best lures for general needs are spinners having red feathers and gang hooks in size No. 4, and regular salmon flies. To hook, fight, and land the big salmon that lie in the deep pools of those Western streams and rivers is an inescapable desire of every angler who wants the ultimate in fly-casting thrills.

At any rate, if you are an angler who cannot be content until you have tried every method and type of lure, you will surely make fly-rod fishing in salt water one of your habitual sports. This is a comparatively new phase of seaside angling that opens the way for much exciting pioneer exploration.

SPINNING FISHING

Spinning casting gear is the newest in the light tackle field. After a slow and awkward infancy as salt-water equipment, spinning tackle has really come of age, and is fast becoming one of the most popular kinds of tackle for light salt-water work. The reason is that spinning tackle is certainly the easiest to use for the beginner and it can be used for the species generally taken by bait casting, but it will give the same thrills as fly casting. (Heavier spinning tackle can be used for surf casting and trolling.) Beginners find that they can cast like experts within a day, and cast well enough to fish in less than an hour. The fine, almost invisible lines fool more and bigger fish, and the automatic drag simplifies the playing of oversized gamesters.

It would be downright ridiculous to claim that spinning is the all-around answer to all kinds of fishing. It is true that under certain conditions it can score heavily. But the spinning rod, reel, and line has, at present, definite limitations in the size of salt-water fish it can handle. So far no spinning reel has been made which will hold large tackle-smashing marlin and swordfish. But there is one niche of ocean fishing into which spinning fits beautifully: the light-tackle division, where the sport-seeking angler fights anything up to moderate-sized ocean-going game fish.

Truly amazing records are being established by spin men these days. For the man who seeks trophy fish in the light-tackle division, the field is wide open. A 150-pound marlin has already been fought to a belly-up finish in running seas with an 8-pound test monofilament line. Another angler, after a two-hour fight, landed a 261-pound mako shark on spinning gear with 12-pound test monofilament line. Giant striped bass, tarpon, salmon, sailfish and many other tackle busters have been licked to a stand-still. With spinning tackle, every ounce of the fish's strength must be exhausted before he can be brought alongside for the gaff or net.

A complete discussion of spinning tackle—reels, lines and rods—will be found in Chapter 2. The terminal tackle used with this spin tackle is also the same as for conventional bait casting except that it is generally slightly lighter in weight. Further information on spin tackle terminal gear will be found in Chapter 3.

Steps required to set the friction drag. With anti-reverse lever set "on," and with line running over line guide, jerk the line hard (*left*). Did the spool turn too easily? Set the drag a bit tighter (*right*) and jerk again. Only experience will tell you when a drag is nicely adjusted. However, when you feel that you have almost reached the breaking point of the line, back off perhaps a half turn on the drag—good line insurance.

Spinning, as referred to in this chapter and throughout this book (except on page 111 where spinning is a method of taking salmon), is simply a way of casting, not a method of fishing. Although it accomplishes the same operation as our bait-casting outfit, there is enough difference in the operation and action of the two kinds of outfit to give them both an important place in the angler's world. Which of the two is preferable depends on the fisherman and the kind of fishing he is doing.

Though the actual manual handling of the spinning reel and line during casting is different from the handling of the conventional revolving spool reel, the mechanics of making the cast are the same. As in any other kind of casting, the weight of the lure and its momentum pulls the line out, and it is the proper flexing of the rod that makes for a good cast.

The basic spin cast with a light rod is the overhead cast. The lure should hang about six inches from the tip of the rod. The first step is to move the pickup device into casting position. With a manual reel you bring the line roller to the top, where you can pick up the line with the index finger of your right hand. Then the line roller is moved out of the way so that it rests at the bottom of the reel. With reels that have finger pickups you do the same thing, turning the handle so the line can be grabbed with the index finger. Then back off or reverse the handle until the finger pickup moves to the bottom of the reel, after which push the finger down, away from the reel spool. For this practice casting, the antireverse should be in the "off" position. When using the full bait pickup reel you turn the handle until the line roller is on top, permitting you to grab the line with your index finger. Then back off or reverse the reel handle so that the line is free from the roller. Finally, using your left hand, push the wire bail down until it is in casting position at the bottom of the reel.

When your reel is ready to cast, rest the line on the ball of your index finger. Next hold the rod at about the 10 o'clock position. Point it at the target. Now bring the rod back fast toward you so that the tip points up into the air above your head at about the 12 o'clock position. Without waiting, you immediately start the rod tip forward. This should be a fast snap. As the rod moves forward it will bend into an arc under the weight of the lure. When it reaches the 10 o'clock position again, the index finger releases the line and the lure shoots out in front of you at a fast speed. When it reaches the target or just above it, you drop your index finger to the lip of the spool to stop the cast. If you have an automatic finger or a bail pickup reel, you can also stop the cast by turning the handle.

If your lure goes high into the air, it means that you released the line too soon. If the lure drops at your feet or a short distance away, this means you released the line too late. It requires a bit of practice before you get the right timing. A good way to get the feel of the rod and lure is to have the line on your index finger ready to cast, then wave the rod back and forth from the 10 o'clock to the 12 o'clock position without releasing the

A

B

C

D

Steps in making spinning surf cast. (*A*) Assume the position indicated here. Note that reel hangs between the second and third fingers of the right hand, pickup bail is in "cast" position, line is caught by right index finger, lure is hanging a foot, or thereabouts below the tip-top, rod tip is pointing at the target area, and you are completely relaxed. (*B*) Bring the rod tip back smartly by lifting with the right hand, sharply propelling the butt away from your body with the left hand. The rod is almost level and the lure is dangling from the tip, almost touching the sand. (*C*) While the weight of the lure is still pulling the rod tip back, building up compression in the rod start the forward casting motion by snapping the butt back toward your body, while at the same time straightening out your right arm. Keep the tip pointed at the lure, and you will reduce line friction to a minimum. (*D*) The cast is completed. The instant the lure hits the water the line should be picked up by the reel ready for the retrieve.

A   B   C

Steps in preparing to cast when using the regular bail pickup. (*A*)
Bring lure to within about a foot of the rod tip-top. Bring the line guide
portion of the pickup bail to the top of the reel (nearest rod handle),
and reach down alongside the line with the right index finger. (*B*) Pick
up line with index finger of right hand. At the same time, with fingers
and thumb of left hand, open pickup bail by swinging it from left to
right until it catches in "cast" position. (*C*) Continue backing off on
the reel handle until the manual pickup is entirely away from the line
where it passes from the reel spool to your finger.

A   B   C

Steps in preparing to cast when using a manual pickup attachment.
(*A*) Bring lure to within about a foot of the rod tip-top. Bring the line
roller to the top of the reel (nearest rod handle), and reach down
alongside the line with the right index finger. (*B*) Pick up line with
index finger of right hand. Back off on reel handle at the same time
you pick up the line. The antireverse lever should be in "off" position,
to allow this movement. (*C*) That's all there is to it. You're ready to
cast. No worry about "level-winding" or backlashes.

line from your index finger. Just go through the motions, waving it back and forth. You will feel the rod flexing under the weight of the lure. Then after a minute or two of this, try releasing the lure at the right moment.

With most heavier salt-water spin rods you must use two hands for casting. The cork handle or butt on these rods is longer, in order to accommodate two hands, and may range from 14 to 30 inches in length. In the two-hand method, you place your right hand above the reel and grasp the end of the butt with your left hand. You release the line from the pickup and hold it with your right-hand index finger as in the overhead cast. To make the two-hand overhead cast you go through the same motions as with the one-hand methods; however, you bring the rod a bit lower in front of you, to a spot slightly above the 9 o'clock position. Then bring it back over your head and let it drop behind you to about the 2 o'clock position. Now, as the lure bends the rod into a big arc, you start the forward cast by pushing with your right hand and pulling back with your left. This is done with a quick snap. When the rod reaches the 10 o'clock position in front of you, let the line go, and the lure will sail out a great distance. Timing here is just as important as in one-handed casting. It will come with practice.

The other method is similar to surf casting with the conventional surf rod. Here you hold the rod behind you, almost parallel to the ground. Then with a fast forward snap you bring the rod over your head and at about the 10 o'clock position in front of you, release the line. This method is best with the heaviest surf spinning rods and with heavy lures.

There are other casts which can be used with the two-hand salt-water spin rods. The side cast—done in the same manner as bait casting (page 210)—is used against a strong wind. When fishing from bridges or piers you often point the rod down toward the water and then flip it out quickly away from the structure. In a boat, or other places where space and movement are restricted, you often do a modified version of the overhead cast by holding the rod up and slightly in front of you. Then you bring it back and forward very quickly, in a short radius, to snap the lure out.

With the light and medium salt-water rods and lighter lures you can hold the line with the ball of your index finger the same as with the one-hand spin rods. But for the heavier rods and lures many anglers prefer to hold the line against the lip of the reel spool.

With the bail pickup model, line is picked up for the retrieve simply by starting to turn the handle in the regular forward direction. The bail automatically flips into the "retrieve" position, with the line in place (Fig. A).

When using the reel equipped with the manual pickup attachment (see Figs. B, C, and D) drop the right index finger against the edge of the spool. The line will catch on the finger. Pick up the line, pulling it back of the path of the manual pickup roller. Then turn the handle in the regular forward direction, and it will cause the roller to pick up the line.

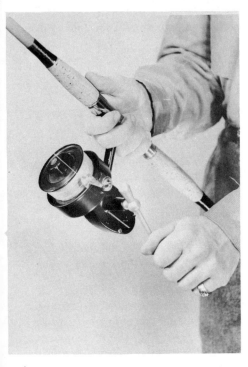

A

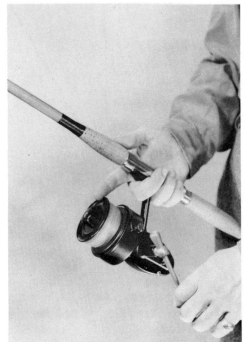

B

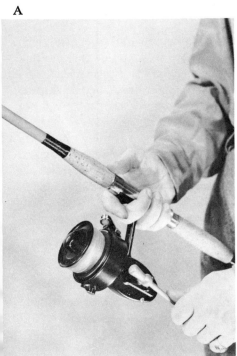

C

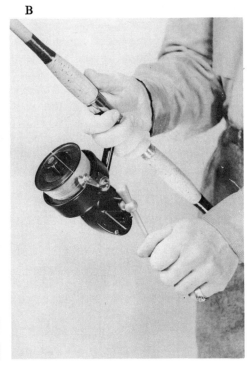

D

Steps in retrieving a line.

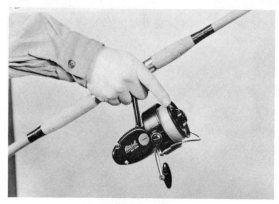

(*Left*) Line control of a spinning reel with the tip of the right index finger. (*Right*) The anti-reverse arrangement on your spinning reel will save many a barked knuckle. It is shown in operation.

Line control while the lure is in flight is simple. Just play the tip of the right index finger on the line or edge of the spool. The amount of pressure you use will determine the amount of braking effect. This same type of line control is useful when drifting a bait. Instead of picking up the line in the "retrieve" position, hold the line with the finger tip. It is then easy to pay out as much or as little line as you want.

Many salt-water spinning reels have an antireverse arrangement which saves plenty of barked knuckles. When a fish strikes, you quickly flip that control lever into the "on" position with your left thumb, at the same time holding firmly to the reel handle. Once the antireverse is on, the handle need not be held. No matter what the antics of the fish, the handle will not turn backward, and the drag can be used with full effectiveness.

The technique of fighting and landing a hooked fish is pretty much the same as the technique described for the conventional bait-casting tackle; but remember that your spinning gear is light, especially the line, and thus you have to do more playing him and tiring him out before you attempt to land him.

Setting the hook with a spinning rig is no more difficult than with heavier rigs. The spinning rod has more "give" and the line more stretch. You must, then, make sure the hook barb is sharp. To make penetration easier, you might want to alter its shape. The left sketch shows the barb as it comes from the factory; the right sketch shows how you may modify it.

CHAPTER 10

Salt-Water Fishing Boats

AFTER READING the previous chapters, you should be convinced that there are few kinds of salt-water fishing in which a boat will not increase your catch. Boats used in salt-water fishing range all the way from tiny 8-foot prams to big inboard cruisers 60 feet in length. There is a time and place for every kind of boat.

Basically, the craft has to be suited to the type of fishing you plan to do. A smaller boat, good for taking weakfish, sea bass, flounders, and the like in coastal waters, has no business far offshore. Conversely, the offshore fishing boat, built to brave high seas, would be far too clumsy in confined shallow waters. Correct size is vital.

A good fishing boat must be seaworthy in design, equipment, and gear. Construction must be the best if it is to have a long useful life without undue stress and strain. The fishing craft, after all, will be subjected to a life far more strenuous than a boat meant only for cruising.

Adequate speed is another important consideration when selecting a fishing boat. Your boat should have enough speed to reach the fishing grounds within a reasonable time. To escape quickly to shelter when a blow comes up is even more vital. You don't need a marine hotrod to meet these requirements; but you'll never regret having adequate power. Your craft must be able to catch up with a fast-swimming school of fish; it must troll slowly and proceed without undue fuss, commotion, or waste of fuel. Its power plant, whether inboard or outboard, must be reliable and safe. Fortunately, most modern marine engines and motors are marvels of efficiency and when they are properly cared for, breakdowns are rare.

HULL SHAPES, DESIGNS, AND MATERIALS

To understand the different types of salt-water fishing boats, you should first know the differences between the various hulls, and the designs and materials employed in their construction.

Hull Shapes

The hull shapes commonly used on all boats are classified as flat, V-, and round-bottomed. Each is good for a specific type of salt-water fishing.

The flat-bottomed hull is best for shallow water, since it has the greatest volume for its draft. Up to 10 mph., it is the most economical type of hull to drive with a motor, while at higher speeds, where planing occurs, it is the fastest of the three forms. However, this type of hull is suitable only for small boats used on protected waters of bays, inlets, and river mouths. In a moderate sea, it tends to pound or bounce. Another disadvantage of the flat-bottomed hull is that it is very difficult to design a good-looking boat when a cabin is required. Since the boat has a shallow draft, an adequately high cabin makes the boat look top-heavy.

The V-bottomed hull avoids most of the difficulties of the flat-bottomed hull. Its forward sections will not pound and, because of its greater draft, it provides good cabin headroom. It is faster than a round-bottomed boat of equal power, length, and displacement. It's also a drier boat to ride in, because the sharp angles between the bottom and sides throw the forward waves out and away from the hull. The V-bottomed hull is well suited for offshore fishing.

The round-bottomed hull is the strongest type of hull and usually results in a better appearance. Because the materials it requires are somewhat smaller than those needed for V-bottomed construction, it is often more economical to build. Many anglers dislike round-bottomed boats because they are said to be "tippy." But boats don't tip by themselves; people tip them. There is no reason why a well-designed, properly built round-bottomed boat with a broad beam—that is, plenty of width in relation to length—should not be a stable rough-water craft. A boat of this kind is normally more easily driven and maneuverable than a flat-bottomed boat. Sometimes two bottom shapes are combined in a single boat: forward the hull may be round or V-shaped, while at the back it may become almost flat or arc-shaped. This combination of shapes makes the boat suitable for both inshore and offshore fishing.

Many kinds of materials may be the skin and skeleton of your boat, from wood and plywood (sheet and molded) to plastic (Fiberglas) and metal (aluminum). Metal is not at present very popular with salt-water anglers. For best performance it is best to use the hull material most commonly employed in the area where you plan to fish.

OUTBOARD BOATS

The outboard motor, or "kicker," as it is called, is the average man's means of powering a fishing boat. It can be attached to practically anything that floats. But for reasonable safety, comfort, and convenience, it is desirable to use an outboard only with a boat specially designed for it. Such boats can range from small open boats 8 feet in length up to 24-foot cabin cruisers.

First, let's consider the smallest and lightest boats made and see how they do in salt-water fishing. These are the 8- to 10-foot pram and dinghy type boats. Such boats aren't very good for salt-water fishing, though they have been used. You can only use them in calm waters and close to shore, because they are not safe in a choppy or rough sea. Most of them are suited only for one-man fishing trips. Their motors are 1.5 to 5 hp—not strong enough to cope with many of the currents and tides found in salt water. About the only places prams and dinghies can be used safely are small, quiet bays, narrow salt-water creeks, and rivers. These boats cost $75 to $150.

Much more practical and easily the most popular salt-water fishing boats are the ordinary flat-bottomed rowboats or skiffs. They cost little and are made mostly in 12- and 14-foot lengths. It is best to get one with a wide beam and high sides. These boats are fairly safe when used in inlets, sounds, bays, and rivers which do not become very rough or choppy. They are dangerous in turbulent surf or ocean where big waves prevail. For the smaller

An ideally designed fishing craft suitable for both still fishing and trolling inshore or near shore. This craft is of lapstrake construction.

rowboats a 3- to 5-hp motor can be used in areas where tides and currents are not strong. The larger boats of this class call for 5½- to 10-hp motors. Fishing rowboats and skiffs vary in price from $150 to $300.

Somewhat more seaworthy because of their high sides and ends is the fishing dory, or half-dory. They are also generally faster and safer than skiffs and rowboats. They come in 14- to 18-foot models and can be used on the larger sounds, rivers, and bays, and the calmer inlets. Outboard motors of 7½ to 35 hp are good for fishing dories. Cost of these boats ranges from $200 to $1,000.

A large utility-type boat is the best for large bays and sounds, tidal rips, surf, and occasional junkets a mile or so offshore on calm days. These boats are 15 to 22 feet long. They have broad beams and high sides, and move fairly rapidly through the water. Most of these boats have decks and windshields, and storage space for equipment to be kept dry. Be sure to purchase a utility boat with a large cockpit so that you have plenty of room to fish. Many manufacturers make special fishing models, which are better for the angler than the sport or racing types. They will take motors of 35 to 110 hp and most of them can be rigged for remote steering. Utility craft cost $300 to $1,800, depending on the number of accessories.

Then there are the outboard cruisers which have become more and more popular in recent years. They are fairly good for fishing if they have large cockpits. They are also ideal for family or group fishing trips where several people have to be accommodated. These boats are often equipped with sinks, galleys, toilets, and bunks. They range from 16 to 24 feet in length and have high sides and broad beams. With outboard cruisers you can bottom fish, troll, cast, or go on long trips in most rivers, inlets, sounds, and bays. On calm days or slightly choppy days you can even fish a few miles offshore. These boats take large motors, 35 to 110 hp, and for extra speed and power the motors are often rigged in pairs. These motor combinations vary, with many skippers pairing 18 hp motors with 35's and 50's, the larger units for speed in getting to the fishing grounds and the smaller for use in trolling. Prices of outboard cruisers range from $1,000 to $3,500.

In southern waters, big outboards are being used more and more in going after the king-sized game fish, including swordfish and marlin, because of their maneuverability. As all who have done any charter-boat fishing will agree, credit for the successful boating of a big fish is often due as much to the captain's handling of his craft as to the angler's skill. By careful maneuvering during the course of the battle, closing in and backing off when necessary, the captain can help the angler out of many a tight spot. It may take a professional seaman to do this with the heavy, inboard-powered craft, but any two-man team of amateurs can learn how to handle an outboard in a relatively short time.

Many large offshore outboards are equipped with forward steering and remote speed-control hookups, devices which owners find are real aids when used carefully. Whether this gear should be installed depends largely on the cockpit design and preference of the skipper. Many claim that forward controls serve very well after a fish is hooked because the man handling the boat is then up front and out of the way of the fisherman working in the stern. But when trolling within a few yards of breaking surf, most veteran outboard fishermen prefer to maintain direct contact with the motor. Steering equipment takes a hard beating in offshore work, so it should be reliable, with all blocks bolted to the hull. The hardware of any boat used in salt-water fishing should be of solid brass—or the more showy chromeplated brass—to resist salt-water corrosion, and it should be bolted, not wood-screwed.

The offshore outboard should be a convertible job with Navy top and side curtains to protect against foul weather and sun. Windshield wipers should be installed and kept in working order. A 25- or 30-gallon permanent Monel gasoline tank, with two 6-gallon tanks for auxiliary use, is recommended. An 8-pound Danforth-type anchor is ideal as a second anchor for the average outboard fisherman. (The first anchor should be of the type recommended by the boat's manufacturer.) This type of anchor can be worked over the side while laying to, eliminating the need to climb out on the bow or over the windshield to work the line. Two or three feet of 5/16-inch galvanized chain made fast to the stock offsets possible buoyant line and allows the flukes of the anchor to take a better bite.

Boat Trailers

One of the main advantages of outboard fishing boats (aside from their low initial cost) is that they can be carried in the newer boat trailers and launched almost anywhere. With a boat trailer, you can expand your boating activities, increasing the range of your fishing and exploration. There are any number of strong, lightweight trailers on the market, especially designed and engineered for carrying boats and equipped with clever launching and recovery devices. More and more communities along the waterfront are building launching ramps, installing dockside boat lifts, and otherwise catering to the itinerant fisherman.

Like everything worthwhile, however, boat trailering requires some work and thought. You have to get the right trailer for your type of boat (your boat dealer will help you), and learn how to maneuver it behind the car, how to secure the boat to the trailer, how best to get it into and out of the water, and how to keep the trailer and its accessories as shipshape as your boat and motor.

There are advantages in having a trailer for your boat besides being able to fish when and where your fancy dictates and as far from your main base of operations as time and money allow. Not the least of these is the advantage of being able to keep the boat at home. There, you are not worrying over whether it is properly looked after, whether it is being used without your permission, whether it has gone adrift or been run down. When the boat is in your back yard or garage between trips, you can repair that loose bow cleat, replace the screw that has jumped out of the floor board, go over the brightwork and touch up the paint where needed. Maintenance costs are lower because it is more convenient for you to do the work yourself. Storage, shed rent, and wharfage fees no longer concern you. From pure economy, it does not take a trailer very long to pay for itself in dollars and cents. And that's not taking into account all the fun and convenience.

When launching ramps, inlets, or sheltered spots are not within convenient trailering distance, an outboard fisherman may find it necessary to launch his boat directly through the surf into the open sea. Since there are several real dangers involved in surf launching, beginners should learn gradually how to do it, on days when the surf is relatively calm. Remember at the outset that going out through the surf is only half the task; the other half is coming back. Before you start, learn to recognize common weather signs; once you start launching, you will be at the mercy of the elements, especially the wind.

Launching the Boat

Successful off-the-beach launching is usually a two-man operation and calls for a boat that can be rowed reasonably well. Oars must be relied upon to get the boat beyond the first few waves, for obviously the motor cannot be used until the craft is far enough out to float freely. The size and power of a motor won't help you here; in fact, motor size and weight may handicap the operation. That is why 5 and 7½ hp models are most popular for off-the-beach launching.

During your learning period, make it a rule to start out early and get back by noon. Summer ocean breezes, which build up the surf, generally reach peak velocity shortly after midday. Before launching, study the surf. You'll notice there are gaps in it—places where the breaking waves are not too high. Choose one of these areas for your launching site, and make note of where it is in relation to some prominent landmark. If possible, mark the place by driving a lengthy piece of driftwood into the sand well up on the beach.

Move your boat to the launching spot just above reach of the waves, and lash in loose gear. Then study the water again. You will see a series of progressively larger waves followed by progressively smaller ones. Try to get your boat in right after the last big one breaks. Fast teamwork is necessary. Once the boat is shoved into the water, the man who is to handle the oars must get aboard quickly, sit down, and get ready to row. The second man, still in the water off the stern, must steady the boat and keep it heading out until the rower is ready to start, then hoist himself in over the transom. Always keep the boat meeting the breakers directly bow on. If you allow it to swing off, a wave may easily heave the boat up and carry it shoreward, possibly spilling out both occupants.

Once the boat is clear of the first few waves, the man in the stern should concentrate on getting the motor started. The rower, meanwhile, should continue to gain distance from the beach and be ready to help at all times until the motor propels the boat to smoother water. This is quite a trick, as you can imagine, and perhaps most outboarders would rather avoid the dangers of surf launching by trailering a little farther and finding a safer way to get to outside fishing grounds. This would be wise if you have a large outboard combination—a boat 15 feet or longer, with a more powerful motor.

INBOARD BOATS

For offshore fishing, the inboard motorboat is tops. An outboard rates first where waves are small and waters are shallow. A craft with sails is the answer for long ocean reaches, where the difficulty of carrying fuel makes motor-only boats impractical. But for extensive offshore fishing, either on the Atlantic or the Pacific Coast, an inboard is your best bet.

The reason is not that inboards are more dependable than outboards; they aren't. An outboard with two motors (the spare is a lifesaver if the first gives out) is often advantageous. Again, outboards are easier to transport. They can be a definite asset where shallow tidal flats are encountered on the way to the ocean. What concerns us most here is that for riding the big waves, away from shore, there·is no substitute for boat size. And outboard motors can't give sufficient power for large boats. For sailing long distances, for carrying bigger loads, for dependability in bad weather, for greater safety as waves roll high and the shore is far off, the inboard is tops.

The most popular inboards for offshore fishing are from about twenty-five to thirty feet long. For most sportsmen any boat over thirty feet means too much loss of maneuverability. Diesels become practical over thirty feet; but they are used for economy, not speed. The gasoline-powered 27-or-so-footer has the speed to get far out enough to find deep-sea game fish, to allow good time to hook and play them, and still to make the round trip in one day. Correctly installed and properly cared for, inboard power can be the ultimate in reliability and can provide you with many desirable safety qualities. Inboard fishing boats cost from $3,500 up to better than six figures.

Facilities and Performance

In a well-designed fishing boat, cabins are not usually very large: the emphasis is on daytime, not nighttime facilities, which permits the aft fishing deck to be of sufficient size. Any fisherman, no matter what the boat size, should allow enough cockpit space for rod handling. There should be no overhanging canopies to catch a rod when pumped upward, no unduly high, exposed cleats or bitts to snag a line. The freeboard from water-line to cockpit top should be low enough to simplify boating a catch, yet high enough to always keep the sea outside.

Any cockpit installation that impedes you when in hot pursuit of fish is uncomfortable and irritating. Stowage space is another essential. On small inboards, it need not be much, yet everything aboard should have its place. The larger the boat, of course, the more gear and therefore the more stowage space are needed.

The minimum cabin accommodations for the average offshore fishing inboard include bunks for two, toilet, stove, and refrigerator. Even the inboard "day cruiser" should have bunks of some sort, since they are practical cabin seats; whether you're seasick-proof or not, you may wish to lie down in the shade out of the wind on a long day junket.

An inboard fishing cruiser should also contain such items as a fish box, a live bait well, outriggers, a fishing or fighting chair, and a hoist or roller. Most sport fishing boats have a fish box across the rear of the transom, capable of holding all ordinary-sized game fish and insulated for a hundred pounds of ice. For keeping the fish box clean, a removable sheet-metal lining is a great asset, as this can be scrubbed and aired thoroughly to remove the obnoxious odor of fish.

A live bait well is optional but not necessary. It comes in handy when angling for fish who are attracted by live bait. Outriggers may be used (see Chapter 7), and hoists and rollers may help in bringing big fish aboard (Chapter 8). The fishing chair, described on page 179, is a necessity in angling for heavy fish.

Exceptional maneuverability is essential to a successful inboard sport-fishing boat. Ease of steering, agility in quick turning, responsiveness in handling—these are invaluable characteristics. The steering or helm position should be fairly close to those doing the catching. Then the man on the wheel can watch the lines astern and prevent a fish from getting tangled under the boat or from snapping a line at the crucial moment. He can help "work" the monsters who frequently try to outswim the fastest boats. For this, and for reasons of navigational safety, the helmsmen must have excellent visibility all the way around the horizon. Visibility is so important that herein lies the reason for dual controls atop a flying bridge in the best examples of the bigger inboard fishing boat. Many big game-seeking craft go further and boast a miniature crow's nest or "tuna tower," a mast higher than the flying bridge, where a lookout can climb to spot swordfish, tuna, and other big fish. Some boats have dual controls placed on top or in the crow's nest; these are not necessary but they are advantageous. In shallow or narrow harbor entrances and areas containing reefs or rocks, a flying bridge or a lookout tower pays off handsomely.

Though slow, nonplaning boats are more efficient if they have a round bottom, at semiplaning speeds the V bottom has a good edge over the round. This is because V's present more planing surface forward, where the weight is likely to be in almost any inboard. Planing round-bottom or lapstrake boats are also seaworthy, efficient, and safe at high speeds. But a fisherman seeking an offshore fishing craft will probably prefer a V bottom, which will give him better speed.

When seas get big, no boat can plane without a lot of pounding; round-bottom, nonplaning (displacement) craft are perhaps at their best in such water. Generally they are smoother riding and take less punishment than V's going the same speed. The objection is often made that many displacement round bottoms have a "seasick roll," but they tend to be very sea-worthy. Round bottoms *are* slow. A 25-foot round-bottom inboard, for instance, can hardly make more than 18 mph; while a planing V bottom the same length can make 25 mph and even more with above-average power. There are many variations among V bottoms some favoring speed, some load-carrying or smooth riding. But there are probably even more variations among round bottoms.

Power

Power may range from about 50 hp—less for some displacement craft—up to several hundred for express sport cruisers. The motor is commonly amidship or somewhat aft. Very often there is a reduction gear between motor and propeller shaft. Modern motors get their speed-giving power by high revolutions per minute, but if the propeller turned at the same high speed, there would be a loss of efficiency. A propeller spinning very fast wastes too much energy in friction. A reduction gear reduces the speed of the propeller to suit the requirements of the boat's design.

Two-motor installation in an offshore inboard craft is popular. Having one propeller revolving one way and the other the opposite is generally more efficient than having both propellers turning the same way. Use of dual inboard power is practical with motors of as low as 50 hp. It has the obvious advantage that in case one motor fails another is left to bring the cruiser in from the ocean, and there is still another advantage: maneuvering is improved. If you try to dock a 30-footer in high winds and waves, with moored boats and moving dinghies close, you will find that you can use all maneuvering aids available. Reversing one motor while the other continues will turn the boat toward the side of the reversed motor. The amount of the turn can be regulated by the throttles on the motors. This is an important aid, because the slower the speed the less effective the rudder. Also the rudder is not very effective when the boat is moving backward. If twin-motor installation is such that the tops of the blades of the propellers normally turn outward, maneuverability is better.

In addition to the old basic choice of inboard versus outboard, there is a strong trend to inboard-outboard or stern-drive power installations in boats that were formerly equipped with large outboard motors or with small inboards (such as utilities and cabin cruisers from about 16 to 27 feet). The motor is permanently installed inside the stern and connected through the transom to an outboard drive, providing advantages of both types. Inboards use less fuel and lubricating oil than the biggest outboards, and there is much more usable space in a boat with the motor out of the cockpit. Diesel-powered motors are used in some of the larger fishing vessels.

Special Equipment

Outfitting a boat correctly is vital to its future worth and utility, as well as its saftety at sea. Startling marine engineering advances have been made in recent years. Depth finders, once unwieldy and expensive, are now more economical every year and they are accurate and reliable. These instruments have several purposes: a skipper can creep into an anchorage during a fog, or at least into shallow water where no larger ship can collide with him. He can use the depth finder as a position location reference to aid in piloting. Hidden reefs that otherwise might possibly sink his boat can be revealed and the practiced operator can determine the type of bottom his vessel is running over. Moreover, schools of fish running beneath the boat can be discovered—roughly, to be sure, with the ordinary type finder, but quite accurately with the bigger editions of the same instrument known as the fish finder. Few of the better sport fishing boats in the large sizes operate without a depth finder or indicator.

Many boats carry radio gear nowadays. Radiophones, too, are becoming better and cheaper every year. Principally a safety measure whereby another nearby craft, or the Coast Guard, may be called in event of trouble, ship-to-shore radio serves also to keep the angler and his companions in contact with home or office. Quite often, matters come up which can be handled by radiophones, making it unnecessary for the sportsman to break off his trip and return home. Skippers of good boats keep in touch with one another, relay weather and fishing information. Weather information is essential to both fishing "luck" and safety in navigation; many boats carry an extra marine band receiver so that weather reports may be heard even if the main set is not operating. Radio direction finders, of priceless value in determining position, are used today on all the better offshore seagoers. In the more modern versions, this fine piece of equipment will not only indicate the location of shore beacon stations and regular shore-side broadcasters, but also can be used to find the position of another boat by beaming in on its radio signal.

Together with the superior compasses now available, these instruments make piloting quite simple. As a direct result, fishing success increases tremendously, and much time is saved. And the already extremely safe sport fisherman is made safer still.

Unfortunately, it is impossible in this book to give complete details on outboard and inboard boat handling, operation, maintenance, the rules of road, and so forth. However, there are many good books available on this subject, and the present author has written two pertinent books: *The Complete Boating Handbook* (McGraw-Hill Book Company, New York,

$4.95) and *Getting the Most from Your Outboard Cruiser* (G. P. Putnam & Sons, New York, $5.95).

UNITED STATES COAST GUARD REGULATIONS

All motorboats more than 16 feet in length, whether inboard- or outboard-powered, that are operated on any body of water classed as "navigable" by the Federal government (all salt-water angling grounds are), must be registered with the Coast Guard and must bear the assigned registration number on its bow. It is a good idea to register any boat. Registration is a simple matter and costs nothing. Check with your local Coast Guard station and ask for an application blank. If you have no Coast Guard station in your community, check with any federal office for directions to the nearest Coast Guard district headquarters.

During your registration period it is not necessary to have your boat inspected; however, any Coast Guard craft may stop you at any time and come aboard to check whether you have the standard equipment required by Coast Guard regulations. The chart shows what must be carried on all powered boats. (It is also a good idea to check with local and state authorities to see if any boat registration is required by them.)

Equipment	CLASS A 0 to 16 feet	CLASS 1 16 to 26 feet	CLASS 2 26 to 40 feet	CLASS 3 40 to 65 feet
Combination light		1 in fore part of boat showing red to port and green to starboard from right ahead to 2 points abaft the beam. Visible at least 1 mile	None	None
Port-side light	None	None	1 on port side, properly screened to to show red from right ahead to 2 points abaft the beam. Visible at least 1 mile	
Starboard-side light	None	None	1 on starboard side properly screened to show green from right ahead to 2 points abaft the beam. Visible at least 1 mile	
Stern light		1 bright white light aft showing all around the horizon. Visible at least 2 miles		
Bow light	None	None	1 bright white light in fore part of boat showing from right ahead to 2 points abaft the beam on both sides. Visible at least 2 miles	

Equipment	CLASS A *0 to 16 feet*	CLASS 1 *16 to 26 feet*	CLASS 2 *26 to 40 feet*	CLASS 3 *40 to 65 feet*
Whistle	None	1 hand-, mouth-, or power-operated, audible at least ½ mile	1 hand- or power-operated, audible at least 1 mile	1 power-operated, audible at least 1 mile
Bell	None	None	1 which produces, when struck, a clear bell-like tone of full, round characteristics	
Lifesaving devices		1 approved life preserver or ring buoy or buoyant cushion for each person on board		1 approved life preserver or ring buoy for each person on board
Flame arrestors		1 on each carburetor of all gasoline engines installed after Apr. 25, 1940, except outboard motors		
Ventilation		At least 2 ventilators with cowls or equivalent capable of removing gases from the bilges in engine and fuel-tank compartments of boats constructed or decked after Apr. 25, 1940, using gasoline or other fuel of a flash point less than 110° F.		
Fire extinguishers	One 1¼-gal foam or one 4-lb CO^2 extinguisher. None required on outboard motorboats	Two 1¼-gal foam or two 4-lb CO^2 extinguishers		Three 1¼-gallon foam or three 4-lb CO^2 extinguishers

NOTE: Under the Federal Boating Act of 1958 all boats propelled by motors of more than 10 horsepower must be registered by the Coast Guard unless the state in which the owner lives has a registration law. Check with the local Coast Guard office or your state conservation department for information.

A good skipper will not only meet the legal requirements and recommendations of the Coast Guard, but, when it comes to lights and life preservers, he'll exceed them. A cork-type ring buoy with 50 feet of 3/8-inch line for emergency use is insisted on by most veteran boatmen. It is also recommended that basic safety equipment include: a portable spotlight with half-mile range; a flare kit with rockets and water dye marker; a reliable compass; charts of the area; a good-capacity manual bilge pump; a first-aid kit; ship-to-shore radio; and two 150-foot lengths of extra line, either 3/8-inch or half-inch manila or nylon, plus two anchors.

RENTING A BOAT

It may not always be advisable or feasible for you to own a boat. The original cost is not the only consideration. Maintenance costs can run into three figures or more a year and, except for an outboard boat with trailer, you must also consider the summer mooring and winter storage expense. Another question you should ask yourself is, "How much use will I get from a boat once I have acquired it?" Well, the Outdoor Boating Club of America has worked out an excellent formula: Count up the average number of days that you've spent on boats over the past few seasons. Double the total and then deduct at least five days for the time you'll have to spend maintaining, repairing, and servicing your craft. A total under twenty would indicate that your investment won't pay a very big dividend, especially if there are a few bad weekends during the season.

If you don't see your way clear to the purchase of some type of craft, you can still have the fun and production of boat fishing by renting a rowboat or motorboat, or by going out in an open party boat or a charter boat. Sometimes it's a good idea to rent such crafts to get their feel before purchasing a boat of your own.

Rental Rowboats and Inboards

Rowboat fishermen generally find quite a few fishing stations near most good fishing spots. For instance, there are more than 250 fishing station liveries from Princess Bay, Staten Island, to Orient and Montauk Points on the eastern tip of Long Island.

The rowboats and skiffs for rent range from 12-foot craft up to 16-foot boats. Many of the bigger fishing stations have more than a hundred of these boats, with a choice of two or three sizes. These rent at $1.50 to $8 a day depending on the size of the boat and whether you want it on a weekday or a weekend. In many spots you can fish a short distance from the fishing station and can row out in a short time. In some places the boat owner will tow you out to the fishing area and bring you back at no extra cost. An outboard motor (available at most of these places) costs an additional $5 to $15, depending on the size and condition of the motor. Most of the boat liveries also sell bait and tackle, and some supply food and drinks. Some even have snack bars and restaurants. Rowboats and skiffs will hold up to three or four anglers safely, depending on the size. Overloading the boat is dangerous, and also makes it difficult to fish in comfort.

A recent trend has been the renting of larger inboard boats known as U-Drives. These range from 16 to 32 feet and are powered by engines of up to 115 hp. These inboard boats are larger and safer; they will accommodate up to five or six people. They are popular with families who want to combine a day's outing with a fishing trip or with a gang from the office who want a get-together and a day's fishing. Many of these boats have a cabin, bunks, toilet, rod holders, life preservers, fishing chairs, compass, and a bait or fish box. They rent for $30 to $50 a day with extra charges for gas and bait.

Almost every salt-water bay, inlet, and popular fishing spot has a boat livery somewhere nearby. On weekdays you will find the fishing water less crowded and your chances of renting a boat much better. If you plan to fish on a weekend, it's a good idea to make a reservation in advance. Rowboat and skiff anglers usually stay close to shore in protected waters. The larger U-Drive craft often venture into the ocean a few miles from shore. As for tackle—boat rods, spinning rods, bait-casting rods, fly rods and even light surf rods can be used. The angler can still-fish with bait; he can troll, drift or cast artificials (see Chapter 5 for details). Most of the fish taken from rowboats and skiffs include flounders, fluke, porgies, sea bass, weakfish, striped bass, bluefish, salmon, croakers, jack crevallé, mackerel, pompano, corbina, rockfish, halibut, and other inshore species.

Party Boats

Open party boats take on as many passengers as their capacity allows at a fixed rate per person and they go out for inshore fishing.

You'll find open party boats wherever salt water and anglers get together. The nation's largest concentration of these craft is in the Long Island–northern New Jersey area. Here party boats fish the bays for fluke and flounders, and the offshore banks and sunken wrecks for blackfish, sea bass, porgies, cod, whiting, ling, or other bottom fish—according to the season. In recent years some party boats in these waters have also concentrated on bluefishing. Party boats ply their trade in Florida where they fish for groupers and other reef fish, and you'll find them pulling out of Gulf ports in search of red snapper. San Diego and the San Francisco Bay area both boast fleets of party boats which fish for the many varieties of food fish such as white sea bass, yellowtails, halibuts, rockfish, and croakers. (For specific information on places where party boats may be found, see Chapters 13, 14, and 15.)

The conventional party boat is usually broad of beam, with a wide, square stern to accommodate as many anglers as possible. The bait tank occupies the center of the afterdeck, handy to all anglers. The pilot house, galley, and any raised deck portion are well forward, permitting ample space for casting on the rear fishing. Some of the newer boats are equipped with benches, enclosed cabins, small snack bars, etc. All these craft are licensed, under strict supervision of the United States Coast Guard and state authorities, and must undergo periodic safety inspection.

Most modern fishing party boats are well equipped, beyond the legally required safety gear. This includes such equipment as radio telephone, depth finders, and compasses. Aboard some of the larger vessels are "fish finders," miniature versions of the Navy's antisubmarine sonar equipment, adapted for searching out fish and reading the character of the bottom. Many boats also boast radio direction finders to help in navigating during thick weather; others also have Loran sets, the Navy's once supersecret long-range radio navigating gear. A few fleet flagships boast radar, the all-seeing eye which pierces fog and night with ultrashort-wave radio beams.

Many party boat captains are veterans of the fishing business, others have grown up in the party boat trade, and all are wise in the ways of the ocean gamesters. The National Party Boat Owner's Alliance, a nation-wide association of party boat owners, says the average age of its captains is approximately forty years. The average captain is on the fourth issue of his "ticket." A "ticket" to operate a boat carrying passengers for hire (all party and charter boats fall into this category) is obtained after passing a Coast Guard examination on navigation, rules of the road, lights, passing signals, fire prevention, vessel safety, and a number of other subjects. Many party-boat captains log well over a thousand hours of boating each year. Most keep logs which describe in great detail the depths of water found in their favorite fishing areas and the effects of tides on the biting habits of the fish found there.

You will find fairly complete listings of the available party boats in the newspapers of nearly all of the great coastal areas. Sport sections of these papers devote considerable space to fishing doings, and a little research there will enlighten the novice as to what fish are running where and who's catching them. Advance reservations are seldom needed on a party boat. You walk on just before sailing time. These boats charge so much a person, usually $3 to $10. Most boats provide free bait, but in some localities the customer purchases his bait either on the dock or on the boat. The passenger provides his own tackle on a party boat. But elaborate tackle is not necessary. Actually, any good boat rod or surf rod will do. (Spinning tackle is often frowned on, since the boats may be crowded and you won't have much of a chance to play a fish.) But if you do not own tackle, you can rent a rod, reel, and rigs for about a dollar a day. The novice can ask the mate or a nearby angler how to fix his rig and bait his hooks. Many boats have accommodations for women.

Some party boats are little launches, licensed for only twelve or so anglers plus the captain and his mate. Larger boats of sixty feet and more may carry fifty or more anglers, each occupying an allotted space at the rail. (This space is strictly a first come, first served affair.) Generally, when the captain decides he has enough fishermen aboard, he sails. Most of them state the sailing time in advance, and a few boats leave as early as 5 A.M., whereas others sail at varying hours up to 10 A.M. They return sometime in the afternoon. During the best fishing months many of the boats also make an additional trip in the evening, leaving about 7 P.M. and returning around midnight or later.

Southern California party boats range from thirty-five to eighty feet in length and take loads of twenty to sixty persons. Bunks and galley services are usually available. If you set out on a live-bait boat (a name for party boats in California) from San Diego, Balboa, Long Beach, or another town in this area, to anchor or drift and try for bottom prowlers, you'll fish according to the rotation plan. This method was devised so that everyone could have an equal opportunity to angle from the most advantageous position on the boat. (Usually the stern is the coveted place, because the chum which the guide tosses overboard drifts astern, and the fish gather around it there.)

In the Santa Monica region the boats have a number arrangement instead of the rotation system. When buying a ticket you are given a number, and when the time comes to load the boat a "dispatcher" calls out these numbers and anglers go aboard in turn. If your number happens to be No. 5, for instance, you'll be the fifth person to step on deck, and you can pick any place that is open along the gunwale and remain there for the day. Naturally, the low numbers, getting first choice, head for the stern.

Further north on the West Coast the party boats are smaller and follow the fishing procedure used along the East Coast. The northern Pacific boats are different in one respect: they are rigged for slow trolling so that it is possible for all on board to fish in this manner. Other party boats do almost all of their fishing either at anchor or else drifting with the current.

In the Gulf of Mexico waters, party boats follow the general system of operation of the East Coast, but the boats are similar in size to those of Southern California.

Barge Boats

Along the California coast, you will find converted sailing vessels or yachts, commonly called "barges," stationed half a mile to three miles offshore. These ships, held firmly in position by bow and stern anchors, remain over selected sites—ordinarily near kelp beds—as long as fishing results are good. Most of them are spacious, comfortable sea resorts, with galley, drinking water, and bunk facilities, live bait tanks, and flood lights for those wishing to fish at nights. A time limit is imposed on some of the barges so that everyone may share in the sport, but on others you can elbow your way to the rail at 6 A.M., if you're lucky, and stay there as long as you wish. If the spirit moves you, and your wallet permits, it is possible to sign up for a stateroom on certain barges and stay afloat for a week or a month. Indeed, some families spend their entire vacations on these ships, and that's really getting away from it all! Meals are generally good, and prices are comparable to those on shore.

Motor launches or tenders, also known as "water taxis," operate on definite schedules between barges and the nearest towns, taking anglers back and forth at frequent (sometimes hourly) intervals. The fare varies from about $2.00 to $5.00 (or from $6.00 to $10.00 on the more swanky barges), depending on local conditions and personal plans. The ticket entitles you to a round-trip passage on the shuttle speedboats, use of tackle and live bait on the barges, and the chance to fish to your heart's content.

Over the barge gunwales come barracuda, yellowtails, white sea bass, bonito, mackerel, halibut, flounders (of which about a dozen kinds wriggle around the California banks), and many other fish. Mackerel bite readily enough in the daytime, but some of the other finners are more cooperative after dark. The Monterey halibut, ranging from 12 to 20 pounds, and a few even up to 50 pounds, is prized by still-fishermen.

Charter Boats

Charter boats are available at various places along our vast coast line. Most cities and towns with good fishing have a fleet. The charter is usually smaller than the party boat—and the rates are much higher. While the party boat anchors for inshore fishing, the charter vessel usually trolls or drifts for the real gamesters—marlin, sailfish, tarpon, tuna, and similar heavyweights. There are two basic types of charter boat.

The smaller of the two types are the guide boats. These range from large outboard rigs equipped with twin power plants to inboard sea skiffs and open motorboats up to about thirty feet in length. Notable guide boat centers are Boca Grande, Florida, and the Puget Sound area, Washington—tarpon and salmon hot spots, respectively. Guide boat fishing generally is for the big inshore game, and you are actually paying more for the guides' knowledge of where the fish are than for the boat itself. The cost, which includes the boat and the services of the guide, is $15 to $45 per day. Lunch, bait, and the inevitable extras must, of course, be added to the cost of a day's outing.

The true charter boat, as opposed to the smaller open guide boat, is an offshore craft ranging of thirty to sixty feet in over-all length, usually equipped with twin gas or diesel engines, outriggers, fishing chairs, live bait wells, fish boxes, ship-to-shore radio, and many of the items that make up the well-equipped offshore fishing boat. Sheltered cabins, bunks, and all the other comforts of yachting are standard. The charter boat is manned by a captain and his mate, both experienced in big-game fishing.

At present, rates for good charter boats range from about $40 per day to $125—and sometimes more. Rates depend upon the season and the quality of the fishing—it's the old law of supply and demand. These figures cover the cost of boat and crew alone; bait, lunch and so on are extra. Some boats charge a small fee for big-game tackle. Remember that the figures mentioned here can be divided by the number of persons in the fishing party. If you go it alone the rates are the same as for four or six. The average fishing party along the eastern seaboard is generally four persons, while on the West Coast, where the charter boats are larger, the parties may reach as many as twenty passengers.

What do you get for your money when you hire a charter boat? First, you get privacy. That is, instead of being one of a big group of party-boat fishermen, mostly strangers, you make up your own group of friends. Next, you get exciting fishing. Instead of the party boat's hand line or boat rod, you use real big-game tackle, and instead of going after bottom fish like flounders, you have the chance to take some of the smashing fighters of the deep, such as sailfish, tuna, swordfish, or marlin. Another benefit of charter-boat fishing not to be overlooked is a chance of education. A day offshore with the skipper who gives you the fishing lore it took him many years to acquire is in itself invaluable. Your knowledge of salt-water fishing will be broadened and you will learn techniques that would be difficult to set down in words. But if you plan to charter a boat, you must make a reservation well in advance—especially on weekends. On weekdays you may find days when the boats are not booked, but even then it pays to make a call in advance to reserve a boat.

Every real salt-water angler should have a go at charter boat fishing at least once in his lifetime. When you do have the opportunity, gather some friends and give it a try. Splitting the cost will make the junket much less expensive. The $12 to $30 your share will cost is well worth every cent. Spread out over your total fishing costs over the years, a few days offshore in a charter boat won't amount to much. You'll bring home a fine store of memories, and—who knows?—you might boat a record-size denizen of the deep.

BOATING SAFETY

As we have said, fishing is a gamble. But there can be another gamble, a more serious one—your personal safety and the safety of others. The fisherman who chooses to accept any odds which are not a hundred per cent in his favor is the leper of the fishing fraternity. You need never risk safety while fishing, for common sense is your guide as well as your guardian angel when you are out in a boat.

Once in a while a genuine accident occurs—one that could not have been prevented—but most are due to stupidity or foolhardiness. Take overloading, for example. I have seen a whole family of five persons happily fishing from one small rowboat, so jammed together that they could hardly handle their rods, let alone the boat. The craft was low in the water and top-heavy. It would have turned over if the least thing had happened to disturb it. In some small boats, three are too many. Because an overloaded boat rides low, it is at the mercy of even small waves if a storm comes up. It scarcely seems necessary to caution anyone against so obvious a danger, but too many such cases are causes of accidents, so— *don't overload a boat.*

Any time you are operating a boat for the first time for a day of fishing, a short "shakedown" run is never out of order. It's good to get the "feel" of a strange fishing boat, to learn the little oddities that might cause trouble if not observed in time. No two boats handle exactly the same way any more than two fish strike or fight alike.

A few reminders: Keep your distance when passing bathing beaches and other craft. Should your boat turn over, it's usually better not to try to swim for it; hang on to the vessel until help arrives. If your boat carries a motor, be extremely careful not to spill gasoline or oil. Raging fires have turned many a pleasure jaunt into a scene of tragedy. Keep your eyes and ears alert for storm warnings, and if bad weather is brewing, postpone that fishing party. If the storm breaks while you are on the water, sail immediately for the nearest shore.

Careless handling of fishing tackle accounts for numerous unnecessary injuries each year. If possible, is good policy to disassemble fishing rods before you carry them. And never carry fishing lines with hooks or plugs attached; you may lose an eye to a snagging hook. Also, don't get so excited at landing your first big one that you clutch happily at the fish as soon as it plops into the boat. A twisting, lively fish can be dangerous, especially when it is still hooked. Those wicked barbs may be driven into your hand.

The "standee" in a fishing boat is as out of place as Mickey Mantle playing in the outfield of the Podunk baseball nine. Few fishing boats are suitable for standing while casting—even if the boat is motionless. It is a very dangerous practice. Overhand casting is a must for boat fishing. It is the "side-wheeler" who usually imbeds the hook of an artificial lure into a companion. This can happen when casting overhand, too, unless care is taken with each backcast. Consequently, it is always wise, when there are two or three casters in a boat together, for all fishermen to cast to the same side of the boat at the same time.

When a hooked fish is brought alongside a boat and is ready for netting or gaffing, unthinking fishermen quickly shift their weight to the side of the boat for a better look at the fish. This is dangerous. Another reminder: it is wise to stun a big fish with a club or a gaff before you haul him in, particularly in the case of a large fish taken on a gang-hooked plug, or a fish that has sharp spines.

It pays to be safe by carrying a first-aid kit on every angling expedition. The most common form of injury results when the point of the hook and the barb become buried in the flesh of the hand, or in other parts of the body. If this happens, don't try to back the hook out of the wound, because the barb will only rip the flesh. Instead, push the point on through the skin so that the shank of the hook can be cut off close to the point where it meets the skin. Then grasp the protruding point of the hook with the pliers and pull it out. Before heading for a doctor, pour antiseptic into the wound and bandage.

In most boat accidents involving drownings one of several things are apparent. In the first place, the mishap probably could have been prevented by foresight or care. Secondly, the victim either was unable to reach the boat or else started immediately to swim toward shore. In the third place, the boat had no life preservers or seat cusions of kapok or some other buoyant material which would serve as a safety device. But, the greatest safety "device" is to stay with the boat. Tie yourself to it if the water is so cold that your hands might become numb.

There is no room for the drunk in fishing. The fisherman who drinks is a menace to himself and to anyone around him. His friends must take their own fishing time to see that he doesn't come to any harm and that he doesn't endanger themselves. The time to have a drink is at the end of the day's fishing.

Seasickness is a problem for a few of our offshore anglers. There are several "seasickness pills" available at your local drugstore and they are generally effective. If you are subject to seasickness, there are several things in addition to pills that you can do to prevent it. Charter boat captains will tell you that most seasick persons have usually had bacon and eggs or orange juice for breakfast. It is best to put to sea on an empty stomach or, at most, grapefruit and a bit of dry toast. For lunch, try some hot chicken broth or consommé with rice and a sandwich. Avoid fried or greasy food. For dessert, if you want it, apples, peaches or pears are best. Coffee is a poor beverage for anyone subject to seasickness. Ginger-ale, Coca-Cola, or a soda drink is far better. Chewing gum between meals is also good.

If you begin to feel seasick on a fishing boat, go topside immediately. Face forward and breathe deeply. Never go below. If you wish to sleep, sleep on deck.

CHAPTER 11

Care and Repair
of Your Equipment

THE PRUDENT salt-water angler will take the best possible care of his fishing gear for two reasons. First, of course, is the dollars-and-cents consideration. More good tackle is ruined by lack of reasonable care than by use. Properly tended reels, rods, and lines last longer and, consequently, need to be replaced less frequently. The second, and equally important, reason is that tackle that is maintained as it should be catches fish. There is no greater angling frustration than the loss of a prize strike caused by faulty gear. If proper maintenance will prevent just one mishap like this each season, it will have amply repaid you for your time and trouble.

CARE OF REELS

Let's begin with your reel, which, of all your investments in tackle, has the largest number of moving parts, takes the greatest beating, and requires the most care for top-flight performance. A good reel, however, demands very little attention in relation to the service it gives. A careful lubrication at frequent intervals and a thorough cleaning at least once a year will keep it in shape for a lifetime.

Most reels can be lubricated quickly, easily, and without special tools. Reel oil and lubriplate or reel grease, obtainable at your local tackle shop, should be used rather than ordinary household lubricants, which will not stand up well under the deteriorating action of water. Household lubricants also offer too much friction for the precision parts of a reel. Lubrication instructions come with most reels, and it is wise to follow these instructions to the letter.

After using your reel in brackish or salt water, be sure to wash the salt from the reel with warm fresh water at the end of each day's fishing. Then wipe the metal parts with a soft, oily cloth to protect their finish. If sand or salt water has gotten into the grease, it will be necessary to flush out the gear housing with a cleaning solution to remove the contaminated grease. Relubricate with clean oil and grease.

Any reel not specifically designed for salt water requires more care than those that are. Its metal parts should be coated with grease beforehand, and the entire reel should be washed in fresh water, dried, and relubricated within twelve hours after use.

Remember to put oil on bearings, grease on gears. Two exceptions to this rule are the handle-knob post, which should receive grease although it is a bearing, and the level-wind screw, which should be oiled although it's a gear. It is also very important not to lubricate your reel too heavily. A drop or two of oil and a speck of grease are all that is required. Never grease-pack gear teeth, but rather give them a fine coating of light grease. Too much lubricant will collect dirt and retard the reel's action. It is also important to keep such parts as the metal and leather washers, used in some reels as a drag device, free of lubricants.

Some fishermen are hesitant to take their reels apart for a thorough cleaning. Perhaps, if their mechanical ability ends at unscrewing a jar lid, it's wise for them to leave the job to a qualified repairman. Most fishermen, however, are creatures filled with curiosity who delight in exploring the internal workings of a reel. Realizing this, manufacturers have taken steps to design their reels with simple take-down features. Every salt-water angler should learn to disassemble his reel; sand or other foreign matter can cause serious damage with a single turn of the handle.

Here are some tips for those who have never tried such a disassembly before. And as elementary as it may sound, the best place to begin is with some instructions on your choice and use of the screw driver, since that simple tool is probably the chief cause of scarred and damaged reels. Many reel manufacturers furnish a combination screw driver-wrench of the proper size for their reels. If there is none, take your reel to a hardware store and find a screw driver of the right size. It need cost no more than ten or fifteen cents since the non-rusting screws used on reels are quite soft and require little force. In loosening a screw, press down fairly firmly with the screw driver, but without unnecessary force, otherwise the tool is apt to jump from the slot, scarring the sides of the screw. Scarred screwheads are the sign of a poor mechanic. Later, in replacing the screw, press down hard again on the final tightening. But don't turn *too* hard; you may twist the soft screw in two—a tough problem for even a good mechanic. Just tighten until it is what is usually called, for lack of a better term, good and snug— no more. Check your reel regularly to be sure all screws are properly tightened.

A wrench is sometimes necessary, chiefly to remove the crank. Again, it should fit the nut. (The use of pliers on the type of soft nut found on reels is plain destructiveness.) Don't use too much force in tightening here, either.

As you take your reel apart, lay each piece down separately and in the order it came from the reel. This will enable you to replace each correctly by reassembling in reverse order. Pay close attention to the sides of each part; they sometimes differ. Also be certain that each is cleaned before putting the reel back together. Stubborn dirt and grease are easily removed with a soft cloth and a cleaning compound two-thirds kerosene and one-third light lubricating oil. You can also use one of the commercial solvents (*not* carbon tetrachloride) or even a very strong soap or detergent. With the latter, rinse the parts afterward in clear water. An old toothbrush makes a good scrubbing tool for such parts as gear teeth, which are difficult to clean. Each moving part should be lubricated as it is fitted back into the reel.

When you reassemble the reel, each part should fit back into place without force. If you meet resistance, you'll usually find that you are doing something wrong. Keep trying stubborn pieces without forcing them; they will inevitably slip into place if you are patient. At worst, they will prove only a minor, if interesting, puzzle for you to figure out.

If any parts are worn and need replacing, order them at once. Try your local dealer or return the reel to the manufacturer. At either place repair charges are minimum for the work involved. When you are sending a reel back to its manufacturer, follow these simple instructions to insure its safe return:

1. Pack the reel carefully	4. Send letter of explanation
2. Address it plainly	5. Fasten letter to parcel
3. Give your return address	6. Insure parcel contents

The best time to return a reel to its manufacturer is during the off season. If you wait until just before the fishing season, when the repairmen are usually swamped with work, you might not get it back when you need it.

A reel should be protected at all times. There should be a padded receptacle in your tackle box or some type of carrying case or bag. Keep the reel in a dry place if you are storing it for any length of time. Also when storing reels, always loosen or back off the drag completely to remove all tension on the drag washers. With the spool in mesh, pull on the line to make sure that the drag assembly is really free. Do not store reels in a damp atmosphere or with the star drag tightened. Either may result in the drag washers sticking to the metal disks and producing a chatter when the reel is put back in service.

CARE OF LINES

Caring for synthetic lines is not much of a problem. To prolong the life of dacron, nylon, or monofilament lines, the following precautions should be taken:

1. The line should be carefully checked each time it's used to make sure there are no worn or frayed spots that might give way at a crucial moment. In most cases, it will show its first signs of wear at the tip or the lure tie-on point. It is a good practice to cut off a foot or so of line when it shows wear at this point.

2. Periodically inspect your rod guides and tip top for "wear-out" or rough spots. These can quickly ruin your line.

3. When reeling in line, keep it away from the edge of the boat or from passing over unnecessary obstructions.

4. When casting spinners or revolving plugs, use a swivel to prevent kinking and twisting your line.

5. When using a nylon line in salt water, it is a good idea to wash it out in fresh water (see page 29).

If you are going to replace a spinning line, it is sometimes wise, especially when only using the gear for inshore fishing, not to pull all the old line off the spool. Instead, peel off 70 to 90 yards and leave the rest of the old line on for backing. Put on enough new line to fill the spool, and you will be equipped to deal with any fishing situation you are likely to meet. Special splicing needles are available at your local tackle shop that make the task of splicing lines together a rather easy task. Spliced lines are usually stronger than those that are tied together with knots.

Fly lines used in salt water usually require a little more care. They should be removed from the reels, washed in clear water, and stored either on a storage spool of large diameter (the round plastic box that most lines come in these days is good for this job) or in loose coils. It is essential that all parts of the stored line be exposed to the air. The storage location should not be excessively hot or humid. If your fly line becomes sticky during storage, it is probably ruined and should be discarded. However, in mild cases of stickiness, soaking the line in lime water may restore it. A fly line left on a reel or coiled up for a long time may have a tendency to take the shape of the coil, causing it to come off curled when you are stripping or retrieving. To straighten the line, unwind it and give it several light tugs. No line, especially a fly line, should ever be stepped upon, nor should it be tightly kinked. Once the smooth coating of a fly line becomes cracked, little can be done to repair the damage.

Wire lines should be carefully inspected for kinks after each outing. Straighten them out gingerly or permanent kinking can result. Some tackle shops sell tools which aid in ridding a wire line of kinks. Tight kinks should be cut out and the line joined with the appropriate splice (see page 74).

CARE OF RODS

Rods of different materials require different kinds of care. In general, modern glass-fiber rods require a minimum of attention. But remember, it is possible to break a glass rod; you should be careful with it even though it will stand a great deal of normal abuse. Careless handling before and after fishing has ruined almost as many rods as casting has. A friend of mine once leaned his rod against the open door of an automobile while he pulled on his boots. A sudden gust of wind slammed the door shut against the rod and ruined it. That thoughtlessness cost him more than twenty dollars. To avoid similar accidents, leave your rod in its case until you are ready to use it. Don't leave it around underfoot where someone might step on a section. The tip of the rod should always stand free and clear. Aboard a boat, stand the rod in a position where it can be neither stepped on nor knocked overboard. If given this kind of treatment, glass-fiber rods will give a lifetime of service.

Beryllium copper rods require little more care than do fiberglass rods. If they accidentally become bent, they can usually be straightened out with no ill effects. Heat should never under any circumstances be applied to a beryllium copper rod, as heat will remove the temper and ruin the rod.

Steel rods should be watched for rust; most of them have a surface coating of some kind, but if it becomes damaged, the rod may rust. If spots of rust appear, they should be removed with a bit of fine steel wool (No. 000), and the bare places covered with rod varnish or touch-up enamel. Rust can be prevented by carefully wiping the rod with a rag lightly soaked in oil or touched with reel grease. Unseated guides on steel rods can sometimes be reseated with solder; but a broken guide is a matter for the manufacturer's repair department.

If you're still using a pet bamboo rod, a season's use will demand much more extensive labors than are required of the glass rod. At any point the protective skin or varnish is bare, the spot is subject to mildew and rot of the all-important bamboo fibers. To prevent this, the exposed point must be varnished over with a rod varnish. Be sure to use a top-grade rod or spar varnish and apply it as directed on the container. But keep in mind that you can't do a good job in applying and drying the varnish if the temperature of the room is below 70° F. Also remember that several thin applications are always better than a heavy one. A single heavy application of varnish tends to check or craze and if the rod is to be extensively covered, the action of the rod can be impaired. Some very expert hands can remove old varnish with a piece of glass or a razor blade. However, for a safer approach, a suitable varnish remover is far better. Bamboo rods tend to become soft and take a set after long use—even those of prime quality. If you are fortunate, you can restore a set rod by introducing it over steam emitted from a tea kettle. You will have to work quickly and over the full length of the rod to do the job correctly. If this fails, consider the rod a family relic and retire it to the attic or your own rod museum.

After a hard season's fishing, every rod, regardless of material, will need some attention, from a few minor repairs to a complete overhaul. However, it's a good idea to check these important points to determine if any work on your rod will be necessary:

1. The condition of guides and ferrules.
2. The condition of windings.
3. The operation of the reel seat.
4. The condition of the cork grip.

Applying Windings

Carefully inspect—perhaps with a magnifying glass—the insides of each guide for grooves caused by the line. Any grooved guide must be replaced since it will quickly ruin new lines. Your local tackle dealer or the rod's manufacturer will be able to supply the proper guide and winding thread to match if you will give him the exact model number.

Nylon thread is the most popular choice for today's rod wraps. The general thread size for new wraps includes sizes A or D on fresh-water type rods, although some wrappers prefer 00 for fly rods and ultralight spinning rods. On salt-water rods, size E is preferred, although EE is used on heavy-duty game and surf rods. The following are the steps required to add new guides and apply the windings properly:

Step 1. Prepare the new guides for mounting by tapering the blunt ends of the guide feet with a whetstone or fine grinding wheel or file (Figure 1). Roughen slightly the top side of the guide foot that comes in contact with the wrap; a better bind of thread to metal results.

Step 2. Make all wraps under tension so that they are tight and even, particularly when using nylon because of its stretch. If a tension device is not available you can make a temporary device by setting a heavy book on the table, placing the spool of thread on the table behind the book in a small open box, and pulling the thread off the spool and running it through the book under a maximum number of pages toward you and the rod (Figure 2).

Step 3. Reset the tip top on the rod with ferrule cement. Align guides to the rod temporarily with cellophane tape, starting with the butt guide first. Cut an 8-inch length of thread from the spool. Put this length aside —you will have use for it later. Then wrap the butt guide first. Start wrap on the shaft ½ inch from the tip of each guide foot. Place end of thread on the rod. Under tension make five or six turns of thread around the rod *and over the end of the thread* (Figure 3). Push turns together with thumbnail away from the guide. As you make your wrap, keep pushing the turns together every five or six turns. This is necessary to prevent bleed of shaft color between the turns when color preserver and varnish are later applied to the wrap. Remember: *Throughout the entire wrap, keep tension on the thread.*

Step 4. When the wrap is three-quarters finished, take the 8-inch length of thread cut from the spool and form a loop. Place the loop on the side of the wrap, extending beyond the partly finished wrap over the blank toward the guide. Holding the loop in place, continue wrap over loop and guide foot until you come to the end of the wrap. Cut thread from spool and insert end of thread into loop (Figure 4).

Step 5. Grip the ends of the loop securely. Pull the loop back, *under wrap and out,* bringing end of thread with it and securing the wrap at this end. Push final turns in toward center of wrap with thumbnail. With a razor edge, trim excess thread from wrap (Figure 5). Use care to cut only the excess thread, not any of the turns. Keep wrap free of dust and dirt. Remove tape from opposite guide foot. Wrap it in the same manner described above. As you wrap each guide make sure the succeeding guides are properly aligned down the shaft. Trim-wraps around ferrules and tip tops are made in the same manner as guide wraps.

The proper procedure to follow when applying a line guide.

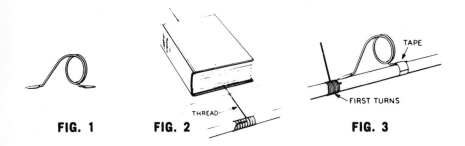

FIG. 1   FIG. 2   FIG. 3

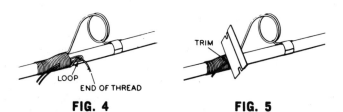

FIG. 4   FIG. 5

Step 6. After all the wraps are made, finishing is the final step. With the tip of a small flame, singe all wraps to remove lint and fuzz. With an artist brush, apply three coats of color preserver to the wraps. Allow a minimum of ten minutes drying time between applications. Now check the entire shaft. Make sure it is smooth and clean, ready for varnishing. Apply two or three coats of glass-rod varnish to the entire shaft, including the wraps, with index finger or artist brush. Allow thorough drying time between applications, up to twenty-four hours if humidity is high. Smooth each varnish application lightly with high-grade steel wool. After final varnish coat dries, your rod is ready for use.

Repairing Ferrules

Worn ferrules are not only a source of annoyance, but may also cause the rod to come apart at the wrong moment and result in catastrophe when a good fish is on the end of your line. Toward the end of the fishing season, they are apt to loosen. This is indicated by a slight knock which you will hear when you are casting. It means that the cement holding the ferrule inside the rod has loosened. If a ferrule is still tight in the slide but has loosened on its seat, it may often be reset by application of a small flame to the metal to melt and redistribute the cement. If this doesn't work, the ferrule must be removed from the rod.

Ferrules that don't fit snugly can often be corrected by applying a coat or two of varnish to them. But if the ferrules are badly worn, it is best to replace them with new ones.

When ferrules are to be replaced, heat the metal and pull the female section by placing the welded end between vise jaws and pulling smartly on the rod. For a purchase on the male section, turn up the thin serrated ends to right angles. If you are using pliers to remove the ferrules, be extremely careful. A flattened ferrule is ruined. Put a wooden plug tightly inside a female ferrule and grasp the plug with the pliers. For a male ferrule, bore and fit a cork ring around it to protect the ferrule from the plier jaws.

Often ferrules can be parted by placing both sections of the rod behind the knees, with the ferrule joined between them. Then squat down, bringing pressure to bear with your knees, and pull the sections apart. When the ferrules are free, clean off the old cement by scraping with a chip of soft wood. Wash them inside and out by soaking in a cleaning solvent such as that described on page 251. New ferrules of the proper size may be purchased at your local tackle dealer.

It is important that new ferrules fit snugly. If they don't, put on a tight wrapping of very fine nylon—try No. 0000 first—to build up the diameter. Then coat the inside of the rod thinly with ferrule cement available from your tackle dealer. Heat the ferrule and press it in gently but firmly. It may have to be heated several times before it is driven into the cap or shoulder. Some surplus usually squeezes out as you press the ferrule home, but you can remove it quickly and neatly with a dab of lighter fluid on a piece of rag or facial tissue.

Often the ferrule trouble lies in the other direction; dirt and corrosion cause the ferrules to stick too tightly. Smooth the ferrules down with fine emery paper or crocus cloth, then give them a few turns on a buffing wheel. Take care not to let them become so heated on the buffing wheel that the cement is loosened.

Never twist a jointed rod that has become stuck; often an application of mild heat from a cigarette lighter on the ferrules is sufficient to free them. Never oil ferrules; rubbing the male ferrule in the hair will provide all the lubrication necessary.

Repairing Reel Seat and Cork Grip

A reel seat with worn threads is a nuisance, and reel seats with a sliding ring often fail to hold the reel securely. It is wise in either case to replace the old seat with a new one. Your local tackle shop will be able to do the job for you.

You can make a cork grip look like new by scrubbing it with any good kitchen cleansing powder, or cleaning it with a pad of steel wool dipped in acetone or common lacquer thinner. Then go over the grip lightly with fine sandpaper. In doing this on a spinning rod, be careful not to remove so much cork as to loosen the reel rings. If the grip is badly worn, your local tackle dealer can replace it, or it can be returned to the factory, as can broken rod sections.

Storing Your Rods

Rods used in salt-water fishing require a little more attention than those used in fresh water. Salt corrodes reel seats and turns guides green; it may even eat into the color preservative on the rod windings and discolor them. To prevent this, wash the rod in fresh water to remove all traces of salt and other grime. Then apply a light coating of oil or grease to all metal parts. All rods should be dried thoroughly before they are stored in their airtight cases.

CARE OF TERMINAL TACKLE

During the fishing season your terminal gear takes a beating—not only from the fish but also from being snagged or knocked about in your tackle box. Your hooks should be sharpened on a honing stone with a special groove (available at your tackle store) to keep them sharp and effective. As has often been stated, dull hooks annually cost anglers more bragging-size catches than they realize. One winter evening's work can spare you many a disappointing experience. Carry a whetstone in your tackle box to cope with on-the-spot emergencies.

Hooks and other steel articles will escape rusting if stored during the winter in a very dry spot. Still, as an extra precaution, it is wise and takes little time to wipe all metal pieces with a greasy rag before putting them away. To simplify the task, use a brush to apply the grease, which should be warmed for easy application.

Check the hooks closely. Long-nosed pliers are helpful in straightening those which have been bent out of shape. Badly rusted hooks should be replaced with new trebles, obtainable in sport shops for a nickel. You may wish to replace the originals with weedless models which cost slightly more than the open treble hooks. Whether they are new or old, be certain that all points are needle sharp. This may mean the difference between hooking and landing a lunker bass or missing a strike entirely.

Spinners and spoons of brass or copper dull quickly in use, which lessens their attractiveness to fish. The simplest and fastest way to polish them is with a little wad of fine steel wool. For highest polish, always rub back and forth in one direction. Spinners and spoons corrode badly in storage, no matter where they are kept. To prevent this, apply a coat of clear lacquer —clear nail polish will do—on the polished surfaces. A thin coat is best since too heavy a coat will peel. If the lacquer is thick, dilute with thinner. Nickel, chrome, stainless steel and other corrosion-proof materials can be brought back to their original brightness with metal polish, jeweler's rouge, or jeweler's polishing cloth.

You'll often hear that plugs are finished to attract fishermen rather than fish. Perhaps so. But cracked or broken finishes expose the body underneath to rusting or rotting. It's a simple matter to touch up chipped spots and to experiment with new finishes. (You might hit on a first-rate combination.) If you give your plug a new paint job, use enamel or lacquer. Lacquer painted over enamel will cause the undercoat to shrivel and peel. Before repainting, replace any rusty screws. If the threads are stripped on the screws, or the holes are worn too large in the plastic or wood bodies of plugs to make a good connection with the screws, replace them with a screw a size larger. Check the double or treble hooks on the lures, too, and straighten them if they have become bent out of shape.

Bucktails and similar feather lures take a fierce beating during the course of a fishing season. However, all but the most severely damaged can be restored to good condition by holding them over a steaming kettle. The matted materials will fluff up instantly, and the fly will appear almost as good as new. When storing, remember that feathers are considered a delicacy by house moths. It is best to store flies with an army of protective moth balls, and to check occasionally during the winter.

At the end of the fishing season, check your leaders. While nylon or synthetic plastic leaders need no particular attention, they sometimes become brittle after heavy usage. There seems to be no treatment to prevent this—and if there were, few would bother with it. New ones are quite inexpensive. Also examine wire leaders for bends and kinks. If straightening out a kink leaves an obvious weak spot, throw the leader away. Before storing, wire leaders should be dried thoroughly with a cloth. Store them in sealed cellophane envelopes or in a wide-mouthed jar filled with talcum powder. Do not leave snaps or swivels attached to leaders when storing.

While not terminal tackle in the true sense, your landing net is the last step in landing your fish. A net that is used heavily may be in bad shape by the end of the season. Wash it with strong laundry soap to remove any slime or odor. Then replace broken sections of the netting with new material. There is no reason to be especially professional about this—just make the repair with simple square knots. Now soak the netting in hot linseed oil for waterproofing that will last another year. Varnish the handle if necessary.

Before we leave the subject of tackle, a word should be said about the tackle box. The average tackle box is a catchall for hooks, plugs, swivels, and sinkers, as well as chipped paint, sand, rust, and rot. Keep the essentials, but get rid of the rest—fast. Scour the insides thoroughly. When it is dry, sand it inside and out. If your tackle box is not already waterproof, make it so by attaching strips of waterproof adhesive tape along the inside seams. Follow this with two complete coats of spar varnish or paint. Remember that dark colors absorb heat and light colors reflect it, so use aluminum paint. If the box is already in good shape, a single coat of spar varnish won't hurt.

While going over your tackle box, you can really make it de luxe by adding a few useful improvements such as these: With waterproof glue and thin sheets of cork, line the bottoms of all the trays. This eliminates noise and clatter and keeps hooks and swivels from getting lodged in the seams. On the bottom, outside, glue two or three rubber mason jar rings. They'll keep the box from slipping, sliding, and scraping on the floor of the boat. A piece of gum camphor in your tackle box will help control moisture.

CARE OF FOUL-WEATHER GEAR, WADERS, AND BOOTS

Even if you fish only occasionally during the season, it is difficult to avoid rain and bad weather. And it's too late to repair holes and rips in your clothing when it begins to pour. So check all foul-weather gear while you can. Wash rubber jackets and raincoats with mild soap and water. Allow them to dry. After that, hold them up in front of a bright light and examine them carefully for punctures. Repair them with light inner-tube patches, or with material furnished by the manufacturer for that purpose.

Waders and boots require slightly different handling. With soap and water, remove any oil or grease that may be on the waders. These are natural enemies of rubber. Rinse and dry them thoroughly. Then, keeping the outside dry, fill them with water and check to see if moisture oozes through anywhere. If holes are evident, repair them with inner-tube patches or, better still, with patches of the same material. When they are dry, stuff them loosely with old newspapers. Hang them feet up or lay them on a flat surface for storage. Some fishermen roll the waders up tight and wrap them heavily with brown paper. To preserve them still better, wrap the paper package with something airtight, such as a plastic bag. Stored in a cool spot when not in use, waders and boots will last the average salt-water angler many years—and won't leak when he uses them.

Most of the new, light plastic gear needs little care. Repair kits are usually furnished with each garment. It has been found that you can get longest wear from these, too, by storing them just as you do your rubber and fabric ones.

When storing your fishing tackle and gear for extended periods of time, be sure to keep them in a completely dry location. Don't just toss them in the corner of a damp basement or garage. By observing all the precautions in this chapter, you will be certain that your fishing tackle is in good condition at all times—ready to catch that really big fish next season.

BALANCING SALT-WATER TACKLE OUTFITS

With so many different combinations of rod, reel, and line, as well as so many different sizes and weights of salt-water fish, it is easy to see that the inexperienced fisherman might acquire, a piece at a time, an outfit which, when set up, would be a most unwieldy affair indeed. This is exactly what used to happen years ago. Over the years, however, the better and more enthusiastic anglers kept trying to standardize outfits so that they would be, as fishermen say, balanced. The upshot was that several terms finally emerged to designate these outfits.

The complete salt-water outfit which balanced best in a certain weight division might be called a 4/6 outfit, for example, or a 6/9, etc. These terms simply tell us what the rod weighs and what size line is on it. The line size indicates the reel size (page 9). For example, a 4/6 outfit means a rod with a 4-ounce tip, on which an 18-pound test line is employed. The following chart explains the meaning of the terms given to the most popular outfits. The average salt-water angler will want one of these outfits.

Outfit	Rod Tip	Line	Reel
2/3	2 oz.	10 lb. test	1/0
3/6	3 oz.	18 lb. test	2/0
4/6	4 oz.	18 lb. test	3/0
6/9	6 oz.	27 lb. test	3/0
9/12	9 oz.	36 lb. test	4/0
10/15	10 oz.	45 lb. test	6/0
12/18	12 oz.	54 lb. test	6/0

There are, of course, numerous other outfits, such as surf tackle (see Chapter 6) and the outfits for big-game fish (see Chapter 8), which are heavier than those in the above chart; but these are seldom designated by similar code numbers.

Numerous salt-water angling clubs divide tackle into light, medium, and heavy classes and base the awards in their contests on the class of tackle with which the catch was made. The rod and the line must meet club specifications but no restrictions are placed upon the reel. But of course a reel is always used which balances the rod and line. Below is a table giving tackle specifications as recognized by most of the world's leading salt-water angling clubs:

LIGHT TACKLE

Rod   Length not less than 6 feet over-all.
Tip   Length not less than 5 feet when seated and weight not over 6 ounces.
Butt Length not to exceed 18 inches.
Line Not to exceed a breaking strength of 30 pounds when wet.
Leader Not to exceed 15 feet in length; no restrictions on breaking strength.
Reel No restrictions; usually a 3/0 or a 4/0 is used.

MEDIUM TACKLE

Rod   Length not less than 6½ feet over-all.
Tip   Length not less than 5 feet when seated and weight not over 9 ounces.
Line Not to exceed a breaking strength of 50 pounds when wet.
Leader Not to exceed 15 feet in length; no restrictions on breaking strength.
Reel No restrictions—4/0 to 6/0 usually used.

HEAVY TACKLE

Rod   Not less than 6 feet 9 inches over-all in length.
Tip   Not less than 5 feet long when seated and weighing not over 16 oz.
Line Not to exceed a breaking strength of 80 pounds when wet.
Leader Not to exceed 15 feet in length; no restrictions on breaking strength.
Reel No restrictions—4/0 to 10/0 depending upon type of fishing.

2/3 and 3/6 outfits are considered a very light outfit. A 4/6 light and a 6/9 medium-light outfit are considered best for general fishing from a boat or bridge where fairly big fellows, but no huge species such as tuna or swordfish, are expected. Naturally, the more expert the angler is, and the more experienced he is in salt-water angling, the lighter an outfit he will dare use for the big fish. But a beginner can have a light or medium-light outfit smashed in a hurry when he hangs a strong fish. This might be great sport—but it will be a short-lived sport, and will prove mighty expensive.

As noted in most of the explanations throughout this book, each item of the tackle, from the hook at one end to the reel at the other, depends upon the properly balanced assistance of every other part. One can attach a heavy leader to a small hook or use a 14/0 reel for 20-pound test line. The results will be very clumsy but not fatal. In matching rod and line, however, each depends on the equal capacity of the other. Successful fishing relies upon the springing capacity of the rod and line, but each spring must have the same power or else the weaker one will try to do all the work—and will fail. Of course, no matter how well you balance your equipment, it won't mean a thing if the tackle is not properly cared for.

CHAPTER **12**

Salt-Water Fish for Dinner

To RECEIVE the fullest enjoyment from salt-water fishing, you must be able to master the art of preparing fish for the table. This is the art of handling of the fish from the moment it is taken from the water to the moment of serving. When properly prepared and cooked, a fish course is a gastronomic delight. Otherwise, it can be an abomination.

PRESERVATION OF SALT-WATER FISH

When fish are first removed from the water they are cool and firm to the touch, lustrous and beautiful to the eye. But unless they are properly cared for, they will soon lose their appeal. Fish deteriorates and decomposes far more rapidly than meat does. However, salt-water fish tend to keep better than fresh-water fish because of their higher salt content. Salt-water bottom fish, such as blackfish, cod, flounders, and fluke keep better than the top-water fish, such as white sea bass, bluefish, striped bass, yellowtail, and weakfish. All salt-water fish are their best when they are cleaned and cooked (or frozen) right after being caught.

In the absence of deep-freeze boxes and dry ice, all salt-water fish will keep better and longer if they are slit. This is done to prevent decay. The fish may have a stomach full of partly digested food when it is caught. If this is not removed, it will begin to rot shortly after the death of the fish and will cause the flesh to turn blue and rancid. To remove the stomach, slit the belly from the vent almost to the gills, but do not split the chestbone. Remove the gills separately, leaving the blood sac along the backbone intact. The sac will turn black and congeal into a solid mass, but it will help to keep the fish fresh and crisp.

It is often necessary to transport the fish a considerable distance from the fishing grounds to your home. Dry ice and deep-freeze units can solve the problem, but these conveniences are not always available. In such cases it is best to use a carryall. This is a long, stout piece of canvas or rubberized cloth with two straps attached to it. It should be lined with some type of insulating material.

Before you begin to prepare fish for the table, you should be sure that it is fresh. A well-developed sense of smell may guide you in determining whether the fish is fresh. There should be no objectionable odor. But since the odor of even the freshest fish may be disagreeable to the novice, there are a number of reliable tests for freshness.

If the eyes are bulging, glassy, clear, full, and bright, the fish is fresh. If the gills are reddish pink, free from slime or odor, the fish is fresh; but it is not if they are faded or discolored. If the flesh is firm and elastic, springing back when pressed, the fish is fresh; but not if the flesh is discolored or dull, and if pressing it with your finger leaves a mark or it separates from the bones. The scales should adhere tightly to the skin, and be bright-colored with their characteristic clear sheen if fresh. A stale fish will usually float when placed in water whereas a fresh one will usually sink. If you are in doubt after having applied these tests, it is best to discard the fish.

Fish are prepared in various ways for different uses. Knowing these forms or cuts is important to the one who must do the cooking. The best-known forms are as follows:

Dressed fish are scaled and eviscerated (entrails removed). The head, tail, and fins are generally removed, and the fish either cut or split into serving-size portions, except for fish intended for baking. Some small fish are frequently cooked with only the entrails removed.

Steaks are cross section slices of the larger sizes of dressed fish. A cross section of the backbone is usually the only bone in the steak.

Fillets are the sides of the fish, cut lengthwise away from the backbone. Sometimes the skin, with the scales removed, is left on the fillets; sometimes the fish is skinned. This form or cut is practically boneless. The most common fillet cut is taken from one side of the backbone and is called a single fillet.

Butterfly fillets are the two sides of the fish corresponding to two single fillets held together by uncut flesh and the skin.

Sticks are pieces of fish cut lengthwise or crosswise from fillets or steaks into portions of uniform length and width.

CLEANING AND DRESSING FISH

To most fishermen, cleaning the catch is an irritating, frustrating job that comes as an anticlimax to the pleasant exhilaration of a successful day out on the water. Some men—a very fortunate few—solve this problem by inveigling their wives into taking on the chore. Just how they accomplish this has long remained a mystery to their less fortunate brethren who far outnumber them and who, though resorting to every wile, are stuck with the task. If you are one of these fellow sufferers, here are the steps to follow to make your job easier.

Scaling

The scales should be removed before the fish is cleaned. Lay the fish on the table and with one hand hold the fish firmly by the head. Then scrape off the scales with the back of a heavy knife (or with a fish scraper), working from the tail toward the head. Hold the knife almost flat against the fish as you scrape. Since scales are more easily removed from a wet fish, it is advisable to soak the fish in cold water for a few minutes before scaling. Take care to remove all the scales near the base of the fins and head.

Cleaning

Cover the working surface with a large piece of heavy paper. Before beginning to work, it is a good idea to rinse your hands in cold water and dip them in salt, in order to prevent slipping. If you have never cleaned a fish before, observe the technique of an expert. To make the task easier, be sure to use a very sharp, strong knife.

Remove the entrails after cutting the entire length of the belly from the vent (anal opening) to the head. Cut around the pelvic fins and remove them. Remove the head, including the pectoral fins, by cutting above the collarbone. However, the head and tail may be left on the fish. If the fish is to be baked the flavor will be enhanced by leaving the head on during the baking; you may remove it, if you wish, before the fish is served. Whether you remove the head and tail before poaching (boiling) is a matter of personal preference, but many people feel that a fish served without tail or head looks peculiar and unnatural. If a fish is to be either broiled or fried, it is generally preferable to remove the head and tail. If the backbone is large, cut down to it on each side of the fish, and then snap the backbone by bending it over the edge of the cutting board or table. Cut any remaining flesh which holds the head attached to the body. Cut off the tail. Remove the dorsal or large back fin by cutting the flesh along both sides of the fin. Then, giving a quick pull forward toward the head of the fish, remove the fin with the root bones attached. Remove the other fins in the same manner.

Never trim the fins off with shears or a knife since the bones at the base will be left in the fish. If the gills have been drawn carefully, the cavity will be perfectly clean except for a line of blood encased in thin skin along the backbone; this is easily removed by scraping with a knife, but be careful not to break the skin. Roll up the gills, fins, entrails, and any other waste in the paper on which the fish was cleaned, and dispose of it so that there will be no odor. (You may want to keep the head, tail, and fins and boil them to make stock.)

Washing

I don't subscribe to the theory that water should never touch fish. I believe that washing or rinsing them does no harm if they are pressed, patted, and wiped dry. But no fish should be washed until the gills and entrails have been removed. Wash the fish in cold running water, removing the blood and any remaining viscera and membranes. Remember that a watery fish is soggy—so wash your fish quickly.

Filleting

Boneless fillets are always a delight, and they are simple to prepare. With a sharp knife, cut through the flesh along the back from the tail to just behind the head. Then cut down to the backbone just above the col-

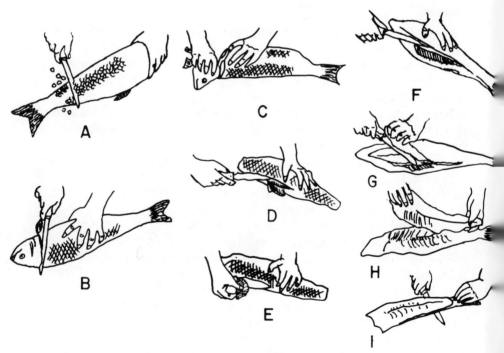

Steps in the proper preparation of fillets.

larbone. Turn the knife flat and cut the flesh along the backbone to the tail, allowing the knife to run over the rib bones. Lift off the entire side of the fish in one piece. Turn the fish over and repeat the operation on the other side.

With flounders, the fillets can be made before the fish is cleaned. Flounders are the easiest fish to fillet, but almost any fish can be boned by the method given above. Fish which have a great many small bones are seldom boned completely, but the fine bones that remain after the backbone has been removed can be pulled out with tweezers. Do not store fillets (or small fish steaks) overnight without first sprinkling them liberally with lime or lemon juice. The flavor soaks in.

Skinning

Skinning is recommended for such fish as eels and the heavy-skinned ocean species. The fish should be scaled and cleaned before skinning, but in order to avoid tearing the shoulder bone, do not slit the belly until after the fish has been skinned. If the flesh is oily, you need not skin the fish until after it has been cooked. For skinning large, tough fish, you will have to use a pair of ridge-jawed pliers.

To remove the skin from a fish, make a slit a short distance below the back of the head. Rub a pinch of sand or salt between the fingers to prevent slipping, and peel off the skin gradually, pulling first on one side and then on the other. You may have to loosen the skin with a knife occasionally in order to avoid tearing the flesh. When the skin has been pulled as far as the lower part of the underfin, reverse the pressure to the opposite side and then pull both sides at once. The rest of the skin should slip from the tail in one piece.

Do not remove the head and tail before skinning a flat fish such as a fluke or flounder. Cut off a thin strip of skin along the center of the back from the tail to the head. Lay the fish flat and cut the skin across the body just above the tail. Work the skin loose gently along the edge and peel it off carefully. Turn the fish over and remove the skin from the other side in the same manner.

If you wish, you may skin fillets, too. Lay the fillets flat on the cutting board or table, skin side down. Hold the tail end with your fingers, and with a knife cut through the flesh to the skin about half an inch from the end of the fillet. Flatten the knife on the skin and cut the flesh away from the skin by pushing the knife forward while holding the free end of the skin firmly between your fingers.

How to Skin an Eel

To divest an eel of its skin, make the first cut right behind the gills on the underside, but be sure this incision is only halfway through the body, stopping when the knife blade touches the backbone. Then, starting at the center of the first cut, slit the eel all the way down the belly. It is important that this incision go through the vent, otherwise the skin will break at that point when it is stripped off. With your knife blade, simply push the intestines out of the belly. Now, grasping the eel firmly with one hand, go back to the very first cut you made and make that incision deeper, cutting through the backbone and flesh. But be careful—do not cut through the skin; you are going to need the eel's head as a handle. While still maintaining your grasp on the eel's head, start to separate the skin from the flesh with the blade of your knife. When the head is attached to the body only by the skin along the back, and skin has been peeled back about an inch or so, you are ready for the actual skinning process.

To get a good grip, wrap a piece of cloth or burlap around the stump of flesh which you exposed by cutting back the skin with your knife. With a good grip on the stump with one hand and the skin flap with the other, start pulling to peel the skin away. It should be pulled in a continuous, steady tug until the entire skin is free. Then lay the eel down on a working surface and cut off the tail. Next, strip off the fins, starting at the tail end. You can begin it with your knife, making a small cut at the base of the fin. Finally, holding the eel with one hand, seize the free end of the fin, pull, and strip it off. If this method seems to give you trouble, an alternative way is simply snip off the fins with a pair of scissors. All you have to do then is scrape the inside of the body clean, rinse the fish off, and allow to drain.

FREEZING FISH

Fishermen find a freezer an ideal place to store their catch, but be sure to freeze only strictly fresh fish. Never let them get warm between the time of catching and freezing. You can keep fish a short time in your refrigerator or on ice, but freeze them as soon as you can.

Wash and prepare fish as you would for eating. Cut them into steaks or fillets. Or you can freeze either large or small fish whole after you behead them and remove the fins, tails, entrails, and scales. Put lean fish steaks, fillets, or whole fish—into a salt solution (½ cup salt per quart of water) for thirty seconds. Do not brine fatty fish like salmon and mackerel; brining will make the fat turn rancid faster, thereby causing wastage.

To package the fish, first wrap each piece, fillet, or steak in a sheet of freezing cellophane. This will keep them from freezing together. Then when you want to use the fish, you can separate the pieces easily for faster thawing and easier handling. Next, put your wrapped fish in a moisture- and vaporproof bag or container and place in your freezer. You also can use any of the sheet materials to package the fish.

COOKING FISH

Unless you like to eat your fish raw (many Oriental people do), a certain amount of cooking is called for. However, the fact that raw fish is edible should be a tip-off for the person who cooks it. It does not require as much cooking time as meat, and there is danger of overcooking. Overcooking will render the flesh dry and tough. At the same time, fish is indigestible if it is underdone. Properly cooked fish is flaky and moist. A fish is done when a fork easily pierces it and separates the flakes of flesh from the bone; however, an experienced cook rarely uses this test because piercing allows the juices to escape.

Since most fish cooking is left to the little woman—and since she usually has her own favorite recipes—we won't go any further into the process of cooking.

SERVING FISH

Razor-sharp knives should be used for cleaning raw fish, but dull, broad ones are better for cutting cooked fish. A spatula is very useful for transferring the cooked fish to the serving platter without breaking it.

The kind of sauce that should accompany a fish course is determined by the manner in which the fish has been cooked and by the fat content of the flesh. Serve a fat-fleshed fish with tartar sauce. In general, serve a lean-meated fish with rich cream sauce, butter sauce, hollandaise sauce, or Creole sauce. However, any fish that has been prepared by frying, or that has been basted with butter or oil during the cooking, requires a tart sauce. Paprika, olives, tomatoes, and finely chopped hard-cooked eggs are popular garnishes for boiled fish. Lime or lemon slices or quarters and cocktail onions are the most popular garnishes for fish that have been baked, broiled, or fried. Parsley, lettuce, or watercress are always good. In order to achieve artistic effects, take color into consideration when you are deciding upon sauces or garnishes.

Dining on fish is an art in itself. Many people will mangle a fine fish into a bone-strewn pulp, especially if it is served whole. This kind of performance is clumsy and unnecessary. Slit a small fish down the back with a fork, and strip the flesh off in one piece. Then, while holding the lower half of the fish down with the fork, gently lift the head with the left hand. Lay the backbone aside and proceed to dine leisurely. If the fish is large, first cut the upper half away from the backbone. Then slice the flesh crosswise every inch or two, and remove it from the body piece by piece. When the first side has been consumed, disjoint the fish and lay aside the backbone. Cut the other side in the same manner.

CHAPTER 13

Where and When to Fish

the Atlantic Seaboard

PART I WENT fully into the "how" of catching the various species of fish that swim our salty oceans, sounds, gulfs, bays, inlets, and rivers. Part II will go into the problem of "where" and "when" to catch these fish. To answer all questions authoritatively, experts have furnished data for the various fishing areas. It is given here without alteration other than for the sake of orderly arrangement.

In this first chapter, let us look into fishing in the Atlantic Ocean from Newfoundland to Georgia.

NEWFOUNDLAND

SUPPLIED BY: Doug Wheeler, Newfoundland Tourist Development Office

Large schools of giant tuna frequent Newfoundland waters from late July until October. Recently the Newfoundland Tourist Development Office purchased two regulation Cape Island–type tuna boats and engaged experienced guides from Wedgeport, N.S., in an effort to develop this sport. Two tuna weighing 620 and 765 pounds were caught during that first season. The larger fish constituted an unofficial North American record for that year. These two government tuna boats, manned by experienced crews, continued the experimental fishing. Sightings of huge schools of tuna in Conception Bay were reported with encouraging regularity, and the tuna boats fished in the areas where concentrations of the big fish were reported.

In many instances, the abundance of food provided by large schools of herring, squid, and mackerel made the giant bluefins extremely choosy about taking the bait. The month of August brought success to the project in a way that left no doubt about the tremendous potential for this exciting sport in Newfoundland waters. Using mackerel and herring baits, fishermen caught ten large tuna averaging 622 pounds—excellent indication of the size of tuna in this area.

There is every reason to assume that a more impressive catch would have resulted from more fishing at the peak of the season. It is safe to predict that the years ahead will see a constant increase of interest in this region from big-game fishermen. Fish weighing more than 1,200 pounds have been harpooned in Newfoundland waters. The Newfoundland Tuna Club is now affiliated with the International Game Fish Association, and all catches are recorded officially.

Swordfish and dolphin also inhabit Newfoundland waters, chiefly in the southwest coastal areas. These, too, provide a challenge to the angler seeking a new thrill in deep-sea fishing. Inshore fish, such as mackerel, halibut, cod, hake, haddock, and pollack, may also be taken in waters around Newfoundland. Further information on fishing here is available from the Newfoundland Tourist Development Office, St. John's Newfoundland.

NEW BRUNSWICK

SUPPLIED BY: R. A. Tweedie, New Brunswick Travel Bureau

Salt-water fishing, in the early stages of development here, is not a large-scale sport as such. However, many of those engaged in commercial fisheries, and others as well, do have boats available and can provide excellent service. This is particularly true in the Bay of Fundy area around St. Andrews and Grand Manan Island. Here, government-inspected charter boats are equipped with the finest fishing gear and are skippered by seamen who know the haunts and habits of the big cod, the fighting mackerel, halibut, haddock, hake, pollack, and ray fish. Bluefin tuna also put in an appearance from time to time in these waters. Boat charters are usually arranged for a five-hour period (weather permitting) and anglers may arrange at extra cost for delicious home-cooked box lunches. Gear and bait are provided. Boat charter rates are generally as follows:

1 or 2 persons $20
3 persons 24
4 persons 28

Boat charters must be made in advance, and can be arranged to suit your convenience. To complete such arrangements, contact the Board of Trade, Grand Manan, N.B., or the Saint John Tourist Bureau, 26 Sydney Street, Saint John, N.B.

In the north of Gloucester County, particularly in the Grand Anse and Caraquet areas, similar trips for cod, mackerel, and pollack may be arranged.

In the Passamaquoddy Bay area, anglers have been enjoying some excellent pollack fishing. These sea fish, relatives of the cod, will seize a feathered jig with the same tenacity as a salmon takes a fly. They weigh up to twenty-five pounds or more. They are most plentiful during active tides, when they chase the schools of herring to the surface. Most pollack fishermen in this area use the trolling method. Another form of angling, gaining in popularity, is offshore fishing with a hand line. This exhilarating sport may be conducted almost anywhere along New Brunswick's 600-mile coast line.

NOVA SCOTIA

SUPPLIED BY: Dan Wallace, Director of Canadian Government Travel Bureau, and Howell E. Rees

The first white men to visit Nova Scotia came for the fish. That was way back in the sixteenth century. They found the ocean surrounding the Nova Scotia peninsula teeming with fish. Year after year they returned, crossing wide and stormy seas to fill their ships from the bounty of the deep. Four hundred years later that bounty remains undiminished. Fishermen of many nations still come to the waters off Nova Scotia, but no longer are they confined to those who make commerce of fishing. Among them are hundreds of sportsmen—and women, too—who fish because they like to fish, and who find in Nova Scotia an abundance and variety of marine life rarely equalled elsewhere. Heading the list is the bluefin tuna, running up to half a ton in weight; Nova Scotia bluefins are giants of the fish realm. Broadbill swordfish are present too, large in size and numbers.

The light-tackle angler shares the enthusiasm of the big-game fisherman, for pollack swarm in every harbor and inlet, as full of fight as the scrappy salmon, and of equal weight. Mackerel are there also, demanding all the angler's wit and skill to bring them to gaff. Those who scorn to bother with rod and reel have unlimited opportunity to tackle halibut, cod, hake, haddock, or a dozen other varieties of bottom fish on a hand-to-hand, come-one-come-all basis. Any shore fisherman is glad to take visitors out in motorboat or dory, and to provide the necessary hand line.

Pollack, cod, haddock, halibut, swordfish, mackerel, or tuna—with no license required to fish them—are always present in offshore waters. There is also no closed season on striped bass and tautog. At present a license is necessary for bass and tautog fishing, but there is the possibility this restriction will be changed. Prospective anglers are advised to check with the

Nova Scotia Travel Bureau before purchasing a license, fee for which is $5 for the season. Minors under fifteen, when accompanied by a resident or nonresident permittee, are not required to have a license.

Sea trout are not classed as salt-water fish, and nonresident anglers must procure licenses. Formerly, anglers were content to wait for these fish to ascend the rivers after their stay in tidal waters, but of late, anglers have been using boats and trolling for sea trout while they are still in salt water, or using spinning equipment from banks at the mouths of rivers, from bridges, or from boats. This type of salt-water angling for sea trout has rapidly become popular in the province.

Striped bass fishermen must have licenses. On the shores of Minas Basin and along the Northumberland Strait, stripers come in on a rising tide, and follow it out again. From half-tide until one hour after high tide has proven the best time for bass fishing—a span of four hours. With two tides every twenty-four hours, visitors are offered eight good hours of fishing each day. Many local fishermen consider the night tide offers best bass fishing, with the stripers feeding on small fish which come closer inshore at night. Good bass fishing can be expected from July 4 through October 31.

In western Nova Scotia, from May 1 to September 30 would appear to be the best time for bass angling; at Round Hill, June 1 to October 15, and at Bear River, July 15 through summer and autumn.

The rise and fall of tide is not as great on the Northumberland Strait shores as on those of the Bay of Fundy, and consequently stripers remain in the deep harbor eddies during slack tide providing extra opportunities for the striper enthusiast via trolling or still-fishing. All rivers emptying into the Northumberland Strait have "narrows" where the best catches have been recorded. Bass are seldom taken in these rivers on a falling tide since they seem to be uninterested in food until they reach the deep harbor eddies.

The Northumberland Strait waters also offer unusual opportunities to catch both mackerel and "tinkers," young mackerel about ten to twelve inches long, which not only provide good fishing but good eating as well. Two methods are used for fishing mackerel—"chumming" and angling from the shore. With the rise of the tide in the harbors, mackerel and tinkers follow small smelts and shiners along the shallow shore waters. The angler has only to chose a vantage point on a sand bar or wharf and begin casting. Live bait is recommended, preferably shiners (easily taken here by dip net). Catches of two dozen mackerel per hour are common in the Northumberland area.

Salt-water pollack fishing has become a popular sport in Nova Scotia, yearly attracting increasing numbers of sportsmen. Pollack "school" in different sizes, and frequent various locations according to size. Six-pound pollack put up a magnificent battle on a trout rod. The best methods of catching them are shore fishing and fishing from a small boat in sheltered coves or shallow water.

For larger pollack, 10- to 30-pounders, a motor boat is used for trolling in deep water at the harbour mouth, and a surf-casting rod with a 30-pound test line is advised.

At Grand Narrows on Cape Breton Island—a stretch of water connecting the Bras d'Or Lakes—pollack can be caught from the shore. On the coast of Nova Scotia's mainland, pollack are everywhere in abundance, and may be taken from wharves, from the shore, or in deep water from boats.

Tautog fishing has only recently been brought to the attention of salt-water fishing enthusiasts in the province. For some years previously, local anglers near Yarmouth, on the southwestern tip of the province, had been catching a fine fighting fish from the estuary of the Tusket River, Yarmouth county, which they were content to call "slippery bass."

Like all salt-water fish in Nova Scotia waters, tuna are found immediately offshore; the season runs from the first week of July until the middle of October. Swordfish reach the waters of Nova Scotia in early July and stay until mid-September.

The whole south and east coast of Nova Scotia is potential tuna fishing ground. The following places have been made popular by the successes of sea-angling explorers in recent years: Wedgeport (site of the International Tuna Cup Matches), Cape St. Mary, Shelburne, Jordan Bay, and Liverpool. Excellent tuna-fishing grounds also lie at the mouth of the La Have River, and may be reached from the town of Bridgewater or from the fishing villages of East La Have, West La Have, Dublin, and Petite Riviere. The waters around the La Have Islands, near the river mouth, are also attractive to light-tackle anglers, owing to the abundance of cod and pollack.

The old seaport of Lunenburg is also popular with deep-sea anglers because of the fine tuna fishing in the bay outside. Chester is a favorite resort of yachtsmen and makes good headquarters for sea angling in Mahone Bay.

Experienced fishing guides and boats equipped for deep-sea sports angling are available at all the more popular fishing spots along the coast of Nova Scotia. In some localities a guides' association or club handles the arrangements for all the guides in the particular area. For further information on fishing in our province, contact the Nova Scotia Bureau of Traveland Information, Provincial Building, Halifax, Nova Scotia.

MAINE

Supplied by: Bob Elliot, Recreation Director, State of Maine

Maine has ideal conditions for salt-water angling. Its magnificent 2,486-mile coast line with its countless bays, inlets, islands; its fine feeding grounds and clear cold waters—all have contributed to make it a fishing ground beyond compare.

The following fish are commonly caught in waters here: *Bluefin tuna.* Range entire coast of Maine, generally well offshore, but often chase bait close to the shore. Best waters are between York Harbor and Muscongus Bay. In these the anglers need go no farther than one to three miles from shore. First tuna appear in Maine's offshore waters during the third week of June. Fishing is at its best in July, August, and first half of September.

Tautog. Good catches have been made in Casco Bay area, from the ledges near Boothbay Harbor, and in Penobscot Bay. These fish move inshore during spring and fall, into deep water during summer and winter.

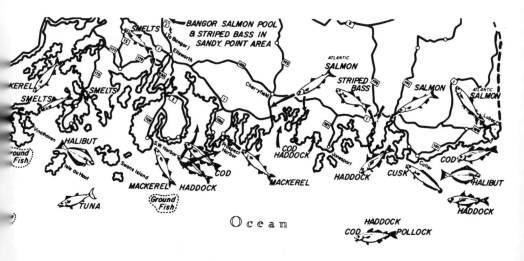

Always frequent rocky and shelly areas, wrecks, and pilings where mollusks abound.

Swordfish. Range entire coast of Maine but nowhere plentiful. One of the great game fish of the sea and one that has never been exploited by sport fishermen off the coast of Maine. Concentrations, if this term can be used, have been observed some ten to twelve miles off Cape Elizabeth during the months of July and August.

Mackerel. Range entire coast of Maine, often very close inshore. They arrive in Maine waters late in May, but rod and reel fishing seldom gets under way until June. The peak of the season is in July, August, and early September.

Striped bass. Range entire coast of Maine. Most often taken in coastal rivers, but are also present in the surf. Ogunquit beach offers surf casting; so do Cape Neddick harbor, lower reaches of Webhannet river at Webhannet, Wells Beach, and the outlet of Branch and Merriland rivers at Wells. All these are between Kittery and Biddeford. Almost any point along the shore as far as Biddeford Pool, just below Biddeford, should furnish fun with striped bass. Beyond that point the coastline is more rugged and irregular, and has fewer places for surf casting. However, there are bass waters in the St. George, Warren, and Oyster rivers near Thomaston, at Belfast, in the famed Atlantic salmon pool at Bangor, at Frankfort where Mash stream enters the Penobscot, and on Narragaugus river at Millbridge. River bass usually show an inclination to hit baits and lures late in May, while surf bass seldom oblige until mid-June or July 1.

Pollack. Range entire coast of Maine. Small harbor pollack swarm close to the shoreline, into harbors and brackish estuaries. Larger pollack chase bait close to shore in spring and fall, and may often be seen breaking water. Concentrations are found in the offshore rips. Best seasons are from mid-May until late fall.

Winter flounder. Range entire coast of Maine, inshore during spring and fall, in deeper harbor and offshore waters during the summer. Winter flounders are often taken in brackish rivers and in shoal areas during the spring.

Cunner. Range entire coast of Maine. Actually, Maine probably boasts some of the largest cunner on the northeast coast. They are plentiful in all coastal areas, inshore and off, wherever there are mollusks to serve as food. They are taken on rocky, shelly bottom, or around wrecks and pilings. Cunner are year-round residents but are most easily taken during the spring, summer and fall.

Codfish and haddock. Range the entire coast of Maine, inshore during the spring and offshore during the remainder of the season. May be taken on offshore banks and in the deeper waters of harbors.

Atlantic salmon. Maine is now the only state in the nation where the sports fisherman can catch the Atlantic salmon, long one of the most famous and favored of game fish. Fishable populations of Atlantic salmon are to be found in seven of the state's rivers: the Machias, the East Machias, the Narragaugus, the Dennys, the Sheepscott, the Pleasant and the Penobscot. Atlantics are caught mainly above tidewater, but some are taken in estuaries and in tidal waters of rivers such as the Sheepscot. The best fishing is in May and June and again in early September. Atlantics are caught mainly on flies. A 6- to 7-ounce rod and English-type salmon flies are recommended. Considerable bank fishing is done on the Narragaugus and Dennys rivers. In some of the eastern rivers, waders are necessary, though pools on the Machias River are most readily fished from boats.

The salt-water sports fisherman in Maine needs no license, except when fishing above tidewater. He may find, however, that Sea and Shore Fisheries Wardens are on duty all along the coast from Kittery to Eastport. These officers have a primary responsibility to the commercial fisheries, but they are always ready to give the sports fisherman a helping hand, provide him with the latest information on fish in the area, or on available boats and facilities. Further information may be had by addressing the Department of Economic Development, State House, Augusta, Maine.

NEW HAMPSHIRE

Supplied by: John Brennan, New Hampshire State Planning and Development Commission

New Hampshire has only eighteen miles of seacoast (at high tide), but is very proud of it. Ocean and other salt- and brackish-water fishing is enjoyed along all the open sea front, in Great Bay, and in waters of the Piscataqua river system to the upper limits of tidewater near Dover. The half dozen beaches are good places to surf cast for striped bass, flounder and other shore feeding species. Stripers also run into bays and brackish waters. Bluefish, mackerel, and pollack like open waters best and many are caught trolling around the Isles of Shoals a few miles offshore. Those waters also yield swordfish and tuna in summer. Good places to fish for tautog are rocky shores such as Great and Little Boars Head between Hampton Beach and Rye Beach. Porgy, flounder, cunner and other species, are caught from wharfs, piers, and from small boats on Great Bay and other protected waters.

Scheduled party boats and charter boats for deep-sea fishing are available at several points, and a number of liveries have small boats for hire. No license is required for salt-water fishing, but you do need a license for oysters and clams and for smelt fishing.

The Seacoast Region Association, Box 807, Portsmouth, New Hampshire 03801, has complete information on the salt-water possibilities in the state. This association also may be contacted for information on the location of party and charter boats.

SPECIES	WHERE	WHEN
Striped bass	Hampton River, Piscataqua River, beach surf	June through October
Tuna	Isles of Shoals, whole coast, Ipswich Bay	July through September
Mackerel	Whole coast, Isles of Shoals	June through September
Pollack	Whole coast, Isles of Shoals, rivers	May through October
Cod, haddock, cusk, hake, wolf fish (cat)	Whole coast, Isles of Shoals	May through October
Flounder	Whole coast, rivers, harbors	May through October
Cunner	Whole coast, rivers	May through October

MASSACHUSETTS

SUPPLIED BY: Lenox E. Bigelow, Massachusetts Vacation Travel Representative

Preeminence of Massachusetts coastal waters for sport fishing has been definitely established within recent years. Consistently, the catch of striped bass, bluefish, and other game species taken by rod and reel has exceeded in size and quantity that of any other state along the northeast Atlantic seaboard. If you look at the map of Cape Cod you will see that it appears as an arm flexed against the Atlantic Ocean. Provincetown is its fist; Chatham its elbow. At the shoulder is the man-made Cape Cod Canal that makes the Cape an island and holds within its tide-scoured length some of the finest striped-bass fishing in the world. South of Cape Cod are Nantucket and Vineyard sounds, both giant bluefish traps in August and September. The old island whaling centers of Martha's Vineyard and Nantucket buffer the Cape against the southerly Atlantic storms and are twin "hot spots" for boat and surf anglers. To the north, in the bight of the arm, is Cape Cod Bay, another great fish trap. Plymouth, Massachusetts, is the westerly jaw of the trap; Provincetown, the easterly. In the bay are giant tuna that Cape anglers are just beginning to learn how to fool.

Along our 1,800 miles of salt-water coastline, there are literally hundreds of "hot" areas for striped bass. At Provincetown and all down the eastern Atlantic Coast, beach buggies are constantly on the prowl for schooling stripers. Now the buggy brigade is getting amphibious: many carry outboards which can be launched through the surf to enable anglers to get beyond the breakers. Planes can be hired to fly you to Monomoy Spit, a desolate storm-washed finger of land stretching toward Nantucket. Other

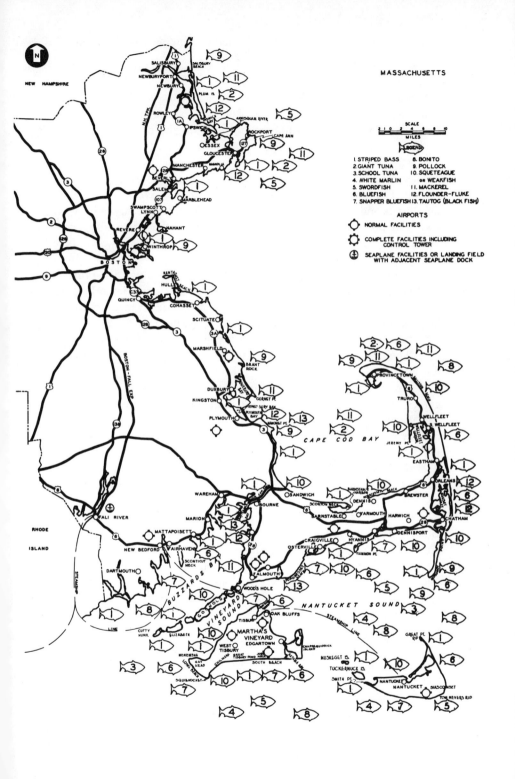

planes fly you low over the surf until bass are spotted. The plane lands on the beach and you cast to the fish.

Boats are now forbidden to troll through the canal. They are considered a menace to big-ship navigation. But surf casters catch good-sized bass from the banks. At the southern entrance to the canal is Buzzards Bay, outboard size at the edges only, but prime striper-trolling country.

Second in popularity on the Cape and Massachusetts are the bluefish. Trollers and surf casters knock them silly (or vice versa) when the runs are on. For the inshore fisherman, the countless rivers, the myriad bays, the sounds and sea itself offer porgies, flounders, weakfish, sea bass, whiting, cod, and pollack. Big fish too are here. From the Vineyard ports, boats meet tuna, marlin, and swordfish in the Atlantic. Offshore waters here have hardly been well scratched.

Any fishing trip in Massachusetts also calls for taking the family along, for there is no better vacation region anywhere. Comfortable lodging, with or without housekeeping facilities, within a price range to meet every budget, are to be found at the seashore or inland areas. Motel, hotel, inn, cottage colony—whatever your choice, you will find them at their hospitable best. There is also every kind of outdoor amusement for those of the family not interested—heaven forbid!—in fishing.

We can also take pride in our charter-boat skippers, both as capable guides and men who maintain their craft for comfort and safety. We suggest discussing disposal of the catch with boat skippers before settling on a charter reservation, that is, if you feel you are going to want to take home the entire catch. Most boat operators work on a small profit margin; thus it is the policy of some to retain a share of a big catch for themselves. Talking over this detail will often prevent misunderstanding, so as not to spoil what should be a perfect fishing day.

The Massachusetts Department of Commerce, 150 Causeway Street, Boston, Massachusetts 02114, will send you free a copy of *Massachusetts' Salt-Water Fishing Guide,* which lists charter boats, outboard launching sites, boat liveries, fishing tournaments, public piers, and the like. Specific questions on the Cape's fish or questions about Nantucket or the Vineyard can be directed to the Division of Fisheries and Game, 73 Tremont Street, Boston 8, Massachusetts.

SPECIES	WHERE	WHEN
Striped bass	Whole coast, surf, rivers	May through October
Giant tuna	Ipswich Bay, Cape Cod Bay, Provincetown	Late July through September
School tuna	South of Cape Cod, off Nantucket Island, Buzzards Bay	Late July through September
White marlin	Nantucket Sound, south of Martha's Vineyard and Nantucket	Late July through September

SPECIES	WHERE	WHEN
Swordfish	Northeast of Cape Ann, Gloucester, Nantucket Sound, south of Martha's Vineyard, Nantucket	July, August
Bluefish	All waters south of Cape Cod and islands, outer Cape Cod beaches. Occasionally north of Cape Cod	August through September
Snapper, bluefish	Waters south of Cape Cod. River mouths, coves, bays	August through September
Bonito	South of Cape Cod, outer Cape Cod waters, Martha's Vineyard, Nantucket	Late July to September
Pollack	Provincetown, Manomet, Plymouth, north to New Hampshire line	May to October. Best runs May and September
Squeteague or weakfish	Cape Cod Bay, Nantucket Sound, outer Cape Cod waters off rapidly shelving beaches, deep bays, estuaries	Late June through September
Mackerel	Whole coast	July through September
Tautog or blackfish	Whole coast. Rocky bottom inshore, bays, harbors, jetties, beaches, breakwaters	May to November
Sea bass	Cape Cod and south. Rocky shores, rocks in water less than 15 fathoms deep around wrecks	Mid-June through September
Scup or porgy	Cape Cod Bay, outer Cape Cod waters from 2 to 20 fathoms, prefer sandy bottom	May through October
Winter flounder	Whole coast. Shoal water, usually sandy bottoms	Year round
Summer flounder or fluke	Whole coast. Best fishing south of Boston	Mid-June through September
Whiting or kingfish	South of Cape Cod. Inshore, often run into fresh water, prefer sandy or hard bottom	May to October
Cod	Whole coast. Deep water. Run inshore during late fall and winter	Year round
Haddock	North of Cape Cod	May to November
Shad	Brackish and fresh water at river mouths	April through June

RHODE ISLAND

SUPPLIED BY: Tom Humphreys, Fishing Editor, *Newport Daily News,* and Leonard J. Panaggio, Rhode Island Development Council

Here in Rhode Island the three most popular fish are striped bass, blue-fish, and blackfish (tautog). These fish can be taken almost anywhere in our waters. To catch them one must have a rough idea where and when they can be found and have a knowledge of what they feed on.

We will start with the striped bass. You will find bass in our waters from the middle of May until late November—the best times being June and September through November. The time of day makes little difference to this fish. You can catch them around the clock. During the day when the baitfish move offshore, the bass come in with them and also at night when the baitfish move back near shore. If there is a heavy sea running, the bait-fish look for shelter in protected coves and inlets. This accounts for the be-lief that the best time to take bass is during a storm. Bass love inlets or the mouths of tidal ponds or marshes, and the deep holes along our rocky coast.

The largest fish are taken at Quonochontaug, Charlestown Beach, Point Judith, and Narragansett—all on the west side of Narragansett Bay. Moving east, Beavertail and the Dumplings on the south end of Jamestown are the hot spots. Farther east, from Brenton's Point along the entire shore to Sachuest Point, and across the Sakonnet River at Sakonnet Point, are all excellent fishing sections. The lures that seem to work best are plugs, tin jigs, and eels. Bait is usually porgies, sand worms, and anchovies.

The bluefish is found in all our waters wherever there is a concentration of baitfish from July through September. The best spots for these are points protruding from our mainland or islands and wherever there is a strong tide or a current. The best spots are considered to be Narragansett, the south end of Jamestown, Prudence Island on the south east side, Hog Island, Newport at Brenton's Point, Ledge Road, Ruggles Avenue, and Sachuest Point. Over in Little Compton, Sakonnet Point is the best spot. These fish feed during the day but they can also be taken on a bright moonlight night. They take eels, tin jigs, feathered lures, and plugs. If you bait-fish for them, large live mummies or cut porgies produce as well as any bait. You must be careful when unhooking bluefish; they have wicked teeth, and unless they are subdued in some way, you will get yourself ripped by their teeth.

Blackfish are found in our waters from April through November. Look for them around wrecks, mussel beds, old piling, and deep holes. James-town, Newport, and Sakonnet are second to no other places when it comes to these fellows. In the spring use a soft bait such as clams or sea worms,

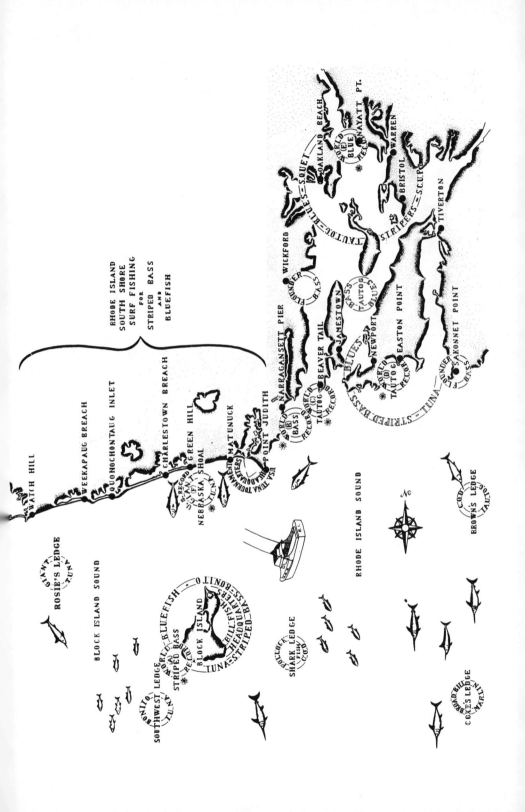

RHODE ISLAND
SOUTH SHORE
SURF FISHING
for
STRIPED BASS
and
BLUEFISH

WATCH HILL

WEEKAPAUG BREACH

QUONOCHONTAUG INLET

CHARLESTOWN BREACH

GREEN HILL

NEBRASKA SHOAL

RECORD (G) GIANT TUNA

MATUNUCK

USA TUNA TOURNAMENT HEADQUARTERS

POINT JUDITH

NARRAGANSETT PIER

FLOUNDER WICKFORD BASS

WORLD (B) BASS

RECORD (C) TAUTOG

BEAVER TAIL

JAMESTOWN

BASS TAUTOG

NEWPORT BLUES

WORLD (D) TAUTOG

EASTON POINT

BLUES

STRIPED BASS

TUNA

FLOUNDER SAKONNET POINT BASS

SQUET

BLUES

OAKLAND BEACH

WORLD (E) BLUE

NAYATT PT.

WARREN

BRISTOL

STRIPERS SCUP

TAUTOG BLUES

TIVERTON

ROSIE'S LEDGE GIANT TUNA

BLOCK ISLAND SOUND

SOUTHWEST LEDGE WORLD (A) RECORD STRIPED BASS BONITO TUNA

BLOCK ISLAND

TUNA STRIPED BASS

BLUEFISH BLUEFISHATTERS BASS BONITO

BILL FISH HEADQUARTERS

POLLOCK SHARK LEDGE FISH COD

RHODE ISLAND SOUND

N

BROWN'S LEDGE COD TAUTOG

COXES LEDGE MARLIN

and as the season gets along use harder baits such as green crabs, fiddler crabs, or sand crabs.

When you are in a locality and you want to know the best spots, ask any bait or tackle dealer and you will get a straight answer, because his existence depends upon you, the fishermen.

Other Rhode Island fish:

White Marlin—June to October, average 50 to 100 pounds. Offshore waters of Rhode Island.

Bluefin tuna—July to October. Schoolfish average 20 to 100 pounds, giants up to 1,000 pounds. Offshore waters. Watch Hill, north and east.

Broadbill swordfish—July to September, average 75-150 pounds. Offshore waters of Rhode Island.

Mackerel—average ½ to 3 pounds, June to November, along entire shoreline and larger bays. Around docks, jetties, inlets, and deep-water shore or rocky ledges.

Weakfish—squeteague ("squit")—average 2 to 10 pounds, May to November, along entire shore line and in all tidal rivers and bays. Inlets, bays, around breaks and eddies of sand bars; in the larger tidal rivers.

Pollack, Boston blue—average 3 to 25 pounds, January to December, same as cod. On outer rocky ledges, wrecks, shoals, tiderips, during May and June; October and December migration inshore along breakwaters, but not in upper bay.

Winter flounder, flatfish—average ½ to 2 pounds, March to December, along entire sandy shore, bays, tidal rivers, and ponds. March to April—upper bays and tidal rivers on muddy or sandy bottoms; around docks, bridges, inlets, and deep holes. May and October—along sandy beaches and breakwaters.

Scup, porgy—average ½ to 3 pounds, May to October, along entire shore line and in larger bays. Along beaches and breakwaters, on all types of hard bottom; in shallow and deep waters.

Codfish—average 2 to 25 pounds, January to December, along entire outer shore. Does not frequent upper bay. On outer rocky ledges, wrecks, shoals. During October and November migration along deep shores and breakwaters.

For information on boat liveries, fishing tournaments, charter boats, public piers, outboard launching sites, etc., write to the Rhode Island Development Council, State House, Providence 2, Rhode Island.

CONNECTICUT

SUPPLIED BY: Connecticut Board of Fisheries and Game

Although always fairly crowded, the salt-water fishing in Long Island Sound on the Connecticut side is popular and productive of excellent sport

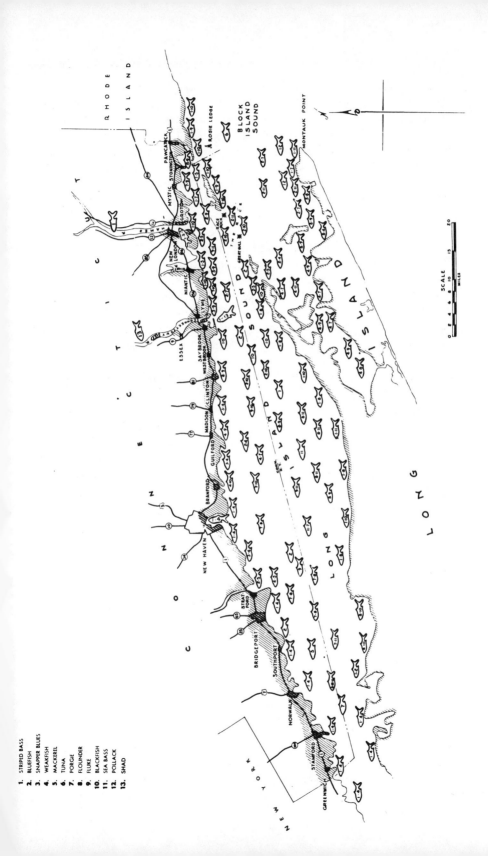

1. STRIPED BASS
2. BLUEFISH
3. SNAPPER BLUES
4. WEAKFISH
5. MACKEREL
6. TUNA
7. PORGIE
8. FLOUNDER
9. FLUKE
10. BLACKFISH
11. SEA BASS
12. POLLACK
13. SHAD

RHODE ISLAND

BLOCK ISLAND SOUND

PAWCATUCK

AOSHE LEDGE

MONTAUK POINT

STONINGTON

MYSTIC

GROTON

NEW LONDON

NIANTIC

ESSEX

SAYBROOK
WESTBROOK
CLINTON
MADISON
GUILFORD
BRANFORD

NEW HAVEN

STRATFORD

BRIDGEPORT
SOUTHPORT

NORWALK

STAMFORD

GREENWICH

CONNECTICUT

NEW YORK

LONG ISLAND SOUND

LONG ISLAND

SCALE

0 2 4 6 8   10   15   20
MILES

at times. The eastern end of the state affords the best fishing. Boats are for hire along the entire Connecticut shore. Most open party boats can accommodate twenty-five to thirty persons on a first-come basis and the cost is usually between $5 and $8 per person for a full day of fishing. This gives you a place at the rail, and bait is usually provided, though not in all cases. These boats leave the dock between 7 A.M. and 8 A.M. and return between 4 P.M. and 5:30 P.M. Open party boats go for bay and offshore bottom fishing for species like fluke, kingfish, mackerel, porgy, sea bass, tautog, and weakfish.

Boat liveries are found at practically every Connecticut fishing port, and skiffs, inboards, and outboards can be rented for $5 to $20 a day, according to horsepower and size. Extra gas is supplied and bait is available. Rowboats can be rented for $2 to $5 per day on weekdays, $3 to $7 per day on Saturday, Sundays, and holidays. Rely on livery owner for up-to-the-minute data plus specific instructions on just where to anchor, drift, or troll.

The New London, Mystic, and Stonington charter boats go out after swordfish and tuna. Charges for charter boats, which accommodate four to six persons, run from $75 to $125 per day depending on the day of the week and port. Tackle and bait are usually included. Information on locations of party boats, boat liveries, and charter boats from the State of Connecticut Board of Fisheries and Game, Hartford 1, Connecticut.

The flat beaches of Connecticut, spotted with stone jetties, are stamping grounds of surf casters. Offshore bars lure weakfish, bluefish, and the surfer's prize catch—the striped bass. We are making a valiant effort to conquer our pollution problems and thus encourage the increase of our highly prized species. Connecticut salt-water fishing is on the upgrade.

SPECIES	WHERE	WHEN
Striped bass	Rocky points, inlets and rivers along entire coast	May through October
Bluefish	Entire coast west to Southport	August, September
Snapper blues	Most inlets and bays along coast	August, September
Weakfish	Most large bays and inlets along coast and Faulkner's Island	Late June through September
Mackerel	Entire coast west to Norwalk	July through September
Tuna	Off Watch Hill and Block Island Sound	Late July through September
Porgy	Entire Sound	May through October
Flounder	Entire Sound and especially in bays and inlets	April through October
Fluke	Along coastline west to Bridgeport	Mid-June through September

SPECIES	WHERE	WHEN
Blackfish (tautog)	Entire Sound on reefs and around rocky points	May through November
Sea bass	Entire Sound west to Bridgeport	Mid-June through September
Pollack	Concentrated north of Montauk Point	May to October (best runs May and September)
Shad	Connecticut River	April through June
Swordfish	Block Island Sound	July, August

NEW YORK

SUPPLIED BY: Glenn E. Anderson

Along the 600-mile coast line of Long Island, the angler has his choice of almost every type of salt-water fishing. These waters contain all the species commonly associated with the north Atlantic, and Montauk Point seems to be the farthest point north for many of the southern species. In other words, in spite of its crowded conditions, Long Island is an excellent spot for good fishing.

For the surf caster, the whole coast line from Montauk Point to Rockaway Point, Shinnecock, Moriches, and Fire Island inlets are good spots in the spring and late fall for striped bass. Other surf-fishing spots are Jones Beach, Short Beach, Point Lookout, Long Beach, Atlantic Beach, and the Rockaways. Striped bass, kingfish, weakfish, mackerel, and tautog are taken along the Long Island shore. June, September, and October are three good months for this area.

There are some 7,000 rowboats and skiffs (plus a few inboard U-drives) for hire at over 235 fishing station liveries stretching from Princess Bay, Staten Island, to Orient and Montauk points at the eastern tip of Long Island. Within the confines of this same "fishy" area there are approximately 170 open boats ranging up to 110 feet, with passenger capacity of 100 or more, and 315 or so charter boats, mainly in the 40-foot class and limited to six or eight fishermen for offshore cruises after the big fellows.

Most of these boats leave from the following ports: Astoria, Atlantic Beach, Babylon, Bay Shore, Canarsie, Cold Spring Harbor, Whitestone, Freeport, Greenport, Hampton Bays, Island Park, Lindenhurst, Mastic Beach, Mattituck, New Suffolk, Montauk, Northport, Seaford, Sheepshead Bay (Brooklyn), and Southhold.

For information about names and locations of fishing stations, boat liveries, and party and charter boat captains, write to the Chamber of Commerce in each of these communities. Another excellent source of information is *Sportsmen's Life,* a monthly publication costing $4 a year. It covers fishing in New York waters. Information can be obtained from *Sportsmen's Life,* 20 Dupont Street, Plainview, New York 11803.

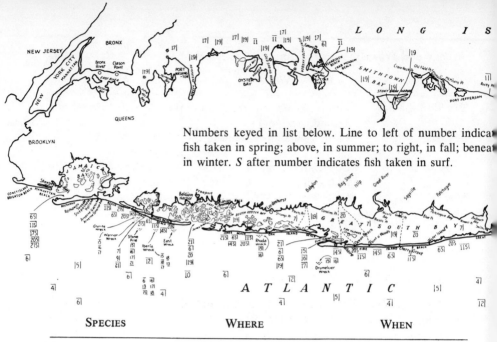

Numbers keyed in list below. Line to left of number indica■ fish taken in spring; above, in summer; to right, in fall; benea■ in winter. S after number indicates fish taken in surf.

SPECIES	WHERE	WHEN
1. Swordfish	South coast from Fire Island to Montauk	June through September
2. Marlin (White)	Entire southern coast	August and September
3. Marlin (Blue or Black)	South coast from Fire Island to Montauk	August and September
4. Tuna (to 150 pounds)	Entire southern coast	July, August, and September
5. Tuna (over 150 pounds)	Entire southern coast	Spring and fall
6. Bluefish	Entire southern and most of northern coast; also most bays and inlets	July through October
7. Snapper bluefish	Most inlets and bays	August to October
8. Mackerel	Deep water on south coast; also Fort Pond Bay	July to November
9. Tinker mackerel	Most inlets and bays	August into November
10. Bonito	Entire southern coast	July and August
11. Striped Bass	Rocky shores on both sides of Island; very good at Montauk	May to December
12. False albacore	Entire southern coast	July through October
13 Pollack	On and over rocky bottoms; very plentiful at Montauk	April, May, and June
14. Kingfish	On sandy ocean or bay bottoms	July, August, and September
15. Sea Bass	On rocky bottoms and wrecks	May through October
16. Porgy	On sandy bottoms and wrecks	June through October
17. Tautog (blackfish)	Off shore and in bays over rocky bottoms and wrecks	Summer and fall
18. Cod	Rocky bottoms—outside	October 1 to April 1

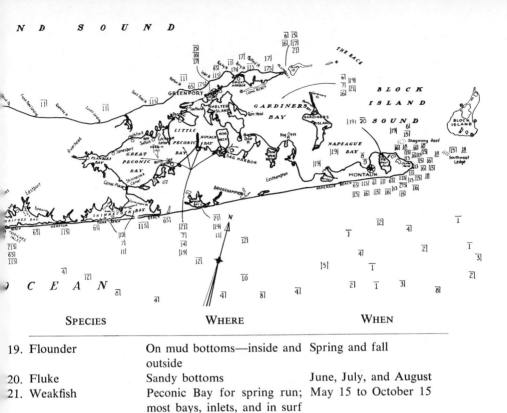

SPECIES	WHERE	WHEN
19. Flounder	On mud bottoms—inside and outside	Spring and fall
20. Fluke	Sandy bottoms	June, July, and August
21. Weakfish	Peconic Bay for spring run; most bays, inlets, and in surf for summer run	May 15 to October 15

NEW JERSEY

SUPPLIED BY: New Jersey Department of Conservation and Economic Development

For the novice or the expert, the salt water of New Jersey's Atlantic coast and inshore coastal bays provides some of the finest fishing in the country. Along the 120-mile New Jersey coast line there is ample opportunity for surf, bank, or ocean fishing. The wide stretches of continuous inland coastal waters offer the angler bluefish, striped bass, porgies, kingfish, flounders, sea bass, weakfish, or croakers. Within sight of the New Jersey coast line are numerous fishing areas where the denizens of the deep are ready to meet the challenge of the most experienced angler. Every species of fish that inhabits the waters of the northern Atlantic Ocean will be found here.

SPECIES	WHERE	WHEN
Whiting	Sea Bright to Cape May	November to April
Marlin (White)	Sandy Hook to Shrewsbury Rocks	August and September

SPECIES	WHERE	WHEN
Tuna (up to 150 pounds)	Sandy Hook to Shrewsbury Rocks	July, August, and September
Tuna (over 150 pounds)	Mud Hole and 17 Fathoms	Spring and fall
Bluefish	Sandy Hook to Cape May	July through October
Snapper Bluefish	Most inlets and bays	August to October
Mackerel	Sandy Hook to Cape May	April to November
Tinker mackerel	Most inlets and bays	August to November
Bonito	Sandy Hook to Cape May	July and August
Striped bass	Sandy Hook to Cape May and Delaware Bay	May to December
False Albacore	Sandy Hook to Cape May	July to October
Pollack	17 Fathoms, Fars, and Sea Bright	April, May and June
Kingfish	Sandy Hook to Cape May and Delaware Bay	July, August and September
Sea Bass	Sandy Hook to Cape May	May to October
Porgy	Sandy Hook to Cape May	June to October
Tautog (Blackfish)	Sandy Hook to Cape May	Summer and fall
Cod	Sandy Hook to Atlantic City	October to end of March
Flounder	Most inlets and bays	Spring and fall
Fluke	Ocean, inlets, and bays	June, July, and August
Weakfish	Ocean, inlets, and bays	May 15 through October 15
Croaker	Barnegat to Delaware Bay	June to October
Dolphin	Sandy Hook to Cape May	July to September
Ocean bonito	Sandy Hook to Cape May	July to September

The New Jersey coastline is long and the beaches are heavily fished by thousands of surf anglers year after year. Starting with Sandy Hook in the north and going south, one finds Sea Bright, Monmouth Beach, and Long Branch. Other beaches are private. Long Branch has numerous jetties that are good locations. South of Long Branch are Elberon, Deal, Avon-by-the-Sea, and Asbury Park, all famous spots for striped-bass fishing. Farther south, Shark River and Manasquan inlets, Barnegat, Beach Haven, Atlantic City, and Ocean City have many surf anglers. Besides the popular striped bass, New Jersey surf fishermen also catch weakfish, bluefish, kingfish, summer flounder, and an occasional channel bass.

New Jersey is equipped to help salt-water fishermen enjoy their fun. Further information may be had by writing to local Chambers of Commerce or to the New Jersey Department of Conservation and Economic Development, Box 1889, Trenton, New Jersey 08625.

DELAWARE BAY

ATLANTIC OCEAN

KEANSBURG
ATLANTIC HIGHLANDS
HIGHLANDS
NAVESINK
SEA BRIGHT
MONMOUTH BEACH
LONG BRANCH
ELBERON
DEAL
ASBURY PARK
BRADLEY BEACH
BELMAR
SPRING LAKE
SEA GIRT
MANASQUAN
BRIELLE
POINT PLEASANT
BAY HEAD
MANTOLOKING
TOMS RIVER
LAVALLETTE
SEASIDE HEIGHTS
SEASIDE PARK
FORKED RIVER
WARETOWN
BARNEGAT
BARNEGAT CITY
HARVEY CEDARS
SURF CITY
SHIP BOTTOM
WEST CREEK
BEACH ARLINGTON
TUCKERTON
BRANT BEACH
NEW GRETNA
BEACH HAVEN CREST
PEAHALA
BEACH HAVEN TERRACE
MOTTS CREEK
SPRAY BEACH
OYSTER CREEK
BEACH HAVEN
HOLGATE
ABSECON
BRIGANTINE
SOMERS POINT
ATLANTIC CITY
VENTNOR
MARGATE CITY
LONGPORT
OCEAN CITY
BAYSIDE
CORSONS INLET
STRATHMERE
LITTLE NECK
PORT NORRIS
SEA ISLE CITY
FORTESCUE
BIVALVE
TOWNSENDS INLET
MOORES BEACH
THOMPSONS BEACH
CAPE MAY
AVALON
REEDS BEACH
PEERMONT
STONE HARBOR
GREEN CREEK
ANGLESEA
NORBURYS LANDING
MIAMI BEACH
WILDWOOD
WILDWOOD VILLAS
WILDWOOD CREST
FISHING CREEK
NORTH CAPE MAY
CAPE MAY POINT
CAPE MAY

N
W   E
S

DELAWARE

SUPPLIED BY: Delaware Game and Fish Commission

The waters along Delaware's coast and inland bays present a fishing paradise for the salt-water angler. The varieties of fish, the different methods of fishing, the excellent facilities, and the occasional springlike days during the winter months virtually guarantee year-round fishing activity. Thousands of anglers from Delaware and nearby states consistently take advantage of this recreation and sports center, and the number of fish caught per hour of fishing matches any other area in the country.

The deep-sea fisherman can find all the accommodations necessary for a day or month of pleasure at the Indian River Yacht Basin or at Roosevelt Inlet, Lewes. Parties have their choice of a variety of fishing. Still-fishing for black sea bass and trolling for blues are the most popular. However, marlin fishing is becoming more commonplace each year.

Party-boat ports along the Delaware Bay at Bowers Beach and the Mispillion Light, near Milford, accommodate thousands of Bay fishermen each season. It is a common occurrence for parties of six or seven fishermen to return to port with two or three hundred sea trout (squeteague), porgies, or croakers. Small-boat owners take advantage of launching facilities created by the Board of Game and Fish Commission to get their private boats into and out of the water. Small boats may be rented from liveries located at Broadkill, Slaughters Beach, Mispillion Light, Bowers Beach, Kitts Hummock, Woodland Beach, and Port Penn.

Ask anyone who has flounder-fished in Indian River Bay or Rehoboth Bay and you will hear it recommended highly. Many 8-10 pounders are taken by hook-and-line fishermen in this area each summer. May through September is considered to be the optimum time for flounder fishing.

Surf fishermen, more numerous every year, are finding sport to their liking along the public beaches south of Rehoboth. Sea trout, flounder, sand perch, and kingfish reward these enthusiasts consistently. Striped bass and other fish offer highly desirable food and fun for surf fishermen.

Over-all, Delaware's marine fishing is tops. It is growing all the time but there is still room and plenty of fish for more people. There are no license requirements and the facilities are excellent. For further information, write to the Delaware Game and Fish Commission, Dover, Delaware.

WHEN THEY BITE

Albacore	May to October
Black drum	May to October
Bluefish	May to July
	September to October
Bonito	May to October

WHEN THEY BITE

Channel Bass	May to July
	September to October
Cobia	June to September
Croaker	July to September
Dolphin	July to September
Flounder	April to November
Blackfish	Year round
Fluke	May to October
Kingfish	June to October
Mackerel	April to June
	September to October
Perch (sand)	Year round
Porgy	May to September
Sea Bass	Year round
Spot	June to September
Striped Bass	Year round
Weakfish	April to November
White Marlin	July to September

MARYLAND

SUPPLIED BY: Earle R. Poorbaugh, Maryland Department of Information

In the 130-mile fishing hole that is Chesapeake Bay, in its estuaries and its twenty-five or more rivers, and in the coastal waters, are over three hundred species of fish. Many are potential tackle-busters, some are speedsters that claw the air when hooked. At least thirty kinds are important commercially and for sport fishing.

Of these, the striped bass is the most sought after. He is the prize of the Chesapeake. At one season or another they can be taken in every portion of the bay. Hardheads, trout, bluefish, Norfolk spot, both kinds of perch, and all the river herring family are available. In places largemouth black bass, catfish, black drum and pickerel are common. In the briny waters of the coast are great white marlin, dolphin, porgies, sea bass, bluefish, channel bass, flounders, sea trout, and kingfish. Now and then slick-skinned mako sharks are boated; also line-stretching tuna and the prized blue marlin.

Although striped bass may be found anywhere in the Chesapeake, most agree they follow a spring-to-fall migratory pattern, thus appearing plentifully at spots, depending upon season and weather. Water temperature, salt content, and availability of food affect migrations. In spring, first important fishing occurs at Sandy Point near the Chesapeake bridge. There, anglers using surf gear often take fish over ten pounds at night. They use bloodworms on bottom rigs.

The migrating schools move northward to eventually fill the lower Susquehanna River. Trolling with June bug spinners, bloodworms, bucktails, or spoons can produce some outsized specimens. Though rock are caught there spring to fall, best fishing is in July and August.

Stripers show all summer in many sections of the bay and anglers converge on famous ports to hire party fishing boats. Among those on the western shore are: Havre de Grace, Baltimore area, Annapolis, Rose Haven, North Beach, Chesapeake Beach, Solomons, and Point Lookout. Eastern shore: Chesapeake City, Betterton, Tolchester Beach, Gratitude, Rock Hall, Kent Island, Claiborne, Tilghman, Taylor's Island, Wingate, Crisfield, and others.

From June through the winter months bay spots such as the following make angling news: Sparty's Lump, Gales Shoal, Tolchester Beach, Pooles Island, Belvedere Shoal, Bay Bridge, Hackett's Bar. Tolly Bar, Gum Thickets, Eastern Bay, Sharp's Island, Choptank River, The Diamonds, Gooses, Cove Point, Patuxent River, Cedar Point, the Middle Grounds, Tangier Sound and others.

Responsible guides can be procured at the ports named, and every old-timer plying the bay is familiar with its hot spots. As a rule, parties of four to six are preferred by most charter-boat skippers, who charge $25 to $40 a day. This includes boat, fuel, guide, and sometimes ice and bait. A few supply tackle if necessary.

Shore and small-boat fishing are also possible in many sections. Stripers are taken by trolling or chumming.

Species other than rock are generally caught by still-fishing or drifting. Chumming is an excellent means of catching black-back white perch, which at certain times virtually fill Eastern Bay. Trout grab small shrimp and bloodworms, as do hardheads (croakers), Norfolk spot, and bluefish. Even cut bait or crab gets these scrappers. Fishing after dark is a good way to catch croakers. Trout, spot, and hardheads seldom move farther up the bay than Poole's Island. Best spots for them are south of the bay bridge, particularly in Eastern Bay, Choptank River, Solomons area, Hooper Straight, and Tangier Sound.

Summer and early fall fishing is excellent. Bluefish are rarely found above the Bay Bridge. Top distribution is south of Annapolis, around Sharp's Island and the Cove Point area. Norfolk spot, the "panfish of the Chesapeake," can be caught by the barrel in places south of the bay bridge during the hot months. Anglers out of Tilghman and Solomons seldom have difficulty "filling up" with spot.

Visitors to the Chesapeake (April to June) have an opportunity to sample some famous shad fishing. At that time many rivers feeding the bay are tinted silver by shad. They live in salt water but migrate to fresh water to spawn, and their springtime runs turn anglers out in droves. Head-of-the-bay rivers and creeks are popular, like the Susquehanna River and North-

MARYLAND

east, Deer, and Octoraro creeks. Others throughout the Chesapeake system receive shad and provide great fishing. Among them are the Choptank River, near Greensboro, and the Patuxent and Wicomico on the western shore. In smaller streams only hickory shad are available, but large rivers have both hickories and whites. They hit artificial lures cast with fly rod, spin, and plug outfits. Small, flashy lures get most shad.

Black drum are the largest fish anglers may expect to hook in the Chesapeake. As a rule they do not appear above Tilghman's Island and Annapolis, being plentiful only in Tangier Sound, near Crisfield. The average black weighs about thirty pounds but each year sixty-pounders are taken and someone always comes up with one of eighty or ninety pounds. Guides can be had at Crisfield, Smith Island, or other points. Black drum are available June to October, with good August angling. Still-fishing with peeler crab or cut bait is preferred.

Coastal anglers find white marlin the ocean's greatest challenge. These billfish are so plentiful off Ocean City that the port is known as the "white marlin capital of the world." More whites are taken there than at any other point on the Atlantic Coast.

The fishing begins about June 15, improves until early August. September fishing can be excellent. Marlin angling is so popular that it is necessary to make boat reservations in advance. Boat, crew, tackle, and bait for four are provided for about $75 a day. Extra anglers can be accommodated at a slightly increased rate. Most marlin are taken in the vicinity of the Jack Spot, a shoal located about twenty-three miles offshore. Squid are trolled to raise the great whites as well as occasional blue marlin, numerous bluefish and dolphin, some sailfish, and mako sharks.

Also offshore are vast schools of bluefish, which arrive by June and are available spasmodically until mid-September. Best fishing is in July. When the blues are in, preceding the major marlin migration, the charter fleet concentrates on them. Parties of six can be arranged at a daily rate of about $65. The fee is slightly higher with more than six. Trolling lures nets quantities of blues weighing up to 7 pounds or more. Porgies, sea bass, kingfish, and trout are also taken offshore, with porgies and bass the mainstay of thousands of bottom fishermen. Charter and party boats are available for this, with ordinary results being a pretzel can full of porgies and bass. The larger party boats, accommodating about thirty anglers, charge $3 per trip. Cut bait, crab, or squid are used.

Inshore anglers concentrate at the Ocean City inlet, the Assawoman and Sinepuxent bays, and along the windswept beaches of Assateague Island. At the inlet, large sea trout are the rule, as well as bluefish, flounders, and striped bass. In the tidal bays flounders provide priority angling. They run up to eight pounds or more. Many troll slowly for them (renting skiffs and outboards), with minnows on bottom rigs. Others still-fish or drift.

On the windswept beach of Assateague Island, red drum or channel bass are an angler's delight. They're taken by surf casting with cut bait, June to October, and the average fish runs about thirty-five pounds. Fifty-pounders are not only possible but probable, and sometimes lucky fishermen get two or more of them in a day. Kingfish, blues, and trout are also caught in the surf and on the same baits used for drum. The island is reached by ferry from South Point, on the Worcester County mainland. Ferry trips are made almost hourly during the season and it is possible to drive autos on the island.

For complete information on guides, accommodations, etc., write to Department of Information, State of Maryland, Annapolis, Md.

VIRGINIA

SUPPLIED BY: J. Stuart White, Virginia Department of Conservation and Development

Salt-water sport fishing! Just take a look at the map of Virginia. On the Atlantic, from Chincoteague to Currituck, is a 120-mile stretch of ocean frontage with long offshore islands, a dozen inlets, and a vast area of channels and bays. From Cape Charles and Cape Henry at its mouth, stretching up to the state of Maryland, the Chesapeake Bay bisects a coastal plain, giving it 300 miles of bay shores. The Potomac, Rappahannock, York and James rivers, salty tributaries and estuaries of the Chesapeake, divide eastern Virginia into historic peninsulas, providing 1,300 miles of tidal shores, with scores of famous creeks and popular fishing grounds.

Bottom fishing is everywhere a popular sport. Hand lines and rods and reels are used with medium-weight lines and enough sinker to hold baited hooks on the bottom. Lines are usually rigged with two hooks, a foot apart, just above the sinker. Peeler crabs, shrimps, bloodworms, cut fish, clams, live minnows, squid, artificial minnows, and flies are used for bait.

Surface and mid-water fishing are done with a variety of methods for fish at the surface and mid-water depths. Live fish, cut fish, artificial lures are used as bait. Chumming is a practice in the Chesapeake Bay.

Surf casting is a popular and rapidly growing sport along the bay and ocean shores. Artificial lures and live and cut fish are used.

Pier fishing attracts thousands at ocean and bay resorts. Fishing piers conduct attractive tournaments and sports events throughout the fishing seasons. Any wharf, jetty, old hulk, or piling in tidewater Virginia is a good spot for a catch.

For the "salty" angler there are the ocean beaches, the inlets, and the deep blue sea. Large bluefish, black sea bass, black drum, bonito, channel bass, dolphin, kingfish, marlin—these are common catches on Virginia's Atlantic Ocean shores.

No license is required for salt-water sport fishing in Virginia, and there is no closed season. Many fishermen prefer the cold weather season, when the striped bass are at their best. Croakers appear in the Bay and lower rivers in April or early May. From then until fall, tidewater Virginia is in the sport fishing game in a big way. Fishing resorts register visitors from all sections of the country, and many return year after year. Guide boats operate out of fifty or more river, bay and ocean harbors. A waterfront resident without a fishing boat is a rarity, and the visitor fisherman is always welcome.

As a rule, guide boats furnish hand lines for bottom fishing. Some furnish rods and reels. Bait is always available. You can rent a small boat and have a day's sport for as little as $3; or you can go deep-sea fishing with your guide or chartered boat, the rates depending on how far you go, how long you stay out, and the size of your party. Or, you can go deep-sea fishing or inshore fishing pro rata with open parties.

In short, due to the extent and variety of its waters, the large number of species, the length of its open seasons, and its tourist attractions and facilities, tidewater Virginia is unexcelled in its advantages for year-round salt-water sport fishing.

For general information on salt-water sport fishing in Virginia, write the Department of Conservation and Development, State Office Building, Richmond 19, Virginia.

SPECIES	WHERE	WHEN
Croaker	Bay and tributaries	June, July, and August
Trout or weakfish	Entire Chesapeake Bay, mouths of tidal rivers & ocean inlets	May, June and October, November
Bluefish	Chesapeake Bay & ocean	June-October
Cobia	Chesapeake Bay	May-September. Best July and August
Rockfish or stripers	Chesapeake Bay and tidal rivers	June-December. Best October and November
Spot	Chesapeake Bay	May-October
Flounders	Chesapeake Bay and tributaries	May-October
Kingfish	Chesapeake Bay, ocean inlets and surf	Summer months
Channel bass	Along coastal beaches and in deep holes in Chesapeake Bay	Spring and fall
Black drum	Along coastal beaches and in deep holes in Chesapeake Bay	Spring and fall
Black sea bass	Chesapeake Bay and ocean	Summer months
Tautog	On rocky bottoms and around lighthouses	May-October

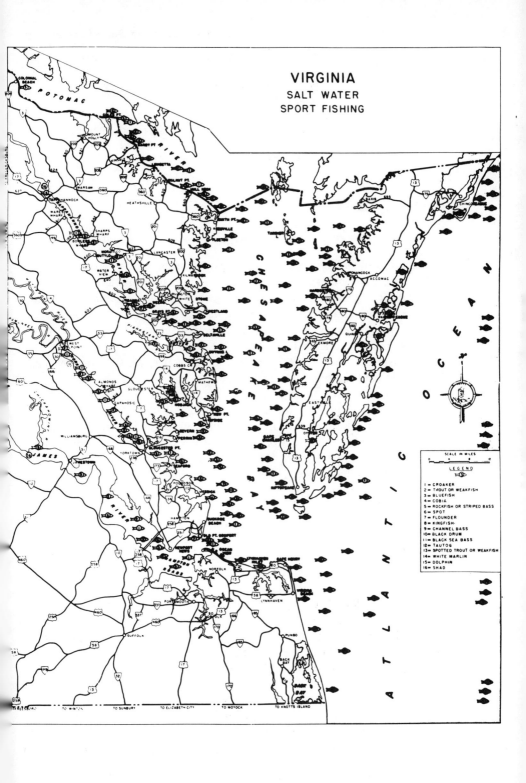

Species	Where	When
Spotted trout or weakfish	Chesapeake Bay and tidal rivers, best at mouth of Lynhaven inlet	Summer months
White marlin	Ocean	July and August
Dolphin	Ocean	July and August
Shad	Upper rivers	March-June

NORTH CAROLINA

Supplied by: Charles Parker, North Carolina Travel Bureau

North Carolina's long coast line has game fish in variety, good facilities, and experienced guides to give salt-water anglers memorable thrills. Prime fishing periods extend from early spring through late autumn, and there is some activity throughout the year. The coastal waters yield more than two dozen varieties of game fish, ranging from small scrappers to line-straining marlin and sailfish of the Gulf Stream. Increasing catches of the billfish in recent years have spurred development of new know-how and facilities to land the big ones.

Names known far and wide among sports anglers dot the North Carolina coast, each with its own special appeal. On the Outer Banks near Nags Head and Manteo, is Oregon Inlet, where the big run of channel bass in late March or early April kicks off the real salt-water fishing season, and in the Cape Hatteras National Seashore Park is Hatteras, where marlin and sailfish are specialties. Marlin catches off Hatteras, where the Gulf Stream swings within a dozen miles of the North Carolina coast, have ranged up to 570 pounds. Oregon Inlet and Hatteras also are favored spots for surf casting for channel bass, as are Ocracoke and Drum Inlet farther down the Banks. In these areas catches in the 50-pound class and better are made every year. Morehead City is the home of the largest sport-fishing fleet in the Tar Heel State. The section is noted for large catches of sailfish, along with other Gulf Stream varieties. A highly prized catch is the large king mackerel, locally called the cero. Nearby is Harkers Island, another center for charter boats. In the southeast are several centers—New Topsail Beach, Wrightsville and Carolina beaches near Wilmington, and Southport, close to the famed fishing area of Frying Pan Shoals. Sailfish boated in this area have topped eight feet. King mackerel also provide fine sport.

Among the twenty fishing centers where boats may be chartered, there are more than two hundred seagoing craft available for fishing offshore or inshore or in the inlets and sounds. Rates per party vary widely, depending on whether fishing is to be done inshore or offshore or for a full or

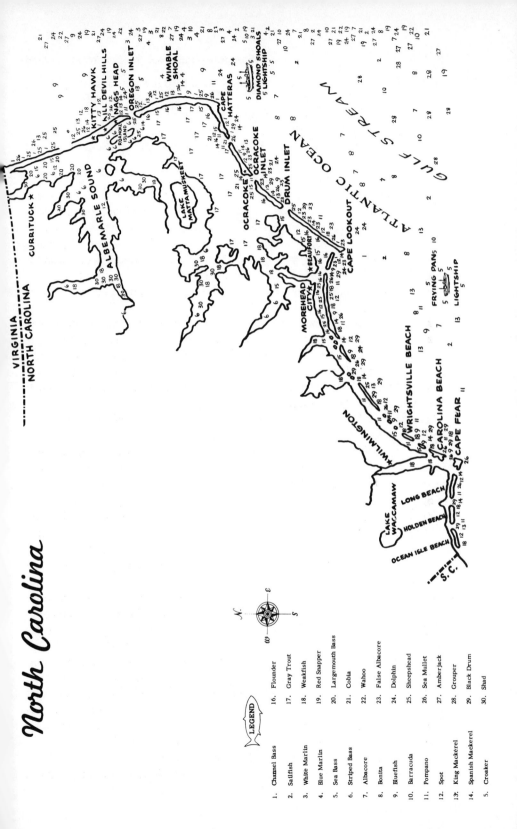

North Carolina

VIRGINIA
NORTH CAROLINA

ATLANTIC OCEAN

GULF STREAM

CURRITUCK ★
KITTY HAWK
KILL DEVIL HILLS
NAGS HEAD
OREGON INLET
WIMBLE SHOAL
CAPE HATTERAS
DIAMOND SHOALS
LIGHTSHIP

ALBEMARLE SOUND
ROANOKE ISLAND
LAKE MATTAMUSKEET
OCRACOKE
OCRACOKE INLET
DRUM INLET
CAPE LOOKOUT
BEAUFORT ★
MOREHEAD CITY
WRIGHTSVILLE BEACH
FRYING PANS
LIGHTSHIP
★ WILMINGTON
CAROLINA BEACH
CAPE FEAR
LAKE WACCAMAW
LONG BEACH
HOLDEN BEACH
OCEAN ISLE BEACH
S.C.

N
E
W
S

LEGEND

1. Channel Bass   16. Flounder
2. Sailfish   17. Gray Trout
3. White Marlin   18. Weakfish
4. Blue Marlin   19. Red Snapper
5. Sea Bass   20. Largemouth Bass
6. Striped Bass   21. Cobia
7. Albacore   22. Wahoo
8. Bonita   23. False Albacore
9. Bluefish   24. Dolphin
10. Barracuda   25. Sheepshead
11. Pompano   26. Sea Mullet
12. Spot   27. Amberjack
13. King Mackerel   28. Grouper
14. Spanish Mackerel   29. Black Drum
5. Croaker   30. Shad

fraction of a day. They may be as low as $30 daily, or range upward to $90 and above. The charges usually include bait and the use of tackle.

There are ocean fishing piers all along the coast, from Kitty Hawk on the northern end to the Southport area nearly three hundred miles to the south. Pier rights usually are $1, with bait available for purchase and tackle for rental.

Game fish from the north and south meet in the waters off North Carolina to provide a wide range of catches. This gives Cape Hatteras its nickname of "Game Fish Junction." Principal game fish include: channel bass (red drum), striped bass (rockfish), sailfish, blue marlin, white marlin, cobia (cabio), Spanish and king mackerel, dolphin, amberjack, black drum, grouper, red snapper, wahoo, albacore, tuna, false albacore, bonito, oceanic bonito, bluefish, sea bass, croakers, flounders, gray and speckled trout, sheepshead, whiting, barracuda, pompano, spot, and sea mullet (Virginia mullet).

Detailed information on fishing and facilities in specific coastal areas may be obtained by writing these information centers: Dare County Tourist Bureau, Manteo, N.C.; Chamber of Commerce, Morehead City, N.C.; Fishing Information Center, New Topsail Beach, N.C.; Greater Wilmington Chamber of Commerce, Wilmington, N.C.; and South Eastern North Carolina Beach Association, Wilmington, N.C.

Experience has shown that areas and seasons for catches can be pretty well predicted. This calendar will be a helpful guide:

March, April, and May. Channel bass run begins in late March or early April at Oregon Inlet, and they appear in large numbers throughout the spring at Ocracoke, Hatteras, Buxton, Drum Inlet, Topsail, and other points. Bluefish schools provide good catches off Frying Pan Shoals (Southport), Hatteras, Oregon Inlet, and Morehead City, and in the surf and off piers. Spanish mackerel appear, especially around Morehead City and Swansboro and as far north as Oregon Inlet. Gulf Stream fishing starts picking up in May. Billfish begin to show up off Cape Hatteras and the Dare Coast.

June, July, and August. There is good channel bass fishing in June from beaches or inlets, especially at Nags Head, Hatteras, Ocracoke, Topsail; falling off and scattered in July, although usually good in southeast. Dolphin and amberjack appear in large numbers off Hatteras, Morehead City, Beaufort, and Southport. Bluefish are caught in ocean and from beaches. Cobia appear at Atlantic Beach, Hatteras, Oregon Inlet; bonito off Southport and Wrightsville Beach; Spanish and king mackerel off Morehead City, Southport, Hatteras. Also, in the Gulf Stream in this season are false albacore, school tuna, oceanic bonito, and barracuda. Red snappers are taken off Cape Lookout and Wrightsville Beach. Sailfish and blue and white marlin begin to make news.

September, October, and November. Offshore fishing is excellent from

Hatteras to Southport and the largest catches of king mackerel, amberjack, dolphin, sailfish, and marlin are recorded during these months. September brings a resumption of surf casting for channel bass at Oregon Inlet, extending—with the advance of cooler weather—to Hatteras, Ocracoke, Drum Inlet, Topsail, and Southport. Large king mackerel are taken off the capes, along with amberjack and dolphin. Striped bass are schooling up in Albemarle and Croatan sounds and adjacent waters. Fishing for speckled trout is unusually good in southeast.

December, January, and February. Increasing catches of striped bass in fresh waters along the coast—in the Neuse, Pamlico, Pungo, Alligator, White Oak, and similar rivers—and in fresh or brackish waters of the Wilmington-Southport area. Puppy drum (small channel bass) appear in salt, brackish, and almost fresh waters from Ocracoke to Cape Fear. Belhaven area reports stripers throughout the winter, and by February they are active all the way to the South Carolina line.

North Carolina has no closed season, and no license is required for salt-water fishing.

SOUTH CAROLINA

SUPPLIED BY: George M. MacNabb, South Carolina State Development Board

Fishing is one of South Carolina's favorite pastimes and a year-round sport. There is always somewhere that the fish are biting, and almost anyone can tell you where to catch a big one.

If you like to just sit and fish, the piers at Myrtle Beach, East Cherry, Grove Beach, McClellanville, Edisto, Murrell's Inlet, Georgetown, Bluffton, and Isle of Palms, the abandoned bridge to Mt. Pleasant, and the Breach Inlet bridge are ripe spots for hauling in spots, croaker, flounders, whiting, sheepshead, and some striped bass.

In South Carolina there are many island and inlets entering into the Atlantic Ocean where surf fishing can be done. Many of these spots are isolated but some like Myrtle Beach, Beaufort, Tilghman Beach, Crescent Beach, Hunting Island, Pawley's Island, the Isle of Palms, Edisto Island, Hilton Head Island, Sullivan's Island, and Folly Beach. Catches of whiting, striped bass, drum, spot, and trout are good at these and other beaches in our state.

Outboards or shallow-draft boats afford some fine fishing spots and are for rent in many places. The Waccamaw, Black, Santee, Cooper, Ashley, Stono, Wando, Edisto, Combahee, Savannah, and Coosawhatchie rivers, and the many creeks that wind from them, are excellent spots for trout in season, rockfish, and channel bass. Bottom-fish for croaker, spot, whiting, and flounders in salty areas of the rivers. Troll and bottom-fish in the Inland Waterway.

South Carolina

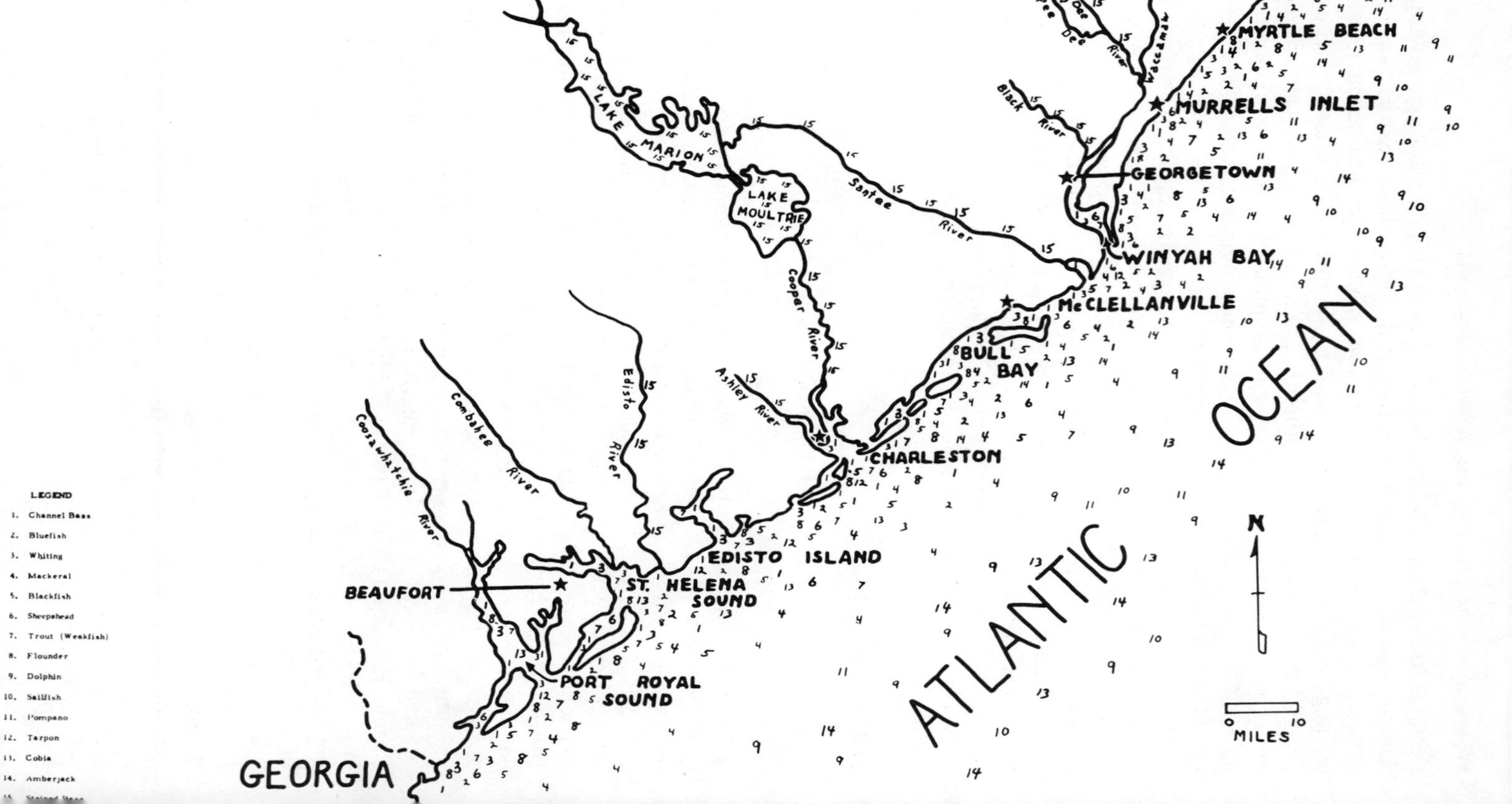

N.C.
LITTLE RIVER
MYRTLE BEACH
MURRELLS INLET
GEORGETOWN
WINYAH BAY
McCLELLANVILLE
BULL BAY
CHARLESTON
EDISTO ISLAND
ST. HELENA SOUND
PORT ROYAL SOUND
BEAUFORT
GEORGIA
ATLANTIC OCEAN
Little Pee Dee
Great Pee Dee River
Waccamaw River
Black River
Santee River
Cooper River
Ashley River
Edisto River
Combahee River
Coosawhatchie River
LAKE MARION
LAKE MOULTRIE
N
0 10 MILES
LEGEND
1. Channel Bass
2. Bluefish
3. Whiting
4. Mackeral
5. Blackfish
6. Sheepshead
7. Trout (Weakfish)
8. Flounder
9. Dolphin
10. Sailfish
11. Pompano
12. Tarpon
13. Cobia
14. Amberjack

Charter boats run out of most major fishing ports for deep-sea fishing, offering the avid fisherman a wide choice of catches. Charter boats cost $50 and up; they all furnish bait and tackle. Party-type boats are also available at several ports. For further information, write to the State Development Board, Columbia, South Carolina.

SPECIES	WHERE	WHEN
Channel bass	Entire coast, but best Charleston to Little River	Best April-July and September-November
Bluefish	All coast, but best Georgetown to Little River	April-October
Whiting	All coast	All year
Mackerel	Entire coast offshore, but best Charleston to Little River	April-October
Blackfish	Entire coast	Summer and fall
Sheepshead	Certain areas on entire coast	Summer months
Trout (Weakfish)	Entire coast	Entire year
Flounder	Entire coast	Entire year
Dolphin	Edges of Gulf Stream	Summer months
Sailfish	Edges of Gulf Stream	Summer months
Pompano	Murrell's Inlet to Little River	Summer months
Tarpon	Edisto Island, Charleston Harbor and Winyah Bay	July-August
Cobia	Beaufort Sound and offshore to north	May-August
Amberjack	Offshore Charleston to Little River	Summer months
Striped bass	Coastal rivers and Santee-Cooper lakes	Winter in rivers, all year Santee-Cooper

GEORGIA

SUPPLIED BY: Georgia Game and Fish Commission

Georgia has a short coast line, but numerous islands which are excellent for surf casting. Many of these islands are difficult to reach or restricted, but a few like St. Simon's, near Brunswick, and Tybee Island, near Savannah, can be fished from the surf. Sea Island Beach is an especially popular spot to cast for channel bass.

Georgia's bays and rivers offer fine catches of tarpon, jack crevallé, drum, winter trout, striped bass, channel bass, whiting, sheepshead, summer trout, and shad. Species predominately caught offshore include eddyfish, albacore, sailfish, Spanish mackerel, cobia, amberjack, angelfish, blackfish, king mackerel, bluefish, and barracuda. Party boats and charter boats are located at Brunswick, Shellman Bluff, and Savannah. Rowboats and outboards are available at these locations and several others along our coast line. Guides can be found at all points and charges are very reasonable. Further information on our salt-water fishing facilities can be had by writing to the State of Georgia Game and Fish Commission, Atlanta 3, Georgia.

SPECIES	TIDES	WHERE AND WHEN
Eddyfish (tripletail)	Low or high slack	Around deep wrecks, channel buoys, beacons, and other shady spots. April to September, but most abundant in early July
Tarpon	Any tide offshore morning and afternoon low water flood inshore	Sounds, inlets, rivers close to ocean, and offshore waters. Last of May to first bad weather in fall (August on), July and August best months
Albacore (little tuna)	Any tide early morning or late afternoon	Offshore waters—seldom closer than edge of Gulf Stream, May through August
Sailfish	Any tide early morning, afternoon after 2 P.M.	Offshore waters—seldom closer than 10-12 miles offshore, May through August
Amberjack	Any tide early morning, middle to late afternoon	Offshore waters, May through August
Jack crevallé (Jackervalle)	Any tide offshore, slack flood inside	Sounds, inlets and offshore waters, summer months
Angelfish	Any tide, morning best	Offshore waters; early spring to late fall
Blackfish (common sea bass)	Any tide	Offshore waters around wrecks, buoys, rock piles, etc.; summer months
Spanish mackerel	High flood inside, any tide offshore	Sounds, inlets, and offshore waters; may through August
King mackerel (kingfish)	Any tide	Offshore waters. Generally while fishing for Spanish mackerel; May through August
Cobia	Any tide	Offshore waters around channel markers, buoys, wrecks, etc., April through November
Bluefish	Any tide offshore, high water flood in inlets	Offshore waters and occasionally in inlets and sounds; two runs lasting approximately 45 days—one in April and May, the other in August to September or October
Drum (black drum)	Slack tide, high or low	Rivers, sounds, inlets and channels usually around piling, buoys,

SPECIES	TIDES	WHERE AND WHEN
		channel markers, wrecks, etc.; April to October
Channel bass	High flood & high slack	Rivers, sounds and inlets around oyster beds; sand bars along beaches in summer; spring and summer into early fall
Whiting (king whiting)	Low ebb or flood inside, low flood on beaches	Rivers close to ocean, sounds, inlets and beaches; caught on bottom, early spring to late fall
Winter trout (speckled sea trout)	Low ebb, high flood	Creeks, rivers, sounds and inlets around oyster beds; October through March, December and January best
Sheepshead	Low water slack best	Creeks, rivers, sounds close to docks, pilings, rock piles, wrecks, etc.; early spring to late fall
Summer trout (weakfish)	Low ebb, high flood	Creeks, rivers, sounds and inlets, around oyster beds; year-round but more evident in summer when winter trout disappear
Barracuda	Any tide	Offshore waters May through August
Striped bass	Any tide, slack flood best	Sounds, rivers, inlets, beaches, creeks; spring months
Shad	Flood best	Caught predominantly in St. Mary's, Altamaha, Ogeechee, and Savannah rivers; January through March

CHAPTER **14**

Fishing Southern and Gulf
of Mexico Waters

IN THIS CHAPTER we will continue to trace the wheres and whens of fishing by exploring the southern Atlantic and the Gulf of Mexico. Then to complete our look at southern waters, we will have a look at the fishing possibilities around the islands of Puerto Rico, the Bahamas, and the Caribbean Sea area.

FLORIDA

SUPPLIED BY: Ernest Mitts, Florida State Board of Conservation

Florida is a magical name to the salt-water fisherman. Regardless of what type of fishing you like, you will find it in Florida. With its hundreds of miles of coast line in both the Atlantic and the Gulf of Mexico, its labyrinths of salt lagoons and bays, Florida offers the angler game fish of all kinds, sizes, shapes, and inclinations—from marlin offshore to snappers and sheepshead under the bridges.

If you like the open sea, you can find your fill of sport in many ways and in many places. On the Atlantic side you can troll the blue-purple Gulf Stream and find white marlin, sailfish, dolphin, bonito, and tuna. The Stream swings in very close to the coast at Stuart and is often plainly discernible from the beach. Sailfish are practically at your front door. Almost the same is true at Palm Beach, while at Miami and down past the Keys, the Stream lies only a few miles offshore. Excellent boats with experienced captains are available at most of the lower east coast ports, and local enthusiasts and tackle shops will be glad to offer suggestions.

308

At Miami's famous Pier, for example, charter boats are available for either Gulf Stream or reef fishing. In the green water over the reefs along the edge of the Stream are amberjack, mackerel, grouper, and barracuda ready to take feather jig, cut bait, or live, small mullet.

Over on the Gulf coast the offshore angler will not find such variety, but there will be plenty to keep him busy. In February and March great schools of king mackerel, or kingfish, work up the coast from Naples to Apalachee Bay and on a good day it is possible to take a thousand pounds of these beautiful fighters trolling a feather jig or a spoon, which is the way the commercial fishermen take them. Far offshore are red snapper, black grouper and red grouper, and occasionally large schools of redfish (channel bass).

Beginning in April and continuing through the summer, schools of tarpon make their way up both coasts, and in famous Boca Grande Pass this fishing is at its height in June. It is only fair to say, however, that tarpon fishing in Florida is generally poor during the winter months. There are some waters where big tarpon may be taken during the winter—places such as Porpoise Creek, Shark River, Cape Sable Creek, and the creeks near the mouth of Broad River. But on the whole tarpon fishing is not good until April or May. During the summer months there is also excellent tarpon fishing on the Atlantic side as far north as the Jacksonville jetties.

When fishing for the silver king in the passes of the Florida west coast, very often the angler ties into a Mexican pompano, or permit. Occasionally a big jewfish will also take hold; then you have a back-breaking job, for these giant groupers weigh up to 500 pounds or more.

Along the beaches of St. Augustine, Daytona, New Smyrna, Vero Beach, and Jensen Beach excellent surf fishing may be expected in the fall. During late August and September there is a good run of redfish and many big ones are taken. The most popular bait is a piece of cut mullet. (Artificial lures, such as are used for striped bass on the north Atlantic Coast, are rarely successful.) Surf enthusiasts can also have much sport trying for pompano with light tackle along the Keys. You will have best luck with shrimp or sand bugs, or by casting a small spoon or clothespin-type plug. The west coast also has many spots which can be fished from shore for a wide variety of fish. Tarpon are popular fish in this area.

For the still-fisherman Florida offers many piers, bridges, jetties, and breakwaters along both coasts where bottom fish and smaller game fish may be taken.

For the light tackle enthusiasts, the number one fish of Florida is the bonefish, found only in the shallow coastal waters from Biscayne Bay south through the Keys. They do not grow very large and do not leap, but they are exceedingly fast and make long runs when hooked. Bonefish are wary and timid and much caution must be used in approaching a feeding school,

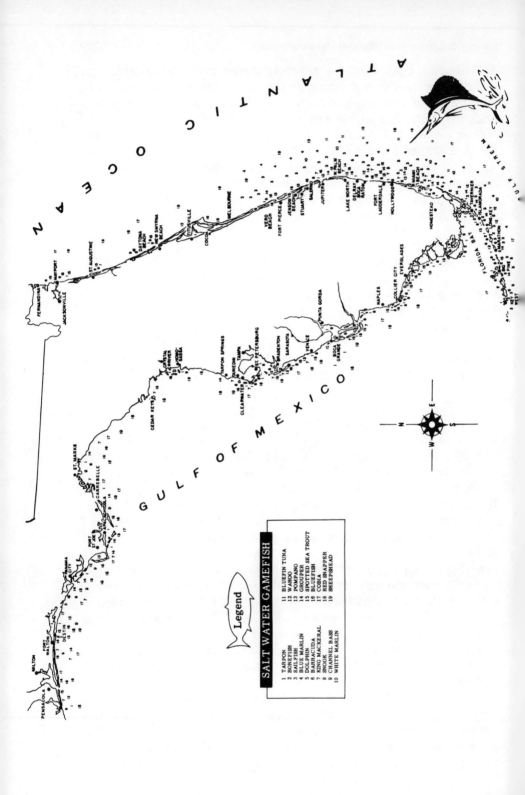

ATLANTIC OCEAN

GULF STREAM

GULF OF MEXICO

PENSACOLA
MILTON
FORT WALTON
DESTIN
PANAMA CITY
PORT ST JOE
APALACHICOLA
CARRABELLE
ST. MARKS
CEDAR KEYS
CRYSTAL RIVER
TARPON SPRINGS
DUNEDIN
CLEARWATER
ST. PETERSBURG
TAMPA
BRADENTON
SARASOTA
VENICE
BOCA GRANDE
PUNTA GORDA
NAPLES
COLLIER CITY
EVERGLADES
HOMESTEAD
KEY WEST
BIG PINE
MARATHON
ISLAMORADA
TAVERNIER
FLORIDA BAY
MIAMI
MIAMI BEACH
HOLLYWOOD
FORT LAUDERDALE
BOCA RATON
DELRAY BEACH
LAKE WORTH
PALM BEACH
JUPITER
STUART
JENSEN BEACH
FORT PIERCE
VERO BEACH
MELBOURNE
COCOA
TITUSVILLE
NEW SMYRNA BEACH
DAYTONA BEACH
ST. AUGUSTINE
MAYPORT
JACKSONVILLE
FERNANDINA

N E S W

Legend

SALT WATER GAMEFISH

1 TARPON
2 BONEFISH
3 SAILFISH
4 BLUE MARLIN
5 DOLPHIN
6 BARRACUDA
7 KING MACKERAL
8 SNOOK
9 CHANNEL BASS
10 WHITE MARLIN

11 BLUEFIN TUNA
12 WAHOO
13 POMPANO
14 GROUPER
15 SPOTTED SEA TROUT
16 BLUEFISH
17 COBIA
18 RED SNAPPER
19 SHEEPSHEAD

which you can often locate by spotting the tails of the fish as they stand on their noses to feed in the shallow water. Occasionally a permit, or great pompano, is encountered while bonefishing, and then you have your hands full. There are many fishing camps along the Overseas Highway to Key West, where good bonefishing may be found, as well as boats for reef fishing and Gulf Stream fishing. For information regarding the great facilities available for the angler, write to the Florida Development Commission, Tallahassee, Florida.

SPECIES	TIDES	LOCATIONS	WHERE FOUND
White grunt	All tides; high best	Entire Florida coast	On all rocky bottoms, inside bays, and large ones on outer reefs
Common pompano	Best on high-slack or incoming		Along beaches and in cuts and inlets, bays, tideways; spring and summer best
Sheepshead	Incoming high	Entire Florida coast	Around pilings, wharfs, rocks, jetties, trestles, etc.
Cero mackerel	High inside, any tide outside	Entire Florida coast	Generally taken offshore
Yellowtail	All tides	Florida Keys	On inner reefs and in deep holes and cuts—spring and summer
Jewfish	High water best; incoming	Entire Florida coast; best Florida Keys	Usually around reefs, wrecks, trestles, rock piles, etc.
Snook (sergeant)	Incoming, high-slack	Entire Florida coast; best from Fort Pierce to the Keys	Inlets to bay, river mouths and up rivers in brackish water; night and morning
Channel bass	Incoming, slack-high	Entire Florida coast	Not common south of Palm Beach; few taken at inlets; surf fishing best sometimes; fall
Sea trout	Incoming, high-slack	Entire Florida coast	In bays, on grass beds and inlets; winter and spring best
Yellow fin grouper	All tides	Florida Keys	Typically a reef species and very seldom taken inshore
Round pompano	Incoming, high-slack		Usually in bays, around islands and Keys, inlets, spring and summer best
Ladyfish	Best on high water	Entire coast, seldom north of Indian River	Taken best at night around trestles and in bays

Species	Tides	Locations	Where Found
Marlin	All tides; late afternoon best	East Coast—Fort Pierce to Miami	Edge of and in Gulf Stream; January to May best; not common
Sailfish	All tides; late afternoon best	East Coast—Fort Pierce to Key West	Usually on edge of stream; sometimes in stream and on outer reef, all year; January to May best
Tarpon	Low water, rising tide, night or early morning best	Entire west coast best. Seasonable, it ranges over entire length of both coasts	Cuts, inlets, rivers, tideways, rips, inside banks, trestles, bays, holes; May to September best
Bonefish	Rising tide, high-slack	Best 140 mile stretch of Keys from Cape Florida to Key West	Mostly on flats and banks, inshore, inlets, bays, etc.; shallow; 6 inches to 2 feet water
Dolphin	Any tide	Ranges the entire Florida coast	Usually around drifting wood, grass, obstructions, on edge and in streams; all times; January to May best
Wahoo	Any tide	Fort Pierce to the Florida Keys best	On edge of outer reef in stream; not common, early spring best
Kingfish	Any tide; high best	Fort Pierce to the Dry Tortugas	Usually school on reefs along shore; always moving; winter and spring best
Spanish mackerel	High-inside, any tide outside	Entire Florida coast	Usually on edge and on inner reef, bays, inlets and along beaches
Bluefin tuna	All tides	Bimini and Cat Cay (see page 324)	Usually taken on the outer reef and in the stream; well offshore
Common bonito	All tides	Entire Florida coast	On outer reef and edge of Stream; all year round; best in spring and summer
Amberjack	All tides, high water best	Both coasts of Florida	On reefs over entire coast; schools at times in localities; spring best
Jack crevallé	Incoming, high-slack	Entire Florida coast	Taken usually inshore around piling, bridges, etc.; spring and summer
Bluefish	Incoming,	Both coasts—	Usually taken in cuts, in

Species	Tides	Locations	Where Found
	high-slack	migratory	surf, and in bays and inlets; late winter best
Barracuda	Outside any tide inshore and bays, low rising	Entire east coast, seldom found on the west coast	Taken almost anywhere in outside waters in fall and winter; inside and bays in summer months
Red grouper	All tides	Entire Florida coast	Taken usually in very deep water; not common in these waters
Mangrove snapper	High water, incoming on inside; any tide or reef	Both Florida coasts	Taken on the reefs outside, in spots where they school; inside about jetties and new pilings, trestles, etc.
Red snapper	All tides	Most abundant in Gulf waters	Taken only in very deep water; not common

ALABAMA

SUPPLIED BY: George M. Kyle, Editor, *Alabama Conservation Magazine*

Although the coast line of Alabama is short, the sport-fishing industry has become increasingly important during the past forty years. At the present time there are probably several hundred or more boats or yachts used in Alabama exclusively for fishing excursions. This is in addition to the thousands of skiffs found all along Mobile Bay. The sport fishing boat that is available for renting is often called a party boat. It is rented for a day or for several days by a group or party and comes complete with captain and crew. Quite often these party boats furnish the special gear needed for deep-sea fishing.

Fish caught by these boats vary with the season. King of all sport fish in Alabama waters is the tarpon. This large, silvery fish, which may attain a length of seven or eight feet and a weight of one to two hundred pounds, is a terrific fighter; a battle of several hours is often required before he can be landed. Cavalla, king mackerel, Spanish mackerel, amberjack, ling, dolphin, and bluefish are other favorites. Deep-sea angling in Alabama attracts many visitors to the area.

Thousands of sport fishermen also enjoy fishing from skiffs in the shallower waters of Mobile Bay and Mississippi Sound, catching incalculable pounds of white and speckled trout, redfish, flounder, croaker, blackfish, sheepshead, drum, and sea catfish.

Alabama offers some surf angling too. The Fort Morgan peninsula, which juts out into the Gulf, is the main surf-fishing area. Channel bass, or redfish as they are called here, run with bluefish, jackfish, spotted weakfish, and pompano.

For further information on fishing in Alabama, write to the Junior Chamber of Commerce, Mobile, Alabama. The Junior Chamber sponsors an annual Mobile Deep-Sea Fishing Rodeo.

SPECIES	WHEN	SPECIES	WHEN
Amberjack—May to September		Mackerel (Spanish)—June to September	
Bluefish—June to October		Mullet (ground)—April to November	
Croaker—May to November		Pompano—June to November	
Dolphin—June to September		Redfish—All year	
Drum (black)—April to October		Red snapper—All year	
Flounder—April to October		Sea catfish—All year	
King whiting—June to September		Trout, spotted—All year	
Grouper—All year		Trout, white—May to October	
Jack crevallé—June to September		Triple tail (blackfish)—June to October	
Jewfish—All year		Sheepshead—April to November	
Ling (cobia)—June to November			

MISSISSIPPI

SUPPLIED BY: Anthony V. Ragusin, author of *Fishing Is Fun,* and Associate Editor of *Down South Magazine*

The stretch of water from Petit Bois Island curving southwest to the eastern mouths or passes of the great Mississippi River Delta is a section of bountiful sea harvest. Fed by waters from Mobile Bay and the Pascagoula River on the east, and the Pearl River and the Louisiana marshes or Mississippi River delta system on the west, this region is one of the nation's finest fish baskets—especially for variety in choice products of the sea.

Many streams and bays help to create this productive stretch of oceanic wealth. One of the sources is the Bay of Biloxi, which receives the waters of Fort Bayou, the Little and Big Biloxi rivers, and the Tchouticabouffa River. Among others are the Bay of St. Louis, Lake Borgne, and Lake Pontchartrain. This constant supply of food-rich fresh water makes possible an untold abundance of marine life. The Louisiana-Mississippi Gulf Coast with its heavily indented shore line, its islands, and its marshes, is one of the greatest oceanic nursery grounds on earth.

Within easy reach of the cities of the Mississippi coast are to be found more than a score of different kinds of fish. In the Back Bay section fishermen sometimes bring both salt- and fresh-water varieties into their rowboats. Strictly salt-water specimens, such as the fighting ladyfish, a close relative of the bonefish, have been landed off the four bridges which serve the Biloxi peninsula. While trolling for speckled trout with plugs off the Old Naval Reserve Park area one afternoon, two fishermen were startled to bring aboard the strange cutlass, or ribbon, fish. Catching a dozen varieties of fish on a day's sport in this area is usual.

The usual cost of a charter boat is $60 per day. One to ten persons are permitted. Bait, tackle, and ice are provided. Departure is usually made at 5 A.M. As many as seventy miles are covered on some of these daily expeditions. Skiffs may be rented at numerous fishing camps along the Mississippi Gulf Coast for a dollar or two. For complete information, write for a free copy of *Angler's Map and Visitor's Guide of the Mississippi Gulf Coast* to the Biloxi Chamber of Commerce, P.O. Box 905, Biloxi, Mississippi.

SPECIES	WHERE	WHEN
Striped Bass	Wolf River, Rotten Bayou, Jordan River, Biloxi River, and Tchouticabouffa River	Spring and fall
Tarpon	Tarpon Hole south of Pass Christian; Gulfport—Ship Island channel; Goose Point on Cat Island; Biloxi channel; Back Bay of Biloxi; Dog Keys Pass	May to October
Flounder	Coast and all islands	April to October
Spanish mackerel	Gulfport–Ship Island channel, Ship Island Pass, Dog Keys Pass, Deer Island, Biloxi channel	June to September
Kingfish	Same as for Spanish mackerel	June to September
Dolphin	Same as for Spanish mackerel	June to September
Sergeant fish (Lemon fish, Ling)	Beacons and buoys in all channels	June to November
Crevallé sea jack	Same as for Spanish mackerel	June to September
Speckled sea trout (summer)	Gulfport–Ship Island channel, Cat and Ship Islands, Biloxi Channel, Back Bay of Biloxi, Bay of St. Louis, oyster beds along coast	In sea from March to October; in rivers from October to March
Speckled sea trout (winter)	In Back Bay	October to March
White trout	All Gulf waters	May to October
Atlantic squebagie	Ship Island channel about beacons, Rock Pile Quarantine Station	September to November
Bluefish	Ship Island, Dog Keys	June to October
Bonito	Ship Island, Horn Island	June to September
Croakers	Front waters and lower reaches of all rivers	May to November

SPECIES	WHERE	WHEN
Sheepshead	Bay St. Louis bridge, pier at Gulfport, Bay bridges at Biloxi	April to November
Whiting (Ground mullet)	Same as above	April to November
Blackfish (Triple tail)	Along beach and beacons in Gulfport–Biloxi channel	June to October
Pompano	Deer Island, Ship Island	April to November
Redfish	Front waters and lower reaches of all rivers	April to November
Black Drum	Akin Pier, Deer Island, and Back Bay	April to November
Spot	Front waters and lower reaches of all rivers	April to November
Ladyfish	Same as for tarpon	June to September

LOUISIANA

SUPPLIED BY: G. C. Ducote, Louisiana Tourist Bureau

The delta of the Mississippi River in Louisiana is a maze of inlets, islands, coves, bays, and swamps, where even the natives get lost at times. However, there are many good spots that are easily available to the salt-water angler. These include the Tchefuncte River, Bayou Lacombe, North Shore, and Grande Isle. The latter is sometimes called the salt-water playground of Louisiana. At Grande Isle, there are charter boats for parties fishing out in the Gulf; some tie up at the offshore drilling platforms for leisurely fishing for bluefish, spadefish, white trout, jewfish, pompano, etc. (These offshore rigs have radically changed the salt-water picture in this area. The artificial banks created by oil rigs have created exciting new fishing, and the variety of fish taken around them is astonishing.) Some boat skippers like to put their anglers to trolling the open waters for Spanish and king mackerel, ling, tarpon, jackfish, and dolphin. Other boats fish the deep waters miles offshore for sailfish, marlin, red snapper, and the latest find: tuna off the deep banks of South Pass.

If the water is right at Grande Isle, the surf angler can have worlds of fun right off the surf, when speckled trout move in for feeding with the

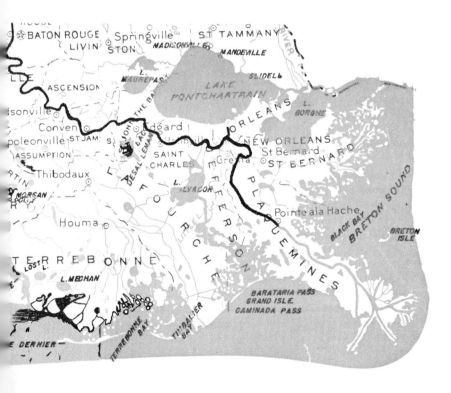

rising tides. Another popular fishing method here is scouting the back bays of the island in search of speckled trout and redfish around the small islands and shell reefs which dot the Barataria and Caminada bays. Such favorites for schooling fish as Monkey and Bird reefs and Middle Bank, are always good spots when water is clear. Those not familiar with the area can always follow other boats that make the run daily during the fishing season, or they may get directions from the operator of their particular boat landing. Rental and bait services are handy on both sides of the Caminada Bridge.

For further information, write to the Louisiana Tourist Bureau, State Capitol Building, Baton Rouge, Louisiana.

SPECIES	WHEN
Bluefish—June to October	
Croaker—May to November	
Dolphin—June to September	
Black Drum—April to November	
Flounder—April to October	
Grouper—April to November	
Jackfish—May to September	
Jewfish—April to November	
Ling—June to November	
Sheepshead—April to September	
Marlin—July to August	
Sailfish—June to August	
Redfish—Year round	
Kingfish—May to September	
Mackerel—May to September	
Red Snapper—Year round	
Speckled Trout—Year round	
White Trout—Year round	

TEXAS

SUPPLIED BY: Fred T. Bennett, Texas Highway Department

Texas offers the angler every type of salt-water fishing. For example, our 624-mile outer beach from Sabine Pass to the mouth of the Rio Grande has many spots for surf fishing: the beaches and breakwaters around Galveston, Port Aransas, and Port Isabel. Tarpon, redfish, spotted trout, and sharks are all caught here.

Most of the Texas coast consists of bays, most of them shallow, some with grassy bottoms, some with shell and sand bottoms. An angler would have to search hard and long for finer fishing than that offered in many of these bays. Fine places are Galveston Bay, Corpus Christi Bay, Nueces

Bay, and the Laguna Madre, which teem with trout, redfish, flounder, drum, and other edible varieties.

A popular method in this area during the summer months is wading out into the water, or taking a boat out to a shallow bar, then getting out and wading. You use a light bass rig and work a spoon at or near the surface, or possibly a floating lure. Speckled trout and redfish seem to go for this treatment and give the angler plenty of excitement.

During cold weather, the speckled trout and redfish move into deep holes in the bays, into ship channels and rivers. There they may be taken by the thousands. Even when it is very cold, they will go for a spoon or a plug worked very slowly and near the bottom. Offshore oil rig platforms, of course, are big fishing areas in Texas.

There are a number of fishing piers along the Texas coast line, notably those at Galveston and Corpus Christi. From these "T-heads" sheepshead, redfish, pompano, ling, trout, drum, flounder, and kingfish are caught. Long rock and concrete jetties, such as those at Isla Blanca Park on Padre Island reach far into the Gulf and offer more excellent spots for fishing.

Charter and party boats are available at such ports as Galveston, Port Aransas, Corpus Christi, and Port Isabel for larger game fish like mackerel, jackfish, kingfish, sailfish, tarpon, and marlin. Of course, tarpon is the big fish in Texas, and while it is generally taken out in the Gulf, it often comes into bays and is taken by fishermen at piers and jetties. Port Aransas and the New Brazos River are tarpon "hot spots" in Texas.

Although Texas does not require licenses for fishing in the tidal waters, there are regulations on the length of salt-water fish which may be taken. The legal lengths of salt-water fish in Texas are as follows:

> Flounder—not less than 12 inches
> Speckled trout—not less than 12 inches
> Redfish—not les than 12 nor over 32 inches
> Drum—not less than 8 inches nor over 20 inches
> Pompano—not less than 9 inches
> Sheepshead—not less than 8 inches
> Mackerel—not less than 14 inches
> Gafftopsail cat—not less than 11 inches
> Redfish—not more than 27 inches without head
> Catfish—not less than 8 inches without head

For complete details write to the Texas Game, Fish and Oyster Commission, Austin 14, Texas.

TEXAS GULF COAST FISHING CALENDAR

Species	Jan.	Feb.	Mar.	Apr.	May	June	July	Aug.	Sept.	Oct.	Nov.	Dec.
Tarpon		FF	FF	GF	BF	BF	BF	BF	BF	GF	FF	
Mackerel			FF	GF	BF	BF	GF	FF				

Species	Jan.	Feb.	Mar.	Apr.	May	June	July	Aug.	Sept.	Oct.	Nov.	Dec.
Kingfish					GF	BF	BF	GF	FF			
Jack crevallé			FF	BF	BF	GF	FF					
Trout	GF	GF	GF	GF	BF	BF	BF	BF	BF	BF	BF	GF
Redfish	GF	GF	GF	GF	GF	GF	GF	BF	BF	BF	BF	GF
Sheepshead	BF	BF	BF	GF	GF	FF	FF	GF	GF	BF	BF	BF
Jewfish			FF	GF	BF	BF	BF	GF	FF	FF		
Shark	FF	FF	GF	BF	BF	BF	BF	BF	BF	GF	FF	FF
Drum	GF	GF	GF	GF	BF	BF	BF	GF	GF	GF	GF	GF
Flounder			FF	FF	GF	GF	BF	BF	BF	GF	FF	
Marlin						FF	BF	BF				
Sailfish						FF	BF	BF				

FF—fair fishing   GF—good fishing   BF—best fishing

Port Isabel season starts one month earlier and stops one month later than rest of coast.

EAST COAST OF MEXICO

SUPPLIED BY: Puerto Rico News Service

On the east coast of Mexico are the famous tarpon grounds of the Panuco River near Tampico, where giant size tarpon are caught, and world's records are regularly chalked up. Here in the month of April the famed tarpon rodeo is staged on the Gulf of Tampico. Other Gulf fish abound in these waters, and vast stretches of lagoons and low surf are readily accessible for light tackle fishing for pompano, sea bass, snapper, and dozens of other species that like the reefs. Boats and guides are very good, as are the hotel accommodations at Tampico.

Fishing for tarpon at Vera Cruz is also excellent, and here they offer their own tarpon rodeo late in April. Reef angling for pargo, barracuda, roballo, red snapper, amberjack, grouper, and others is unexcelled in this area. Boats and guides are fair to good, but hotels and food are excellent.

To the south, Coatzacoalcos, deep in Mexico's tropics, is the home of schools of tarpon, amberjack, snook, tenacious grouper, and the whole gamut of Gulf of Mexico fighters. In the Gulf of Campeche off the coast of Yucatan there are also some interesting keys and reefs which are worth exploration by big-game anglers. For information on fishing on Mexico's Pacific Coast, see page 343.

PUERTO RICO

SUPPLIED BY: Rosellen Callahan, Puerto Rico News Service

Deep-sea fishing, virtually unknown in Puerto Rico a few years ago, is rapidly becoming the island's favorite sport. Puerto Rico has an abundance of every variety of the better-known game fish—albacore, barracuda, bonito, bonefish, dolphin, all kinds of grouper and jack, kingfish, blue and white marlin, sailfish, snook, tarpon, and tuna. According to the IGFA world records, Puerto Rico is second in the world in the number of record catches. Due to its subtropical climate, always tempered by the trade winds, Puerto Rico is one of the few fishing centers that can boast a year-round season. There are many good ports from which deep-sea fishermen may put out in search of game. San Juan, Mayaguez, Aguadilla, La Parguera, Ponce, and Fajardo, are the most popular, although the ardent fisherman can shove off from practically every inlet and find himself an exciting time.

At present, the major charter fleet operates in the San Juan area. Other boats are available at the tiny fishing village of La Parguera near the southwest tip of the island. Rates run from $45 to $100 for six, including tackle. Elsewhere, arrangements can be made for fishing trips from many of the coastal cities.

The big fish of the island is the blue marlin. Best fishing for this species is from April through November, the earlier months being the best. The big blues are there all the year through and have been known to grab a trolled whole mullet or bonefish in every month of the year. A brief rundown of the offshore seasons would include sailfish from August to January; white marlin from April to August; Allison tuna from April through November; blackfin tuna, known locally as albacore, during the same period; bonito and king mackerel, both of which can also be taken inshore, from April up until the middle of January. These seasons represent the peaks only; all species mentioned can be taken inshore also from April on, provided you have patience and luck. Add to the total also those fish that apparently have no fixed seasons at all—wahoo, dolphin, and a host of others that are caught "accidentally" while fishing for billfish.

Deep-water angling is not confined to the northern coast by any means. South, east, and west, the same species roam—and pay even less attention to the seasons prescribed by custom. Since Puerto Rico and its surrounding small islands are merely the tops of vast, submerged volcanic mountains rising sheer from the ocean, at no point along the coast is blue water very far away. And where the depths lie, the big game fish lie also.

Armed with spinning or bait-casting rods, many of the local light-tackle addicts have discovered that surf fishing will bring amazing results. The species sought are snook, tarpon, and ladyfish, with a few barracuda thrown in for good measure. Just which other species will fall for this technique is still unknown. Here once again the field is wide open for the angler who wants to do a little experimenting. Since deep-water fish work close to the beach, angling sensations are not only possible, but probable.

As summer approaches, both tarpon and snook are likely to work on a low tide around the countless river mouths of the island. Wading out in bathing trunks and casting to these fish is as exciting as it is unusual. The Santo and Loiza rivers to the east of San Juan, and the Anasco and Guana-jibo rivers near Mayaguez, are favorites for this type of angling, but there is no reason why equal success cannot be had at any of the fifty-odd river mouths elsewhere around the island.

Snook and tarpon are at their best from May to November, but they can be taken in almost all months. River fishing, particularly for snook and tarpon, has not been fully explored, although a few experimenters have had amazing results with spinning and fly rods. Ladyfish also come well within reach of the light-tackle angler working from shore or river. Ladyfish apparently are most plentiful in September and October, but here again the season limits cannot be closely defined. Jack crevallé hit artifi-cials best from May through October and will take live bait at any time of year. Grunt, snapper, runner, and countless other species feed inshore and are taken both by light tackle and other methods.

Undoubtedly the least popularized species of Puerto Rico are the glamor fish of the light-tackle world—permit, pompano, and bonefish. Their feeding habits and seasons are virtually unknown, but they are there in abundance. Because there are more flats and shallows along the southern coast, these speeders are most common in that area, although they are taken from time to time all around the island.

Squidding with surf tackle and artificial lures is practically unknown in Puerto Rico, but it is a safe bet that it will become popular when bait casters and spinners find they can reach feeding fish that lie out of range of their lighter rods. Like much of the island's sport fishing, it has not been fully explored.

It is easy to get to Puerto Rico. You fly there in five and a half hours from New York—less than four hours from Miami. You need no pass-port. The currency is the United States dollar. Hotels are modern and air-conditioned. For further information, write to the Puerto Rico Visitors Bureau, 666 Fifth Avenue, New York 22, N.Y.

BAHAMAS

SUPPLIED BY: Don McCarthy, author of *The Fisherman's Guide to the Bahamas*

One of our finest salt-water fishing grounds—perhaps *the* finest—is that vast Atlantic area that surrounds the Bahama Islands. These 70,000 square miles of nearly virgin waters teem with most of the world's popular species of game fish. Some of the spots have rarely been fished, and many others have yet to be explored.

The Bahamas consist of an extensive chain of nearly 700 low and rocky limestone islands. The surrounding waters are filled with countless marine fish. These fishing grounds are truly an angler's paradise. They will meet the approval of the most particular salt-water angler, whether he prefers to fish the shallow crystal-clear waters of the flats for speedy bonefish, or to troll the outer reefs for the larger gamesters. Proof of the quality of Bahamas angling can be found in the number of IGFA records chalked up in the Bahamas.

The Bahamas offer all of the modern facilities necessary to accommodate the sport fisherman, whether he specializes in one species of fish, such as marlin, bluefin tuna, or bonefish, or takes on all comers, from amberjack and grouper to dolphin and wahoo. The guides are men of wide experience, wise in the ways of fish, and know intimately which fishing grounds are the most productive in the various seasons and weather conditions. Boats and guides are available for charter on a daily basis ($50 to $100 per day) or for extended trips throughout the picturesque cays and islands that comprise the Bahamas archipelago.

Few fishing grounds in the world can match those of the Bahamas for year-round, action-packed, sure-fire light tackle angling. The inshore and offshore waters teem with a fascinating variety of game fish, and some are undoubtedly of world-record size. In the winter months wahoo, kingfish, and dolphin course the indigo depths in search of food. Striking hard and decisively, fighting in furious zigzag runs, they set a sizzling pace that leaves the angler breathless from tension and speechless with admiration. Through the summer the albacore, tuna, and bonito hold the spotlight. Miniature counterparts of the bluefin, these fish—taken on light gear— are as tough as their heavier relatives.

The cavern-pocked weed-patched fern-dotted reefs that flank the countless islands and cays of the Bahamas harbor an amazing variety of sturdy battlers. Among them are barracuda and grouper, snapper and yellowtail, runner and mackerel. Some cruise close to the surface; others hug the bottom. Most of them will take a trolled lure; all will snatch a live bait. Those that can be taken by trolling make perfect prey for the 3- and 6-thread fishermen. When caught off the bottom from an anchored boat, they will extend a 9-thread line to its limit. Meat-on-the-table fish, they are nevertheless ready strikers, strong fighters, and colorful antagonists, well able to give the angler a day of thrills and sport.

Many of the bays, passes, inlets, creeks, and beaches of the Bahamas offer fast and consistently steady fishing for the fly fisherman, plug caster, and spinning enthusiast. Small amberjack, barracuda, grouper, jack, mackerel, runner, snapper, tarpon, and occasionally bonefish will strike almost any type of artificial lure. Off rocky points where reefs lie just below the surface, the angler, using weighted lures worked close to the bottom, will have a busy time with several species of snapper and grouper, jack and houndfish. When the sea is calm and the tide is in, the caster can wade the sandy beaches, taking runner, palometa, and sometimes a

bonefish on streamer flies or a bucktail. Tarpon in bays and creeks will rise
to surface plugs.

The Bahamas are the nearest group of foreign islands to the United
States—the closest island, New Providence, is some forty-three miles east
of Florida. From Miami it is only a forty-five-minute trip by air to Nassau,
the capital. The accommodations on the islands are excellent, and offer
a wide variety of hotels, guests houses, cottages, and camps. For further
information, see your travel agent or write the Nassau, Bahamas Development Board, Bay Street, Nassau, Bahamas.

SPECIES	WHERE	WHEN
Amberjack	Berry Islands, Bimini, Cat Cay, Exumas, Green Turtle Cay, Walker Cay	November through April
Albacore tuna	Berry Islands, Exumas, Nassau	May through September
Allison tuna	Berry Islands, Exuma Sound (eastern edge), Nassau	December through May
Barracuda	All the Bahamas	Year-round
Bluefin tuna	Bimini and Cat Cay	May to June
Bonefish	Abaco Cays, Andros (Fresh Creek and Bang Bang Club), Bimini, Joulter Cays, Rock Sound (Eleuthera), Walker Cay	Year-round
Bonito	Berry Islands, Exuma Cays, Nassau	May through September
Dolphin	Andros, Berry Islands, Bimini, Nassau, Powell's Point (Eleu-thera), Walker Cay	December through March
Grouper	All the Bahamas	Year-round
Kingfish	Berry Islands, Bimini, Cat Cay, Exumas, Green Turtle Cay, Nassau, Walker Cay	January through June
Sailfish	Andros, Berry Islands, Bimini, Cat Cay, Walker Cay	November through April
Tarpon	Andros	Year-round
Wahoo	Andros, Berry Islands, Bimini, Cat Cay, Powell's Point (Eleu-thera), Nassau, Walker Cay	November through April
White marlin	Andros, Berry Islands, Bimini, Cat Cay, Walker Cay	November through April
Blue marlin	Andros, Berry Islands, Bimini, Cat Cay, Walker Cay	May through September

CARIBBEAN SEA AREA

All the islands in and the countries bordering the Caribbean Sea are a veritable angler's paradise. This area has often been called a "new frontier" of angling adventure—an opportunity to explore hundreds of thousands of miles of foreign, mostly unfished, virgin waters. All the ports and harbors along the coast of northern South America, Central America, and the entire West Indies are good fishing grounds. There is no closed season for the deep water in this region.

It would be virtually impossible to mention all the good fishing spots in the Caribbean area. Much of the general information given earlier on Puerto Rico and the east coast of Mexico (both considered in the Caribbean area) holds good for most of the region. For specific data on where to go and how to get there, write to the Caribbean Gamefishing Association, P.O. Box 366, Coral Gables, Florida 33134. This organization is "an international brotherhood of anglers and marine scientists dedicated to the exploration, development, and preservation of sport fishing in the Caribbean Sea area."

CHAPTER 15

Fishing the Pacific Coast

Roving through the surf, bays, coves, channels, and deep outer basins along the Pacific coast from Alaska to Mexico, sweeping among the numerous rocky islands that afford sheltered waters, and invading the great tributary rivers of the Pacific seaboard, a multitude of salt-water fish await the fisherman eager for sport.

Point Conception, California, about forty-five miles west of Santa Barbara, seems to mark a dividing line for kinds of fish and ways of angling. Most northern fish stay in the colder climes, while the southern species seldom stray far above Point Conception.

Each region boasts its special attractions. The sea routes off Alaska, British Columbia, Washington, and Oregon are famous for salmon, steelheads, and cutthroat trout; the stretch from Monterey Bay, California, to Coos Bay, Oregon, is renowned for striped bass; the beaches are popular surf-casting centers for corbina, spotfin, yellowfin croakers, surf perch, and others. Central California ensures good results with bottom feeders—yellowtail, tuna, albacore, and sea bass. Farther south are marlin, sailfish, swordfish, and dolphin in season.

At many of the ports over these grounds, completely equipped party and charter boats are ready to take passengers out for trolling, casting, and still-fishing. Or fishing barges may be anchored some distance offshore. And there are always the piers, where bait nabbers offer amusement for young and old alike, every day of the week.

CALIFORNIA

Supplied by: State of California Department of Fish and Game

Starting at San Diego, you will find every type of deep-sea fishing—open party boats, charter boats, barges. San Diego's harbor is superb. Here you can get in on the best roundup of smaller species to be had anywhere along the coast. Farther out, there are yellowtails, bluefin tuna, white and black sea bass, Pacific barracuda, striped marlin, and swordfish, to name a few. Marlin put San Diego on the big-game angler's map, for these powerful fighters roam not far from the mainland.

Fishing gets into high gear in southern California about the first of June, and holds strong until around the middle of September. San Diego is a main focal point for the yellowtail fleet. Thousands of anglers head for the Coronado Islands when runs of these desirable scrappers are on. Big ones up to forty pounds and more are taken, and rivalry becomes fast and furious, especially while San Diego's Yellowtail Fishing Derby is in progress.

For a change of scenery you can have fun in Mission Bay, tickling the palates of corbina, croakers, mackerel, sea perch, bass, and halibut with baits and lures either from boats or the shore.

Should you wish to cast or still-fish for bottom feeders, take your stand on one of the piers that extend several hundred feet out into the ocean at Ocean Beach, Pacific Beach, Del Mar, and Oceanside.

Detailed information on rates, schedules, licenses, and lodging in this neighborhood will be sent on request by the San Diego–California Club, 499 West Broadway, San Diego, California.

You can count on good results in the region with mackerel, white sea bass, and bonito. Tuna, marlin, and swordfish are active from about the first of July to the latter part of October. Yellowtail and barracuda are most plentiful from April to October. The bottom fish—including kelp bass, rock cod, grouper, halibut, and sheepshead—take live baits the year around. Surf casting is profitable from April into October, with the summer months yielding the heaviest strings. Corvina, croakers, and surf perch are frequently beached at this time.

Up at San Clemente you can take part in live-bait boat, barge, pier, and surf fishing. Sea bass, barracuda, bonito, halibut, and panfish such as corbina, flounder, perch, halibut, and croakers are caught from March to late fall, with the peak from June through September.

Another leading center is the Balboa-Newport Beach area, where catches, boats, and guide services are all first-class. Party boats leave for the day, roaming local waters or going over to Santa Catalina Island, and charter boats set out for the marlin and swordfish grounds. You can rent rowboats and skiffs to troll with artificial squids and jigs for barracuda, yellowtail,

CALIFORNIA

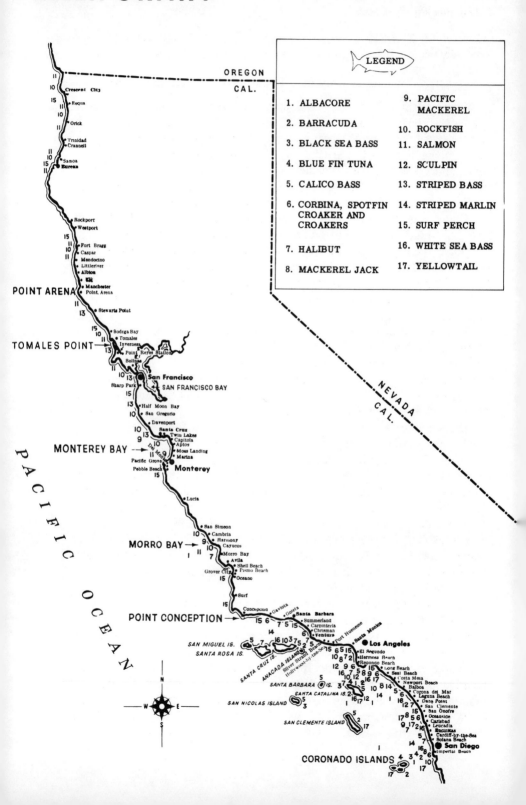

LEGEND

1. ALBACORE
2. BARRACUDA
3. BLACK SEA BASS
4. BLUE FIN TUNA
5. CALICO BASS
6. CORBINA, SPOTFIN CROAKER AND CROAKERS
7. HALIBUT
8. MACKEREL JACK

9. PACIFIC MACKEREL
10. ROCKFISH
11. SALMON
12. SCULPIN
13. STRIPED BASS
14. STRIPED MARLIN
15. SURF PERCH
16. WHITE SEA BASS
17. YELLOWTAIL

OREGON
CAL.

NEVADA
CAL.

PACIFIC OCEAN

POINT ARENA

TOMALES POINT

MONTEREY BAY

MORRO BAY

POINT CONCEPTION

Crescent City
Requa
Orick
Trinidad
Crannell
Samoa
Eureka

Rockport
Westport
Fort Bragg
Caspar
Mendocino
Littleriver
Albion
Elk
Manchester
Point Arena
Stewarts Point
Bodega Bay
Tomales
Inverness
Point Reyes Station
Bolinas
San Francisco
SAN FRANCISCO BAY
Sharp Park
Half Moon Bay
San Gregorio
Davenport
Santa Cruz
Twin Lakes
Capitola
Aptos
Del Monte
Moss Landing
Marina
Pacific Grove
Pebble Beach
Monterey

Lucia

San Simeon
Cambria
Harmony
Cayucos
Morro Bay
Avila
Shell Beach
Pismo Beach
Grover City
Oceano
Surf

Concepcion
Gaviota
Goleta
Santa Barbara
Summerland
Carpinteria
Chrisman
Ventura
Port Hueneme

SAN MIGUEL IS.
SANTA ROSA IS.
SANTA CRUZ IS.
ANACAPA ISLANDS
Silver Strand Beach
Hollywood-by-the-Sea
Santa Monica
Los Angeles
El Segundo
Hermosa Beach
Redondo Beach
Long Beach
Seal Beach
Costa Mesa
Newport Beach
Balboa
Corona del Mar
Laguna Beach
Dana Point
San Clemente
San Onofre
Oceanside
Carlsbad
Leucadia
Encinitas
Cardiff-by-the-Sea
Solana Beach
San Diego
Imperial Beach

SANTA BARBARA IS.
SANTA CATALINA IS.
SAN NICOLAS ISLAND
SAN CLEMENTE ISLAND

CORONADO ISLANDS

N
W E
S

and albacore, or you may still-fish in Balboa Bay for croakers and halibut.

At Huntington Beach and Long Beach there are barges, live-bait boats, piers, and long stretches of surf. Barge fishing, especially at night, is a big enterprise here. Charter boats will take you to the Catalina Island for the sort of rod-and-reel adventure you have dreamed about.

San Pedro has two landings, one at Twenty-Second Street and another at Cabrillo Beach. Barges and party boats await anglers from all corners of the land. You won't lack for action in this vicinity.

The burning desire of many big- and small-game fishermen is to wet their lines in the sunlit waters surrounding the world-renowned Catalina Islands. Said to be the birthplace of salt-water sports fishing, these islands (comprising Santa Catalina, San Clemente, and San Nicholas) are in the midst of a fertile basin harboring giant tuna, marlin, and swordfish. Yearly some of the most celebrated rodmen living come here to pit their skill and endurance against these leviathans. Headquarters is picturesque Avalon, site of the famous Catalina Tuna Club. You don't have to be a club member to fish from Catalina. Party boats tied to public wharves will take you where bottom species may be landed by hand lines and rods, with sardines for chum and bait.

Continuing up the coast from San Pedro, you come to Redondo Beach, Ocean Park, Long Beach, Mission Beach, and Santa Monica. At all these places you can fish from barges and piers or hire live-bait boats for half- or full-day trips. The nearby grounds provide fine catches most of the year, with March through September being a banner period for barracuda, white sea bass, mackerel, and bonito.

At La Jolla, jewfish have been caught from the Biological Station pier. From the rocks or cliffs one may pick up rock bass and sand bass, sculpin, cod, moonfish, sheepshead, and garibaldi perch. From Pismo Beach to Santa Cruz, the most likely species are rockfish, surf perch, kelp greenling, and halibut.

From Santa Barbara, charter boats work out around the offshore islands (Santa Cruz, Santa Rosa, San Miguel, and Anacapa) on a search for marlin, tuna, and other deep-water surface fish. At times there are exceptionally large runs of marlin in the Santa Barbara Channel.

New and exciting prospects for sport and unusual catches are in store for you wherever you dip your line along the coast north from Monterey Bay and San Francisco. You come into striped bass, salmon, steelhead, and cutthroat trout territory, and that means tops in action.

At Santa Cruz, for instance, during the summer and early fall you can have fine results surf casting for striped bass at the mouth of the San Lorenzo River. Spring and fall also bring stripers to the shore of Monterey Bay, near the Salinas River. Big striped bass are also taken above Santa Cruz.

On the stretch of beach at San Francisco there is good surf casting where holes and sloughs have formed. These are usually evident by the absence of breakers. When the bass do not respond here, the coves and straight segments of beaches south of the city—at Sharp Park, Rockaway Beach, or San Pedro Point—are possible. The best surf-casting harvests occur from June into September.

When the stripers have forsaken the surf, you may induce them to strike live or artificial lures by trolling, bait casting, or still-fishing at different points in San Francisco and San Pablo bays, and in the delta section of the Sacramento and San Joaquin rivers. At Rio Vista, up the Sacramento River, a one-day Striped Bass Derby is held annually that attracts about ten thousand people. Some exceptional salmon lurk in this region, too. Ed Neal, outdoor editor of the San Francisco *News,* writes: "Some of the finest salmon trolling in the country is available right at San Francisco's front door—in the ocean off the Golden Gate." The season runs for nine months, from the first of April to the end of December, with April and May and again from late July through mid-October the peak periods.

North from San Francisco, the beaches between this city and Bolinas are hot spots for striped bass surf casting from June into September. Fair killings can also be made by following the beaches up to the Russian River. Sizable stripers are caught every year in this section. Their northern limit seems to be Coos Bay, Oregon, where splendid bass are lodged.

An important fact to bear in mind is that striped bass, salmon, and other species are protected by law, according to size and daily catch limits, seasons, license requirements, sale restrictions, etc. Angling regulations and other fishing dope may be obtained from the California Department of Fish and Game, 722 Capitol Avenue, Sacramento, California.

SPECIES	WHERE	WHEN
Albacore	San Diego to Morro Bay from close in to as far as 65 miles out	July to October
Barracuda	San Diego to Point Conception	Year round; summer best
Black sea bass	Coronado Islands (below San Diego) northward to Point Conception	Year round
Bluefin tuna	San Diego to Point Conception	Summer best
Calico bass	San Diego to Point Conception	Year round
Corbina, spotfin croaker, and croaker	San Diego to Morro Bay	Year round; summer best
Halibut	San Diego north up whole coast	Year round

SPECIES	WHERE	WHEN
Mackerel (Jack)	San Diego to Point Conception	Summer
Pacific mackerel	San Diego to Point Conception	Year round
Rockfish	San Diego north up whole coast	Year round
Salmon	Morro Bay north	Year round; closed November 13 to February 15 south of Tomales Point
Sculpin	Point Conception south	Year round
Striped bass	Monterey Bay north	Year round
Striped marlin	San Diego to Point Conception	Late summer
Surf perch	Entire coast	Year round
Yellowtail	Point Conception south— best off San Diego and Coronado Islands	Early summer
White sea bass	South of Point Conception	Year round; summer best

OREGON

SUPPLIED BY: Gene Maudlin, Oregon State Highway Department

Our state's salt-water fishing may be divided into four zones:

Zone 1 (coastal rivers and bays and deep-sea fishing). Principal game fish taken in coastal rivers and bays include chinook salmon, silver salmon, steelhead, and striped bass. There are both spring and fall runs of chinook salmon, but except in the larger rivers—the Columbia, Umpqua, and Rogue—the spring runs are not of sufficient size to offer much attraction. Fall chinook and silver salmon are taken from late August to mid-November, with a peak in October. They are taken primarily by trolling, casting, or still-fishing. Spinners, artificial minnows, wobblers, and cluster eggs are suitable lures. Jack salmon may be taken on cluster eggs while still-fishing from shore.

Steelhead, the sea-run form of the rainbow trout, enter most coastal streams after the fall rains commence, and fishing is at its peak from December through February. Boat and bank angling are equally popular; boat liveries are available on most of the larger streams and rivers. Cluster eggs, spinners, and spinning lures are used. Although winter temperatures are not severe, warm and water-repellent clothing is a necessity.

Striped bass are taken in Coos Bay and lower Coos River. The months of July through October provide the best angling. Fish are taken both from the bank and from boats. Artificial plugs, frozen pilchard, herring, and sculpins are used. At Coos Bay, the stripers average around six pounds.

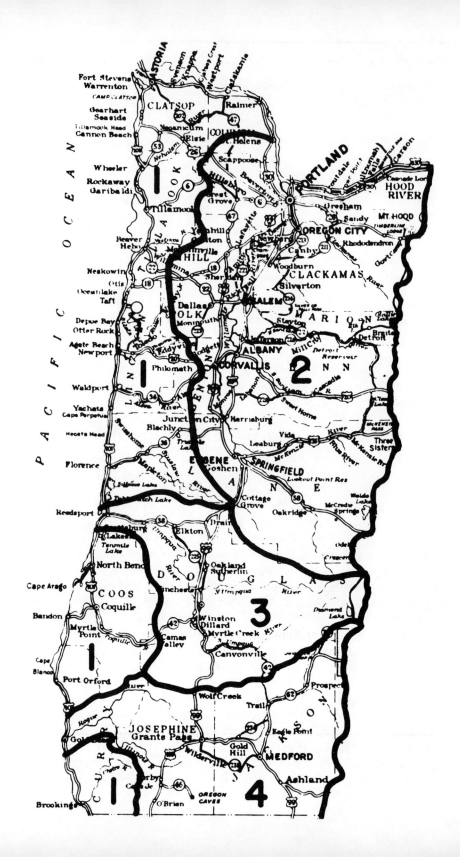

Rock and surf fishing is enjoyed all along the Oregon coast. (A license is required only for trout, salmon, shad, and striped bass.) Perch, flounders, rockfish, sea bass, ling, cod, and many other species are taken by sport anglers.

Salmon fishing offshore in private and charter boats is growing in popularity in the summer months. Jetty fishing is claiming additional converts each year. Boats and guides may be obtained at most of the major coastal communities. Tackle is provided, if desired.

Zone 2 (Columbia River system). This zone includes the Columbia River and its major tributaries, the Willamette, Sandy and Hood rivers. In spring, huge schools of king salmon begin their journey up the Columbia River system to the spawning beds. The best runs usually take place in April, May, and June.

From August to the middle of September, fall runs of kings enter the Columbia at Astoria and excellent results are experienced when trolling at this place. An annual Salmon Derby is sponsored by the Astoria Regatta Association, with cash awards for the largest fish caught.

Beginning in July or August, until shortly after the peak is reached in October and November, silver salmon migrate up the Columbia River and into streams of western Oregon. Sport fishing is tops at this time.

Chum salmon also enter the Columbia River in late summer and continue until November, going only short distances. Simultaneously, bands of sockeyes are to be found working upstream.

Winter steelhead are taken from January to June, with the later fishing occurring in the upstream tributaries. Summer steelhead are taken in the Columbia River in June and July, with bank angling providing a favorite pastime.

Boats, motors, and tackle can be rented at moorages along the Willamette and Columbia. The Game Commission maintains a regional office at Route 1, Corvallis, Oregon. Inquiries on fishing in the northwest part of the state can be directed to that office.

Zone 3 (Umpqua River system). The Umpqua River drainage is one of two major stream systems heading in the Cascades and cutting through to the Pacific Ocean. The river branches near Roseburg into the North and South Forks. Approximately 5,500 square miles are included in the drainage, and the distance from the mouth at Winchester Bay to the headwaters is nearly 250 miles.

Excellent salmon fishing is had at Winchester Bay from June through August. The fish are taken by trolling various types of plugs or baitfish. Charter boats and skiffs are available in the area. Spring chinook are taken from the river in April and May. Spinners or cluster eggs are the usual lures. Fall chinook angling is best in September and October, from the bay to the forks, using similar equipment. Sea-run cutthroat trout are taken in the main river below the forks and in the lower river tributaries, primarily in August through October. Flies or spinners produce most of the catches. The Reedsport Chamber of Commerce can provide additional tourist and fishing information. The Game Commission maintains an office at P. O. Box 977, Roseburg, Oregon. Inquiries on fishing in the southwestern section of the state can be directed to that office.

Zone 4 (Rogue River system). The Rogue River system, in the southwestern part of the state, is the other major drainage heading in the Cascades. Actually the famed Rogue River is headquarters for some of the finest king and silver salmon, and steelhead trout, fishing in the world. King salmon may be caught from early March until late October (best April to June and September), and silver salmon in the fall. Fly fishing for steelheads begins on the riffles in June or July, and continues through the fall (best in late August and September). Angling for these species may be done from boat or shore.

To stimulate interest in hanging up large trout and salmon, several contests are held at certain leading grounds in Oregon. One of the most popular is the annual Lower Rogue River Salmon and Steelhead Derby. This is staged by citizens of Gold Beach and Wedderburn, and extends from April 1 to October 15. Other notable contests in Oregon are the Nehalem Bay Salmon Derby in late September and early October, and the Waldport Silverside Salmon Derby on the Alsea River at approximately the same time. Details may be obtained by writing to the chambers of commerce at Gold Beach, Nehalem, and Waldport, respectively.

WASHINGTON

SUPPLIED BY: F. W. Mathias, Washington State Department of Commerce & Economic Development

Salmon fishing is easy fishing in the Evergreen State of Washington. You can step from your car on the waterfront of any of the cities that border Puget Sound, rent an outfit, and test your skill against a salmon. Or you can drive over scenic highways to more isolated resorts, such as Hope Island with its tide-swept channel, where fifty-pounders are not uncommon and where seventy-pound giants have been caught; Neah Bay, where you put out from an Indian village and look across towering ocean swells into the teeth of the Pacific; Westport, on historic Grays Harbor, where you can charter a boat to take you to the offshore banks; or any one of many other equally picturesque and productive fishing areas.

Great masses of salmon migrate from Alaska, and upon reaching the Strait of Juan de Fuca the formations break up and spread to different localities. Schools of sockeyes head for Fraser River, in British Columbia. Other salmon assemble at the Forty Mile Bank off Neah Bay, and from there multitudes of chinooks and silvers move on to the Columbia and southward, while the rest, accompanied by humpbacks (in the odd-numbered years) and chums, push farther into Puget Sound. They all head for the same rivers in which they were born.

Puget Sound offers salmon the entire year, but the twelve areas which have been designated as special fishing grounds vary in some respects, depending upon local conditions. A few details about these sites may help in planning your campaigns.

Strait of Juan de Fuca Area

Through this gateway come the first runs of adult king and Coho salmon, en route to the inland spawning beds. These silvery fish are in top physical form, ready to give you a rugged time on suitable tackle. The chinooks start forging into the strait early in May, and the procession fluctuates in number throughout the summer until it tapers off toward the middle of September.

Farther to the east, out from Port Townsend, there is another derby, and wonderful catches are made in this vicinity. Immature (blackmouth) and mature kings and silvers are presented in abundance from June into October. Boats, guides, cabins, tackle, and other accommodations are ready for service at resorts and towns along the Washington shore line of the Strait.

September and October are highlighted by the remarkable strings of silver salmon that may be secured, particularly in the waters around Sekiu and Clallam Bay, where natural basins favor concentrations of these fish. Salt-water bottom species and halibut may also be landed here on all occasions.

Though trolling is the method most used, experience has shown that this is also a good place to try your skill in bringing salmon to gaff by fly casting. Such lures as spinner and fly combinations, streamer and bucktail flies, and regular wet flies of Royal Coachman, Jock Scott, Durham Ranger, Silver Doctor, Golden Spinner, Salmon Fly, Western Bee, Silver Wickerson, Babcock, and Umpqua Fly patterns may be cast profitably at various periods of the season. These are also effective when tied on hooks. In the same pools and riffles and quiet expanses of Puget Sound, these lures also account for many fine steelhead and cutthroat trout.

Due to the rough weather in the Strait of Juan de Fuca during the winter, most of the angling activity at that time is carried on around sheltered Port Angeles. However, prospects are highly favorable over in the Neah Bay section, and outdoorsmen who are hardened to the winds and rains reap fine specimens of winter blackmouths.

San Juan Islands Area

After leaving the Strait of Juan de Fuca, you turn northward toward Bellingham and come to the San Juan Islands. Throughout the year, but especially during the late spring and summer months, salmon can be taken in the hundreds of shielded coves provided by the many islands.

Fifteen miles west of Bellingham, at Fisherman's Cove, the prospects are excellent for gathering in large kings, silvers, blackmouths, and humpbacks from February through October, and there are fine boat, guide, cabin, camp ground, restaurant, and other accommodations. At Fisherman's Cove, spinning is very effective.

The fishing off Orcas Island, reached by auto ferry from Anacortes to Orcas, is good for blackmouths in March and April, for kings from May through July, and silvers and humpbacks from July through September. Obstruction Pass, on the southern end of attractive Orcas Island, above Blakely Island, is another good spot for spinning. Tidal eddies create excellent spinning grounds, for they drive baitfish into close formations, which in turn cause blackmouths and silvers to gather for a feast. Moreover, the flow of water makes the spinning bait act lifelike.

Sea bass, rock cod, ling cod, some halibut, and many bottom fish are available the entire year among the San Juan Islands.

Hope Island Area

Trolling southward in your tour of the prominent salmon sites, try the waters around Hope Island. Located in Skagit Bay near Whidbey Island, this small island is located in one of the best areas in Puget Sound for huge king salmon.

In this area, embracing the north shores of Whidbey Island, the southern limits of Fidalgo Island, and Deception Pass, the fishing is generally above average for a longer period than elsewhere in the Sound—from April through September. Cabins, trailer spaces, community kitchens, boats, and tackle are obtainable. The best runs of kings and silvers in the Pass extend from June 1 to the middle of September.

Whidbey Island Area

On the southern end of this elongated island, you come to Possession Point. This is a stronghold for salmon from March through October, with a heavy run of big kings in evidence from the middle of July to September. Silvers run rampant from May to October. Due to the action of the tide, spin fishing is effective off Possession Point. Whidbey Island, approximately fifty miles in length, has several productive stretches of shore line. There is a ferry from Mukilteo to Columbia Beach, and this puts you in contact with the grounds off Possession Point, Langley, Holmes Harbor, and the western shore. You will find excellent resorts equipped with boats, bait, tackle, guides, cabins, and other conveniences. At Sandy Point, below Langley, there are good spinning beds.

At the northeast entrance to Holmes Harbor you'll find a fertile spot for blackmouths all year, particularly during February, March, and April. In the spring there is a run of cutthroat trout, and silvers hold sway from

July to October. At Dines Point, in Holmes Harbor, salmon are usually taken by spinning from March to July. For variety, all kinds of bottom fish may be brought to net at nearly any time of the year.

Along the southwest shores of Whidbey Island—out from Bush Point, Mutiny Bay, and Double Bluff—you may gather in kings, silvers, blackmouths, and humpbacks in season from May 1 through mid-October. This is a noted place for taking silvers by means of fly fishing, as well as by trolling and spinning.

Everett—Cameo Island Area

From both the mainland and island shores of this area there is some of the best cutthroat-trout fishing in Puget Sound during the spring months. Hermosa Point on Tulalip Bay, seven miles west of Marysville, is a hangout for these trout, and blackmouth, king, silver, and humpback salmon are on hand until October. And the same is true off Hat Island and Camano Head. Out from McKee's Beach, located on Port Susan northwest of Marysville, blackmouth may be caught from January into March by spinning, and the same method brings good results off Mission Beach.

As the adult kings and silvers pause before the mouths of the Snohomish and Stillaguamish rivers, you can bring aboard some heavy fellows; and lively blackmouth are there in the spring and fall months. Up at Kayak Point, northwest of Marysville, kings and silvers are ready to strike from July to the middle of September.

From the town of Stanwood you can drive across the bridge to Camano Island and swing over to the western beach. There are several resorts and fine salmon grounds along this shore. Blackmouths are in abundance from February to October, silvers from June through October, kings from June through August, and humpbacks during August and September.

East Mainland—Point No Point—Kingston Area

In this district of Puget Sound, easily reached from Seattle, thousands of anglers have their greatest fun with salmon from March to October. Those who troll along the mainland shores hook into vast numbers of young kings and silvers during March, April, and May. Then they move up to the beds off Point No Point and Possession Point, where the runs of adult salmon also come through.

Out from Whidbey Island, Foulweather Bluff, and Point No Point there are tidal eddies, and here the method of spinning is practiced extensively, bringing better results than trolling. Kings and silvers linger here from May to October 15, and in the odd-numbered years the humpies are here in August and September.

From Edmonds you can take the ferry to Kingston, where blackmouths are available all year, and large kings, silvers, and humpbacks pass through in season. The situation is similar as you move up to Edlon and on to Point No Point. The usual species of salt-water bottom fish may be caught around the calendar.

Seattle Area

Each year more than a hundred thousand people compete in the king and silver salmon derbies held in Elliot and Shilshole Bays within the city limits of Seattle. Salmon may be boated the entire year, but the peak of the season extends from about the first of August to the middle of November. This applies principally to adult kings and silvers, for black-mouths are present in generous quantities from about November 15 to the middle of May. Out from Ballard, in Shilshole Bay, big silver salmon are played and landed on fly-fishing and standard spinning outfits, especially during October and November.

Tacoma Area

Continuing your swing around the special salmon-fishing sites of Puget Sound, you reach the area which embraces such scattered grounds as the trolling routes off Tacoma itself, Point Defiance, Dash Point, and Brown's Points; Commencement Bay and the Narrows; Gig Harbor and Wollochet Bay; and the trolling routes skirting the northern shore of Fox Island. Finally, there are the spinning holes off Anderson Island where black-mouths congregate. This whole area can keep you busy and contented every month of the year.

From Point Defiance and in the Narrows you can tie into salmon of all sizes and all kinds of bottom fish, the year around. Many of the big fellows are taken by spinning off Point Defiance. In Commencement Bay adult kings, silvers, and humpies are most plentiful in the summer and fall. In Gig Harbor, you can catch dog salmon on light tackle, which is an exceptional feat since these fish are shy at attacking lures. The dogs may be taken from November through January.

In this same harbor you will find blackmouth all year, silvers in the fall, and sea-run cutthroat trout in the summer. The bulk of the blackmouths are most obliging from the middle of November to the middle of March, with your day's efforts showing up best when spinning.

Olympia Area

Unfortunately, due to harmful local practices, the salmon fishing in this most southern district of Puget Sound has not measured up to that of other areas. One of the best spots, however, is around Johnson Point, about ten miles from Highway 99, where boats may be rented and black-mouths caught from September through June, and silvers taken mainly during September and October. Other places to try are at Boston Harbor and around Steamboat Island.

Bremerton—Port Orchard Area

Turning northward from Olympia to try some of the favorite spots along the western side of Puget Sound, you pause opposite Seattle to fish in the area covered by Manchester, Port Orchard, Bremerton, and Suquamish. Here you find salmon grounds around Plake Island, Manchester, Rich Passage, Port Orchard Narrows, Agate Pass, and Yukon Harbor.

Upper and Lower Hood Canal Area

From its wide entrance at Port Ludlow and Foulweather Bluff, the Hood Canal cuts southward into Washington for more than sixty miles. Along its course there are several outstanding salmon beds, affording worthwhile results the year around. This is one of the most popular vacation sites in the Puget Sound country for visiting sportsmen and cottage owners, with many well equipped resorts located on both sides of the Canal.

Schools of active, feeding blackmouths are present during most of the year. Runs of adult kings are strong in July and August, and silvers from September into December.

In the upper Hood Canal, off Lawter's Beach near Seabeck, you may catch blackmouths from February through April, and silvers from September through November. A short distance to the south the Maple and Scenic beaches also offer commendable fishing.

Up in Dabob Bay, near Quilcene, your best chances for boating young kings are usually in March and April, and silvers in the summer and fall. In this same bay, near the Dosewallips River by Brinnon, the noted Seal Rock run of blackmouths, some weighing as much as twenty-five pounds, supplies plenty of action from February through April, with adult kings, silvers, and humpies abundant in September and October. At Seal Rock you'll make some of your top catches by spinning, in March and April.

Below this section you enter the long arm of the lower Hood Canal, where cabin camps and resorts have every facility for the comfort and success of the angler. At Holly Beach a substantial run of kings occurs in July and August, and silvers in the fall.

In the vicinity of Hoodsport and in the stretch of water from Eldon to Lilliwaup there is excellent fishing for kings from July to September, silvers from September to December, blackmouths all year but particularly from September to February, and bottom fish at any time.

At famous Bald Point you have an opportunity to fish the year around, with special emphasis on blackmouths from February through April, silvers from September through December, and cutthroats during May and June. Boats, bait, tackle, and cabins may be rented, and you set out to troll or spin for salmon in beautiful surroundings.

Across the Canal, in the vicinity of Union, young kings and silvers are present all summer and fall, and the adults pass through from August to November. The customary salt-water bottom fish are there also to give you varied sport.

If the capturing of mammoth and vigorous Pacific salmon is your ambition, you should not miss coming to the magnificent Puget Sound region. Besides salmon, salt-water species include halibut, ling, cod, black cod, rockfish, and albacore. The last-named is not normally considered a cold-water fish, but it has been reported recently.

No license is required for salt-water fishing in Washington State. For other angling information, write to the Department of Fisheries, Olympia, Washington.

BRITISH COLUMBIA

SUPPLIED BY: Ed O'Hara, author and former guide in this area

While many species of bottom fish are taken along the salty coastline of British Columbia, salmon is the number one fish. In this province the king salmon is usually called tyee, an Indian name meaning "chief," and the celebrated Tyee Club on the Campbell River of Vancouver Island has set a low limit of thirty pounds for these fish. Below that weight they are regarded as spring salmon. In some rivers of British Columbia there is a fairly continuous run of kings from spring until fall. Best results in the Campbell River, where world record tyee salmon are taken, usually occur during the first three weeks of August. By early September the kings have turned black and lost their vigor. The kings of this river are said to be larger than those found elsewhere along the seacoast, averaging around forty pounds.

Anglers who troll in this vicinity often do so in the Strait of Georgia close to the mouth of the Campbell River, but this may be accomplished only for short periods, for the most part, due to the strong winds and heavy tides.

The first spring run of the British Columbia tyee is generally along the headwaters. Fall tyee assemble in the bays and inlets in late summer, to wait there until rains have raised the river levels so they may ascend. Their journeys begin in July or August, and this activity increases as the weeks advance. These fish like the larger streams of the lowlands, where the fishing is good from about mid-September through November or December, with October being especially favorable.

Silver salmon are often caught during this same period, for they like similar types of bottom and depths of water. The weather is generally clear in early fall, and quite rainy in November and December, but there are numerous excellent salmon days at this time of the year. Like other salmon, silvers are bright-colored when in the sea and turn darkish after being in fresh water awhile. Many of them do not enter the rivers until October or November—as in some of the coastal streams of British Columbia—and then they spawn over an interval lasting through February. They usually deposit their eggs in the lower reaches, at short distances from the sea, but at times they go to the upper tributaries of large rivers. Silvers have a normal life cycle of three years, one in fresh water and two in the ocean—the youngsters migrating to the ocean in April or May after a little over one year of stream existence.

In British Columbia the adult sockeyes start entering the rivers in early summer and continue until as late as August. The famous Fraser River, however, receives periodic runs even into November. The fish approach the headlands of Vancouver Island at the eastern end of Juan de Fuca Strait, move to the southern end of San Juan Islands, turn up through Rosario Strait into the Gulf of Georgia, and crowd into the Fraser River. From salt-water the sockeyes come in on the flood tide, revealing themselves by breaking water and leaping. The early schools make for the lakes located at headwaters of rivers.

The Sproat River on Vancouver Island is another excellent salmon site. This is a brawling stream that lends plenty of action and thrills as the fish are seen jumping and surging against the current. An equally wild and beautiful water is the Stamp River, outlet for Great Central Lake, which joins the Sproat River and empties into Alberni Canal at Port Alberni. The Canal and its tributary streams are top-flight salmon grounds, producing kings up to fifty and sixty pounds. The Cowichan, Nimpkish, Courtenay, Salmon, and Bear rivers are also good tyee habitats.

The coastal waters around and near the city of Victoria offer some of the best salmon fishing in the Pacific Northwest. In these waters around Victoria the fishing is for springs, which run to great weight, and for cohos averaging about ten pounds apiece. Since the cohos play on the surface, they often provide even more sport than the bigger springs. Angling for grilse is also enjoyed in this area, mainly in the Saanich Arm some twelve miles from the heart of Victoria. These young salmon go from about one to three pounds in weight, and are caught with a trout rod and bucktail fly from boats in the open ocean.

As a note of interest, steelhead fishing is an outstanding sport in many of the rivers of Vancouver Island, where the fish weigh anywhere from five to fourteen pounds, with an average of about seven or eight pounds. The steelheads are taken on fly-casting tackle, and the best season is during April, May, June, September, and October in most of the rivers.

Cutthroat trout are caught at the mouths of many coastal rivers during the winter, with certain legal restrictions. They spawn in convenient streams from around February to May. While in the ocean the cutthroats eat a variety of small fish, including sandlance, rockfish, salmon, sea perch, sculpins, and flatfish; and in the rivers their food consists of insects, shrimps, and minnows. They may attain a length of over two feet, and weight of about forty pounds, but the average in most rivers is around six pounds. These trout are mainly caught by fly-fishing with wet and dry flies, streamer and bucktail flies, fly-and-spinner combinations, plain spinners, and small spoons. Bait casting with ordinary wooden and plastic plugs, using a regular casting outfit, is also effective.

Further information on salt-water fishing in British Columbia may be obtained by writing to the Game Commission, 567 Burrard Street, Vancouver, British Columbia.

ALASKA

Data reprinted in part from an article that appeared in the *Ashaway Sportsman*

The largest state in the union is one of the best salmon areas in the world. Unspoiled by man's so-called civilized advance, there are scores of streams, rivers, and bays in all coastal districts, capable of producing record fish and guaranteed to supply real fishing. But this uncivilized character has its disadvantages, too. Boats, guides, and accommodations are scarce. Now that Alaska is a state, new growth is expected, and the fishing facilities should also become better.

In the southeastern district, the best known and publicized, the angler can find fairly good accommodations and have a good chance to tie into a king salmon or a hefty cutthroat. This district, with Juneau in the north and Ketchikan in the south, is crammed with hundreds of islands nesting under the eastward 10,000-foot British Columbia Rockies. You could not begin to cover in one season all the numerous bays, streams, and rivers of the famous Inland Passage water. In June, the tackle-busting king, or tyee, salmon commence their rampage in the tide slicks and whether you are trolling a plug or spoon, or bait-strip fishing, you will have little time on your hands to worry about income taxes or what have you. In August a new menace to the tranquillity of the salt channels puts in its appearance in the form of the coho salmon—a first-class acrobat and worthy of far more praise from sportsmen than has been bestowed. Land one out of three of these aquatic streaks of lightning and you are doing all right.

Seven hundred and fifty miles west of Juneau is the city of Anchorage, the railroad, highway, and airplane center of the state. South of Anchorage and only minutes away by air (the favorite means of transportation up here) is the renowned Kenai Peninsula where the much-publicized moose have overshadowed some of the finest trout and salmon fishing in the world. Approximately three hundred miles from Anchorage is the commercial salmon center of Naknek. Swarming out of the Bering Sea into

Bristol and Kirchak bays, millions upon millions of salmon gladden the hearts of cannery men and sportsmen.

Rockfish, Alaska pollack, starry flounder, lemon sole, Atka mackerel, ling cod, greenling, sea trout, and other bottom fish are often taken along the coast of Alaska.

Alaska's fishing regulations are generous. For most of the state there is no closed season on game fish. Bag limits and possession limits vary. There is no closed season or limit anywhere on the five species of Pacific salmon. Complete regulations may be obtained by writing the Alaska Development and Planning Commission, Box 2391, Juneau, Alaska 99801.

It is really not fair to pick out districts or select spots when writing of salt-water fishing in Alaska. We have skipped over and omitted many worthy places. Outside of a small district around Point Barrow, there is excellent sport for anglers in every section of Alaska's coastline.

WEST COAST OF MEXICO

SUPPLIED BY: Ignacio Bonilla Vazquez, Director-General of Fishing

From Cape San Lucas around to Acapulco are some of the greatest big-game fishing grounds in the world. Here are found the Mexican sailfish, marlin (both striped and black), papagallo, dolphin, yellowfin tuna, wahoo, rooster fish, yellowtail, giant bass—in fact, virtually every big game fish sought by anglers. Following is a roundup of the better salt-water spots, starting with Ensenada on the Pacific side of Lower California, working around the west and east coast of the Gulf of California, down the west coast of the Mexican mainland fronting on the Pacific Ocean.

Ensenada. This town is approximately seventy miles below Tiajuana by paved highway. Big-game fishing is better in other sections of Mexico, but there are marlin (July to October), tuna (June to October) and occasional swordfish (August to October). Albacore (July to October), yellowtail, and other game fish of the San Diego area are prevalent at about the same seasons, sometimes a little earlier. Accommodations are good here.

Surf angling is good all along the coast from Tiajuana, mainly for croaker, surf perch, corbina, and halibut. Rosarito Beach (eighteen miles below Tiajuana) and Estero Beach (six miles below Ensenada) are the best locations for this sport. Fishing offshore for white sea bass, barracuda, yellowtail, and marlin is good at these spots. San Quintin (125 miles south of Ensenada) also has excellent surf casting, but accommodations are primitive.

Las Cruces. Gulf fishing is at its best here; sailfish and marlin are numerous in season. It is not at all unusual to be fighting one of these big fish within five minutes after leaving the dock. Boats from La Paz do most of their fishing in these waters—opposite Cerralvo Island and just below Espiritu Santo Island. Accommodations are very good.

San Felipe. Located on the Gulf side of Lower California, this village is the base of a commercial shrimp fleet and the home of the great totuava (Mexican white sea bass), fierce fighter which may go better than 150 pounds and is excellent eating. Besides totuava, there are white sea bass, grouper, pinta, bonefish, cabrilla, trigger fish, Mexican bass, red snapper, sierra mackerel, and others.

Guaymas. This is situated halfway up the Gulf of California on the western mainland coast. April to July are top months for sailfish and marlin, but fishing for them goes on all summer. From October to May, there are all types of bass, including totuava, yellowtail, jewfish, pompano, Spanish mackerel, silver sea trout, and others. May to September, there are rooster fish, swordfish, tuna, dolphin, and sharks. In mid-June, there is a Fishing Fiesta; in mid-October, the International Fishing Rodeo.

Mazatlan. This is on the mainland of the west coast of Mexico, just opposite Cape San Lucas. It is Mexico's largest Pacific seaport and is in the heart of an excellent fishing area. Sailfish and marlin are the big attractions, the former running from mid-April or May to November, the latter from December to April or later. Good hotel and boat accommodations are available.

Acapulco. In recent years this town has gained a great deal of renown as a leading fishing spot. November to May are the top months (the International Fishing Rodeo is in mid-April), but you can get sailfish on into the summer. Big marlin and sailfish are the chief targets, but dolphin, yellowtail, amberjack, red snapper, mackerel, rooster fish, pompano, palometa, bonito, tuna, barracuda, and shark are plentiful. Snook fishing with light tackle is excellent. The hotel accommodations and the boats are excellent, too. For information on Mexican fishing, write to the Dirección General de Turismo, Avenida Juárez, 89, Mexico, D. F.

HAWAII

While some mention of big-game angling in our fiftieth state has been made in Chapter 8, the over-all picture of fishing among the islands is not included within the scope of this chapter. For information on fishing in our newest state, which by the way is excellent and most rewarding, write to the Hawaii Visitors Bureau, 2051 Kalakaua Avenue, Honolulu, Hawaii 96815.

APPENDIX A ALL TACKLE RECORDS

WORLD RECORD MARINE GAME FISHES

Record Catches for Both Men and Women

Fish	Scientific Name	Weight	Length	Girth	Place	Date	Angler	Line lbs.
ALBACORE	Thunnus germo	69 lbs. 2 oz.	3' 10"	32"	Montauk, N.Y.	Aug. 21, 1964	Larry R. Kranz	80
AMBERJACK	Seriola lalandi	149 lbs.	5' 11"	41¾"	Bermuda	June 21, 1964	Peter Simons	30
BARRACUDA	Sphyraena barracuda	103 lbs. 4 oz.	5' 6"	31¼"	West End, Bahamas	1932	C. E. Benet*	80
Calif. Black Sea BASS	Stereolepis gigas	557 lbs. 3 oz.	7' 4¼"	78"	Catalina Island, Calif.	July 1, 1962	Richard M. Lane	50
Calif. White Sea BASS	Cynoscion nobilis	83 lbs. 12 oz.	5' 5½"	34"	San Felipe, Mexico	Mar. 31, 1953	L. C. Baumgardner	30
Channel BASS	Sciaenops ocellatus	83 lbs.	4' 4"	29"	Cape Charles, Va.	Aug. 5, 1949	Zack Waters, Jr.	50
Giant Sea BASS	Promicrops itaiara	680 lbs.	7' 1½"	66"	Fernandina Beach, Fla.	May 20, 1961	Lynn Joyner	80
Sea BASS	Centropristes striatus	8 lbs.	1' 10"	19"	Nantucket Sound, Mass.	May 13, 1951	H. R. Rider	50
Striped BASS	Roccus saxatilis	73 lbs.	5'	30½"	Vineyard Sound, Mass.	Aug. 17, 1913	C. B. Church*	50
BLACKFISH or TAUTOG	Tautoga onitis	21 lbs. 6 oz.	2' 7½"	23½"	Cape May, N.J.	June 12, 1954	R. N. Sheafer	30
BLUEFISH	Pomatomus saltatrix	24 lbs. 3 oz.	3' 5"	22"	San Miguel, Azores	Aug. 27, 1953	M. A. da Silva Veloso	12
BONEFISH	Albula vulpes	19 lbs.	3' 3⅝"	17"	Zululand, S.A.	May 26, 1962	Brian W. Batchelor	30
Oceanic BONITO	Katsuwonus pelamis	39 lbs. 15 oz.	3' 3"	28"	Walker Cay, Bahamas	Jan. 21, 1952	F. Drowley	50
COBIA	Rachycentron canadus	102 lbs.	5' 10"	34"	Cape Charles, Va.	July 3, 1938	J. E. Stansbury*	130
COD	Gadus callarias	74 lbs. 4 oz.	5' 6"	43"	Boothbay Harbor, Me.	June 2, 1960	James J. Duggan	50
DOLPHIN	Coryphaena hippurus	76 lbs. 12 oz.	5' 10½"	35"	Bimini, Bahamas	May 28, 1964	Charles J. Costello	50
Black DRUM	Pogonias cromis	94 lbs. 4 oz.	4' 3½"	42"	Cape Charles, Va.	Apr. 28, 1957	James Lee Johnson	50
FLOUNDER	Paralichthys	21 lbs. 4 oz.	3' ½"	35"	Maitencillo, Chile	Dec. 8, 1959	Daniel Varas Serrano	50
KINGFISH or TANGUIGUE	S. cavalla C. commersonii	81 lbs.	5' 11½"	29¼"	Karachi, Pakistan	Aug. 27, 1960	George E. Rusinak	80
Black MARLIN	Name being revised	1560 lbs.	14' 6"	81"	Cabo Blanco, Peru	Aug. 4, 1953	Alfred C. Glassell, Jr.	130
Blue MARLIN	Makaira ampla	814 lbs.	13' 8"	69"	St. Thomas, Virgin Islands	July 26, 1964	John Battles	80
Pacific Blue MARLIN	Name being revised	1095 lbs.	13' 10"	81"	Kona, Hawaii	May 30, 1964	Jack Whaling	130
Striped MARLIN	Makaira mitsukurii	465 lbs.	10' 6"	65"	Mayor Island, New Zealand	Feb. 27, 1948	James Black	130
White MARLIN	Makaira albida	161 lbs.	8' 8"	33"	Miami Beach, Fla.	Mar. 20, 1938	L. F. Hooper	80
PERMIT	Trachinotus goodei	50 lbs.	3' 7"	34½"	Miami, Fla.	Mar. 27, 1965	Robert F. Miller	12
POLLACK	Pollachius virens	43 lbs.	4'	29"	Brielle, N.J.	Oct. 21, 1964	Philip Barlow	50
Rainbow RUNNER	Elagatis bipinnulatus	30 lbs. 15 oz.	3' 11"	22"	Kauai, Hawaii	April 27, 1963	Holbrook Goodale	130
ROOSTERFISH	Nematistius pectoralis	114 lbs.	5' 4"	33"	La Paz, Mexico	June 1, 1960	Abe Sackheim	30
Atlantic SAILFISH	Istiophorus americanus	141 lbs. 1 oz.	8' 5"		Ivory Coast, Africa	Jan. 26, 1961	Tony Burnand	130
Pacific SAILFISH	Istiophorus greyi	221 lbs.	10' 9"		Santa Cruz Is., Galapagos Is.	Feb. 12, 1947	C. W. Stewart	130
SAWFISH	Pristis pectinatus	890 lbs. 8 oz.	16' 1"	92"	Fort Amador, Canal Zone	May 26, 1960	Jack Wagner	80
Blue SHARK	Prionace glauca	410 lbs.	11' 6"	52"	Rockport, Mass.	Sept. 1, 1960	Richard C. Webster	80
Mako SHARK	Isurus oxyrhynchus I. glaucus	1000 lbs.	12'		Mayor Island, New Zealand	Mar. 14, 1943	B. D. H. Ross*	130
Man-Eater or White SHARK	Carcharodon carcharias	2664 lbs.	16' 10"	9' 6"	Ceduna, So. Australia	Apr. 21, 1959	Alfred Dean	130
Porbeagle SHARK	Lamna nasus	400 lbs. 8 oz.	7' 9½"	57½"	Fire Island, N.Y.	May 16, 1965	James T. Kirkup	80
Thresher SHARK	Alopias vulpinus	922 lbs.			Bay of Islands, N.Z.	Mar. 21, 1937	W. W. Dowding*	130
Tiger SHARK	Galeocerdo cuvier	1780 lbs.	13' 10½"	103"	Cherry Grove, S.C.	June 14, 1964	Walter Maxwell	130
SNOOK or ROBALO	Centropomus undecimalis	52 lbs. 6 oz.	4' 1½"	26"	La Paz, Mexico	Jan. 9, 1963	Jane Haywood	30
SWORDFISH	Xiphias gladius	1182 lbs.	14' 11¼"	78"	Iquique, Chile	May 7, 1953	L. Marron	130
TARPON	Tarpon atlanticus	283 lbs.	7' 2⅗"		Lake Maracaibo, Venez.	Mar. 19, 1956	M. Salazar	30
Allison or Yellowfin TUNA	Thunnus albacares	269 lbs. 8 oz.	6' 9"	53"	Hanalei, Hawaii	May 30, 1962	Henry Nishikawa	180
Atlantic Big-Eyed TUNA	Thunnus obesus	295 lbs.	6' 6½"	40"	San Miguel, Azores, Portugal	July 8, 1960	Dr. Arsenio Cordeiro	130
Pacific Big-Eyed TUNA	Parathunnus sibi	435 lbs.	7' 9"	63½"	Cabo Blanco, Peru	April 17, 1957	Dr. Russel V. A. Lee	130
Blackfin TUNA	Thunnus atlanticus	36 lbs.	3' ¼"	28⅞"	Bermuda	July 14, 1963	Joseph E. Baptiste, Jr.	50
Bluefin TUNA	Thunnus thynnus	977 lbs.	9' 8"	94½"	St. Ann Bay, Nova Scotia	Sept. 4, 1950	D. McI. Hodgson	130
WAHOO	Acanthocybium solandri	149 lbs.	6' 7¾"	37½"	Cat Cay, Bahamas	June 15, 1962	John Pirovano	130
WEAKFISH	Cynoscion regalis	19 lbs. 8 oz.	3' 1"	23¾"	Trinidad, West Indies	Apr. 13, 1962	Dennis B. Hall	80
Spotted WEAKFISH	Cynoscion nebulosus	15 lbs. 3 oz.	2' 10½"	20½"	Ft. Pierce, Fla.	Jan. 13, 1949	C. W. Hubbard	50
YELLOWTAIL	Seriola dorsalis or S. grandis	111 lbs.	5' 2"	38"	Bay of Islands, New Zealand	June 11, 1961	A. F. Plim	50

*Line not tested.

Courtesy of International Game Fish Association

These are the major world records as of January 1, 1966. For records in other classes (20-, 30-, 50-, 80-, and 130-pound Line Test) write to the International Game Fish Association, 1112 Dupont Building, Miami, 32, Florida.

ALL TACKLE RECORDS
Women's Records

Fish	Scientific Name	Weight	Length	Girth	Place	Date	Angler	Line lbs.
ALBACORE	Thunnus germo	55 lbs. 4 oz.			Catalina, Calif.	Sept. 1927	Mrs. L. M. Doxie*	30
AMBERJACK	Seriola lalandi	106 lbs. 8 oz.	5' 5''	39''	Pinas Bay, Panama	July 9, 1960	Helen Robinson	80
BARRACUDA	Sphyraena barracuda	66 lbs. 4 oz.	5' 10''	25½''	Cape Lopez, Gabon, Africa	July 17, 1955	Mme. M. Halley	80
Calif. Black Sea BASS	Stereolepis gigas	425 lbs.	7' 2¼''	64¼''	Coronado Island, Calif.	Oct. 8, 1960	Lorene Wheeler	80
Calif. White Sea BASS	Cynoscion nobilis	62 lbs.	4' 9''	28''	Malibu, Calif.	Dec. 6, 1951	Mrs. D. W. Jackson	20
Channell BASS	Sciaenops ocellatus	69 lbs. 8 oz.	4' 3½''	33¼'' (30-lb. record for men & women)	Cape Hatteras, N.C.	Nov. 16, 1958	Jean Browning	30
Giant Sea BASS	Promicrops itaiara	366 lbs.	7' 4½''	68''	Guayabo, Panama	Feb. 8, 1965	Betsy B. Walker	80
Sea BASS	Centropristes striatus	5 lbs. 1 oz.	1' 8½''	16''	Panama City Beach, Fla.	July 21, 1956	Mrs. R. H. Martin	50
Striped BASS	Roccus saxatilis	64 lbs. 8 oz.	4' 6''	30'' (30-lb. record for men & women)	North Truro, Mass.	Aug. 14, 1960	Rosa O. Webb	30
BLACKFISH or TAUTOG	Tautoga onitis	16 lbs. 8 oz.	2' 6''	22''	Seventeen Fathoms, N.Y.	Nov. 1, 1953	Edna De Fina	50
BLUEFISH	Pomatomus saltatrix	19 lbs. 4 oz.			Long Island Sound, N.Y.	Oct. 19, 1958	Elanor Plasko	30
BONEFISH	Albula vulpes	15 lbs.	2' 8½''	18½''	Bimini, Bahamas	Mar. 20, 1961	Andrea Tose	12
		31 lbs.	2' 11''	24''	Kona, Hawaii	June 16, 1963	Anne H. Bosworth	130
Oceanic BONITO	Katsuwonus pelamis	31 lbs.	2' 10½''	24½''	San Juan, P. R.	Dec. 26, 1954	Gloria G. de Marques	50
		31 lbs.	2' 11''	24¾''	Nassau, Bahamas	Jan. 25, 1956	Mrs. Barbara Wallach	80
COBIA	Rachycentron canadus	97 lbs.	5' 6½''	33'' (80-lb. record for men & women)	Oregon Inlet, N.C.	June 4, 1952	Mary W. Black	80
COD	Gadus callarias	71 lbs. 8 oz.	4' 10''	31'' (20-lb. record for men & women)	Cape Cod, Mass.	Aug. 2, 1964	Muriel Betts	20
DOLPHIN	Coryphaena hippurus	73 lbs. 11 oz.	4' 11½''	43½'' (30-lb. record for men & women)	Baja, Calif., Mexico	July 12, 1962	Barbara Kibbee Jayne	30
Black DRUM	Pogonias cromis	93 lbs.	4' 2½''	42''	Fernandina Beach, Fla.	Mar. 28, 1957	Mrs. Stella Moore	50
FLOUNDER	Paralichthys	20 lbs. 7 oz.	3' 1''	29½''	Long Island, N.Y.	July 8, 1957	Mrs. M. Fredriksen	60
KINGFISH or TANGUIGUE	S. cavalla C. commersonii	78 lbs.	5' 6½''	28½'' (50-lb. record for men & women)	Guayanilla, P.R.	May 25, 1963	Ruth M. Coon	50
Black MARLIN	Name being revised	1525 lbs.	14' 4''	80''	Cabo Blanco, Peru	Apr. 22, 1954	Kimberley Wiss	130
Blue MARLIN	Makaira ampla	730 lbs.		60¾''	Cat Cay, Bahamas	June 6, 1939	Mrs. Henry Sears*	80
Pacific Blue MARLIN	Name being revised	555 lbs.	11' 11''	58½''	Kailua-Kona, Hawaii	Aug. 9, 1964	Mrs. R. H. Baldwin	80
Striped MARLIN	Makaira mitsukurii	430 lbs.	10' 8½''	54½''	Mayor Is., New Zealand	Apr. 9, 1955	Mrs. H. J. Carkeek	80
White MARLIN	Makaira albida	152 lbs.	8' 3''	40'' (130-lb. record for men & women)	Bimini, Bahamas	Mar. 14, 1936	Mrs. Marion Stevens*	130
PERMIT	Trachinotus goodei	38 lbs.	3' 4''	30½''	Islamorada, Fla.	Mar. 21, 1954	Mrs. W. K. Edmunds	20
		38 lbs.	3' 7''	33''	Islamorada, Fla.	June 11, 1961	Louise Meulenberg	20
		38 lbs.	3' 7''	31''	Key West, Fla.	Apr. 9, 1963	Helen Robinson	30
POLLACK	Pollachius virens	29 lbs.	3' 6''	24¼''	Manasquan, N.J.	Nov. 3, 1958	Ann Durik	50
Rainbow RUNNER	Elagatis bipinnulatus	23 lbs.	3' 6''	19½'' (50-lb. record for men & women)	Oahu, Hawaiian Islands	May 9, 1961	Lila M. Neuenfelt	50
ROOSTERFISH	Nematistius pectoralis	99 lbs.	4' 11½''	34½''	La Paz, Mexico	Nov. 30, 1964	Lily Call	30
Atlantic SAILFISH	Istiophorus americanus	104 lbs. 8 oz.	7' 11''	31''	Miami Beach, Fla.	Mar. 22, 1939	Ruth Edmands Pope*	80
Pacific SAILFISH	Istiophorus greyi	196 lbs.	10' 7''	40''	Acapulco, Mexico	Feb. 9, 1951	Mrs. F. Bart	80
SAWFISH	Pristis pectinatus	134 lbs.	8' 10''	·32'' (20-lb. record for men & women)	Long Key, Fla.	Mar. 27, 1963	Olive M. Senn	20
Blue SHARK	Prionace glauca	334 lbs.	10' 8''	47½'' (130-lb. record for men & women)	Rockport, Mass.	Sept. 4, 1964	Cassandra Webster	130
Mako SHARK	Isurus oxyrhynchus	911 lbs. 12 oz.	11' 2''	70''	Palm Beach, Fla.	Apr. 9, 1962	Audrey Cohen	130
Man-Eater or White SHARK	Carcharodon carcharias	1052 lbs.	13' 10''	72½''	Cape Moreton, Australia	June 27, 1954	Mrs. Bob Dyer	130
Porbeagle SHARK	Lamna nasus	271 lbs.	8' 2''	49'' (130-lb. record for men & women)	Looe, Cornwall, England	Aug. 18, 1957	Mrs. Hetty Eathorne	130
Thresher SHARK	Alopias vulpinus	729 lbs.	8' 5''	61''	Mayor Island, New Zealand	June 3, 1959	Mrs. V. Brown	130
Tiger SHARK	Galeocerdo cuvier	1314 lbs.	13' 9''	89''	Cape Moreton, Australia	July 27, 1953	Mrs. Bob Dyer	130
SNOOK or ROBALO	Centropomus undecimalis	52 lbs. 6 oz.	4' 1½''	26'' (30-lb. record for men & women)	La Paz, Mexico	Jan. 9, 1963	Jane Haywood	30
SWORDFISH	Xiphias gladius	772 lbs.	12' 10''	70'' (80-lb. record for men & women)	Iquique, Chile	June 7, 1954	Mrs. L. Marron	80
TARPON	Tarpon atlanticus	203 lbs.	7' 11''	44''	Marathon, Fla.	May 19, 1961	June Jordan	80
Allison or Yellowfin TUNA	Thunnus albacares	254 lbs.	6' 3''	52''	Kona, Hawaii	Aug. 19, 1954	Jean Carlisle	130
Atlantic Big-Eyed TUNA	Thunnus obesus	182 lbs.	5' 8''	56''	Cat Cay, Bahamas	June 2, 1958	Mrs. Pablo Bardin	130
Pacific Big-Eyed TUNA	Parathunnus sibi	336 lbs.	7' 3''	56½''	Cabo Blanco, Peru	Jan. 16, 1957	Mrs. Seymour Knox III	130
Blackfin TUNA	Thunnus atlanticus	31 lbs. 4 oz.	3' 1⅞''	26¼''	Bermuda	June 23, 1963	Mary Anne Eve	30
Bluefin TUNA	Thunnus thynnus	882 lbs.	9' 2''	83½''	Wedgeport, N.S.	Sept. 6, 1947	Mrs. A. D. Crowninshield*	130
WAHOO	Acanthocybium solandrii	110 lbs.	6'	29''	Walker Cay, Bahamas	Apr. 1, 1941	Mrs. A. D. Crowninshield*	130
		110 lbs.	6' 1½''	36½''	Port Eades, La.	June 22, 1964	Mrs. Homer J. Moore, Jr.	130
WEAKFISH	Cynoscion regalis	11 lbs. 12 oz.	2' 7¾''	18''	Newport R., N.C.	Oct. 29, 1950	Mrs. L. A. Denning	50
Spotted WEAKFISH	Cynoscion nebulosus	10 lbs. 8 oz.	2' 7½''	15''	Jupiter, Fla.	May 30, 1964	Jane H. Cole	30
		10 lbs. 4 oz.	2' 6½''	16''	Jupiter, Fla.	June 1, 1958	Nancy Dukes	12
YELLOWTAIL	Seriola dorsalis or S. grandis	81 lbs.	4' 9½''	32½''	Cape Brett, New Zealand	May 18, 1960	Kura Beale	80

*Line not tested.

12-1b. LINE TEST RECORDS
(Up to and including 12 pounds)
Record Catches for Both Men and Women

Fish	Scientific Name	Weight	Length	Girth	Place	Date	Angler
ALBACORE	Thunnus germo	29 lbs. 8 oz.	3' 1''	24½''	San Diego, Calif.	Oct. 5, 1963	Jane Holland
AMBERJACK	Seriola lalandi	48 lbs. 4 oz.	4' 4''	26½''	Key West, Fla.	Apr. 11, 1965	Mrs. Charles O. Frasch
BARRACUDA	Sphyraena barracuda	39 lbs.	4' 9''	21''	No. Key Largo, Fla.	Jan. 29, 1959	Mrs. Walter Bell
Calif. Black Sea BASS	Stereolepis gigas						
Calif. White Sea BASS	Cynoscion nobilis	52 lbs. 6 oz.	4' 6''	27¾''	Newport Harbor, Calif.	June 3, 1959	Ruth Jayred
Channel BASS	Sciaenops ocellatus	51 lbs. 8 oz.	4' 2¼''	29''	Cape Hatteras, N.C.	Nov. 19, 1958	Joan S. Dull
Giant Sea BASS	Promicrops itaiara	110 lbs.	4' 10½''	39½''	Islamorada, Fla.	Aug. 2, 1961	Mrs. Gar Wood, Jr.
Sea BASS	Centropristes striatus	2 lbs. 8 oz. (12-lb. record for men & women)	1' 5½''	12½''	Block Island, R.I.	July 12, 1957	Mrs. C. Shanks
Striped BASS	Roccus saxatilis	47 lbs.	4' 1½''		Umpqua R., Ore.	Aug. 21, 1958	Mrs. Margaret Hulen
BLACKFISH or TAUTOG	Tautoga onitis						
BLUEFISH	Pomatomus saltatrix	16 lbs. 10 oz.	3'	19''	Montauk, N.Y.	June 24, 1961	Gloria Better
BONEFISH	Albula vulpes	15 lbs. (12-lb. record for men & women)	2' 8½''	18½''	Bimini, Bahamas	Mar. 20, 1961	Andrea Tose
Oceanic BONITO	Katsuwonus pelamis	24 lbs. 6 oz. (12-lb. record for men & women)	2' 6½''	21''	Walker Cay, Bahamas	Mar. 26, 1965	Patricia E. Church
COBIA	Rachycentron canadus	37 lbs.	3' 10''	22½''	Panama City Beach, Fla.	Apr. 20, 1960	Mrs. Curtis G. Bane
COD	Gadus callarias	14 lbs. 7½ oz.	2' 11''	17½''	Nova Scotia, Canada	July 9, 1963	Janet D. Wallach
DOLPHIN	Coryphaena hippurus	55 lbs. 2 oz. (12-lb. record for men & women)	4' 11¾''	32½''	Mazatlan, Mexico	Oct. 18, 1964	Marguerite H. Barry
Black DRUM	Pogonias cromis	58 lbs. 12 oz.	3' 9¾''	36''	Atlantic Beach, N.C.	May 8, 1959	Juel W. Duke
FLOUNDER	Paralichthys	12 lbs. 2 oz.	2' 7¼''	25¼''	Avalon, N.J.	Sept. 8, 1957	Mrs. Alfred J. Bernstein
KINGFISH or TANGUIGUE	S. cavalla C. commersonii	41 lbs. 8 oz.	4' 6''	23''	Pompano Beach, Fla.	Jan. 15, 1961	Margaret A. Paine
Black MARLIN	Name being revised						
Blue MARLIN	Makaira ampla	223 lbs. 1 oz.	10' 2½''	42''	Bimini, Bahamas	Apr. 9, 1960	Suzanne H. Higgs
Pacific Blue MARLIN	Name being revised						
Striped MARLIN	Makaira mitsukurii	210 lbs.	9' 6''	40''	Las Cruces, Mexico	June 20, 1959	Lynn F. Lee
White MARLIN	Makaira albida	122 lbs. (12-lb. record for men & women)	8' 3''	44''	Bimini, Bahamas	Mar. 30, 1953	Dorothy A. Curtice
PERMIT	Trachinotus goodei	36 lbs.	3' 6''	29''	Content Key, Fla.	Mar. 16, 1964	Lynette G. Siman
POLLACK	Pollachius virens	15 lbs. 7 oz.	2' 9¾''	19''	Nova Scotia, Canada	July 9, 1963	Janet D. Wallach
Rainbow RUNNER	Elagatis bipinnulatus						
ROOSTERFISH	Nematistius pectoralis	45 lbs.	4' 4½''	30''	San José del Cabo, Mex.	June 11, 1951	Mrs. W. G. Krieger
Atlantic SAILFISH	Istiophorus americanus	83 lbs.	6' 11¾''	32¼''	Key Largo, Fla.	Apr. 4, 1965	Helen K. Grant
Pacific SAILFISH	Istiophorus greyi	146 lbs. 8 oz.	9' ½''	35½''	Palmilla, Mexico	Nov. 14, 1962	Evelyn M. Anderson
SAWFISH	Pristis pectinatus	102 lbs. 12 oz. (12-lb. record for men & women)	8' 6''	29''	Grassy Key, Fla.	June 23, 1961	Marjorie M. McClellan
Blue SHARK	Prionace glauca	150 lbs.	8'	32''	Montauk, N.Y.	July 22, 1962	Dorothea L. Dean
Mako SHARK	Isurus oxyrhynchus	52 lbs. 5 oz.	4' 6½''	27¼''	Montauk, L.I., N.Y.	Sept. 11, 1953	Anne Bowditch
Man-Eater or White SHARK	Carcharodon carcharias						
Porbeagle SHARK	Lamna nasus						
Thresher SHARK	Alopias vulpinus						
Tiger SHARK	Galeocerdo cuvier						
SNOOK or ROBALO	Centropomus undecimalis	32 lbs. 8 oz. (12-lb. record for men & women)	3' 9''	24''	Jupiter, Fla.	Aug. 2, 1957	Mrs. Nancy Neville
SWORDFISH	Xiphias gladius						
TARPON	Tarpon atlanticus	103 lbs. 8 oz.	6' 6''	34''	Islamorada, Fla.	June 16, 1958	Mrs. H. M. Roach
Allison or Yellowfin TUNA	Thunnus albacares	70 lbs.	4' 5''	33''	Sydney, N.S.W., Australia	May 30, 1965	Signa Paton
Atlantic Big-Eyed TUNA	Thunnus obesus						
Pacific Big-Eyed TUNA	Parathunnus sibi						
Blackfin TUNA	Thunnus atlanticus	26 lbs. 12 oz.	2' 11''	23½''	Bermuda	Oct. 18, 1957	Mrs. L. Edna Perinchief
Bluefin TUNA	Thunnus thynnus	39 lbs. 8 oz.	3' 8½''	28''	Tasmania, Australia	May 27, 1963	Mrs. Bob Dyer
WAHOO	Acanthocybium solandri	64 lbs. 8 oz. (12-lb. record for men & women)	5' 5''	26''	Exuma, Bahamas	Apr. 12, 1958	Mrs. Anne Archbold
WEAKFISH	Cynoscion regalis	8 lbs. 14 oz. (Tie 12-lb record for men & women)	2' 8''	15''	Fire Island, N.Y.	June 19, 1954	Mrs. M. S. Hirsch
Spotted WEAKFISH	Cynoscion nebulosus	10 lbs. 4 oz.	2' 6½''	16''	Jupiter, Fla.	June 1, 1958	Nancy Dukes
YELLOWTAIL	Seriola dorsalis or S. grandis	32 lbs.	3'11''	23''	Ponto Inlet, Northland, New Zealand	Jan. 18, 1959	Patricia Low

12-lb. LINE TEST RECORDS

(Up to and including 12 pounds)

Women's Records

Fish	Scientific Name	Weight	Length	Girth	Place	Date	Angler
ALBACORE	Thunnus germo	39 lbs. 8 oz.	3' 7½"	32½"	Balboa, Calif.	July 23, 1958	Dr. R. S. Rubaum
AMBERJACK	Seriola lalandi	76 lbs. 10 oz.	4' 9"	32"	Challenger Bank, Bermuda	Sept. 8, 1963	Joseph Henry Stubbs
BARRACUDA	Sphyraena barracuda	49 lbs. 4 oz.	4' 8"	21½"	Margarita, Venezuela	Jan. 9, 1960	Gerardo Sanson
Calif. Black Sea BASS	Stereolepis gigas	112 lbs. 8 oz.	4' 9"	44"	San Francisco Is., Mex.	June 12, 1957	D. B. Rosenthal
Calif. White Sea BASS	Cynoscion nobilis	65 lbs.	4' 10"	28"	Ensenada, Mexico	July 8, 1955	C. J. Aronis
Channel BASS	Sciaenops ocellatus	60 lbs. 8 oz.	4' 2¾"	29¾"	Kill Devil Hills, N.C.	Oct. 24, 1954	A. Clark, Jr.
Giant Sea BASS	Promicrops itaiara	110 lbs.	4' 10½"	39½"	Islamorada, Fla.	Aug. 2, 1961	Mrs. Gar Wood, Jr.
Sea BASS	Centropristes striatus	3 lbs. 8 oz.	1' 6½"	13¼"	Panama City Beach, Fla.	Aug. 4, 1960	Roy H. Martin
Striped BASS	Roccus saxatilis	61 lbs. 10 oz.	4' 5"	30"	Block Island, R.I.	July 5, 1956	L. A. Garceau
BLACKFISH or TAUTOG	Tautoga onitis	12 lbs.	2' 1½"	20½"	Block Island, R.I.	Oct. 18, 1952	D. V. Marshall
BLUEFISH	Pomatomus saltatrix	24 lbs. 3 oz.	3' 5"	22"	San Miguel, Azores	Aug. 27, 1953	M. A. da Silva Veloso
BONEFISH	Albula vulpes	15 lbs.	2' 10¼"	18¾"	Islamorada, Fla.	Feb. 28, 1961	Nat Carlin
		15 lbs.	2' 8½"	18½"	Bimini, Bahamas	Mar. 20, 1961	Andrea Tose
		15 lbs.	2' 8"	23"	Bimini, Bahamas	Feb. 7, 1953	Sam Snead
		14 lbs. 12 oz.	2' 8¾"	22½"		Apr. 14, 1954	D. H. Braman, Jr.
Oceanic BONITO	Katsuwonus pelamis	24 lbs. 6 oz.	2' 6½"	21"	Walker Cay, Bahamas	Mar. 26, 1965	Patricia E. Church
COBIA	Rachycentron canadus	70 lbs.	5'	31½"	Gulf of Mexico, Texas	May 13, 1955	H. A. Norris, Jr.
COD	Gadus callarias	55 lbs.	5' 6"	38"	Plum Island, Mass.	July 6, 1958	W. C. Dunn
DOLPHIN	Coryphaena hippurus	55 lbs. 2 oz.	4' 11¾"	32½"	Mazatlan, Mexico	Oct. 18, 1964	Marguerite H. Barry
Black DRUM	Pogonias cromis	68 lbs.	4'	36"	Canova Beach, Fla.	Mar. 28, 1958	G. Miller
FLOUNDER	Paralichthys	16 lbs.	2' 10¾"	17¼"	Beavertail, R.I.	Aug. 14, 1958	C. Martorelli
KINGFISH or TANGUIGUE	S. cavalla C. commersonii	52 lbs. 4 oz.	4' 11½"	25½"	Miami, Fla.	Apr. 13, 1958	H. Marin
Black MARLIN	Name being revised	186 lbs. 8 oz.	8' 9"	42¾"	Piñas Bay, Panama	Jan 19, 1963	Ray Smith
Blue MARLIN	Makaira ampla	224 lbs. 8 oz.	9' 2½"	42"	Bimini, Bahamas	Apr. 16, 1960	Harry W. Barton
Pacific Blue MARLIN	Name being revised						
Striped MARLIN	Makaira mitsukurii	250 lbs.	10' 1"	46"	Palmilla, Baja Calif.	Apr. 16, 1965	R. M. Anderson
White MARLIN	Makaira albida	122 lbs.	8' 3"	44"	Bimini, Bahamas	Mar. 30, 1953	Dorothy A. Curtice
PERMIT	Trachinotus goodei	50 lbs.	3' 7"	34½"	Miami, Fla.	Mar. 27, 1965	Robert F. Miller
POLLACK	Pollachius virens	29 lbs. 12 oz.	3' 7"	24½"	Montauk, N.Y.	May 10, 1962	Donald F. Leydon
Rainbow RUNNER	Elagatis bipinnulatus	18 lbs. 12 oz.	3' 2⅞"	20½"	La Cruces, Baja Calif.	May 31, 1961	Bing Crosby
ROOSTERFISH	Nematistius pectoralis	50 lbs. 11 oz.	4' 8"	32"	Guerro, Mexico	Jan. 15, 1961	Joseph Krieger, Jr.
Atlantic SAILFISH	Istiophorus americanus	85 lbs.	7' ½"	31"	Carayaca, Venezuela	July 15, 1962	Guillermo Yanes Pares
Pacific SAILFISH	Istiophorus greyi	159 lbs.	9' 11"	36"	Piñas Bay, Panama	July 23, 1957	J. Frank Baxter
SAWFISH	Pristis pectinatus	102 lbs. 12 oz.	8' 6"	29"	Grassy Key, Fla.	June 23, 1961	Marjorie M. McClellan
Blue SHARK	Prionace glauca	312 lbs.	10' 7"	47"	Montauk, N.Y.	Oct. 28, 1963	John S. Walton
Mako SHARK	Isurus oxyrhynchus I. glaucus	261 lbs. 11 oz.	7' 4"	44½"	Montauk, N.Y.	Oct. 1, 1953	C. R. Meyer
Man-Eater or White SHARK	Carcharodon carcharias	96 lbs. 10 oz.	5' 7"	27½"	Mazatlan, Mexico	Apr. 30, 1964	Ray O. Acord
Porbeagle SHARK	Lamna nasus	66 lbs.	4' 10"	30"	Montauk, N.Y.	June 8, 1958	M. H. Merrill
Thresher SHARK	Alopias vulpinus	92 lbs. 8 oz.	4' 9"	31"	Long Beach, Calif.	Dec. 12, 1959	D. F. Marsh
Tiger SHARK	Galeocerdo cuvier						
SNOOK or ROBALO	Centropomus undecimalis	37 lbs.	3' 11"	24½	Boynton Beach, Fla.	June 18, 1959	Durling Drake
SWORDFISH	Xiphias gladius						
TARPON	Tarpon atlanticus	170 lbs. 8 oz.	7'	40"	Big Pine Key, Fla.	Mar. 10, 1963	Russell C. Ball
Allison or Yellowfin TUNA	Thunnus albacares	94 lbs. 8 oz.	4' 7¼"	36¼"	The Peak, N.S.W., Australia	May 2, 1965	Phillip W. Bensted
Atlantic Big-Eyed TUNA	Thunnus obesus						
Pacific Big-Eyed TUNA	Parathunnus sibi	13 lbs. 8 oz.	2' 6½"	18⅞"	Cabo Blanco, Peru	Apr. 23, 1963	Stanley W. Good, Jr.
Blackfin TUNA	Thunnus atlanticus	19 lbs. 6 oz.	2' 8"	21¾"	South Shore, Bermuda	May 17, 1956	Frank C. Gamble
Bluefin TUNA	Thunnus thynnus	56 lbs.	3' 11½"	32"	S. Neptune Is., Australia	Apr. 12, 1965	Eldred H. V. Riggs
WAHOO	Acanthocybium solandri	64 lbs. 8 oz.	5' 5"	26"	Exuma, Bahamas	Apr. 12, 1958	Mrs. Anne Archbold
WEAKFISH	Cynoscion regalis	9 lbs. 2 oz.	2' 7½"	17"	Tuckerton, N.J.	May 15, 1963	Melvin Parker
		9 lbs. 2 oz.	2' 7½"	15¼"	Oak Beach, N.Y.	Oct. 16, 1953	B. L. DeClue
		9 lbs. 3½ oz.	2' 5"	16½"	Ocean City, Md.	May 26, 1954	Bob Gilbert
		8 lbs. 14 oz.	2' 8"	15"	Fire Island, N.Y.	June 19, 1954	M. S. Hirsch
Spotted WEAKFISH	Cynoscion nebulosus	13 lbs.	2' 10½"	18"	Jupiter, Fla.	July 19, 1956	L. R. Dukes
		13 lbs. 4 oz.	2' 9"	18½"	Cocoa, Fla.	Mar. 13, 1957	R. L. Fink
YELLOWTAIL	Seriola dorsalis or S. grandis	45 lbs. 12 oz.	4' 4"	26½"	Coronado Is., Baja Calif.	June 25, 1964	S. Robert Hettenbach

COMMON NAMES OF SALT-WATER FISH

There are literally thousands of species in our oceans. It would, of course, be impossible to list all the names of salt-water species. But happily, since certain rare or unpopular kinds bite only occasionally when fishing is specifically directed at them, we need only mention the ones most popular with salt-water anglers. The methods of catching the various species are described in Chapter 5 through Chapter 9.

The names of fishes are often confusing. Many hot arguments have been held about the proper name for a given fish. It usually turns out that both sides are right; a fish may have a certain popular name in one part of the country and a different one somewhere else. What we call the weakfish, for example, is also known as the sea trout, squit, squeteague, gray trout, drummer, shad trout, gray weakfish, summer trout, northern weakfish, sun trout, and salt-water trout. Efforts to straighten out this confusion have recently been made by the Outdoor Writers Association of America, the American Fisheries Society, and the Board of Conservation of Florida, in cooperation with the University of Miami. Each has published a valuable check list of fish that includes a careful selection of popular names. Since it is clearly impossible for us to list all the multitudinous synonyms for the most common salt-water fish, we have followed these authorities, especially the first, in our choice of popular names. The scientific name for each species is given in parenthesis, while the "non-standard" names—those which refer to more than one fish or which are of local use only—are listed beneath:

Albacore (Germo alalunga)
Baby tuna, atun, germon, bonito de norte, tuna, chicken-of-the-sea, long-finned albacore, thon blanc.
Albacore, False (Euthynnus alletleratus)
Bonito, little tuna, Atlantic bonito, oceanic bonito, tuna, blue-finned tuna, frigate mackerel, alilonghi, germon, long-finned albacore, blackfin tuna.
Amberjack (Seriola dumerili)

Amberfish, almicore, jack, pez limon, rock salmon, medregal, horse-eye bonito, coronado, great amberfish.

Amberjack, Pacific (Seriola colburni)
California yellowtail, coronado, jack, pez limon.

Angelfish (Chaetodon ocellatus)

Barracuda, Great (Sphyraena barracuda)
Brocket de mer, cuda, kaku, ono, picuda, salt-water muskellunge, salt-water pike, sea pike, sennet, short-finned bass, becuna, sea tiger, Florida barracuda, berry.

Barracuda, Northern (Sphyraena borealis)
Brocket de mer, cuda, kaku, ono, picuda, sea pike, sennet, short-finned bass, tigerfish.

Barracuda, Pacific (Sphyraena argentea)
Brocket de mer, California barracuda, cuda, kaku, ono, picuda, salt-water muskellunge, salt-water pike, sea pike, sennet, short-finned bass, becuna, scooter.

Bass, California Black (Stereolepis gigas)

Bass, California Kelp (Paralabrax clathratus)
Cabrilla, calico bass, kelp bass, sand bass.

Bass, California Sand (Paralabrax nebulifer)
Sand bass.

Bass, California White Sea (Cynoscion nobilis)
Corbina, croaker, white sea bass, sea trout, king croaker, Catalina salmon, Pacific squeteague.

Bass, Red Spotted Rock (Paralabrax maculatofasciatus)
Spotted bass, spotted cabrilla.

Bass, Giant Sea (Promicrops itaiara)
Black sea bass, California black sea bass, giant bass, jewfish, Pacific jewfish.

Bass, Sea (Centropristes striatus)
Bass, blackfish, black harry, black perch, black will, bluefish, hannabil, rock bass, rock fish, tallywog.

Bass, Channel (Sciaenops ocellata)
Bar bass, puppy drum, ratine, red bass, red drum, redfish, reef bass, salt-water bass, sea bass, sergeantfish, bull redfish, drum, branded drum, red horse.

Bass, Striped (Roccus saxatilis)
Greenhead, lineside, rockbass, rockfish, sea bass, squidhound, streaked bass, white bass, striper, rock.

Blowfish (Tetraodon maculatus)
Sea squab.

Bluefish (Pomatomus saltatrix)
Ballerino, blue, blue runner, blue snapper, burel, elf, enxova, greenfish, lufar pez azul, salmon argentino, shad, snapper, snapper blue, snapping mackerel, tassergal, anchoa, fatback, skip mackerel, tailor.

Bonefish (Albula vulpes)
Bananafish, bonyfish, grubber, ladyfish, macabi, macaco, sanducha, O'io.

Bonito, Atlantic (Sarda sarda)
Bloater, blue bonito, bone-eater, bonejack, bonito, bonite, Boston mackerel, frigate mackerel, little tunny, pelmid, skipjack, African bonito.

Bonito, Pacific (Sarda lineolota)
  California bonito, skipjack.
Bonito, Oceanic (Katsuwonus vagans)
  Aku, arctic bonito, bonito, cachoretta, leaping bonito, listao, oceanic skip-jack, skipjack, striped tuna, watermelon tuna, striped bonito.
Cabezon (Scorpaenichthys marmoratus)
  Bullhead, sculpin.
Catfish, Gafftopsail (Bagre marinus)
Catfish, Sea (Galeichthys felis)
Chub, Bermuda (Kyphosus sectatrix)
Cobia (Rachycentron canadus)
  Bacalao, black bonito, black kingfish, black salmon, cabia, cabio, cavio, crab eater, cubby-yew, ling, seakin, sergeantfish, coalfish, lemon fish, seakin.
Cod (Gadus morhua)
Cod, Pacific (Gadus macrocephalus)
Coney (Cephalopholis fulvus)
  Graysby.
Corbina, California (Menticirrhus undulatus)
  Barge, California whiting, corbina, corvina, sand sucker.
Croaker (Mocropogon undulatus)
  Blanca, chut, corbina, corvina, crocus, hardhead, ronco, roncodina.
Croaker, Black (Sciaena saturna)
Croaker, Spotfin (Roncador stearnsi)
Croaker, Yellowfin (Umbrina roncador)
Cultus (Ophiodon elongatus)
  Blue perch, lingcod, longcod, perch.
Cunner (Tautogolabrus adspersus)
  Bergall, bergylt, chogset, nipper.
Dolphin (Coryphaena hippurus)
  Coryphene, dorado de Altura, dourade, mahimahi, dorado.
Drum, Black (Pagonias cromis)
  Bass, big drum, big porgy, butterfish, channel bass, corvina negra, drum, little drum, porgy, sea drum, striped drum.
Eel (Anguilla bostoniensis)
Flounder, Sand (Lophopsetta maculato)
Flounder, Starry (Platichthys stellatus)
Flounder, Summer (Platichthys dentatus)
  Broil, doormat, figleaf, flatfish, flounder, fluke, giant flounder, northern fluke, sand dab, sole, southern flounder, turbot flounder, plaice, puckermouth.
Flounder, Winter (Pseudopleuronectes americanus americanus)
Gag (Mycteroperca microlepis)
Graysby (Petrometopon cruentatus)
  Coney, cabrilla.
Greenling (Hexagrammos decagrammus)
  California sea trout, kelp greenling, greenling seatrout.
Grouper, Black (Mycteroperca bonaci)
  Agaugi, black rockfish, bonaci arara, grouper, jewfish, longboned sunfish, Warsaw, Warsaw grouper, common rockfish.

Grouper, Nassau (Epinephelus striatus)
   Hamlet, cherna criola.
Grouper, Red (Epinephelus morio)
   Cherna, mero, mero quajiro.
Grouper, Rock (Mycteroperca venenosa apua)
   Red rockfish.
Grouper, Yellow (Mycteroperca venenosa)
   Yellowfin grouper.
Grunt, Blue Striped (Haemulon sceurus)
   Yellow grunt.
Grunt, French (Haemulon flavorlineatum)
   Yellow grunt.
Grunt, Gray (Haemulon macrostomum)
   Black grunt, pigfish, striped grunt, sailor's choice.
Grunt, Margate (Haemulon album)
   Bream, sailor's choice.
Grunt, White (Haemulon plamieri)
Haddock (Melanogrammus aeglefinus)
   Egrefin, haddie, schellfisch.
Hake, California (Paralichthys californicus)
Hake, Silver (Merluccius bilinearis)
   Whiting.
Halibut, Atlantic (Hippoglossus hippoglossus)
   Giant sea bass, halibut.
Halibut, California (Paralichthys maculosus)
   Chicken halibut.
Halibut, Pacific (Hippoglossus stenolepis)
   Halibut.
Herring, Common (Clupea harengus)
Hind, Red (Epinephelusgus guttatus)
   Mero quafiro, rockhind, cabrilla.
Hind, Rock (Epinephelus adscensionis)
   Grouper, cabra mora.
Jack, Bigeye (Caranx marginatus)
Jack, Crevallé (Caranx hippos)
   Cavalla, crevallé, pompano, skipjack, toro, ulua, xareo, horsejack, jack,
   jack crevallé, horse crevallé, cavally, jackerville.
Jack, Green (Caranx caballus)
   Jurel.
Jack, Horse-eye (Caranx latus)
   Green jack, goggle-eye jack, jurel de ojo gordo.
Jewfish, Black (Garrupa nigrita)
   Grouper, mero, guasa.
Jewfish, Spotted (Promicrops itaiara)
   Black grouper, black jewfish, black sea bass, Florida jewfish, giant sea bass,
   grouper, mero, Warsaw, Warsaw grouper, June fish.
Kingfish, California (Genyonemus lineatus)
Ladyfish (Elops saurus)

Bananafish, banding, big-eyed herring, bonyfish, chiro, chiro ladyfish, horse mackerel, lisa, menangen, skipjack, ten-pounder, awa-aua, flip flap, silver-fish.

Leatherjack (Dliogoplites sarus)

Mackerel, Atlantic (Scomber scombrus)
Bullseye mackerel, chub mackerel, common mackerel, mackerel, northern mackerel, tinker mackerel.

Mackerel, Cero (Scomberomorus regalis)
Painted mackerel, pintada.

Mackerel, Chub (Pneumatophorus grex)

Mackerel, King (Scomberomorus cavalla)
Cavalla, cero, horse mackerel, king cero, kingfish, pinado, tazza, sierra, sierra canaiera, carite, cierra.

Mackerel, Pacific (Pneumatophorus diego)
Caballa, cape mackerel.

Mackerel, Spanish (Scomberomorus maculatus)
Cavalla, cero, houndfish, mackerel, spaniard, spotted mackerel, bay mack-erel, sierra.

Marlin, Black (Makaira nigricans marlins)
Saku voro waga.

Marlin, Blue (Makaira nigricans ampla)
Aguja, Bimini blue marlin, Cuban black marlin, swordfish, marlin swordfish, spearfish, espada.

Marlin, Silver (Makaira nigricans tahitiensis)

Marlin, Striped (Makaira mitsukurii)

Marlin, White (Makaira albida)
Aguja, aguja blanca, billfish, skellygoelle, great bellfish.

Mullet (Mugil cephalus)

Palometa (Trachinotus glaucus)

Perch, Barred (Amphistiohus argentius)

Perch, White (Marone americana)

Permit (Trachinotus goodei)
Big pompano, crab crusher, Mexican pompano, palometa, round pompano, Key West pompano, Key West permit.

Pigfish (Orthopristis chryopterus)
Sailor's choice.

Pollack, Alaska (Theragra chalcogrammas)
Coalfish.

Pollack, Atlantic (Pollachius virens)
Coalfish, quoddy, pollack, greencod, Boston bluefish, saithe.

Pompano (Trachinotus carolinus)
Carolina pompano, cobblefish, cobbler, crevallé, palometa, permit, butter-fish.

Pompano, Africa (Hynnis cubensis)

Pompano, Round (Trachinotus falcatus)
Palometa, permit.

Pompon (Anisotremus surinamensis)
Black margate.

Porgy, Grass (Calamus arctifrons)

Porgy, Jolthead (Calamus bajonado)
Porgy, Northern (Stenotomus chrysops)
 Ironsides, maiden, paugy, scup, scuppang, fair main.
Porgy, Southern (Stenotomus aculeatus)
 Peje pluma.
Queenfish (Seriphus politus)
Roosterfish (Nematistius pectoralis)
Runner, Blue (Caranx crysos)
 Jack crevallé, cojinua.
Runner, Rainbow (Elagatis bipinnulatus)
 Runner.
Sablefish (Anoplopoma fimbria)
Sailfish, Atlantic (Istiophorus americanus)
 Aguja voladora, bannerfish, pez vela, spearfish, sail, spikefish, billfish, boo-
 koo, guebucu, saku laca, aguja prieta, boohoo.
Sailfish, Pacific (Istiophorus greye)
 Pez vela, spearfish, spikefish, sail, billfish, saku laca.
Sailor's Choice (Haemulon parra)
Salmon, Atlantic (Salmo salar salar)
Salmon, Chinook (Oncorhynchus tshawytscha)
 King salmon, quinnot salmon, spring salmon, tchavicha, tschawytscha, tyee,
 tule, Sacramento River salmon, Columbia River salmon, blackmouth salmon.
Salmon, Chum (Oncorhynchus keta)
 Dog salmon, keta, calico.
Salmon, Humpback (Oncorhynchus gorbuscha)
 Pink salmon, humpy.
Salmon, Silver (Oncorhynchus kisutch)
 Coho salmon, silversides, white salmon, Skowitz, Pacific salmon.
Salmon, Sockeye (Oncorhynchus nerka)
 Red salmon, blueback salmon, Kokanee, kickaninny.
Sawfish (Pristis pectinatus)
 Serrucho.
 (Hardly a sport fish, but it has been taken often enough with rod and
 reel off the Texas coast to deserve a place in this check list.)
Sculpin (Acanthocottus octpdecemspinous)
 Hacklehead, pigfish, sea toad.
Seatrout (Cynoscion regalis)
Seatrout, Sand (Cynoscion arenarius)
Seatrout, Silver (Cynoscion nothus)
Seatrout, Spotted (Cynoscion nebulosus)
 Spotted trout.
Sandfish (Diplectrum formosum)
 Sand perch.
Shad (Alosa sapidissima)
Shad, Hickory (Pomolobus mediocris)
Shark, Atlantic (Isurus oxyrinchus)
Shark, Blue (Prionace glauca)
Shark, Bonito (Isurus glaucus)
Shark, Hammerhead (Sphyrna zygaena)

Shark, Large Black-tip (Eulamia maculipinnis)
    Spinner-shark.
Shark, Lesser Black-tip (Eulamia limbatus)
Shark, Mako (Isurus glaucus or Isurus oxyrhynchus)
    Mackerel shark.
Shark, Nurse (Ginglymostoma cirratum)
Shark, Porbeagle (Lamna nasus)
Shark, Sand (Carcharias taurus)
    Dogfish, sand tiger.
Shark, Thresher (Alopias vulpinus)
Shark, Tiger (Galeocerdo arcticus)
Shark, White (Carcharodon carcharias)
    Man-eating shark.
Sheepshead (Archosargus probatocephalus)
    Sargo raiado, convict, bajonado.
Sheepshead, California (Pimelometopon pulcher)
    California redfish.
Snapper, Dog (Lutjanus jocu)
    Pargo colorado, jocu.
Snapper, Lane (Lutjanus synagris)
    Biajaiba, redtail snapper, spot snapper.
Snapper, Mangrove (Lutjanus griseus)
    Caballerote, pargo prieto, red snapper, gray snapper.
Snapper, Mullet (Lutjanus aratus)
    Anding, loban, striped mullet.
Snapper, Muttonfish (Lutjanus analis)
    Mutton snapper, pargo, pargo criallo, red snapper.
Snapper, Red (Lutjanus backfordii)
    Acara aija, Mexican snapper, pargo colorado, Pensacola red snapper, pargo
    criollo.
Snapper, Schoolmaster (Lutjanus apodus)
    Black snapper, caji, dog snapper.
Snapper, Yellowtail (Ocyurus chrysurus)
    Florida yellowtail, Key West yellowtail, rabirrubia.
Snook (Centropomus undecimalis)
    Pike, robalo, sergeant, sergeantfish, brochet de mer.
Sole, Lemon (tsettichthus melanostictus)
Spiny Dogfish (Squalus acanthias)
Spot (Leiostomus xanthurus)
    Lafayette.
Surfperch (Phanerodon furcatus)
        (This species includes a number of similar small fish found in the surf.)
Swordfish (Xiphias gladius)
    Albacora, broadbill swordfish, vehuella, sofia, espada.
Tarpon (Tarpon atlanticus)
    Grande ecaille, sabalo, tarpum, savalle, savanilla, silver king.
Tautog (Tautoga onitis)
    Bergall, blackfish, black porgy, chub, moll, oysterfish, white chin.
Tripletail (Lobotes surinamensis)

Blackfish, black perch, black tripletail, buoyfish, chobie, flasher, sunfish.

Tuna, Allison (Thunnus albacares)

Tuna, Atlantic (Thunnus secundodorsalis)

Tuna, Atlantic Big-eyed (Thunnus obesus)

Tuna, Atlantic Blackfin (Thunnus atlanticus)

Bermuda tuna, black-finned albacore, albacora.

Tuna, Atlantic Yellowfin (Neothunnus argentivitatus)

Allison tuna, atun, long-finned tuna, thon, thon rouge, tunny, yellowfin tuna, yellowtail.

Tuna, Bluefin (Thunnus thynnus)

Atun, giant tuna, school tuna, thon, thon rouge, jubaan, horse tuna, horse mackerel, leaping tuna, great albacore, tuny.

Tuna, Pacific Big-eyed (Parathunnus sibi)

Tuna, Pacific Yellowfin (Neothunnus macropterus)

Atun, long-finned tuna, tunny, yellowtail.

Tomcod (Microgadus tomcod)

Tomcod, Pacific (Microgadus proximus)

Wahoo (Acanthocybium solandri)

Becane, bonito negro, guarapucu, Pacific kingfish, ono, peto, queenfish, relee, ocean barracuda.

Weakfish (Cynoscion regalis)

Gator trout, gray squeteaque, gray trout, salt-water trout, sand squeteaque, sea trout, silver squeteaque, Northern weakfish, squeteaque, sun trout, trout, squit, drummer, summer trout.

Weakfish, Sand (Cynoscion arenarius)

Sand trout.

Weakfish, Silver (Cynoscion nothus)

Weakfish, Spotted (Cynoscion nebulosus)

Gator trout, salt-water trout, sea trout, southern weakfish, southern sea trout, spotted squeteaque, spotted sea trout, sun trout, trout, salt-water trout, speckled sea trout.

White fish, Ocean (Caulolatilus princeps)

Whiting, Northern (Menticirrhus saxatilis)

Barb, hogfish, kingfish, king whiting, sea mink, sea mullet, sea perch, northern kingfish, hake, black mullet

Whiting, Silver (Menticirrhus littoralis)

Ground mullet, gulf kingfish.

Whiting, Southern (Menticirrhus americanus)

Barb, corvina, gulf kingfish, hogfish, kingfish, king whiting, sea mink, sea mullet, sea perch, southern kingfish.

Yellowtail, Pacific (Seriola dorsalis)

Dorado, jaurel, kingfish, saga, yellowtail, yellow-finned albacore, white salmon.

GLOSSARY OF SALT-WATER FISHING TERMS

AGATE GUIDES. Rod guides with rings of agate through which the line passes.

AGATINE GUIDES. Rod guides consisting of rings of glass mounted in metal rings.

ANADROMOUS. Ascending from salt to fresh water for spawning (striped bass, shad, salmon, and some trout). Opposite of "catadromous."

ANTIBACKLASH. A reel with a device to keep it from backlashing or forming tangles.

ANTIREVERSE. A device on a spinning reel that prevents the handle from turning backward.

ANTITWIST KEEL. A lead or plastic fin-shaped device with its largest part off center. It is usually used with a swivel directly behind it and is attached to a line ahead of the lure, preventing the line from being twisted or kinked by the action of the lure.

ARTIFICIAL BAIT *or* ARTIFICIAL. Any kind of manufactured lure except a fly.

BACK CAST. Cast behind the angler to develop energy for the forward throw of the line or lure.

BACKING. Line placed on the reel under the casting line to fill up the reel. It is available as reserve line for playing large fish.

BACKLASH. A tangle or snarl caused when a reel spool revolves faster than line passes off it.

BAIL. A hinged loop on the front of a spinning reel that picks up the line for retrieving; used instead of a pickup finger.

BAIT CASTING. Method of fishing employing a weighted lure, a multiplying reel, and a short rod, usually six feet or less in length.

BAIT FISHING. Fishing with a natural lure or any form of manufactured lure except a fly.

BAIT RIG. Hook or hooks assembled on a line or leader for the purpose of holding bait.

BALANCED TACKLE. A general term meaning that the component parts of a fishing outfit (rod, reel, and line) work together in harmony.

BALE HOOK. A gaff-type hook used to help land large fish by pulling the fish's tail out of the water.

BALLOON. A rubber device occasionally used as a float—especially with the large baits used in big-game fishing.

BANK SINKER. An elongated sinker with an eye cast into its slim end.

BARRACUDA. A feather jig with an eye on the top of the head for attachment to a leader. (Also the name of a fish species.)

BARREL SWIVEL. A swivel similar to the BOX SWIVEL but with the inner ends of the wires enclosed in a barrel-shaped structure.

BEACH BAG. A carry-all bag used by the surf angler to hold his tackle.

BEACH BUGGY. An automobile or truck especially fitted with large tires for transporting surf anglers along sandy beaches.

BIG-GAME FISH. Fish species of large size and fighting ability. Examples: swordfish, tuna, marlin, sailfish, and shark.

BILL A FISH. To grasp a billfish by the spear in order to boat the fish.

BIRD'S NEST = BACKLASH.

BLADE. The part of the rod other than the handle.

BOTTOM FISHING. Angling for bottom-feeding fish with a hook held near or on the bottom by a sinker.

BOX SWIVEL. A swivel shaped like an open box with a hole at each end. In each hole is an eyed wire, with the end of the wire enlarged so that it will not pull out. The wires rotate freely and prevent line twist.

BOW. Forward part of a boat.

BRACKISH WATER. A combination of both salt and fresh water.

BREAKING STRAIN. Strength of fishing line; see POUND TEST.

BREAK OUT. For a fish to show itself on the surface of the water.

BUCKTAIL. A fly with wings of fur or hair. It is normally a long fly and is usually placed on a long-shanked hook.

BUG. A lure characterized by a thick and rather clumsy body much heavier than the typical fly.

BUTT. The handle of a rod.

BUTT GUIDE. The guide next to the grip on the bottom section of a fishing rod.

BUTT JOINT. The bottom section of a fishing rod that is in two or more sections.

CABLE. Wires twisted to form a single strand.

CATADROMOUS. See ANADROMOUS.

CHARTER BOAT. A boat for hire, available to an angler or a group of anglers by the day, week, or month.

CHUMMING. Attracting or holding fish by throwing whole or cut pieces of fish into the water.

CHUM POT. Screened container filled with ground fish or other bait and lowered to the bottom. Bait particles and odor seeping through screen attract fish.

CHUNKING. CHUMMING with large pieces of fish or with whole fish.

CLINCH SINKER. A deeply grooved lead weight. The line is placed in the groove, and the sides are pinched together on the line.

CRADLE REEL. A reel with a mounting that puts the reel spool on the same plane as the rod blade.

CRIPPLES. Injured fish.

CROSS WINDING. A method of spooling the line in some spinning reels so that each turn of the line crosses the previous turn and produces a crisscross pattern.

CRUISER. Large craft in the small-boat class, powered by either outboard or inboard engine.

CUTTYHUNK. A twisted linen line, each thread of which has a wet test of three pounds; the threads are in multiples of three, from 6-thread to 72-thread. Named for Cuttyhunk Island, Massachusetts.

DAY CRUISER. Stripped-down version of the standard cruiser, usually without sleeping accommodations.

DIPSEY. A pear-shaped sinker with a flat bottom and a revolving wire tie-on through its middle.

DISGORGER. A metal or plastic instrument used to remove a hook from the mouth of a fish. It backs the hook out, then protects the point of the hook as it is withdrawn.

DOUBLED LINE. In big-game fishing, the part of the line attached to the leader is doubled, sometimes for as much as thirty feet.

DRAG. A brake on a reel.

DRAIL. A hook whose shank is covered with lead. It is generally used in deep trolling.

DRIFT FISHING. Angling from a drifting boat with bait or lure trailing.

DROPPING BACK. The pause before setting the hook, permitting line to unwind from a reel after certain big-game fish take the bait.

EDDY. A circular movement of water at the junction of two opposing currents.

EEL BOB. A whole eel, with head removed, attached to a lead head and used for surf casting.

EELSKIN LURE. An eel's skin fastened to a metal head which has a hole in it to allow a flow of water to inflate the eelskin.

EELSKIN SQUID. A metal squid with a ring attached, to which an eelskin is fastened.

EGG SINKER. A sinker somewhat tapered at both ends into an egg-shaped form.

END PLATE. The round plates at the ends of a reel.

END TACKLE = TERMINAL TACKLE.

FEATHER JIG. A jig with a bullet-shaped metal head followed by a bunch of feathers.

FERRULE. The plug and socket used at the joint of a rod.

FINGER = PICKUP FINGER.

FISH STRINGER. A string or chain on which live fish are kept.

FLAPPER. A lure with a spinner blade attached so that it flaps and waves rather than spins.

FLAPTAIL. A lure with a FLAPPER at the terminal end.

FLASHER. A shiny metal lure that flashes to attract fish.

FLIP CAST. Cast in which the rod tip is flipped down and up in a short, quick movement to send lure forward.

FLOAT. A device which is attached above the hook on the line, and, by its actions, warns of a fish's presence. Floats are made of a variety of materials, cork and plastic being the most common.

FLOATERS. Lures which float when at rest, no matter whether they run upon the surface or underwater in retrieve.

FLY. A lure, an imitation of an insect or some other fish food, constructed of feathers, thread, and tinsel.

FLY CASTING. Method of fishing in which extremely light lures (mainly flies) are carried out by the weight of the line. A long rod, generally over seven feet, is used.

FOOT = REEL FOOT.

FOUL *or* FOULING. The snarling of any part of an angler's gear.

FOUL HOOKED. Applied to a fish hooked other than through the mouth.

FREE FISH. Fish (especially big-game) sighted but not hooked.

FREE-SPOOL CLUTCH. A clutch on a reel that allows the spool to revolve independently of any other mechanism.

FREE-SPOOL REEL. A reel in which the spool runs freely on the cast, the rest of the mechanism (including the handle) not being actuated.

GAFF. An instrument which holds a fish while he is being landed.

GAME FISH. Any species of fish known for its fighting qualities.

GATHERING GUIDE. The large butt guide on a spinning rod that gathers up the spiraling line and funnels it onto the next guide.

GEAR RATIO. The ratio of gears in a reel to produce a certain number of revolutions of the spool or retrieving mechanism for each turn of the handle.

GIMBAL. A socket, usually of leather, into which a rod butt fits; it helps an angler in holding the rod while playing a large fish. One type is fastened to the fishing chair; another, the girdle gimbal, is worn directly on the angler's belt.

GIN POLE. A stout, short mast fitted with a block and tackle at the upper end, used to load big-game fish aboard a boat.

GREYHOUNDING. A series of long, low jumps, as often made by a hooked marlin, and occasionally by a sailfish.

GUIDE. (1) A fitting mounted on a rod through which the line passes; a series of such fittings being fastened to the rod at intervals to direct the line from the reel to the tip of the rod. (2) An angling assistant or helper familiar with a particular location.

GUNWALE. The edge where the deck meets the sides and stern of a boat.

GUT. Material used for leaders, processed from silkworms.

HAND LINE. Baited hook and line manipulated by hand rather than from a rod.

HARNESS. Gear worn by a big-game angler to aid in transmitting muscular power to the rod or to absorb strain.

HEART-SHAPED SINKER. A thin, flat sinker which, when unattached, resembles the outline of a heart; pinched onto the line, it becomes a keeled sinker.

HIGH GUIDE. A big-game rod guide constructed so that the line is carried an inch or more from the rod surface.

HOOK HONE. A small stone used to sharpen fish hooks. Many have a groove in the center into which the point of the hook fits.

HORSE IT IN. To pull in a fish as rapidly as possible without giving him a chance to fight.

HOT SPOT. A good fishing area or location.

HUMPING. A fish showing part of his back above the surface.

ICE CREEPERS. A spiked shoe or foot covering worn by surf anglers to obtain secure footing when climbing slippery rock or wood jetties, etc.

IGFA. Abbreviation for International Game Fish Association, organized to promote better sport in big-game fishing by establishing rules and regulations and to register record catches of big-game fish.

INSHORE. Close to the shore, or toward the shore.

INSHORE FISHING. A type of angling done near the shore.

INTEGRAL KEEL. A keel built into a lure, especially popular in spinning lures.

JAPANESE JIG. A feathered jig having a shiny metal head followed by a bunch of feathers.

JERK-TURN. A method of retrieving a plug in the surf, popular on the West Coast.

JETTY. A structure, usually made of wood or wood and stone, that is built out into the water from the shore.

Jig. A bullet-shaped metal head followed by a bunch of feathers, a bucktail, etc.

Jigging. A method of angling in which a lure is raised and lowered rapidly on the bottom to make a fish strike.

Keel. A metal or plastic device used to keep the line from twisting; fastened between the leader and the line.

Keel-swivel = keel.

Knuckle-duster. An old-style salt-water reel, the handle of which turned when the line was running out.

Landing net. A bag-shaped net used in landing fish.

Lead = sinker.

Leader. A connecting length of line between the line proper and the lure, or between the hook and the snap (or swivel) at the end of the line. The leader is usually of stronger test than the line.

Leather drag. A flap of sole leather hinged to the crossbar of a reel, used to control spool speed in casting or as a brake in playing the fish.

Lee. The side opposite that from which the wind is blowing.

Leeward. The lee side.

Left-hand wind. A revolving-spool reel with the handle on the left side or a spinning reel with the handle on the right side.

Leg. The connecting rod between the foot of a spinning reel and the reel proper.

Level wind. A mechanism that spools the line evenly over the spool.

Lever. The device which actuates a free spool clutch on a reel.

Line capacity. The amount of a certain size and type of line that a reel spool will contain; often used to designate the size of a reel.

Line clip. A small spring clip of metal or plastic that snaps around the spool of a spinning reel to keep the line in place when the reel is not being used.

Line dryer. A device to hold line in large coils while it dries, or to assist the angler in changing lines from one reel to another, or for line storage.

Line guide. The eye of metal, agate, or glass which holds the line in place on the rod.

Line marker. An object, such as a piece of thread, fastened to a line at measured intervals to indicate how much line is out.

Line spool. The spool on a reel that contains the line.

Line test = pound test.

Live bait. Food used in luring a fish to a hook, as distinct from artificials, which are imitations of food designed to achieve the same purpose.

Live line. A line that is baited but unweighted, moved to or from the angler by currents, tides, and waves.

Loose hook. A hook which is fastened to a leader wire by means of a loop threaded through the eye of the hook, permitting it to swing loosely. Conversely, a solid hook is one that is fastened to the leader in such a way that it cannot move independently of the leader.

Low guide. A guide which carries the line close to the rod surface.

Lure. Live or artificial bait used to attract fish.

Manual pickup. A system of retrieving used on a spinning reel whereby the line is picked up by the fingers and engaged in the retrieving mechanism.

Matched outfit. A rod, a reel, and a line that work well together.

Metal squid. An artificial lure shaped to resemble a salt-water minnow, usually a sand eel or mullet.

MONEL. A rustproof alloy, largely composed of nickel, used for fishing lines.

MONOFILAMENT. A synthetic plastic material in a single strand used for lines and leaders.

MONOLON. A type of line consisting of fine wire braided around a nylon monofilament core.

MOOCHING. A method of catching salmon used on the West Coast.

MULTIPLYING REEL. A reel the spool of which revolves more times than does the handle.

OFFSET HANDLE. A rod handle with some portion, usually the reel seat, not in a direct line with the rod blade.

OFFSHORE. Well beyond the surf and the middle ground, therefore deep water. Not necessarily out of sight of land.

OFFSHORE FISHING. Fishing roughly a mile or more away from the shore.

ONSHORE FISHING. A type of fishing wherein the angler fishes from the shore at such places as jetties, piers, breakwaters, etc.

OPEN BOAT. Any small craft which is not decked over, or has no more than a very short bow deck forming a small bow locker.

OPEN PARTY BOAT. A fishing boat available to anglers which sails on regular daily schedules—as contrasted with a charter boat, which sails only when specifically hired by an individual or group.

OUTFIT = TACKLE.

OUTRIGGER. A framework extending outboard from the side of a boat, used primarily in trolling for big-game fish.

OVERHEAD CAST. Casting method in which the rod tip travels through a vertical, overhead arc.

OVERRUN = BACKLASH.

PARALLEL WINDING. A method of spooling the line in a spinning reel in which each turn of the line is almost exactly parallel to the previous turn. The opposite of CROSS WINDING.

PAY OUT. Releasing line from the reel, usually while the lure or bait is being trolled or carried by a fish.

PERSUADER = PRIEST.

PICKUP. The device for picking up the line in a spinning gear; it may be finger, bail, or manual.

PICKUP FINGER. A curved, fingerlike member on the front of a spinning reel which picks up the line after a cast and guides it while it is being spooled.

PINCH-ON LEAD = CLINCH SINKER.

PLAIN-THREADED KEEL. An anti-twist keel having holes through which the line is threaded.

PLAYING A FISH. Fighting a hooked fish to tire it out before landing it.

PLUG. A lure of wood or plastic primarily intended to be cast out and retrieved. May also be trolled or used in still-fishing.

PLUG CASTING; PLUGGING. Bait casting.

POP A LINE. To snap a line.

POP CASTING. Bait casting with a surface lure, which is now and then made to "pop" or disturb the water by a sudden twist of the rod tip.

POPPERS. Lures with hollowed-out heads which produce a popping noise when retrieved in jerks.

POUND TEST. A term indicating the dead weight that a line or leader will support. This is a standard way of classifying lines.

PRIEST. A weighted billy club used to kill a fish by hitting it on the head; some have a knife blade in the handle.

PROPELLER BLADE. A type of spinner blade resembling the propeller of an airplane.

PUMPING. Reeling in a fish by raising the rod tip, then dropping it suddenly, and taking up the slack line thus created.

PURIST. A fisherman who uses nothing but artificials.

PYRAMID SINKER. A lead sinker in a sharp pyramid shape.

QUADRUPLE MULTIPLYING REEL. A reel the spool of which revolves four times for every turn of the handle.

RACE. A strong, surging tide or current.

RAISE A FISH. To attract a fish to a trolled bait.

REEL. A spool set in a frame, usually of metal, which is attached to the rod butt near the hand for the purpose of controlling line movement when angling.

REEL FOOT. The part of a reel that fits against the reel seat; a term especially used with spinning reels.

REEL HARNESS. A harness of leather which helps an angler hold large rod and reel.

REEL HOOD. A ring around a reel seat with an overhang under which the shoe or foot of the reel is placed.

REEL SEAT. The area of the rod handle or grip where the reel is fastened. It is generally provided with a device to hold the reel in place.

RELEASING FISH. There are three ways of freeing a fish which has been brought alongside the boat. It may be unhooked; or the leader wire may be cut reasonably close to the fish's mouth; or, when using light leader wire, the angler then may take a wrap of the light wire around his gloved hand and yank hard in order to break the leader at the eye of the hook. The latter two methods are preferred.

RETRIEVING SPEED. The speed at which a reel retrieves line; in a spinning reel, the speed is generally given in inches retrieved for each turn of the handle.

REVERSIBLE HANDLE. A spinning reel handle that may be turned in toward the main housing of reel for convenience in transportation, storage, etc.

RIG. Colloquial term for a fishing unit, such as a surf-casting rig, spinning rig, big-game rig, etc.

RIGGED EEL. A whole eel rigged with hooks for casting in the surf.

RIP. Disturbed water caused by one current meeting another flowing in a different direction, or a current meeting comparatively still water.

RISE. A visible disturbance on the surface of the water which indicates that a fish is feeding or rising to inspect food.

ROD. A manufactured stick, in one piece or in two or more sections joined together by ferrules, which tapers progressively from butt to tip and is fitted with guides, hand grasp or grasps, and reel seat.

ROD BELT. A rod support used especially by surf anglers. The butt of the rod fits into a cup on the belt and allows the angler to use the rod and reel to best advantage.

ROD BLADE = BLADE.

ROD CARRIER. A device for holding one or several rods on the top of an automobile. The carrying supports, usually two, are clipped to the rain gutter, and the rods are held in place by pressure or by being tied.

ROD CLAMP. A device, frequently a ring with a tightening nut, to hold a reel onto a rod.

ROD GIMBAL = GIMBAL.

ROD GRIP. The portion of a fishing rod grasped by the hand or hands.

ROD HOLDER. A device which holds a rod off the side of the boat for still-fishing or trolling; another type jams into the ground or dock and holds the rod for still-fishing. They are generally adjustable as to height and angle.

ROD WINDER. A spooling device used for winding the line on a rod evenly and neatly.

ROLL = BREAK OUT.

ROLLER. The small, spool-shaped metal roller, found on most spinning reels, over which the line passes while being spooled.

ROLLER GUIDE. A guide consisting of a metal roller mounted on an axle, sometimes on ball bearings; it is used on big-game rods.

ROLLER TIP. A rod tip consisting of a metal wheel revolving on an axle; it is used to reduce friction on big-game rods.

RUN. (1) Movement of a hooked fish in going to or from the angler, or (2) abundance of a species of fish in an area, often occurring periodically.

RUSH. The first dash of a hooked fish away from the angler.

SALMON FLY. Typically, an elongated wet fly of highly elaborate design; as many as two dozen different materials may be used in one fly.

SALMON REEL. A sturdily constructed, single-action fly reel of large capacity.

SAND SPIKE. A tube-like rod holder used by surf anglers to hold their rods when not in actual use. It consists of a spike that is pushed into the sand and a hollow sleeve in which the rod is held.

SCALER. A metal instrument for removing the scales from a fish.

SEAT = REEL SEAT.

SECTION. One of the pieces of a jointed rod.

SELF THUMBER. A reel provided with a device to prevent backlashing or overrunning.

SET. A bend or curvature of the rod blade.

SETH GREEN RIG. A rig consisting of a sinker above which a series of leadered hooks are fastened at regular intervals; it is used for still-fishing and trolling.

SET THE HOOK. To strike the fish with a tight enough drag on the reel to drive the point of the hook deep into the fish's jaw.

SHANK. The portion of a hook extending from the eye to the bend.

SIDE CAST. Cast made with the rod swinging parallel to the water.

SIDE SWIPER = SIDE CAST.

SINGLE ACTION REEL. A reel the spool of which turns at the same rate as the handle.

SINKER. A lead weight used to keep the line and lure on the bottom or to give additional weight to a line and lure.

SNAP. A fastening device to facilitate the quick changing of terminal tackle, generally found on one side of the leader.

SNAP SWIVEL. A swivel with a snap connector used to prevent line twist and to expedite changing of lures.

SNELL. A section of gut, nylon, wire, or other material attached to a hook shank; it serves as a leader for small fish.

SNELLED HOOK. A hook attached to a piece of gut or nylon.

SOLID HOOK. See LOOSE HOOK.

SOUNDING. The deep diving of a hooked fish.

SPECIFICATION ROD. A rod of a specified weight and length, to fit into a given class of salt-water angling. The different clubs and associations have their own specifications.

SPIN CASTING. A method of casting in which the line peels from a reel spool that does not turn, in an action similar to that of pulling thread from one end of an ordinary sewing machine spool. This "frictionless" casting permits long casts with extremely light lures.

SPINNER. A blade of metal or other material that spins when drawn through the water, used as a lure.

SPINNING. (1) A variety of fishing employing a fixed spool reel and a thin line. (2) A method of angling for West Coast salmon.

SPINNING REEL. A fixed spool reel with the axis of the spool in line with the rod; the reel is hung under the rod. Spinning reels are generally wound with the left hand.

SPLIT-HOLE KEEL. An ANTITWIST KEEL having a split above each hole through which the line is forced, making it possible to attach the keel without threading the line through the hole.

SPLIT RING. A ring used as a connector. It can be opened by running the split section of the ring through a hole or wire loop.

SPLIT-SHOT LEAD. Small, round sinkers, from BB size on up, with a deep groove into which the line is inserted; the sinker is then pinched onto the line.

SPOOL. The cylindrical device on which the line is wound in a reel.

SPOON. A large spinner or a wobbler.

SPREADER. A bow-shaped wire device used to keep hooks separated. Hooks are attached at either end, and the line is attached to a center swivel.

SPRING BUTT. A rather long, flexible butt used on a surf rod.

SQUID. A metal, usually block tin, imitation of a squid or baitfish, used as a lure.

SQUIDDING ROD. A rod used for the casting and retrieving of artificial lures in the surf.

STAR DRAG. A brake to prevent the pulling out of line from a reel, generally adjusted with a pronged wheel somewhat similar to a star in shape.

STERN. The after part of a boat.

STILL-FISHING. Fishing (usually with live bait) from a boat anchored and lodged at a set place. Bank, jetty, dock, and bridge fishing is also considered by many to be still-fishing.

STOP DOG. An antireverse device used on a spinning reel.

STRAIGHT HANDLE. A handle all parts of which are in line with the rod blade.

STRAIGHT OFFSET HANDLE. A rod handle with the reel seat out of line with the rod blade, but with the grip in line.

STREAMER. An elongated wet fly; specifically, such a fly with feather wings.

STRIKE. The contact of a fish with the bait.

STRIKING A FISH. Hooking a fish by giving the rod a jerk or twitch, or by braking the reel spool.

STRIP BAIT. A thin, diamond-shaped strip of flesh cut from the lower side of a fish, used in trolling. Also known as cut bait and flesh strips.

STRIP THE LINE. To pull line rapidly off a free-spool reel, or when the drag is reduced to a minimum.

SURFACE. For a fish, especially a hooked fish, to break the surface (though not necessarily to jump), or to swim sufficiently close to the surface so that it can clearly be seen.

SURFACE-RUSHING. The action of big-game fish when hooked in swimming off near the top of the water. Opposite of SOUNDING.

SURF BOTTOM FISHING. Fishing from a beach or jetty with tight line and with live bait lying on the ocean bottom.

SURF CASTING. Fishing from a beach or jetty with artificial lures.

SWELLED BUTT. An increase in the diameter of the rod just above the grip or handle.

SWELLED HANDLE. A rod handle thick in the middle and tapering at the ends.

SWIRL. Whirling motion on water surface caused by a fish.

SWIVEL. A connector constructed so that the eye at either end will revolve freely without turning the opposite end.

TACKLE. All manufactured items that the angler requires for fishing.

TACKLE BOX. A waterproof box used to carry lures, hooks, reels, and other items of tackle.

TAILED UP FISH. A fish whose tail has become fouled up in the leader wire, and is thereby hampered in swimming or cannot swim at all.

TAILER. A stick with a noose on one end which is slipped over the tail of a fish to land it.

TAILING. The emerging of a fish's tail above the water surface. In shallow water, a sign of feeding fish. Big-game fish, swimming close to the surface, often expose their tail.

TAIL ROPE. A short, stout length of rope used to land a big-game fish after he has been gaffed.

TAIL WALKING. Hooked fish skipping over the water surface on their tails, their bodies vertical, in an effort to shake the hook.

TAP. The strike of a swordfish, marlin, or sailfish; they seem to tap the bait with their bills instead of striking like other big-game fish.

TAPER. The decrease in size of a rod from butt to tip.

TEASER. An extra-large plug (12 to 16 inches in length) without hooks that is towed astern on a short line to attract fish to the surface where they will more readily see trolled baits.

TEMPTER = TEASER.

TERMINAL TACKLE. Any items of tackle such as leaders, sinkers, swivels, snaps, and hooks, used at the end of a line to aid in catching fish.

TEST = POUND TEST.

THREAD. The unit of a linen line; each thread in a standard line has a wet test of three pounds. Lines are made in multiples of three threads.

THREAD LINE. (1) Linen fishing line; (2) very fine spinning line.

THREE-WAY SWIVEL. Three swivels in the shape of a "Y"; the line is attached to one end, a sinker to another, and the bait to the third.

THROW A HOOK. A fish's shaking itself loose from a hook.

THROW LINE = HAND LINE.

THROW-OFF LEVER. The lever on a reel used to throw the mechanism into free spool.

THUMBING. Thumb pressure on a moving reel spool to prevent its moving faster than the unrolling line.

TIDEWATER. That part of any body of water connected to the ocean, as a bay, a river, an inlet, or a sound, which shows the effects of the tide.

TIE-ON. A ring-shaped device on a plug or sinker, to which the leader or line is fastened.

TIGHT LINE. A line kept taut; usually means a taut line after a fish is hooked.

TINNED WIRE. Steel wire with a tin plating.

TIP-ACTION ROD. A rod which, when under stress, bends mainly in the tip.

TIP GUIDE. A guide on the tip section of a rod.

TIP JOINT. Terminal joint of a fishing rod.

TIP TOP. The guide at the tip of a rod.

TOP-WATER LURE. A lure which stays on the surface of the water while being retrieved.

TRACE = LEADER.

TRANSOM. Part of the hull upon which motors are mounted, in the extreme stern of the boat.

TROLLING. Fishing by towing a lure behind a boat at slow speed.

TROLLING KEEL. A KEEL-SWIVEL attachment used to prevent a trolled lure from twisting the line.

TURN A FISH. To cause a hooked fish to alter course, generally 90 degrees or more, either by applying pressure on the fishing line or by changing the angle of the line.

TURN ON A FISH. A manoeuvre performed in big-game fishing in which the boat is brought about quickly in order to be in a position to follow a fish.

TWISTED WIRE. Line consisting of thin strands of wire twisted into a cable.

UNDERHAND CAST. A cast made by dangling line below the rod tip and swinging the lure back and forth like a pendulum before releasing it.

WADERS. An article of wading equipment that extends to the chest; made of rubber, plastic, or nylon, or a combination of all three.

WADING SANDALS. A light sandal with a felt sole; worn over wading shoes to give the angler extra protection against slipping on rocks or moss.

WADING SHOE. A heavy shoe used for wading. There are two general types: a leather shoe with a felt or metal-hobbed sole and a canvas shoe with a felt sole.

WADING STOCKING. A heavy part-wool stocking worn under the wading shoe.

WEIGHTED KEEL. A keel made of a heavy material, as against one made of plastic.

WET FLY. A fly designed to sink when cast.

WET TEST. The amount of dead weight that a line will support when wet.

WHITE WATER. Foaming water at the beach where the surf is breaking.

WINDINGS. The thread wrapped around a rod to hold in place guides, etc.

WIRE LINE. Wire used as a fishing line.

WOBBLER. A lure of curved metal or other material that darts and wobbles erratically when drawn through the water.

APPENDIX D

READY HOOK AND BAIT REFERENCE GUIDE
FOR INSHORE AND BOTTOM FISH

The following reference guide is a composite. It offers suggestions regarding hook sizes and bait which are based on selections made by many fisherman over the years. (The same information for game fish can be found in Chapters 7 and 8.)

Species	Hook	Bait	Method*
Angelfish	No. 4 to 6	Bits of shrimp and crab	S
Bass, California kelp	No. 1 to 1/0	Sardines, anchovies, clams, mussels, sea worms, shrimp	T, C, S
Bass, giant sea	12/0 to 14/0	Whole or cut barracuda, mullet, sardine, mackerel	T, S
Bass, sea	1/0 to 5/0 Sproat	Squid, clams, sea worms, crabs, killies	T, S, D
Bocaccio	1/0 to 4/0 O'Shaughnessy	Cut baits, mainly sardines, and silvery metal lures	T, S, J
Catfish, gafftopsail	No. 4 to 2/0	Mullet, shrimp; jigs, plugs, spoons	T, S, C
Cod	7/0 to 9/0 Sproat	Clams, conch, crabs, cut fish	S
Croaker	4/0 to 6/0 for big fish; No. 1 to 10 for smaller ones	Sand bugs, mussels, clams, sardines, anchovies, sea worms	T, S, C
Cultus	4/0 to 5/0 O'Shaughnessy	Squids and crustaceans	S
Eel	No. 6 to 1/0 Carlisle	Killies, clams, crabs, sea worms, spearing	S, J, D
Flounder, starry	1/0 to 3/0 O'Shaughnessy	Killies, spearing, shrimps, sea worms	S, C, D
Flounder, summer	4/0 to 6/0 Carlisle and Sproat	Killies, sea worms, clams	S, C, D
Flounder, winter	Long shank Chestertown 7 to 12	Bloodworms, clams, mussels	S
Greenling	No. 4 to 2/0	Clams, mussels, shrimps, sea worms	T, S, J
Grouper	4/0 to 12/0	Squids, mullet, sardines, balao, shrimp, crabs; plugs and spoons	T, S
Grunt	No. 3 to 1/0	Shrimp, crab, sea worms	S
Haddock	1/0 to 4/0	Clams, conch, crabs, cut fish	S
Hake, California	2/0 to 6/0	Clams, conch, crabs, cut fish	S
Hake, silver	1/0 to 4/0	Squid, herring, sea worms	S
Halibut, California	1/0 to 3/0	Killies, crabs, sea worms, shrimp, squids	S, D
Halibut, Pacific	3/0 to 10/0	Killies, crabs, sea worms, shrimp, squids	S, D

Species	Hook	Bait	Method*
Jewfish	10/0 to 12/0 Shark	Mullet, small baitfish	T, S
Ladyfish	1/0 to 5/0	Killies, shrimp; plugs, flies, spoons	T, S, C
Leatherjack	No. 6 to No. 1	Sardines, seaworms; spoons, plugs	T, S
Ling	No. 4 to 2/0 Sproat	Clams, conch, crabs, cut fish	S
Mackerel, Atlantic	No. 3 to No. 7 Carlisle	Shiny jigs, spinners, spoons, with or without baitfish	T, S, D
Perch, barred	No. 1 to 2 (hollow)	Pileworms, clams, mussels, pieces of minnows	S, C
Perch, white	No. 2 to No. 6 Sproat	Sea worms, shrimp, spearing; flies, spoons	S, C
Pompano	No. 1 to No. 4	Sand bugs, flies, bucktail jigs and plugs	T, S, C
Porgy	No. 4 to 1/0 Sproat, Virginia, O'Shaughnessy	Squid, clams, sea worms, crabs, mussels, shrimp	S
Rockfish, Pacific	1/0 to 8/0	Herring, sardine, mussels, squid, clams, shrimp	S, J
Sailor's choice	No. 1 to No. 9	Shrimp and all types of cut bait	S
Sculpin	No. 1 to 3/0	Clams, cut baits	S, J
Snapper, mangrove	1/0 to 6/0	Cut baits, shrimp	T, S
Snapper, red	6/0 to 10/0	Shrimp, mullet, crabs	T, S
Snapper, yellowtail	No. 4 to 1/0	Shrimp, mullet, crabs	T, S
Snapper blues (baby bluefish)	No. 1 to No. 4 Carlisle	Spearing, killies, spoons	S, T
Sole, Lemon	No. 4 to No. 6 Snelled	Clams, sea worms	S
Spot	No. 8 to No. 10 Carlisle and Sproat	Clams, sea worms, crabs	S, D
Tautog	No. 6 to No. 8 Virginia	Sea worms, clams, shrimp	S
Tomcod	No. 6 to No. 8 Carlisle and Sproat	Clams, mussels, shrimp	S
Tripletail	No. 1 to 4/0	Squids and crustaceans	T, S
Weakfish	No. 1 to 4/0 Sproat, Eagle Claw, Carlisle, O'Shaughnessy	Shrimp, squid, sea worms	T, S, C, J, D
Whitefish	3/0 to 6/0	Crabs, sea worms, clams	S
Whiting, northern	No. 4 to 1/0 Sproat and O'Shaughnessy	Sea worms, clams	T, S, C

*T--trolling	S--still fishing	C--casting	J--jigging	D--drifting

Index